Development or Destruction

Published in cooperation with the
United States Man and the Biosphere Program

Development or Destruction

The Conversion of Tropical Forest to Pasture in Latin America

EDITED BY
Theodore E. Downing,
Susanna B. Hecht,
Henry A. Pearson,
and Carmen Garcia-Downing

Westview Press / BOULDER • SAN FRANCISCO • OXFORD

Westview Special Studies in Social, Political, and Economic Development

The opinions, conclusions, and recommendations expressed in United States Man and the Biosphere publications are those of the authors and do not necessarily reflect the views of the participating agencies and institutions.

This Westview softcover edition is printed on acid-free paper and bound in library-quality, coated covers that carry the highest rating of the National Association of State Textbook Administrators, in consultation with the Association of American Publishers and the Book Manufacturers' Institute.

Published in 1992 in the United States of America by Westview Press, Inc., 5500 Central Avenue, Boulder, Colorado 80301- 2877, and in the United Kingdom by Westview Press, 36 Lonsdale Road, Summertown, Oxford OX2 7EW

Library of Congress Cataloging-in-Publication Data
Development or destruction : the conversion of tropical forest to pasture
    in Latin America / edited by Theodore E. Downing, Susanna B. Hecht,
Henry A. Pearson, Carmen Garcia-Downing.
        p.   cm. — (Westview special studies in social, political, and
economic development)
    Includes bibliographical references and index.
    ISBN 0-8133-7824-9
    1. Deforestation—Latin America.   2. Pastures— Latin America.
3. Beef cattle—Latin America.   4. Forests and forestry—Latin
America.   5. Rural development—Latin America.   I. Downing, T. E.
II. Hecht, Susanna B.   III. Pearson, Henry A.   IV. Garcia-Downing, Carmen.
V. Series.
SD418.3.L29D48   1992
333.75'98—dc20   89-32692
                                                                          CIP

Printed and bound in the United States of America.

The paper used in this publication meets the requirements
of the American National Standard for Permanence of Paper
for Printed Library Materials Z39.48-1984.

10   9   8   7   6   5   4   3   2   1

Contents

Part Three
Environmental Impacts
Carmen Garcia-Downing

Part Four
Social Impacts
Theodore E. Downing

Part Five
Production Alternatives
Carlton H. Herbel

Part Six
Developers' and Donors' Perspectives
Gary R. Evans

Part Seven
Community Perspectives
Carmen Garcia-Downing

Part Eight
Comments and Recommendations

Tables and Figures

Figures

Foreword

One of the most dramatic changes in landscape in the last years of the millennium has been the conversion of Latin American forest to pastureland. The United States Man and the Biosphere (U.S. MAB) conference in Oaxaca, Mexico, in October 1988 examined the dynamics underlying this complex and destructive process. In an effort to identify alternatives, it enlisted multiple perspectives of agronomists, foresters, social scientists, corporate loggers, and those of peasant farmers.

The range of debate was ample, with a place for impassioned advocates and cautious analysts. The goal, of course, was and is to identify options which could simultaneously conserve natural resources and enhance human welfare both short and long term. The problem is too vast and complex for a simple consensus to have emerged or for the problem just simply to have been solved. But clearly the chapters which follow, authored by various authorities, represent the continuing discussion which is the necessary precursor to more sensible treatment of shrinking tropical resources.

Thomas E. Lovejoy
Assistant Secretary for External Affairs
Smithsonian Institution

Preface and Acknowledgments

After innumerable delays, the first technical workshop on the conversion of tropical forest to pasture in Latin America convened in Oaxaca, Mexico in early October of 1988. The workshop was organized by the United States Man and the Biosphere program (U.S. MAB). As the plans evolved, we sought to bring together diverse perspectives, not just those of the scientific community. Consequently, sixty-seven people from 10 countries participated, including scientists, technicians, private sector interests, environmentalists, writers, administrators, and peasants. Following the meeting, fourteen of the twenty-five papers presented at this workshop were extensively revised for this book.

Special thanks are extended to those that helped prepare the proposal for the Oaxaca workshop, including two previous aborted attempts to obtain financial support. The progenitors of the volume include, in alphabetical order, Charles F. Bennett, Theodore E. Downing, A. J. Dye, Gary R. Evans, Carmen Garcia-Downing, Susanna B. Hecht, Carl F. Jordan, Ariel E. Lugo, Henry A. Pearson, John Peterson, Paul F. Randel, Marianne C. Schmink, and Richard W. Rice. Henry Pearson and Susanna Hecht merit special credit as project leaders and co-chairpersons of the program. Richard Rice, chair of the U.S. MAB Grazing Land Directorate, coordinated the Oaxaca meeting. He was assisted by Theodore E. Downing, Carmen Garcia-Downing, and Nemesio Rodriguez, who made local arrangements in Oaxaca, including finding representatives from Oaxacan forest communities, rapport building, and conducting a preconference field trip to rural Oaxaca. The Hotel Victoria in Oaxaca provided excellent facilities, including a spectacular view of the archaeological ruins of Monte Alban and its deforested hinterland. Ivan Restrepo, director of the Centro de Ecodesarrollo, was named president of the workshop in recognition of his steadfast defense of tropical forest research and forest peoples. Roger E. Soles, executive director of U.S. MAB, encouraged the transformation of the workshop drafts and papers into a book and Cecile W. Ledsky, U.S. MAB program director, made invaluable suggestions for improving the manuscript. Susana Albasi Fletcher and Deanna Hammond volunteered their translating services. Finally, we appreciate the financial support of U.S. Man and the Biosphere Program and thank Downing and Associates of Tucson for the layout and preparation of the manuscript.

Nuestros sinceros agradecimientos a todos .

The Editors

1

Introduction

The conversion of forest to grasslands in the humid tropics is one of the most profound land transformations of the 20th Century, with major consequences for biodiversity, global and regional climates, soil resources, and local populations. Tropical forests encompass nearly 1.9 billion ha of the planet. Few forests are logged with any silvicultural management system to insure adequate regeneration. As forests shrink, croplands and pastures expand, often accelerating forest degradation.

Deforestation in Latin American lowlands is substantially higher than the global average of 1.8 percent. More than 53% of the annual deforestation, some 74,400 km^2, is cleared in Latin America's moist forests. Much of the cleared area is being seeded directly for pasture. At the peasant frontiers, new clearings are likely to end up as pasture as soil nutrient declines, pest problems and labor constraints take their toll on the land. The rich realm of tropical forests — providers of latex, nuts, fibers, medicinals, wild meat, timber, and the diversified economies that depend on them — is lost at an ever increasing pace.

Multiple and increasing demands are being made on the forest. Many feel that something must be done to maintain a proper balance of forest, pasture, crops, and other amenities for the good of man and the environment. But who or what is responsible? What is the nature of the conversion problem? Who should act? What should they do? Proper management of forests and pastures is imperative and few tasks can be more crucial than understanding in better detail the processes that drive forest to pasture conversion.

The shrinking size of the tropical forest has stimulated considerable international concern. Of the estimated world tropical forest, 1.2 billion ha are closed forest and 0.7 billion ha are open tree formations. Latin America possesses about a quarter of the world's tropical forests. In 1989, its tropical forests were being reduced 76,300 square kilometers per year. More disturbing is the unfortunate trend of increasing rate of deforestation which has risen, on the average, by 76% between 1980 and 1990. Conversion of forests to pastures was a significant part of this process.

Unfortunately, this process generated several disastrous consequences and many victims. Displacement of forest peoples and the loss of their knowledge about forest management was certainly one casualty. Incineration of forests and thus the genetic heritage of the planet was another. Latin America's tropical forests are host to wild cousins and local land races of corn, manioc, sweet potatoes, beans, arrow roots, yams, squashes, peppers, rice, and others, that are central for maintaining the genetic complexes necessary for breeding programs of commercial varieties of these food crops. Cacao, pineapples, avocados, guavas, rubber, numerous palms are but a few of the fruits from tropical zones that play a major role in international commerce. One out of every four drug or pharmaceutical purchases derives in one way or another from tropical plants. Animal habitat was destroyed, eliminating critical pollinators and dispersal agents of forest species.

And there are global victims. Tropical forests contain from ten to a hundred times more carbon in their vegetation and soils than tropical crops or pastures, so when forests are replaced by non-forest land uses they ultimately release CO_2 into the atmosphere. Deforestation throughout the developing tropics accounted for some 10% of total CO_2 emissions. Tropical Latin America supplied about half of the total.

Although there are many victims, identifying the villains is not so easy. The villians are not simply personages, but processes and policies. Forests fall for any number of reasons. Peasants migrate to forest zones to make their fortune. The acute landlessness or land insufficiency in many Latin American countries is a potent force driving peasants to tropical frontiers. Often they follow in the wake of logging, construction, mining development, or dam construction. Government colonization projects have also stimulated this migration. Speculators, large and small, have cleared, claimed and profited from deforested land. Credit incentives and land concessions also stimulate the large scale clearing associated with the large holdings. As inflation levels become stratospheric, land — occupied land — becomes a valuable hedge against increasingly worthless currencies. Livestock are essential to peasants' survival and the profits of the wealthy. In brief, when faced with the complexity of tropical forests, and the minimal general knowledge available for managing them sustainably, the low input, low labor, adaptable cow is an attractive solution. Compounding the risks and costs in agriculture, livestock was a rational land use choice.

In the following sections, we explore distinct perspectives of the overall situation from the perspective of environmental policy, bio-economic costs, and livestock economics (Hecht, Ledec, Toledo, Sere and Jarvis). Lugo, Laarman, and Halhead examine forest uses, demand for forest products, and the associated socio-political context. The possible climatological and terrestrial impacts of the conversion of forest to pasture are reviewed by Salati and Nations, respectively. And Barkin and MacDonald discover some unexpected social reverberations of the conversion process. In an attempt to discover solutions, the contributors emphasize sustained production systems and offer several alternatives (Serrao and Toledo; Venator, Glaeser, and Soto; Restrepo; and Trujillo).

Examination of this problem would be incomplete without the perspective of the donors, developers, and the local forest communities. In the final two sections, Svanqvist offers a perspective from the international timber industry and Moran explains the challenging idea of a debt-for-nature swap. The forest dweller's perspective is the most difficult to capture. Peasants don't normally prepare papers on their problems. Their voice is a critical element in the deforestation equation. To cover this lacuna, we developed an innovative approach. Several peasants and community representatives were invited to attend the Oaxaca Workshop and listened to early versions of many of these chapters in this book. Shortly thereafter, the editors encouraged them to prepare tape recordings or notes on their perspective, which were subsequently edited by Garcia-Downing so as to provide a community perspective. An interview with Osmarino Rodrigues, the secretary of the Rubber Tappers Council, describes what the expansion of pasture has meant in the Acrean forest. Next, the editors summarize the recommendations of the sixty-seven participants in the Oaxaca workshop and offer an overview of what this book has accomplished. Finally, Theodore E. Downing suggests an answer to the question so often asked by those concerned with deforestation - "what can I do?"

— The Editors

PART ONE
OVERVIEWS

Critics from the developed nations like to point to tropical forest conversion as a major cause of global warming due to increases in carbon dioxide in the atmosphere and identify cattle as the principal agent of deforestation. Such a simplistic analysis absolves developed nations from their responsibility for global climatic changes. By applying economic, political, and social pressure on the tropical forest converters, they (we) can divert attention and delay responsibility for the consequences of the non-sustainable lifestyles of developed societies.

This section documents the overwhelming long-term ecological, economic, and environmental costs of tropical forest conversion. The contributors make it clear that no simple answer suffices. The reasons are to be found in a complex cluster of economic, political and biological factors related to the international and national development problems. The conversion is caused by the actions of people and their institutions, with cattle being their instruments of destruction.

— Richard W. Rice

2

Logics of Livestock and Deforestation: The Case of Amazonia

Susanna B. Hecht

Most land cleared of forest in Latin America's lowland tropics eventually ends up as pasture. This transformation of high biomass forests into relatively unproductive pasture is one of the most salient environmental transformations of the last 25 years. The incineration of large areas of forest in Amazonia currently generate 10 - 15% of the total carbon additions from biomass burning to the atmosphere (Dickinsen 1987) and banishes from biological history several species every day. Local impacts include siltation of smaller creeks and rivers, and sharp changes in microclimates as well as potential shifts in the hydrological regimes (Salati and Vose 1984).

The environment is not the only victim. Forest peoples, native people and forest product extractors also routinely watch their lives, livelihoods and complex agricultures reduced to ashes in the process of forest conversion. Peasants are often displaced by cattle ranchers in violent conflicts, or are part of a process of short term cropping on land on its way to pasture.

This chapter analyzes the logics and the economics of livestock in Amazonia by evaluating the various means of profit making from land and natural resource capital. I also elaborate for Amazonia how the livestock sector is closely linked to virtually every other rural development activity. In so doing, I establish a framework for analyzing deforestation patterns that qualify some of the current explanations of this process. Finally, the analysis focuses on current approaches to diminishing this destructive land use.

Conversion of forest to pasture is a logical process for both large and small scale owners, but the logic requires understanding the deficiencies of many of the current models of explaining deforestation, and to contextualize the role of cattle in light of contemporary lowland tropical development in the Amazon.

Why Forests Fall: A Quick Overview

One of the most common explanations of pasture driven deforestation focuses on the international beef market. The so-called "hamburger connection" focused on the idea that the international commerce for beef was stimulating the patterns of forest conversion for grassland that became so disturbing during the last 25 years. This perspective was informed by the work of Nations and Komer (1987) for Central America where this model was influenced for much of the 1970s and widely disseminated by a popular article by Norman Myers (1981). Nations and Komer contextualized the play of markets in grassland expansion within the context of Central America's land tenure patterns, regional development strategies and the relation of pasture to land speculation. The local features are often lost from the "hamburger connection" story when extrapolated to explain other livestock related deforestation patterns. This is especially true of Amazonia. International market dynamics have very little to do with the expansion of livestock production in the Amazon lowland forests. Amazon herds are a very small portion of national herds (usually less than 5%); *aftosa* (foot and mouth disease) is endemic to the region and thus their products are ineligile for international export. Livestock from all areas in Latin America, tropical and temperate, represents a small proportion of the export portfolio of primary products — again usually less than 5% (Jarvis 1986).

If deforestation were primarily a result of the workings of commodity markets, then the solutions would be straight-forward: reduce demand. This is exactly the strategy proffered by those who ascribe to the hamberger connection model. It is worth noting that U.S imports of Latin American beef are generally less than 5% of the total beef imports, which are eclipsed by meat purchased from Australia, New Zealand and the EEC. However, international exports of beef have generally declined from tropical areas in national terms and as a portion of market share, reflecting the surge in production by the European community. Economic crises have also reduced domestic demand as the Latin American middle class saw its buying power plummet. In spite of such contretemps in the livestock sector in Latin America, deforestation for pasture has increased at dizzying rates.

The Malthusian Specter

Another way of explaining the conversion of forest to pasture invokes population. While overall rates of population increase have slowed some-what in South America (Brazil's birth rate is now 1.8%), lowland tropical areas have in fact witnessed an increase in population. This has been due to aggressive colonization programs, the advance of the agricultural frontiers, infrastructure development (especially roads) in the service of economic integration, and national security concerns. More to the point, however, is that lowland tropical frontiers are generally more urbanized than previous frontiers, and, because of the ecological constraints of tropical zones (poor soils, pest problems), and the impressive increases in production in already developed agricultural areas, the lowland frontiers do not play a large role in food supply (Muller 1991). The movement of populations to these lowland areas has less to do with demographics per se than the factors that marginalize small farmers in Latin America. These include structural change in agriculture, expulsion by violence, excessively small holding sizes, and contraction of rural labor markets with increased mechanization — all of which tend to make small farms less viable (Muller 1991).

Another powerful draw into Amazonian forests in recent years pertains to the handsome returns (by peasant standards) to be made from the cultivation of coca. As agricultural and urban options contracted and as the regional economies faltered, illegal drug production on the Amazon flanks of the Andes attracted millions of migrants to the new growth sector. In a similar manner, dirt farmers also began to pursue the allurements of the gold rush, as strikes abounded from the gold fields of the Gurupa in the Eastern Amazon to Ecuadorian and Colombian jungles. It was not increasing human numbers, so much as the shifts in economic opportunity that began to make the Amazon gamble considerably more interesting as a migration target than it had been in previous decades.

Current pasture driven deforestation in the Amazon and other lowland tropical zones is the outcome of complex local processes, regional policy and national economics in which cattle and their pastures have an economic flexibility and low risk unmatched by other more ecologically appropriate land uses. Attempts to control pasture expansion will be a more arduous task than changing consumption patterns or birth control, although these efforts are worthy.

Making Money from Land and Resources

There are three main ways of capturing value through land and natural resources. The first involves **extraction**, which can take two basic forms: renewable and "irrevocable" extraction. Both renewable and irrevocable extraction involve extracting some product of value to human society from the natural world. They can be primary products (ore for example) where numerous transformations transpire between the natural product and its forms of use, or final products, like fish, which are not generally processed very much before they are finally consumed. While labor and markets both contribute to the way that value is generated with these natural commodities, there are also essential chemical or biological characteristics, perhaps one could call this inherent natural capital, which are the defining features of its value. Renewable exploitation concentrates on appropriating a certain level of biological productivity for human uses in ways that do not undermine the basic productivity of the resource. Vast literatures in resource management and economics focus on what are sustainable economic and biological levels of extraction, and what pushes actors into over-exploitation. The general types of explanations can include population (Ehrlich 1984), lack of private property systems under market conditions (Hardin 1967), market driven over-exploitation, misery driven over-exploitation (Sen 1986), prisoner dilemma models, and subsidy driven exploitation (cf. Repetto and Gillis 1988) among the many analytic options. Some of these models have been extrapolated to non-renewable extraction, although the central focus of much of the analysis of non-renewable resource extraction is concerned with optimal exploitation rates. An emerging body of Marxist scholarship that analyzes the historical patterns and determinants of exploitation is now gaining a great deal of attention (Blaikie and Brookfield 1987).

The second way to make profits, **production**, involves more direct intervention in the manipulation of biological processes through the application of energy, labor, and capital to generate products of use to human societies. Capital can include the standard economic understanding of the term: machinery, money, etc., but it also implies biological/environmental capital in the form of genetic resources or soil properties, and human capital embodied in knowledge systems and individual skill. Production implies far more complex and organized forms of intervention in the natural world, and incorporates the idea that energy and resources are applied to land to generate something of value not entirely inherent in the land resource itself.

The final way to make money via land and natural resources is through their ability to capture **financial resources**, through speculation, their usefulness as means of capturing institutional rents, such as credits and subsidies, and as a means for claiming other assets. In this case, the value of the resource or land has little to do with its own characteristics, or the labor and resources applied to it. The value of the resource/land is linked to this ability to generate returns through a variety of structural features in the larger economy. Bhagwati (1982) has called these activities "directly unproductive Profit seeking activities" (or DUP's). Value is determined less by inherent environmental characteristics (although theses are not completely absent, as in the value of timber stocks), than by institutional factors such as validity of title, for example, or spatial characteristics, like proximity to roads. In DUPs land/resources become objects of strategies conditioned by the larger economy that are often non-productive, profit seeking activities . They represent ways of making a profit, but produce little by ways of goods and services through increased production. Bhagwati's initial formulation focused on tariffs where the use of DUP activities would not, in principle, carry with them large externalities, but when the DUP strategy is transferred into the tropical forest, DUPs can use up real resources. Livestock ranching is not exactly a pure case, since it is possible to capture a return to animals in some circumstances (cf Hecht et al. 1988, Browder, 1988), but the range of benefits that flow to livestock often fall on the DUP rather than on the production side of the resource use gradient.

Livestock and Wealth

This short discussion on extractive, productive and profitable but large-ly unproductive forms of appropriating value from land/resources is necessary for understanding how cattle and their pastures are not limited to producing wealth as commodities generated through productive activities. In the Brazilian case, pastures and livestock have served as a means of claiming land, tax breaks and a variety of other forms of financial benefits such as subsidies and immense speculative gains (Mahar 1989, Browder 1988, Hecht 1985, 1982, Hecht, et al. 1988).

The reason that pastures and livestock have played such a seminal role in the conversion of forest to pasture is that these are among the best ways in which all three forms of capturing value — extractive, productive and DUP — can be achieved, especially in the lowland tropical context of high environmental and economic risk. Moreover, it is a strategy in which both large and small actors can participate. The underlying logic of livestock investment will vary at different scales of production but but are based primarily on 1) the biological flexibility of the animal; 2) the economic flexibility which permits the owner to decide the time of sale; 3) the ability to occupy large areas with little labor; 4) the importance of land as a means of capturing other assets, all of which reduces risk in highly uncertain rural activities. All these combine to produce explosive expansion of a land use that produces fewer calories, proteins and direct monetary returns per unit area with enormous environmental degradation.

The Logic of Livestock

Large Owner

The Amazon case represents one of the most comprehensive analyses of the economic dynamics of large ranching enterprises. Most of the litera-ture on cattle production in Amazonia focuses on the Eastern Amazon (cf Hecht 1982, 1985; Mahar 1979, 1989; Browder 1988; Gasques and Yakimoto 1986). The focus of corporate ranches was facilitated by the relative ease of obtaining such information because the documentation of these enterprises could be tracked through public materials held in the Superintendency for

Amazon Development (SUDAM). The current number of ranch projects is 579 according the SUDAM data from 1987 (SUDAM 1987) but this includes modernization, expansion and modification of many existing projects, as they were sold or required further or different funding, or new parts of a project were developed on existing holdings. Thus, 303 projects are in reformulation and amplification, and 276 are in the implantation or modernization phase. This data contrasts with that of Gasques and Yakimoto (1986) who say that there are 621 projects, and Browder (1988) who indicates 470. The confusion is due to the reformulation of parts of projects and whether a ranch with several reformulations counts as one or many projects. The high percentage of abandoned projects − 30% (Gasques and Yakimoto 1986) − imply that we have no idea currently of how many SUDAM ranches there really are at this time. The studies that were produced from SUDAM information, thus gave the incorrect impression that only highly subsidized livestock operations were involved in the tremendous transformation of forests to grasslands in Amazonia. There is no question that the SUDAM jumbo ranches have been important in the deforestation dynamic since they formally control some 8,763 sq. km. In areas where they dominate, such as southern Para and Northern Mato Grosso, they have been responsible for 30% of the clearing, according to the figures from INPE, the Brazilian Institute for Space Studies (Tardin et al., 1982).

The recent data on clearing, however, suggest new trends. The explosive deforestation in Rondonia, Mato Grosso and Para suggest several patterns other than the large ranch model. Areas dominated by middle size holdings, with few SUDAM holdings such as those in Paragominas, Para, are currently experiencing deforestation rates greater than 1.5% per year (Woodell et al., 1988).

These SUDAM ranches were highly subsidized in several ways:

- **Fiscal incentives:** SUDAM ranches received grants of up to 75% of the ranch development costs in order to encourage corporate groups to invest in the region.
- **Tax holidays** of up to 100% of a corporations tax bill were forgiven if these monies were invested in holdings in the Amazon region or the dry Northeast. The net effect of these holidays was to permit corporations to use their monies as though they were venture capital, or simply to divert them into other more lucrative activities.
- **No import taxes** were exacted for equipment used on these ranches.
- **Subsidized credits** were widely available at essentially negativeinterest rates. Thus, while inflation leaped ahead well over

50% of the credits were granted at 8 to 12 %. Because these credit lines were largely granted by public banks and were initially designed to favor small farmers, the kinds of loans for land development (*investimento*), unlike those for short term costs (*custeio*), or marketing, often had 6 to 8 year grace periods under a twelve to 15 year amortization period. Many of the contracts signed in the early 1970s were not adjusted when policies shifted, resulting in a "founders rent" for early borrowers. Under the prevailing inflation rates, such funds were often diverted into the short term financial markets ("overnights") or other kinds of investments with a rapid and high return.

- **Land Concessions** were provided in many areas or lands were provided at nominal cost. Indeed, EMBRAPA (the Brazilian Ministry of Agriculture) economic analyses generally do not incorporate a land price. The ensemble of benefits directly tied to the clearing of forest ostensibly for cattle ranching made this activity enormously attractive, and, indeed, they were designed to lure investors and capital into the region. The dynamic entrepreneurs from Southern Brazil were given extraordinary favors in part because they helped craft the terms of the incentives and because they were to take on the "*mission civilizatrice*" of taming the Amazon.

As Mahar (1979, 1989) suggested in his studies of Amazonian frontier policy, livestock became a vehicle for capturing these kinds of extraordinary financial benefits. Whether the land use was sustainable, economic or appropriate made very little difference in this context.

Subsidies and Land

The SUDAM cases could probably be argued on the basis of subsidies and tax holidays alone, and indeed this line of argument has become central in policy circles. Here, the distortions caused by SUDAM subsidies drive virtually all the pasture expansion with predictably dire results (cf Repetto and Gillis 1988). And "getting the prices right" — reducing or eliminating subsidies and credits — would bring the producer cost more in line with the real costs and make the heedless conversion of immense areas from forest to pasture land less likely. This form of subsidy has its roots in a longer history of gentlemen's agreements between the cattle sector and government policy makers (cf Hecht 1982, Pompermeyer 1978) and were revoked in a "policy triumph" under President Sarney's "Nossa Natureza" program only when subsidy contracts had largely terminated for most of the estab-

The point of the immense subsidies was to develop regional breeding herds and for this reason cow-calf operations as well as fattening steers were always included, and indeed were an important justification for the incentives. Cow-calf operations are costly — they require more labor, more fencing, more management, and more medicines. Moreover, fodder demands of lactating and pregnant cows are often 25% higher than that of steers. Fattening operations, on the other hand, require minimal labor, perfunctory vaccinations and far less fencing and management. Losses are less likely because young steers are already quite robust.

Thus, using a strategy of importing steers from producer areas — Goias and Southern Mato Grosso in the case of the Southern Amazon flanks and the Island of Marajo in the Paragominas area, and the Roraima grasslands and the riparian zones for the Manaus region drastically reduced the production costs for many livestock operations, and if one was given to overgrazing and maximizing production in the first few years when pasture quality is better, these operations often were profitable, albeit for fairly short periods of time.

The focus on a few hundred mega-ranches has obscured the fact that there are more than 50,000 livestock operations in Amazonia at all scales of production. In addition to the emphasis on fattening steers, the economic impacts of regional development strategies, subsidized credits, inflationary pressures in the Brazilian economy that place premiums on real property, the potential revenues from timber, or the possibility of gold strikes set into play an intense rise in the speculative value of lands. The stratospheric rise in land values also reflected specific large scale infrastructure investment patterns: the development of extensive highway systems, and the clear commitment by the Brazilian government to sustain investment in Amazonia through its growth pole strategy and "Jumbo" projects such as the Carajas area and Tucurui hydropower dam. A whole industry has developed around clearing land for pasture and then selling that land as quickly as possible, pocketing the gains and moving on into new forest zones, the famous *industria de posse.* The value of land as a commodity itself rather than as an input into production helped fuel the murderous land conflicts that now characterize the Brazilian Amazon.

Land ownership in Amazonia has been characterized by extensive fraud and overlapping and competing claims. While land fraud stories verge on the folkloric with archives ablaze and state governors selling title to areas that exceed the areas of their states (cf Asselin 1982), there are several fundamental problems that reflect the existence of colonial titles, emphyteusis rights, squatters rights, the exceptionally rapid creation of capitalist land markets in Amazonia, and a rather chaotic, often corrupt, emission of definitive title. (Pompermeyer 1978, Bunker 1985, Hecht 1986).

Since those who clear land have a stronger legal claim to a parcel than those who do not, there is ample incentive to clear as much land as possible. Moreover, legal claim to an area six times the size of the clearing is permitted under the laws of INCRA (the Institute of Agrarian Reform). Thus, should there be interesting timber on adjacent sites or potential mineral finds, these, too, could be secured through clearing. Finally, under the threats of agrarian reform, land in "effective use" — that is to say — cleared, cannot be expropriated under the terms of the new 1988 constitution.

Production

Cattle ranching as a "productive" economic activity is very tenuous. A study carried out by the Brazilian Institute for Economic Analysis (IPEA) on SUDAM ranches showed that the actual production and sale of livestock was a mere 15% of projected productivity in large operations that were running at capacity, while those ranches that were still developing generated a mere 8% of estimated production which was based on the general stocking rate of one animal unit per hectare (Gasques and Yakimoto 1986). Take-off rates have hovered at about 10%, one of the lowest herd cull rates in the world. Formation and management of pastures is quite expensive, pastures are not usually sustainable, and the value of the final animal product often does not repay the investment costs. Browder (1988) suggests that cattle repay about 25% of their production costs based on a 15% take off rate, based on SUDAM ranch types.

In a simulation study of livestock economics under various price regimes, with and without subsidies, and with and without speculation, and with different types of technologies Hecht et al. (1988) showed that the economic returns to cattle production alone (without credits, no overgrazing, and no land appreciation) was only economically viable under very specific conditions in the cattle cycle. Overgrazing improved the economic scenario somewhat, but the real gains to the enterprise were realized through capital gains linked to the rise in land values and the subsidies. The returns to cattle production are overshadowed by the spectacular returns obtained by land speculation, and the rents associated with subsidies. This is not to say that the revenue derived from the sale of cattle is unimportant, only to point out that largest portion of the revenue associated with livestock will not be generated by returns to **production** but rather through **financial** or **DUP** machinations such as I have described.

Extraction

Irreversible extraction can also have a role in livestock expansion in two ways. The first, already mentioned involves using livestock as a way to claim lands. A recognized land claim permits the holder to assert royalty rights on subsurface minerals which are technically owned by the Brazilian state. Areas adjacent to gold strikes frequently experience vigorous clearing. Cattle claim what is under their feet. Another way in which extraction is linked to pasture expansion is through the use of valuable timber to subsidize pasture development costs (Uhl and Buschbacher 1986). This is a more recent phenomenon due to the improved infra-structure, expanding timber markets, and relatively recent policy changes, and is more widely used by smaller ranching operations.

Larger scale livestock operations appropriate value from natural resources through their ability to capture financial resources and to claim extractive ones. They can generate revenue as producers of beef, but this rarely covers the costs of production. The fusion of all three forms of accumulation through a given land use is not limited to cattle ranching but it does have special appeal: the low cost of pasture compared to agriculture or perennial crops like cacao, its low labor demands and most importantly, through the rapid and extensive occupation of land.

Chayanov meets the cow: The Logic of Livestock for Peasants

The discussion of large scale livestock operations has dominated the analysis of cattle and deforestation, and indeed the impact of big operators is probably more important for deforestation patterns in the Basin as a whole. However, the highest rates of deforestation currently occur in the state of Rondonia, where colonists and small producers are also intimately involved in the expansion of livestock. The increase in Rondonia's herd was more than 3,000% in the period between 1970 and 1988, and it has come to dominate the cleared areas.

Why should livestock figure so prominently in the strategy of small farmers? There are several reasons that pertain to the biological flexibility of the animals and their unusual economic features within the context of rural and national economies. Cattle, and livestock more generally, have been one means of evening out risk in agriculture. As part of a household income portfolio they provide an income supplement in the form of milk or calves, and if there are agricultural disasters, as is often the case in the Brazilian Amazon, they provide a large "lump" of income when sold. Thus ready local market for animal products where beef fetches the highest price of any source of protein, and the highest per kilo value of any basic food commodity. Cattle provide these market benefits with less labor cost than rice, beans, corn, manioc or tree crops. Animals are capable, unlike the crops, of transporting themselves. The timeliness of animal harvest is determined by household need or market opportunity and not by the biological demands of the crop production which often work against small farmers since all bring their main crops to market simultaneously.

Cattle production also extends the economic life of a given cleared area. Sites that have been planted to crops go out of production within three years and are usually planted to grass. This land is grazed until it becomes choked with weeds or so degraded that no forage will grow. While the productivity of these pastures is among the lowest in the Amazon, they provide marginal return on a piece of land that would otherwise be generating nothing for the colonist household. This may be a minor increment, but for poor households its importance should not be dismissed, especially since the labor costs are relatively low and the returns on the output quite respectable.

In highly inflationary economies, such as those of most Amazon countries, investing in animals is a way of protecting assets for peasants as it is for large owners. For people who may not be comfortable with banks, and where interest rates do not accompany inflation such a strategy is completely reasonable.

Colonization projects have frequently produced credit lines for small scale producers of cattle. In this case, the obvious benefits of buying a valuable asset with borrowed money whose value is evaporating while that of the animal is at least maintaining if not exceeding that of inflation are quite clear.

The role of cattle as a means of claiming land is well developed for small holders and follows roughly the same logic as that of large owners. Throughout the Amazon, pasture is the cheapest and easiest way to claim occupation rights. If, as often happens, peasant households inhabit a parcel of questionable title, and this land is adjudicated, the larger the cleared area the greater the indemnification if they are expropriated. As areas that have been cleared for pasture have a value that is about one third greater than that of forest, their ability to speculate with these lands is also enhanced. Among colonists land speculation, and indemnification by the state or larger landowners occurs with some frequency. Finally, given the nature of windfall profits in Amazonia, a lucky gold strike or generous profits in coca production may produce immense surpluses for a rural household. In this case, one of the few means of diversification in the regional economy involves investing in land with cattle. For example, in the Guaviare areas of

Colombia, famed for its coca production, only about 5,000 ha are given over to coca cultivation, while most of its forests fall for the creation of pasture, which now occupies some 100,000 ha (Corporacion Araracuara 1986).

The diversity of economic ends that can be served by cattle make them very compelling for colonists. Whether these advantages center on their convenience for the household as it struggles along day to day, or in the way livestock can be used to mitigate larger macroeconomic pressures, cattle have an extraordinary benefits vis a vis what many consider more appropriate land uses, such as perennial crops. It is not surprising that peasants everywhere clamour for cattle, and are intent on clearing pasture for the day when they can add to their humble herds. Livestock are important in helping to guarantee the livelihoods of peasants by reducing risk, protecting assets, providing milke and meat, extending land parcel life all with a minimum of effort, and a relatively inexpensive and accessible investment. Within the wider economic dynamics, they once again capture financial benefits.

Cows must be seen in the context of the numerous roles they fill in these very uncertain rural and national economies. For both large and small operators, their advantages are inescapable. Unfortunately these private benefits have quite disastrous public costs in terms of their environmental costs and their implications for the regional economy.

The Ecological Dimensions of Pastures

Pastures in the Amazon do not remain productive for very long (Hecht 1982, Serrao and Toledo, this volume). The high biomass forests survive on very poor acid soils because they have complex systems of nutrient cycling. Most of the ecosystem nutrients are held in the biomass itself, not in the soil, so physiological features of the plants, structural features of the plants and symbiotic relationships with other organisms keep nutrient circulating within the living materials. When forests are cleared for pasture there is a nutrient flush as elements held in the biomass are released to soils. However, with leaching, runoff and uptake by the pasture plants, soil nutrients decline rapidly to levels below those necessary for maintaining pasture production. The nutrient value of the grasses falls off, and shrubby weeds begin to invade the pasture. Soils become compacted. Cleaning the pastures by chopping down the bush, burning, and fertilizing can give pastures a new, albeit short lease on life, although the economics of maintaining pastures versus clearing new ones works against managing existing cleared land (Serrao and Toledo, this volume). Thus new areas are constantly being cleared as old ones go out of production. Pastures in the Amazon are degraded, they are frequently abandoned in ten years (Hecht 1982, 1985).

These degraded lands are exceedingly difficult to recuperate. As the size of clearings get larger, it is increasingly difficult for forest seeds to establish themselves (cf Uhl et al. 1988). There are several reasons for this. First, fire is an integral part of pasture formation and maintenance. Tropical forest trees are rarely able to tolerate fire. Seed in the soil, or stump sprouts are thus regularly killed. Next, many forest seeds are large and need to be carried by animals. If the dispersal agents are killed or flee because of habitat destruction, this also reduces the number of seeds that enter a field. If by some lucky chance, seeds somehow arrive in a field, they are often subject to very extensive predation by leafcutter ants. The environmental conditions of pastures, high heat, low humidity, compacted soils make it hard for a seedling to establish itself, let alone survive the various onslaughts, of fire, drought and ravaging predators (Uhl et al. 1988). These factors also make pasture areas very difficult and expensive to recuperate. Thus the clearing for pasture in the end often condemns land to waste, and more than 50% of the areas cleared have been abandoned.

In terms of regional economies, cattle generate ephemeral employment in the clearing phase, and for brush management, but they do not absorb much labor at any scale of production. This is a private advantage for both peasants and large landowners, but for the regional economy it is a disaster because livestock occupy vast areas but generate very little employment. The standard *fazenda* uses about 1 cowboy for every 1500 ha cleared. The linkages to other parts of the regional economy are fairly weak. Implements, seed, wire, animal supplements and veterinary products all come from southern Brazil. Local urban centers do consume Amazon beef, and some employment is generated in the small slaughterhouses and butcher shops, but the bulk of the labor linked to pasture development is in the clearing stage for casual labor, with little permanent employment. Tax revenues generated from the sales of animal is very low. In the case of the SUDAM ranches, these revenues were only about 2% of the value of incentive money they were granted (Gasques and Yakimoto 1986).

What is to be done? Current Approaches, Problems and Hints

Policy and Politics

One of the current emphases in international circles as mentioned earlier is to reduce cattle subsidies and their distortions, the gains will evaporate and livestock would lose its attractiveness as an investment. This view constitutes the major analytic contributions of World Resources Institute (cf Repetto and Gillis 1988) and the World Bank (Mahar 1989). This perspective views development processes as largely mechanistic, and underemphasizes the fact that regional development processes which are incorporated into livestock development take on a life of their own and interact with a number of dynamics within the local and macro-economy. The irony of course is that deforestation rates have increased as subsidies to the sector have declined (Figure 2.1). One of the central problems with this model has been the excessive focus on the impact of super subsidies to a relatively small set of producers and the extrapolation of this view to all cattle operations in the Amazon. Even in the SUDAM ranches, between 60-70% of the total fiscal incentive resources were concentrated in 35 large corporate groups who often had more than one SUDAM project. While these ranches were important in initiating a regional clearing dynamic, the withdrawal of subsidies now probably comes too late.

The regional economy responds synergistically to a number of factors that are now beyond the control of one set of policies. What drives land speculation now are high inflation rates, the relatively low entry costs for land in Amazonia, the clear commitment to infrastructure development, colonization programs on the part of the Brazilian government, the non-renewable resource potential (the gold mining and mineral development), the threat of disappropriation of uncleared land, and the concerted promulgation of doctrines of national security, national integration and manifest destiny. As the rest of the Brazilian economy goes into a tailspin, the "Amazon Card" is seen as an important means of resolving internal social tensions and assuring continued accumulation for entrepreneurs who are not able to participate in urban investments particularly well. Given the difficulty of the other land uses in Amazonia, and the high rates of failure in short spaces of time, livestock is a relatively secure investment. There is a large, and politically powerful constituency that will support and encourage the continued occupation of the Amazon, no matter what the environmental or social cost.

Technological Fix

A popular line of argument suggests that environmental problems in Amazonia could be substantially mitigated if better pasture and livestock practices were implemented (Serrão and Toledo, this volume). If each area cleared stayed in production, the need for clearing would diminish. Research institutes throughout the Amazon engage in careful field testing and fertilizer trials, germplasm selection in order to find the combination that permits sustainable pasture production. While certainly a laudable goal, it assumes that the pasture management problems mainly reflect improper technologies, and that the desultory and destructive pasture management is largely the outcome of poor existing technologies. While better manage-

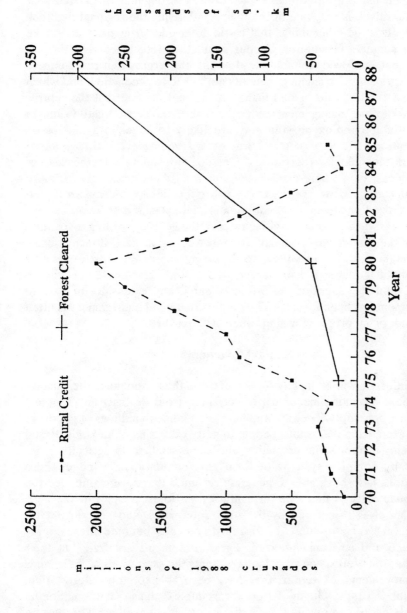

FIGURE 2.1 Rural credit and forest cleared in Amazonia 1970-88

Source: Banco do Brasil (credit data) and Setzer (1988)

ment could make a difference, I have argued throughout this article that production itself is only one of the logics underlying the regional livestock economy. It is the other things that cattle do besides grow meat that make them of singular fascination. In our simulation (Hecht et al. 1988) we showed that improved technologies do not yield returns that can compete with overgrazing. The ancillary benefits not linked to production, and which will accrue under good or bad management, and the fact that the returns are higher to bad management under the time frame of most cattle runners means that technological solutions are likely to have little impact on deforestation patterns, a pattern borne out by the low levels of adoption of improved technologies (Serrao and Toledo, this volume). In the case of Paragominas, Para where extensive research has been underway for more than a decade, and where the best pasture technology systems are tested and subsidized, the technology adoption is minimal, and deforestation rates have increased above the prevailing rates of the 1970s, according to Thomas Stone of the Woods Hole Amazon Remote Sensing project. If technologies would make a difference they would do so there, due to the relative proximity of the large Belem market, where production could conceivably pay off, and the enormous effort in research and extension on pasture management has been focused. The point is that good management is often of secondary importance for landowners with pasture.

Social Movements

Rainforests will ultimately survive because those who make their livings from them have organized to protect them from destruction. Tropical forests are not empty. They are and have been home to millions of people in the Amazon, from indigenous people to petty extractors of all kinds. Based on systems of renewable extraction and some small scale agriculture, informed by complex systems of local environmental knowledge, these populations have been able to generate revenues that have maintained the Amazonian elites in fine style for centuries. As forest peoples increasingly find themselves threatened by livestock enterprises, and government infrastructure development, their resistance has become increasingly politicized and environmentalized. These movements are frail, but their concerns about forest conservation represents the aspirations of indigenous social movements. Moreover, they have been able to stop deforestation. The Rubber Tapper Union of Acre for example, claims that 1.2 million ha of forests have been saved by their direct actions. In southern Para, where goldmining, timber mining and ranching have obliterated one of the Amazon's richest forests and its fauna, the only areas that have not been routinely ravaged have been within the Kayapo and Xingu reserves.

While there is often a romantic *frisson* associated with the emergence of resistance movements, it is worth mentioning that these movements are frail, and the history of Amazonia has been written in crushed aspirations (Hecht and Cockburn 1989). Nonetheless these types of movements, beleaguered though they may be, have managed to form alliances within the national political context and with international environmental groups to bring pressure to bear at many levels. In the end, however, it is the development of the non-violent "empates", where people prohibit deforesters to enter that will directly stop the forest destruction. This is not without consequences, as the death of Chico Mendes makes clear.

Final Comments

In this chapter I have tried to show how value can be extracted from natural resources via extractive, directly unproductive but profitable economic strategies. This has been framed within an analysis of the logics of livestock for both large and small scale producers. By concentrating on strategies and rationales, I have placed far less emphasis on the usual ways of explaining deforestation in Amazonia: Malthusian pressures, commodity markets and policy mistakes. At least in the case of Brazil, the demographic model of deforestation is not valid because more than half the population is urban (IBGE 1988) and the migratory pressures reflect economic forces at least as much as demographic ones. The classic and well loved "hamburger connection" and influence of international beef markets simply do not operate in the current Amazonian context. Amazonian beef is rife with aftosa and prohibited into US markets, even if the Amazon were not a net beef importer. The current emphasis on policy and subsidy distortions incorporates more complexity, but it comes a bit late, and the empirical data show that as credits contracted, deforestation increased. Models that focus on beef commodities cannot capture the broader dynamics of livestock stimulated deforestation throughout the humid Latin American tropics. Land markets, value of ancillaries and the larger macro-economic context and individual economic strategies must also be included. Livestock are an unusual commodity, and their biological, market, and ancillary features make them quite unlike other commodities like coffee or rice.

Control over the processes of deforestation will evolve at the national and not the international level. It is important to understand that the Amazon Basin is not a first world colony, and that the destiny of the region will be shaped through local and national politics to a greater degree than international pressure. This does not mean that one needs to throw up ones hands in frustration, but rather to realize that the logic behind livestock is immensely compelling, and likely to become more so, particularly since the alternatives, forestry, agriculture, and agroforestry lack the variety of mechanisms, extractive, productive and DUPs, through which value can be captured.

References Cited

Asselin, V. 1982. *Grilagem: Corrupcao e violencia em terras do Carajas.* Petropolis: Vozes.

Bhagwati, D. 1982. Directly unproductive, profit seeking activities. *Journal of Economics, 90 (5) 988-1002.*

Blaikie, P. and H. Brookfield. 1987. *Land degradation and society.* New York: Methuen.

Browder, J. 1988. The social costs of rain forest destruction. *Interciencia* 13 (3) 115-120.

Bunker, S. 1985. *Underdeveloping the Amazon.* Chicago: University of Chicago Press.

Dickinsen. R., ed. 1987. *The geophysiology of Amazonia.* New York: Wiley for The United Nations University.

Ehrlich, P. 1984. *The Cassandra Conference.* New York: Harpers.

Gardin et. al. 1982. Relatorio de desmatanmento. INPE. Sao Jose dos Campos.

Gasques, J. and C. Yakimoto. 1986. *Resultados de 20 anos de incentivos fiscais na agropecuaria da Amazonia.* ANPEC, Brasilia.

Hardin, G. 1967. The tradegy of the commons. *Science 162:243-1248.*

Hecht, S.B. 1982. Cattle ranching development in the Eastern Amazon. Ph. D. Thesis University of California.

_____ 1985. Environment, development and politics: here Capital accumulation & the livestock sector in Eastern Amazonia. *World Development* 13(6), 663-684.

Hecht, S.B. and A. Cockburn. 1989. *Fate of the forest.* London: Verso.

Hecht, S.B., R. Norgaard, G. Possio. 1988. The economics of cattle ranching in the Eastern Amazon. *Interciencia* 13(5) 233-240.

IBGE. 1988. Censo agropecuario. IBGE. Rio de Janeiro, Brasil.

Jarvis, L., 1986. *Livestock in Latin America.* New York: Oxford University Press.

Mahar, D. 1989. *Government policies and deforestation in Brazil's Amazon region.* Washington, D.C.: World Bank.

_____ 1979. *Frontier policy in Brazil: A study of Amazonia.* New York: Praeger Publishers.

Millikan, B. 1988. Dialectics of Deforestation. MA Thesis. University of California.

Muller, C. 1991. Dianamica, Condicionantes e impactos socio-ambientales ha evolugao da fronteira agricola no Brasil. Brazil: ISPN (Instituto Sociedade, Populacao e Natureza).

Myers, N. 1981. The hamburger connection: How Central America's forests become North America's hamburgers. *Ambio*.

Nations, J., and D. Komer. 1987. Rainforests and the hamburger society. *The Ecologist* 17(14/15) 161-167.

Pompermeyer, M.J. 1979. The state and frontier in Brazil. Ph.D. dissertation, Stanford University.

Relatorio Corporación Araracuara. 1986. Bogata. Columbia.

Repetto, R. and M. Gillis. 1988. *Public policies and the misuse of forest resources*. New York: Cambridge Press.

Salati, E. and P.B. Vose. 1984. Amazonia: A system in equilibrium. *Science* 225: 129-138.

Sen A. 1986. *Resources, values and science*. Cambridge: Harvard University Press.

Sen, A. 1986. *Natural Resource Economics*. Cambridge: Cambridge University Press.

Setzer, A. W., M. C. Pereira, A. C. Pereira Jr., and S. A. O. Aleida. 1988. *Progress Report of the IBDF-INPE "SEQUE" Project 1987*. Instituto de Pesquisas Espaciais. May. INPE-45-34 RPE 565.

Stone, T.A. 1989. Personal Communication.

SUDAM (Superintendencia du Desenvolvimento da Amazonia) 1987. Fiscal Incentive Spread Sheets.

Tardin Et al. 1982. Relatorio Projeto: Desmatamento Convenio IBDF/Cnpq-INPE. Sao Jose dos Campo: Sao Paulo, Brazil.

Uhl, C. and Buschbacher, R., 1986, A disturbing synergism between cattle ranch burning practices and selective tree harvesting in the Eastern Amazon. *Biotropica* 17: 265- 8.

Uhl, C., R. Bushbacher and A. Serrao. 1988. Abandoned pastures in the Eastern Amazonia. *J. of Ecology* 76:663- 681.

Uhl, C. and G. Parker. 1986. Is a quarter pound of hamburger worth a half ton of rainforest? *Interciencia* 11 (5): 210.

Woodell, G., T.A. Stone, and R. Houghton. 1988. *Deforestation in Para, Brazilian Amazon Basin*. Report to ORNL. Woods Hole, Mass: Woods Hole Research Center.

3

New Directions for Livestock Policy: an Environmental Perspective

George Ledec

Large-scale cattle ranching has become the dominant feature of livestock development in Latin America. Governments in the region, with the encouragement and assistance of international development agencies, continue to promote cattle ranching enthusiastically. However, serious environmental and other social costs accompany much of the cattle raising. For this reason, it is necessary to examine closely the prevailing pro-cattle policies as well as the social costs of the continued pasture expansion which these policies promote.

This chapter examines livestock policies in Latin America (including the Caribbean) from primarily an environmental and normative perspective. It documents the importance of cattle pasture expansion to tropical deforestation. It discusses the significance of the various environmental and other social costs of the deforestation that results from cattle ranching. It describes some of the other social costs (besides deforestation) of cattle pasture expansion. Most importantly, it recommends a variety of major changes in both livestock policies and complementary policies, so that the deforestation and other social costs of cattle pasture expansion can be minimized.

Importance of Cattle Ranching to Deforestation

To a very great extent, the deforestation problem in Latin America is the problem of cattle pasture expansion. Consequently, deforestation generally cannot be controlled unless the spread of cattle ranching is somehow controlled.

Deforestation defined

It is important to understand what "deforestation" means. "Deforestation" is the more or less permanent removal of most of the natural tree cover from an area. In naturally forested areas, deforestation is usually synonymous with land clearing.

Logging usually implies forest modification (or degradation), rather than outright deforestation. Most commercial timber from natural tropical forests is selectively logged, for only certain tree species and size classes. Depending on the number of trees removed per hectare and the felling and extraction techniques used, such logging can cause major forest disturbance and modification, changing average tree size and density, as well as species composition. If "high grading" is done without leaving enough high-quality seed trees to provide for adequate regeneration of commercially valuable species, the long-term economic value of the forest resource declines. However, selectively logged areas are still forests, albeit ecologically modified and often commercially degraded. Even the clear-felling of forest patches is not deforestation per se, since some type of forest will naturally regenerate, provided that enough standing forest remains in the area to serve as a seed source, that the soil is not severely eroded as a result of the logging or associated road-building and that the land is not repeatedly burned, grazed, plowed, or otherwise disturbed. While most commercial logging does not directly cause deforestation, the construction of logging roads frequently leads to deforestation by "opening up" forested areas to settlement and land clearing.

The Significance of Cattle

In the Latin American tropics, cattle raising is responsible for substantially more deforestation than all other production systems combined. For example, Panamanian agricultural census data indicate that more than 70% of the country's deforested land is in cattle pasture; all of this country's banana, sugar cane, coffee, rice and other cash and food crop production collectively account for less than 30%. Similarly, about 70% of all of the deforested land in Costa Rica is in pasture (Hartshorn *et al.* 1982). Examination of land use data for most mainland tropical countries is very likely to yield similar results. The main exceptions to this rule may be Guyana, Suriname and French Guiana, where cattle ranching has not emerged as a major land use. Not surprisingly, these are also the only tropical Latin American countries where deforestation pressures are still negligible (Table 3.1).[1]

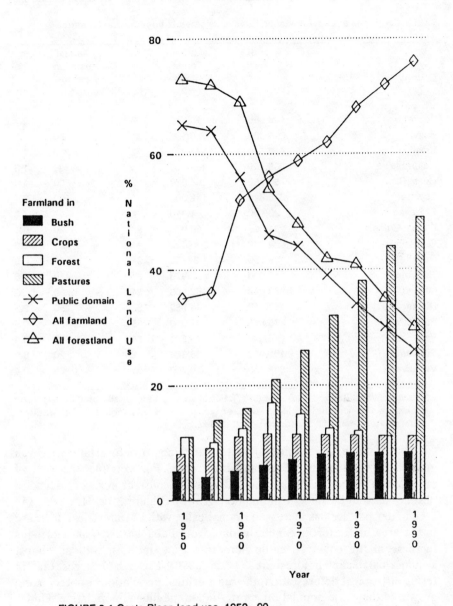

FIGURE 3.1 Costa Rican land use, 1950 - 90

Note: post 1975 extrapolations from Tosi 1974

TABLE 3.1 Forest area deforestation rates in selected Latin American countries

Country	Land Area km²	Natural Forest Area km²	Area %	Annual Deforestation Rate km²	Area %
Belize	22,965	13,540	59	90	0.7
Bolivia	1,084,390	440,100	41	870	0.2
Brazil	8,456,510	3,574,800	42	59,230	1.7
Columbia	1,038,700	464,000	45	8,200	1.8
Costa Rica	50,660	163,980	32	650	4.0
Ecuador	276,840	142,500	51	3,400	2.4
El Salvador	20,720	1,410	7	40	2.8
French Guiana	91,000	89,000	98	10	0.0
Guatemala	1,084,300	44420	41	720	1.6
Guyana	196,850	1,84750	94	20	0.0
Honduras	111,890	37,970	34	480	1.3
Mexico	1,923,040	462,500	24	4,700	1.0
Nicaragua	118,750	44,960	38	1,250	2.3
Panama	759,90	41,650	55	360	0.9
Peru	1,280,000	696,800	54	2,600	0.4
Suriname	161,470	148,300	92	20	0.0
Venezuela	882,050	318,700	36	1,250	0.4

Sources: World Resources Institute (1987). Forest area data are for all closed-canopy forest types, whether undisturbed, logged-over, or secondary. Deforestation data for Brazil are inferred from Mahar (1989), for the period 1980-88.

The relative importance of cattle ranching to deforestation is even greater if we consider recent land use trends. For example, the area of cropland in Costa Rica has remained virtually constant in recent decades, despite substantial human population growth (Figure 3.1). However, the area under pasture has increased dramatically, with a symmetrical decrease in the area under forest. Similarly, data from Panama reveal an enormous increase in the country's cattle herd in recent decades, with an almost symmetrical decline in forest area (Ledec 1990). These data suggest that, in terms of tropical deforestation, the most critical population problem is the growth of the cattle population, more so than the human population. Under prevailing cattle stocking rates, every new cow or bull requires roughly one hectare of pasture land, which typically implies that one more hectare of forest disappears.

It is also important to note that frontier colonization zones, the "terminal" use of most deforested land is cattle pasture, even though it is often

TABLE 3.2 Export receipts of land devoted to agricultural commodities (1980)

Country	Export Receipts ($Millions)	Area Utilized (Km2)	Export Receipts per Km2 (US$)
GUATEMALA			
Coffee	433.0	2,480	1,745.97
Sugar	53.3	740	722.97
Cotton	192.4	1,220	1,577.05
Beef	41.1	8,700	47.24
Bananas	48.0	N.A.	N.A.
HONDURAS			
Coffee	196.6	1,300	1,514.62
Sugar	N.A.	750	N.A.
Cotton	N.A.	130	N.A.
Beef	60.8	34,000	17.88
Bananas	199.9	N.A.	N.A.
NICARAGUA			
Coffee	199.6	850	2,348.24
Sugar	19.6	410	478.04
Cotton	148.0	1,740	850.57
Beef	67.7	34,200	19.80
COSTA RICA			
Coffee	252.0	810	3,111.11
Bananas	169.0	280	6,036.71
Beef	65.0	15,580	41.72
Sugar	37.0	480	770.83

Source: Leonard 1987

preceded by several years of subsistence or other cropping. Comparable patterns are reported in the lowlands of southeastern Mexico (Nations and Komer 1983), the Peten region of Guatemala, and the Atlantic lowlands of Honduras (Jones 1985), Darien province and other settlement frontiers in Panama (Heckadon 1984, Joly 1989), as well as most of Amazonia (Hecht 1983, Uquillas 1989). Thus, while it is commonplace to describe deforestation as "expansion of the agricultural frontier," a more accurate description would be "expansion of the cattle frontier."

In terms of deforestation pressure, cattle ranching in tropical Latin America is in a class by itself — fundamentally different from any other type of food or cash crop (including small livestock). This is because cattle raising is so incredibly land-demanding compared to all of these other (non-forest) production systems. Per land area deforested, cattle raising produces much smaller economic or social benefits than any other production system — whether these benefits are measured as foreign exchange, financial revenues, employment, calories, or animal protein.

As an example, look at the foreign exchange earned per square kilometer deforested for five major agricultural export commodities in Central America: coffee, sugar cane, cotton, bananas and beef (Table 3.2).

These data show that a dollar's worth of beef requires the deforestation of between 37 and 119 times more land than a dollar's worth of coffee [2]; also 15-24 times more land than sugar, 34-43 times more land than cotton, and about 145 times more land than bananas! In the Brazilian Amazon, only about one job is created for each $63,000 invested in cattle ranches (Skillings and Tcheyan 1980); this represents the lowest employment-to-expenditure ratio of virtually any type of development project (Goodland 1980). A typical large Latin American cattle ranch employs roughly one person for every 31 km^2 of deforested land (Rainforest Action Network 1988). Even if animal protein is the objective, small livestock such as pigs, goats and chickens or other poultry, as well as fishponds, are much more efficient in terms of meat production per hectare than are cattle. This is true even if the land requirements for growing grain or other feed for these small livestock are considered (Ledec 1990).

The following example perhaps best illustrates the extreme land demands which cattle ranching places on the Latin American tropics. Even though cattle pasture expansion is widely acknowledged as the most significant cause of deforestation in the Brazilian Amazon, this region is still a net beef importer (Hecht, this volume). Thus, all of the incredibly vast areas of Amazonian rainforest thus far cleared for pastures (as dramatically demonstrated by recent satellite imagery) are not even sufficient to supply the beef demand of Manaus and other Amazonian cities.

Even these initial low levels of productivity are often not sustained after the first 5 to 10 years of pasture establishment. Fearnside (1980) and Hecht (1981) point out that many cattle ranches in the Brazilian Amazon have been abandoned because of the declining productivity of pastures caused by soil erosion, compaction by cattle hooves, nutrient depletion (scarce minerals such as calcium and phosphorus are exported in cattle carcasses), and the inevitable invasion by noxious weeds that soon compete with introduced pasture grasses. While this pattern of degradation also prevails over much of the recently deforested land of Central America, cattle ranches are usually not abandoned because of the prestige, social security and speculation value of owning land (even if the land is very degraded) — instead, cattle continue to be grazed at very low stocking rates (Hecht 1981).

Assuming that a typical Latin American pasture on deforested land is productive for 8 years before serious degradation and abandonment, Uhl and Parker (1986) calculate that each quarter-pound hamburger produced from such a pasture implies the deforestation of roughly 55 square feet of land — the size of a small kitchen. They add:

Such a space could contain one vigorous tree, 60 feet tall and weighing about 875 pounds. Below the tree might be some 50 saplings and seedlings in some 20-30 different species (another 120 pounds). Several of these plant species might be extremely rare with limited distributions. Living in the vegetation would be thousands of insects in more than a hundred species (as much as 2 pounds). Several of these insects would likely belong to species not yet known to science. Dozens of bird, reptile, and mammal species would regularly pass through and use this patch of forest (2 pounds). Finally, an almost unimaginable diversity and abundance of mosses, fungi, and microorganisms would be associated with leaf surfaces, bark, roots, and the soil (1 pound). All told, millions of individuals and thousands of species inhabit that patch of tropical forest represented by a single [quarter-pound] hamburger (Uhl and Parker 1986).

Prospects for Intensification of Cattle Production

Since cattle raising normally requires so much land per unit of economic benefit, it is important to evaluate the prospects for intensification. Intensification of cattle production refers to any change in cattle raising technologies which sustainably increases the output of cattle products (principally beef or milk) per unit land area utilized for forage. Such intensification might come from increased sustainable stocking rates — cows or "animal units" (AU) per hectare and/or increased output of beef or milk per AU.

Technologies which might conceivably achieve successful intensification include improvements to existing pastures (such as planting more productive forage species, fertilization, weed control or drainage), improved rotation of cattle on pastures, higher-yielding genetic stock of cattle, improved control of diseases and parasites, and minerals or other nutritional supplements. However, the track record of such attempts at intensification has not been very impressive for tropical beef production. Typical sustainable stocking densities are usually only 1 AU/ha — often appreciably less in frontier areas or on degraded pastures. One of the best-managed, large private cattle ranches in Panama has a stocking density of 1.5 AU/ha, on relatively high-quality agricultural land (i.e., potentially more productive than most Panamanian pasture lands). Thus, barring an unforeseen technical revolution in tropical pasture management, it is difficult to envision that most tropical pastures could economically sustain more than 1.5, or at most 2, free-ranging cattle per ha, any time soon. Similarly, future increases in beef or milk output per AU are not likely to change dramatically the very low ratio of economic benefit per land area deforested that is characteristic of tropical pastures.

Since even the hope of doubling beef or milk output per hectare on most tropical pastures may be optimistic, such intensification offers no viable solution to the problems of pasture expansion and deforestation, although it may produce some marginal improvements. This is in spite of the sizable investment in pasture intensification research by international agricultural research institutes such as the Centro Internacional de Agricultura Tropical (CIAT) in Colombia, or national ones such as the Instituto de Investigacion Agropecuaria de Panama (IDIAP).

The one case for which impressive gains in AU/ha have been sustained for grass-fed cattle is with cultivated pastures that are hand-cut and fed to penned-up dairy cattle. This system (in Spanish, *pasto de corte*) is characteristic of small landholdings in the fertile highlands of Costa Rica, Colombia, and other countries. In places such as Monteverde and parts of the Meseta Central in Costa Rica, this system sustains stocking densities of 7-10 AU/ha. By contrast, typical highland pastures with free-roaming dairy cattle sustain only about 1-3 AU/ha. In large measure, these cultivated, hand-cut pastures are so much more productive per land area cleared because the soil is not compacted and the growing grass is not trampled by cattle hooves. Also, the cultivated pastures are fertilized, and in general treated as a valuable crop. As a rule, intensive dairying with cultivated pastures and enclosure-fed cattle is the only form of cattle raising in Latin America that generates a relatively high economic return per land area deforested.

Natural Grazing Lands versus Induced Pastures

From an environmental standpoint, it is important to distinguish between natural grazing lands and induced pastures. Natural grazing lands are areas which can be grazed without removing any existing trees or shrubs; these are principally natural grassland and savanna ecosystems. Induced pastures, on the other hand, are created by humans through the clearing of forests (or other natural woody vegetation, such as woodlands or shrublands). When natural grazing lands are grazed by cattle or other livestock, they undergo a variety of ecological changes (such as in the composition of dominant grass species). However, these lands still retain their basic ecological structure under grazing (as well as many or most of their original

fauna and even flora), if they are not severely degraded through overgrazing, excessive burning, or other mismanagement. Thus, well-managed cattle
raising does modify natural grazing land ecosystems, but it does not
eliminate them. By contrast, all cattle grazing on induced pastures occurs
through the elimination of the forest (or other original woody vegetation).
From an environmental perspective, it is much more desirable to raise cattle on natural grazing lands than on induced pastures; the former implies
only a modification of the original natural ecosystem, while the latter requires its complete elimination.

Natural grazing lands occurring in Latin America include a variety of
grassland ecosystems in north-central Mexico, the *llanos* of parts of
Venezuela and Colombia, the high-altitude *puna* of the Andes in Peru and
Bolivia, the *cerrado* of central Brazil, and the temperate grasslands of Argentina and Uruguay. Conversely, some Latin American countries do not
have any natural grazing lands. For example, prior to human settlement,
about 99.8% of Costa Rica's land surface was covered by natural forest
(Hartshorn et al. 1982). Similarly, the best available evidence indicates that
Panama also used to be almost completely forested − this includes the
so-called "savanna" zone of lowland Pacific western Panama, which was
probably covered by tropical dry forest prior to human settlement. Thus,
while cattle raising in parts of Latin America takes place on natural grazing
lands, in many areas it takes place exclusively at the expense of forest.

The Social Costs of Deforestation

Although there is major variation by country and region, deforestation
in Latin America is generally proceeding at a rapid and alarming pace.
Table 3.2 indicates estimated deforestation rates for most Latin American
countries (using essentially the same definition of "deforestation" as in this
paper). It should be noted that deforestation estimates vary somewhat, due
to the varying definitions of "forest" and "deforestation" (cf. Myers 1980,
Dourojeanni 1980, UNEP 1982, Molofsky et al. 1986a). For Latin America
overall, Wolf (1987) estimates that by the end of this century, only 52% of
the original forest area will remain. Certain tropical forest zones are particularly critical because they have already been reduced to relatively small
patches and/or are suffering from particularly rapid deforestation. In Latin
America, these zones include the Selva Lacandona in Chiapas, Mexico; the
Mosquitia forest along the Honduras-Nicaragua border; Darien province in
Panama; the Choco region in northwestern Colombia; the lowland coastal
forests of Ecuador; the Atlantic coastal forests of Brazil; and the southern
and eastern Brazilian Amazon (Ledec and Goodland 1988).

There are numerous environmental and other social costs arising from deforestation for cattle pasture. These costs are very high and often irreversible; to a large extent, they will be borne by future generations.

Loss of Wood Production

Perhaps the most obvious social cost of deforestation is the destruction of a valuable timber resource. As Latin America's forests continue to diminish, it will become increasingly difficult and costly to obtain adequate building materials, paper, fuelwood, and other wood products. Shortages of wood for building houses have already been noted in El Salvador, which has lost almost all of its primary forest cover (Leonard 1987). Although Costa Rica is presently a wood exporter, it will need to import about $200 million annually in unprocessed wood products by 1995, if deforestation and domestic demand trends continue (IDB 1987).

Aside from the high costs of wood imports or substitute products, large-scale deforestation implies the loss of a major economic "comparative advantage." The tropical countries of Latin America are mostly naturally forested, and have ideal ecological conditions for growing a wide variety of timber trees relatively quickly. By contrast, many of the forested lands now being cleared are not ecologically suitable for sustained cattle production (Fearnside 1980, Hecht 1981, Leonard 1987). Thus, the potential long-term economic benefits from well-developed forest industries are being sacrificed for the largely ephemeral revenues from cattle ranching. Browder (1988) calculates that the opportunity cost of marketable timber which is destroyed for cattle pastures in the Brazilian Amazon is more than five times the market value of the beef produced. Roughly $5 billion in marketable timber has been destroyed by deforestation (mostly for pasture) in the Brazilian Amazon during the past decade (SAF 1988).

Loss of Environmental Services

Most of the direct, present-day economic benefits provided by Latin American forests are not wood products, but a variety of environmental services that are important to sustained economic development. Environmental services are functions performed naturally by forests, such as maintenance of water flow patterns, protection of the soil, and support of economically important living resources. Despite their economic value and importance to meeting human needs, environmental services are frequently overlooked or underestimated because they are usually public goods, not priced in the marketplace (Ledec and Goodland 1988). Many of the environmental services provided by forests relate to their watershed protection and soil conservation functions. The loss of forest cover often contributes to floods and landslides during the rainy season; water shortages during the dry season; more rapid siltation of hydroelectric dams, irrigation canals, harbors, and other water works; reduced quality of drinking water; and decreased downstream agricultural production, among other development problems (IUCN 1980, Baum and Tolbert 1985, Ledec and Goodland 1988). Even though the main thrust of present-day frontier settlement is in the lowlands, many steep areas continue to be deforested for cattle pasture. Serious degradation of important watershed areas is often the result.

Many Latin American countries rely heavily on hydroelectric power to meet their growing electricity needs. For example, the proportion of electricity generated by hydropower is about 71% in Costa Rica, 68% in Colombia, 57% in Bolivia and Honduras, and 54% in El Salvador (World Bank 1983). Nonetheless, many hydroelectric projects worth hundreds of millions of dollars are being seriously damaged through the deforestation of their watersheds, often by a relatively few cattle ranching families. When hydroelectric watersheds are deforested, accelerated sedimentation due to erosion from deforested slopes reduces the storage (and electricity-generating) capacity of many reservoirs. Furthermore, substantially less water may be available during the dry season, either because the extra deforestation-related runoff must be released from the reservoirs during the wet season, or because montane "cloud forests" (which capture the moisture from dry-season clouds) had been cleared. Examples of hydroelectric reservoirs which suffer from accelerated sedimentation and a shortened economic life due to watershed deforestation (primarily for cattle pasture) include *Cinco de Noviembre* in El Salvador (Leonard 1987), *Chixoy* in Guatemala and *El Cajon* in Honduras (World Rivers Review 1988), *Arenal* and *Cachi* in Costa Rica (Leonard 1987, World Rivers Review 1988), Madden (*Alhajuela*) in Panama (Panama 1986a, Alvarado 1985, Robinson 1985), and *Bajo Anchicaya* (Farvar and Milton 1972) and *Chivor* (*La Esmeralda*) in Colombia (ISA 1986). It should therefore be remembered that many tropical forests are valuable energy resources, not if they are burned for fuel but if they are left standing intact for watershed protection.

One of the most dramatic examples of how deforestation for pasture threatens important infrastructure is the case of the Panama Canal, still Panama's greatest single economic asset (Panama 1986b). Deforestation is jeopardizing the Canal's long-term viability, resulting in heavy siltation and lack of sufficient water during some dry seasons to operate the locks for the larger ships (Panama 1986a, USDS 1978). There are fears that the losses from sedimentation will be much greater within a few decades if deforestation continues on the Canal watershed's many steep slopes (Panama 1986a, Alvarado 1985, Robinson 1985). The main cause of deforestation in the

Canal watershed is land clearing for cattle pasture (Heckadon 1986, Robinson 1985). Millions of dollars are spent annually by the governments of both Panama and the United States for military defense of the Panama Canal. By contrast, comparatively little money has been invested to control the spread of cattle ranching, which seems to pose a more certain long-run threat to the Canal than any military foe (Voelker 1988).

In addition to their soil conservation and water regulation functions, Latin American tropical forests are important to the economic productivity of many fisheries. In Amazonia, fallen fruit from seasonally flooded varzea forests is necessary to the survival of many species of fish. Substantial clearing of this forest may permanently damage this fishery resource, along with the livelihoods of local people (Goulding 1980). In Costa Rica, heavy sedimentation due to deforestation (for pasture) has been identified as the major cause of the severe recent deterioration of two major coral reef systems (Cahuita and Limon). As a result, many fishermen are now struggling while others are out of business. Commercial lobster production has markedly declined. The tourist sport fishery around Tortuguero (an important source of foreign exchange) also appears threatened (USAID 1987).

Besides fisheries, Latin America's tropical forests support a variety of other economically important living resources, often in remarkable ways. The production of Brazil nuts (*Bertholletia excelsa*) depends on a variety of poorly-known forest plants and animals. The pollinating insects are not fully known, but several species of Euglossine bees visit the flowers. Male Euglossine bees attract females before mating only after gathering organic compounds from certain species of epiphytic orchids, but depend on other flower species for food (nectar). The hard fruit case (pyxidium) enclosing the nuts is opened naturally only by agoutis (*Dasyprocta* – large forest-dwelling rodents), which thereby enable seed dispersal to take place (Prance and Mori 1983). Thus, maintaining Brazil nut production appears to require conserving enough natural forest to protect Euglossine bee nesting habitat, bee food plants, certain orchids and the trees upon which they grow, the insects or hummingbirds that pollinate the orchids (and all their necessities in turn), and agoutis. The Brazil nut industry exports more than US$16 million to the United States alone (Caufield 1982). Smoke from adjacent forest burning has been suspected of decreasing Brazil nut yields by interfering with the pollinators (Ledec and Goodland 1988).

Loss of Biological Diversity

One of the most far-reaching and irreversible consequences of large-scale deforestation is the imminent extinction of numerous plant and animal species. Tropical forests are the most biologically diverse ecosystems on the planet. For example, a country as small as Panama has over 880 species of birds, more than the United States and Canada combined (Ridgley 1976). The Amazon rainforest contains perhaps 20% of all higher plant species found on earth (Wetterberg et al. 1981). In many respects, the tropical forests of Latin America are even richer in species than their counterparts in Asia and Africa. Tropical America is estimated to contain roughly 90,000 species of flowering plants, compared to about 30,000 for sub-Saharan Africa and 35,000 for tropical Asia, Australia, and the Pacific (Myers 1979). Many tropical species of plants and animals have very localized distributions and cannot survive if their forest habitat is eliminated. Rapid forest clearing for cattle pasture can therefore cause the extinction of numerous plant and animal species virtually overnight; most of these species are not yet even known to science (Myers 1979, 1983; NAS 1980b).

Why is preserving biological diversity important? There are compelling economic, scientific, aesthetic, and ethical reasons for humanity to be alarmed about the rapid loss of species. The economic reason is that numerous wild plant and animal species are "undeveloped resources," in that they have economic potential that is currently undiscovered or underutilized. Biological resources are essential to human existence, and the preservation of biological diversity is necessary for the maintenance and improvement of agriculture, animal husbandry, forestry, fisheries, medicine, industry, and tourism (Plotkin 1988, Fitter 1986, Prescott-Allen and Prescott-Allen 1983, Myers 1983, 1984). For example, a recently discovered species of wild perennial corn (*Zea diploperennis*) may become important for increasing food production, even though it seemed at first to be "just another weed" growing on a single forested hillside in Jalisco, Mexico (Iltis 1988). Human society is likely to be better off because this apparent weed was not eliminated by conversion of all of its natural habitat to agriculture or other uses.

Similarly, over 25% of modern prescription drugs sold in the United States contain one or more active ingredients originating from wild species, particularly tropical plants (Farnsworth 1988). In some cases, it is impossible or more costly to synthesize these compounds than to obtain them from living sources; in other cases, it would not have been possible to know what compound to synthesize without first having the natural model.

Wild animal and plant species are also important to industry, providing tannins, resins, gums, oils, dyes, and other commercially useful compounds. Even the rubber tree (*Hevea brasiliensis*) was once just another Amazonian tree species of unknown value. Though impossible to quantify, there is substantial potential for new industrial products from currently unknown or poorly-known plant and animal species. These even include renewable sources of hydrocarbons. For example, *Copaifera langsdorfii*, a tree that grows only in northern Brazil, produces 20 liters of sap per tree every six months. It was recently discovered that this sap can be used directly as a fuel in diesel engines (EEB 1982). There has been little systematic screening of wild plants for many of the types of products used by modern society; some plants naturally manufacture such products in considerable quantities.

These few examples serve to indicate the potential economic value of many wild species. Nonetheless, less than 20% of the world's tropical species of plants and animals have been inventoried and scientifically named, and even fewer have been assessed for possible human uses (NAS 1980). Biological resources (unlike petroleum and other fossil fuels), are completely renewable, but only if care is taken not to destroy them before their value can be realized. Eliminating much of the world's vast wealth of biological diversity for short-term expediency has been likened to "burning the world's libraries for one winter's warmth" (Kirchner et al. 1985).

The scientific reason for species preservation is that we cannot understand the interactions of life forms and their environments unless we can observe how they function in the absence of significant human intervention. It is therefore necessary to conserve comprehensive samples of ecological systems in an undisturbed state. Moreover, the physiological, biochemical, and population characteristics of each species are unique; the study of these characteristics is an aid to unraveling many of life's mysteries.

The aesthetic reason is that many wild species of plants and animals are irreplaceable sources of wonder, inspiration, and joy to humans because of their beauty, intriguing appearance, variety, or fascinating behavior. The French anthropologist Claude Levi-Strauss described wild species as "an irreplaceable marvel, equal to the works of art which we religiously preserve in museums" (discussion, Special Commission on Internal Pollution, London, October 1975). This aesthetic value has only partially been measured in terms of economic value, through such activities as bird watching and wildlife photography. However, many people derive enrichment merely from knowledge of the existence of many wild species they never see; this "vicarious satisfaction" has no market value. In the context of Latin America, it is noteworthy that a large proportion of the birds which breed in the United States (245 out of 645 species) migrate to spend the northern winter in Latin America and the Caribbean; at least 57 of these depend strictly on tropical forests for their survival (Ehrlich et al. 1988, WWF 1982).

Finally, the ethical reason for species preservation is that a growing number of people believe that human beings do not have the right to obliterate other species of living things at will— even those species not known to have any practical value to humankind (Rolston 1985). This ethical value has been called the "Noah Principle" (Ehrenfeld 1981). While this value is not universally shared, extinction is a completely irreversible process, and to extinguish other species is to deny the options available to all future human generations. For one or two generations of cattle ranchers to eliminate a sizable proportion of the diversity of life on Earth is, at the very least, an act of considerable arrogance. Thus, although human societies are confronted with numerous, pressing short-term problems, any actions with such profound and everlasting consequences as causing mass extinctions must be weighed very carefully.

In the following statement, Wilson (1985) provides an ecological perspective on the significance of massive, human-induced species extinctions:

> The worst thing that can happen — will happen — is not energy depletion, economic collapse, limited nuclear war, or conquest by a totalitarian government. As terrible as these catastrophes would be for us, they can be repaired within a few human generations. The one process ongoing in the 1980s that will take millions of years to correct is the loss of genetic and species diversity by the destruction of natural habitats. This is the folly our descendants are least likely to forgive us. (Wilson 1985:20-21).

Climatic Stability

There is growing scientific evidence that Latin America's tropical forests are major factors in maintaining regional climatic stability. Reduced rainfall in northwestern Costa Rica and central Panama has been attributed to forest removal for cattle pasture (Windsor and Rand 1985). On a larger scale, it is feared that, because the Amazon Basin forest generates approximately 50% of its own rainfall, deforestation in the Basin might initiate irreversible climatic changes throughout the rest of Brazil. A drier climate, with increased frosts and damage to crops, has been recently observed in southern Brazil and linked to Amazonian deforestation (Salati and Vose 1984). Even when it does not actually decrease rainfall, deforestation can result in water shortages for rain-fed agriculture. For example, rain-fed crops in the lowlands of Pacific western Panama are now surrounded by large areas of pasture, as the area has been almost totally deforested. During the dry season, strong, hot winds greatly decrease soil moisture and potential crop yields. If these croplands were surrounded by patches of forest rather than by open pastures, these winds would have much less effect in drying out the soils, and crop yields would probably significantly increase (Ledec 1990).

Effects on Forest-dwelling Peoples

Although it is by no means the only disruptive consequence of settlement by outsiders, deforestation can quickly destroy the livelihoods (and even the lives) of forest-dwelling peoples, particularly Amerindians. These ethnic minorities, only partially or not at all acculturated into the dominant national society, are extremely vulnerable to being forced off their traditional lands by immigrant settlers. Examples of this process are strikingly evident in many parts of Amazonia (Davis 1977, Uquillas, 1989), as well as in the lowlands of Chiapas, Mexico and parts of Central America (Nations 1985, Nations and Komer 1983). Joly (1989) and Jones (1989) point out how cattle-raising *latino* settlers in Panama continually encroach upon and displace populations of both Indians and Afro-hispanics. Both of the latter groups deforest comparatively very little land for their livelihoods; not surprisingly, they also generally do not raise cattle.

Aside from its serious ethical and human rights implications, the cultural (or physical) demise of these Indian groups can produce a serious setback to efforts to obtain increased economic gain from tropical forest lands. Over the millennia, forest-dwelling tribal people have accumulated an impressive amount of knowledge concerning how various tropical plants and animals can be used for food, medications, and other products. Moreover, these people have learned many useful lessons about how the forest ecosystem can be successfully manipulated for food production and meeting other subsistence needs (World Bank 1982a). Modern scientists confess their substantial ignorance about many aspects of managing lands in the lowland humid tropics for sustained economic production (NAS 1980). Consequently, there is a sense of urgency about studying how tribal peoples utilize the forest ecosystem, to ensure that this knowledge is not irretrievably lost.

Other Social Costs of Cattle Pasture Expansion

Besides the many effects of large-scale deforestation, cattle ranching and the associated pasture expansion in Latin America entails a variety of other high social costs. As with deforestation, the seriousness of these other social costs has largely been overlooked by development planners.

Displacement of Crop Production and Agricultural Labor

Not all pastures are created by directly clearing forest. Pastures frequently take over active or fallow cropland (thereby often creating pressures to clear roughly an equivalent area of forest to replace the lost cropland). Moreover, many cattle pastures are in areas of relatively fertile soils and high agricultural potential. In most Latin American countries, non-frontier lands which could support more intensive agriculture are often used very extensively, especially for cattle pasture (Leonard 1987, Shane 1986, Goodland et al. 1984). Much more so than in the densely-populated tropics of Asia and even parts of Africa, the "population pressure" for land settlement can largely be attributed to a maldistribution, rather than absolute shortage, of existing good-quality agricultural land.

The prevalence of cattle grazing on high-potential agricultural lands results in a number of serious social problems. There is often a high economic opportunity cost to the loss of more valuable crop production; for various social reasons, agricultural land markets are often neither economically efficient nor rational. Because of grazing on prime agricultural lands, subsistence and small holder crop production are typically pushed to marginal lands, where yields per hectare are lower and serious soil erosion or loss of fertility often result (thereby implying still more deforestation). Major employment opportunities are lost when high-potential agricultural lands are used for cattle ranching, which absorbs so little labor. The result is increased poverty and out-migration, typically to overcrowded cities or forested frontier areas.

Frontier living conditions are frequently very harsh for settlers displaced from other agricultural lands. This is particularly true in lowland humid tropical areas with their many endemic diseases. In Rondonia, Brazil, for example, at least one member of every settler family contracted malaria in 1980 (Goodland 1984).

Costs of Low-density Settlement Patterns

Because cattle ranching requires much more land than most other production systems to support each household, it results in very low-density patterns of land settlement. A strong case can be made that such low-density settlement is socially more costly and frequently undesirable (apart from the above-mentioned problems of deforestation and displacement of indigenous peoples). When people live at these low densities, it is much more costly per capita to provide them with roads, schools, health centers, and other social infrastructure. As a result, governments or aid donors must pay much higher costs per person served in a cattle-ranching zone than, say, a coffee, banana, or rice-growing zone. Furthermore, the people living in low-density zones must often do without vital services, because the nearest clinic or school is too far away.

While substantial, these costs of low-density settlement are usually ignored by development planners. It is important to incorporate such costs within economic analyses of development projects that promote low-density settlement patterns. Examples of such projects include forest penetration roads in frontier settlement areas, as well as livestock credit or other cattle promotion schemes.

Costs of Subsidies

Throughout Latin America, livestock credit is promoted and subsidized on a large scale by governments and international development agencies. Brazilian 1977-78 subsidies for agricultural credit amounted to 3.3% of Gross Domestic Product, 32% of treasury revenue (World Bank 1984), and roughly 25% of government expenditures at all levels — federal, state, and local (Sayad 1983). During this period, nearly 25% of these agricultural credit subsidies was earmarked for cattle (World Bank 1982b). In Panama, the proportion of subsidized agricultural credit allocated to cattle approaches 50%. The high investment opportunity cost of cattle credit should not be overlooked. Browder (1988) calculates that every metric ton of beef produced in the Brazilian Amazon represents about $1,050 in rural credit subsidies.

Another type of subsidy granted to cattle ranching is reduced land taxes for cattle pastures. The largest-scale example of this type of subsidy was the tax credit program of SUDAM, Brazil's Amazonian development agency, which provided the equivalent of hundreds of millions of U.S. dollars in tax relief to cattle ranchers during the 1970s (Browder 1988). Forest penetration roads that promote cattle ranching also represent costly subsidies for cattle ranching. Both penetration roads and subsidized cattle credit are financed largely by international loans, particularly from the World Bank and Inter-American Development Bank. These types of loans represent a "double blow" to Latin American countries: at the same time that they promote the destruction of a valuable and irreplaceable forest resource, they add to the country's heavy foreign debt burden.

Recommended Livestock Policy Reforms

From an environmental perspective, new directions for livestock policy are urgently needed. The basic guiding principle should be to encourage cattle raising only on natural grazing lands (in those countries which have them), or in very intensive systems (such as cultivated pastures and enclosure-fed dairy cattle). On the other hand, cattle ranching that implies using extensive areas of deforested pasture land should be strongly discouraged, in favor of less extensive and more forest conserving agricultural production systems.

Encourage Alternative Livestock Species

In the Latin American context, the words "livestock" and "cattle" (*ganado*) are often used interchangeably, reflecting the heavy emphasis which cattle raising receives relative to other species of livestock. Nonetheless, small livestock have an important role in agricultural systems. Pork production is of growing importance in most of Latin America; there are about two domestic pigs for every human being in South America (Goodland et al. 1984). Pigs require much less land than beef cattle per kilogram of meat produced, whether they are fed grain, cassava, or other crops in large-scale commercial operations, or agricultural residues in small-scale peasant household production. The same can be said of chickens, turkeys, ducks, or other poultry, which figure prominently in many Latin American diets. Goats, which are prominent in a number of Latin American countries (including Bolivia, Jamaica, Peru, and Venezuela), also require much less land than cattle per kg of meat produced (Ledec 1990). Unlike cattle, goats can thrive on the shrubby second-growth typical of shifting cultivation systems and do not require pasture establishment for their production. (The bad environmental reputation of goats is mainly due to their ability to over-browse semi-arid zones, but this criticism is much less relevant in the humid tropics). Other small Latin American livestock which require relatively little land per kg of meat produced include rabbits, iguanas (being domesticated in Panama) and capybaras (Venezuela). There is also major potential for growth in fish production through small-scale aquaculture.

Despite their presently substantial and potentially much greater role in satisfying meat demands all of these small livestock have received substantially less credit and other development assistance than have cattle. This is unfortunate from an environmental standpoint, because (in the absence of natural grazing land) cattle require the deforestation of much more land per kilogram of meat produced than any of these other alternatives. Small livestock are also more amenable to production by poor rural households, who frequently lack the relatively large amount of capital or land required to support a herd of cattle. For both environmental and social reasons, governments and international development agencies should greatly increase their support for small livestock production, which is an excellent alternative to extensive cattle ranching on induced pastures.

Discourage or Prohibit Bank Credit for Pasture Expansion

In most of Latin America, cattle ranchers receive subsidized credit from governmental banks—for example, the Banco Nacional de Panama and Banco de Desarrollo Agropecuario in Panama. These governmental banks obtain their funds for cattle lending largely from international loans, particularly from the Inter-American Development Bank (IDB) and World Bank. Private commercial banks also lend money for cattle ranching in countries such as Panama, frequently at subsidized rates mandated by the government. Millions of U.S. dollars' worth of subsidized cattle credit in Latin America have been justified largely in terms of promoting intensification of cattle production. Nonetheless, the effect of this credit in countries such as Panama has largely been to promote pasture expansion, either directly or indirectly at the expense of forest (Ledec 1990).

In any case, institutional cattle credit is heavily regulated (and frequently subsidized) by Latin American governments. It is therefore possible for governments to change existing policies and restrict or even eliminate institutional cattle credit for ranching on induced tropical pastures. Some of the policy options for doing this are listed below.

Eliminate or Reduce Institutional Cattle Credit. The most effective (but most controversial) means to avoid promoting deforestation through cattle credit is to eliminate credit subsidies outright, or even to prohibit banks from lending for cattle at commercial interest rates. However, less drastic reductions or restrictions in cattle credit are also possible. The general thrust of rural credit policy should be away from cattle raising on induced pastures, and towards small livestock, crop or forestry production. Aside from the environmental benefits, reallocating agricultural credit towards crops and small livestock would also be progressive in distributional terms, since rural Latin Americans with cattle tend to be wealthier than those without. Alternatively, the funds could be used in other sectors or for servicing the foreign debt.

In addition to their cattle, many ranchers raise some crops (subsistence or commercial). This poses the problem of fungibility − possible use for cattle of credit intended for crops or small livestock. It would therefore be more effective to eliminate or reduce agricultural credit to anyone who owns more than a few cattle, rather than merely specifying that the borrower may not use any of the credit for cattle.

Limit Credit to Areas Deemed Best Suited for Cattle Production. Cattle credit could be prohibited for protected forest areas (which nonetheless often have settlers or private "inholdings" within their boundaries), very steep zones, high-quality agricultural land, and other areas that are particularly ill-suited for cattle ranching. Such "redlining" could be at a macro level (e.g., no cattle credit for the most forested states, provinces, departments, or other administrative units), or at a micro level (checking the ecological suitability of each applicant's landholdings). The exact form of these lending restrictions would depend on the detail of the land capability data base, as well as the administrative capabilities of the banks.

Raise Interest Rates on Cattle Credit. Some businessmen undertake cattle ranching merely to qualify for subsidized credit, and then divert the funds to non-agricultural investments, which are not legally eligible for comparable credit subsidies. This process often leads to deforestation for cattle pasture to obtain the cheap credit. This problem could be easily corrected by raising interest rates for cattle credit to commercial levels, simply by cutting existing governmental subsidies.

Provide Cattle Credit for Intensification Purposes Only. One approach would be to designate cattle credit only for those inputs that are most closely related to intensification, rather than pasture expansion. For example, veterinary care and mineralized salt are closely related to intensification, while chainsaws (for forest cutting) are intimately linked to pasture expansion. However, many inputs (such as fencing and breeding stock) can arguably be used for either intensification or expansion. Moreover, the effectiveness of this approach would be severely limited by fungibility.

Another (perhaps more promising) approach would be to prohibit borrowers from clearing any remaining forest on their landholdings. Disbursements could be terminated if the borrower clears additional forest. In countries such as Panama, bank representatives already visit and inspect the land of each borrower, so that the marginal administrative costs of this approach would not be high. On the other hand, it might lead to some "pre-emptive" forest clearing by borrowers before they apply for the credit.

Establish Cattle-free Development Zones

A variety of relatively sustainable development options exist for forest frontier areas in the humid tropics of Latin America. These include sustained-yield timber harvest; extraction of various "minor forest products," including Brazil or other nuts, chicle, wild rubber, and others; a large variety of tree or shrub crops; various agroforestry systems which combine field crops with trees or shrubs, simultaneously or sequentially; small livestock; fisheries, including aquaculture; and nature-oriented tourism, among others. However, all of these potentially sustainable and environmentally more benign land uses are precluded by large-scale cattle pasture establishment. It would therefore be very desirable for Latin American governments to designate "cattle-free development zones" in which the raising or transportation of cattle would be prohibited. Such zones would enable other, more sustainable and environmentally desirable production systems to develop and flourish.

To some degree, such a zone presently exists in the section of Darien province in Panama close to the Colombian border. In this zone, the transportation of cattle is prohibited, because of the risk of spreading hoof-and-mouth disease (aftosa) from Colombia to Panama (and then to Central and North America). As a result of this prohibition on moving cattle to the lucrative Panama City market, pasture development has been discouraged, while alternative production systems, including the commercial cultivation of cassava and plantains, predominate. As a result, less forest is cleared per unit of economic value (and per settler family) in this zone than in the rest of Darien province. While this special zone was established for animal health reasons, rather than environmental ones, it shows that "cattle-free zones" in some form can be feasibly implemented, and that the resulting land use pattern is different (most notably, less forest is cleared).

Redefine Economic Comparative Advantage of Cattle Raising

Despite the very high environmental and other social costs of cattle ranching on induced tropical pastures, this activity continues to be enthusiastically promoted by international development advisors, particularly livestock economists. Their prescription is that Latin American governments should do even more than they are doing now to promote both beef and dairy production, with the objectives of achieving domestic self-sufficiency and/or exporting as much of a surplus as possible. For example, a recent World Bank (1985) country study for Panama recommends increased emphasis on cattle ranching, despite this country's almost complete lack of natural grazing lands. A major World Bank livestock study states that "most countries in Latin America probably have a comparative advantage not in poultry and pork but in beef and milk because of their substantial pastoral resources (Jarvis 1986)." However, for most tropical Latin American countries, these "substantial pastoral resources" are largely or entirely dependent upon substantial deforestation.

This pro-ranching advice, which continues to be so destructive to the forests, is based on a very incomplete assessment of the beef production costs that are used to calculate economic comparative advantage. Only the market-based production costs for beef on induced tropical pastures are considered; the numerous environmental and social "externalities" are completely ignored. A partial list of these externalities includes the loss of timber production; extinction of numerous animal and plant species, many with potential economic value; soil erosion and loss of fertility; increased flooding and landslides during the wet season and water shortages during the dry season; reduced economic output of hydroelectric reservoirs and other water development projects; increased dredging costs for harbors and canals; damage to inland and coastal fisheries; the cultural and even physical extinction of forest-dwelling peoples; potentially disastrous and irreversible climatic changes; displacement of crop production from high-quality agricultural lands; displacement of agricultural labor, with resulting poverty and out-migration; increased costs and decreased availability of many social services, due to very low-density settlement; and the investment opportunity costs of a variety of explicit or "hidden" cattle subsidies.

It is methodologically very difficult to incorporate all of these very real costs within the cost-benefit framework of neoclassical economics, due to such problems as measurement and valuation difficulties, discount rate selection, and irreversibility (Goodland and Ledec 1987). There is a major need to revise the methodology for calculating the economic comparative advantage of cattle raising . Meanwhile, the environmental and social case against cattle ranching on induced pastures is so strong that the following "interim" guidelines should be used. In Latin America, a comparative advantage for beef production may exist for those countries or regions endowed with abundant natural grazing lands, but it clearly does not exist for countries or regions where cattle ranching occurs primarily or exclusively on induced pastures, created at the expense of forests. Similarly, a comparative advantage for dairy production may exist for natural grazing lands, or for very intensive dairying systems (particularly with cultivated pasture forage and enclosure-fed cows), but it does not exist for relatively extensive dairy production (including so-called "dual-purpose" beef-milk ranching) on induced tropical pastures.

Discourage Beef Consumption in Countries Lacking Natural Grazing Lands

Many Latin American governments continue to promote domestic beef consumption, particularly through price controls on various cuts of beef [3] (Jarvis 1986). Such policies treat beef as a staple which should be made available in ample supply, even to lower-income groups. However, no credible nutritionist today would claim that beef is necessary for a healthy diet, even though it is tasty and culturally popular. Moreover, the social costs of beef consumption are very high, whenever that beef is produced on induced pastures at the expense of tropical forests. From an environmental perspective, such beef should be viewed as a wasteful and costly luxury, rather than as a product whose consumption should be strongly encouraged.

While Latin American livestock policies have focused on supply management, it is important to consider demand management as well. For those countries where natural grazing lands are either absent or extremely limited (including all of Central America and the Caribbean), there is a strong divergence between the private and social costs of beef consumption. The beef consumer only pays the market price of beef, which does not include the many environmental and other social externalities (outlined above) of beef production on induced pastures.

Three basic, complementary public policy approaches are available to help correct this serious "market failure." First, the other policies outlined in this paper to minimize further pasture expansion will tend to constrain beef production, thereby raising consumer prices (which should definitely not be subsidized). Second, public policies should promote both the production and consumption of alternative forms of animal protein, including pork, goat meat, chicken and other poultry, eggs, fish, and even "unconventional" small livestock such as iguanas or capybaras; these all require much less land to produce each kilogram of meat than does beef. Jarvis (1986) indicates that sufficient cross-price elasticity of demand exists between beef and other meats, so that consumers would probably respond strongly to a major, longer-term shift in relative prices. Third, a special beef tax could be imposed to discourage both consumption and production, particularly in those countries where all beef production has high environmental costs because no natural grazing land exists. (A general beef tax would penalize all of a country's beef producers, not just the most ecologically "inefficient" ones.)

Revise Dairy Production Goals

It is more difficult to argue that dairy products are a luxury food than is the case with beef (even though the importance of dairy products to human nutrition is often greatly overstated). Many Latin American countries are substantial (dried) milk importers; for example, Panama imports about 50% of its domestic consumption. To the extent that import substitution (or, for some countries, export) goals for milk can be attained through highly intensive production (particularly cultivated pastures and enclosure-fed cows), the environmental costs are not likely to be high. On the other hand, increasing dairy production through land-extensive systems (involving relatively low stocking rates) would probably cause considerable further deforestation. If increasing domestic dairy production is tantamount to increasing deforestation, a more environmentally desirable strategy for countries lacking natural grazing lands is to accept continued milk imports (or to avoid milk export promotion). A close analogy is with wheat. Many tropical countries, such as Panama continue to import most or all of their wheat flour, because they admittedly lack (for ecological reasons) a comparative advantage in wheat production. Similarly, if the high environmental costs of extensive dairy production are fully considered, countries lacking natural grazing lands probably also lack a comparative advantage in dairy production.

Complementary Policy Reforms

No less important than the above-mentioned livestock policy reforms are a variety of complementary policy changes to encourage forest conservation and discourage deforestation for pasture expansion. Many of these complementary policy reforms are outlined below.

Establish and Strengthen Protected Forest Areas

Protected forest areas that have been established in various Latin American countries include biosphere reserves, national parks, biological reserves, natural monuments, strict nature reserves, ecological stations, wildlife refuges, forest reserves, and indigenous reserves (Ledec and Goodland 1988). While the preferred management system and desired degree of human intervention in these areas varies by type of category, country, and location, these areas are all intended to maintain intact stands of native forest or other natural vegetation. One very basic strategy to limit the damage done by deforestation for cattle pasture is therefore to set aside legally protected areas where forest clearing is not allowed. In the case of Costa Rica, this approach towards controlling deforestation is the only one that has succeeded to any significant degree. The country has one of the best protected systems of National Parks and equivalent reserves, yet outside these "islands of conservation," it has suffered probably the highest relative rate of deforestation (mostly for pasture) of any country in Latin America (USAID 1987, 1988; Fundacion Neotropica 1988; Tosi 1988; Boza 1986; Hartshorn et al. 1982).

Table 3.3 indicates, in absolute and relative terms, the amount of land which different countries in the Americas have legally set aside for the conservation of forests and other natural ecosystems, as of 1985. While the establishment of legally protected forest areas has been vitally important in reducing species extinctions and the other social costs of deforestation, it suffers from two major deficiencies. First, many unique tropical forest types still lack legal protection. For example, Fundacion Neotropica (1988) indicates that of Costa Rica's 53 different natural vegetation types (mostly forest types), 17 are not represented in strictly protected areas, and 8 are not in any type of protected area. This is even though Costa Rica is internationally known for its relatively well-developed system of protected areas. For Latin America overall, Wolf (1987) projects that 66% of all rainforest plant species will eventually become extinct if the only rainforests that survive are those presently in protected areas. Second, many of the legally protected areas are "paper parks," receiving little or no on-the-ground protection from deforestation or other illegal activities (Ledec and Goodland 1988).

Fortunately, both deficiencies are amenable to policy change. It is important for Latin American governments to set aside new protected areas, as well as to improve the on-the-ground management of existing ones. In this respect, an encouraging development is the World Bank's recently adopted policy on wildland management. This policy commits the Bank to supporting explicit natural forest protection components within any future Bank-financed projects which either cause deforestation, or depend upon existing natural forests for their proper functioning (World Bank 1986). The United States Agency for International Development (USAID) now has an active program for supporting the conservation of biological diversity in host countries, including natural forest conservation projects in Costa Rica and Peru (Schaffer and Saterson 1987).

Highways and Rural Roads

Perhaps the most influential policy variable concerning deforestation is the construction of forest penetration roads (whether major highways or small rural roads). These roads are usually a prerequisite to major cattle pasture expansion, since they provide the only convenient access to forested lands for most colonists, including cattle ranchers. Throughout most of tropical Latin America, the mere building of a road into a forested area is usually sufficient to encourage spontaneous colonization and forest clearing. Even paving or otherwise improving an existing road can have this effect, by providing would-be colonists with improved access to markets. It should be remembered that the massive POLONOROESTE land settlement program in Rondonia and Mato Grosso, Brazil, consisted primarily of the paving of an existing road between Cuiaba and Porto Velho. This program may ultimately account for the clearing of 100,000 km^2 of natural

TABLE 3.3 Legally protected wildland areas in the western hemisphere

Country	National Area km²	Protected Wildlands km²	National Area Protected %	Protected Areas
Argentina	2,766,890	25,944	0.94	29
Bahamas	13,940	1,225	8.79	4
Barbados	430	0	0.00	0
Belize	22,965	53	0.23	2
Bolivia	1,098,581	47,077	4.29	12
Brazil	8,511,960	118,943	1.40	50
Canada	9976,140	229,491	2.30	78
Chile	756,950	127,343	16.83	64
Colombia	1,138,981	39,588	3.48	30
Costa Rica	50,900	4,125	8.14	21
Cuba	113,198	243	0.21	4
Dominica	750	68	9.07	1
Dom. Republic	48,730	2,198	4.51	5
Ecuador	270,670	26,274	9.27	12
El Salvador	20,988	0	0.00	0
French Guiana	91,000	0	0.00	0
Grenada	340	0	0.00	0
Guatemala	108,980	596	0.55	2
Guyana	214,970	117	0.05	1
Haiti	27,750	50	0.18	2
Honduras	112,090	4,226	3.77	4
Jamaica	10,990	0	0.00	0
Mexico	1,967,180	9,384	0.48	29
Nicaragua	130,000	173	0.13	2
Panama	77,082	6,609	8.57	6
Paraguay	406,750	11,205	2.75	9
Peru	1,285,220	24,076	1.87	11
St. Lucia	620	16	2.58	1
Suriname	163,820	5,824	3.57	9
Trinidad and Tobago	5,130	165	3.22	8
United States (inc. Puerto Rico)	9,372,360	649,461	6.93	251
Uruguay	176,220	288	0.16	6
Venezuela	912,050	73,889	8.10	34
TOTAL	39,854,535	1,408,651	3.53	687

Source: Area and number of protected areas, adapted from IUCN (1985); national area from Molofsky et al (1986) or others. Includes all Strict Nature Reserves, National Parks, Natural Monuments, Wildlife Sanctuaries, Protected Landscapes, Biosphere Reserves, and World Heritage Natural Sites, but not Resource Reserves, Anthroplogical Reserves, or Multiple Use Management Areas, as defined by IUCN (1985).

vegetation, mostly rainforest (Goodland 1984). This area is roughly twice the size of Costa Rica, and five times the size of El Salvador.

Perhaps the most effective way in which Latin American governments and development aid agencies can control deforestation is by controlling the construction and improvement of highways and rural roads. Roads intended to facilitate settlement of forested areas are justified only if the lands to be settled are likely to be utilized in a sustainable and relatively intensive or forest-conserving manner. Since this is rarely the case in Latin American land settlement, it would be desirable for governments to impose a moratorium on further road construction of this type, emphasizing instead more intensive agricultural and infrastructure development in zones that have already been heavily deforested.

If new roads are built primarily to connect population centers (rather than to promote forest settlement), they should be situated so as to avoid crossing vulnerable forest areas. Where such road alignment is not feasible, the government should provide guard stations or other measures to restrict spontaneous settlement and deforestation. This measure was taken by the government of Costa Rica in connection with the building of a new highway to connect Guapiles with San Jose. To prevent spontaneous settlement of a steep forested area, the government extended the boundaries of the Braulio Carrillo National Park to include most of the area traversed by the new highway (Ledec and Goodland 1988). However, such strong forest conservation components of new road projects are still very much the exception, rather than the rule.

Land Tenure Laws

Although they vary by country, formal and customary (unwritten) land use laws and traditions strongly endorse the practice of forest clearing. Clearing the forest is often a prerequisite for obtaining land title or official usufructuary rights. In fact, landowners or land claimants who do not clear the forest often risk losing their legal rights to the land (Ledec and Goodland 1989). It is worth noting that cattle ranching is generally the preferred production system for demonstrating "productive use" of deforested land, because it enables the landholder to "utilize" the maximum amount of land, with a minimum of family or hired labor, or purchased inputs.

This "use it or lose it" legal tradition of forest clearing is rooted in the perception that natural forest has no value unless it is cleared or otherwise directly exploited by people. This perception implies that forests which may be serving important societal functions such as watershed preservation, soil conservation, habitat for rare species, or climatic stabilization are considered "unutilized," while ephemerally productive, poorly managed or degraded pasture lands are not. To environmentalists, this view of tropical forests is an anachronism; it fails to take into account the numerous negative effects of deforestation.

There is thus an urgent need for a thorough reform of existing land tenure laws, so that landholders or squatters are not compelled to deforest land to demonstrate their "productive use." It is essential that such a reform take place "on the ground" and not just "on paper" in each Latin American country. For example, Colombia (Ortega 1986) and Costa Rica (Arias 1987, Costa Rica 1986a, 1986b) have both recently enacted strong forest conservation laws which explicitly repeal land clearing as a necessary condition of productive use. Nonetheless, deforestation to claim land possession is still very prevalent in both countries.

A related issue is the lack of efficient land titling and adjudication procedures in most of Latin America. A large proportion of private landholdings are without formal title; many titles are disputed or overlapping. The resulting land tenure insecurity discourages forestry or similar long-term investments in land management.

Land Taxes

In many Latin American countries, very low land taxes have encouraged massive land speculation, and forest clearing to acquire land rights is an integral part of the land speculation process. Furthermore, low taxes on lands of high agricultural potential often keep such areas underutilized (that is, under extensive grazing rather than some type of agriculture which would generate higher rural employment), thereby increasing the pressures for agricultural expansion onto marginal forested lands.

A differential land tax structure, in which cleared land would be taxed at a much higher rate than forested land, would be most desirable from an environmental standpoint. This tax reform would encourage intensified production (and often a shift from pasture to crop production) on cleared lands. At the same time, it would help discourage further clearing of forested lands. In terms of economic efficiency, such a tax structure can be justified in terms of supporting the numerous non-market public goods provided by forests, and as a "second best" means of compensating for many years of other, "anti-forest" government policies.

Forestry Policy Reforms

In many Latin American countries, forest landholders receive only a small fraction of the value of wood extracted from their lands. If rural people were to find forest management more profitable, they might be less likely to convert their land to pasture or low-quality cropland. Governments can promote a variety of policies to raise the price of wood paid to landholders, or to promote improved forestry through other means. These policies include, among others:

- Organizing forest landholders into their own groups, to bid up the price paid to loggers, truckers, or sawmill owners. Although strict supply cartels might not succeed, looser organizations could still raise consciousness among landholders of the real financial value of their wood.
- Encouraging vertical integration in the forest industry. For example, very few forest landowners in the Latin American tropics also own sawmills or other substantial wood-processing facilities.
- Encouraging the development of an integrated mix of wood products from each site. These products can include lumber, poles, furniture, handicrafts, pulp and paper, particle board, and perhaps charcoal. Such integration helps to maximize the commercial value of the wood harvested from each forest plot.
- Providing forestry assistance to landholders: Such assistance should include forestry extension and other forms of technical assistance, as well as credit for environmentally justified, long-term forestry investments.
- Raising stumpage taxes: Low stumpage taxes in many Latin American countries have encouraged careless, environmentally damaging logging practices and less complete utilization of felled wood. Besides encouraging improved logging and timber utilization practices, higher stumpage taxes could generate greater revenues for financially stressed forestry and natural resources agencies.

Promote Alternative Employment Opportunities

Since most direct forest clearing is done by the rural poor (often on behalf of wealthier cattle ranchers), providing attractive alternative forms of employment (whether rural or urban) can reduce the pressure for forest clearing. It would lower the demand for settling and clearing forest land, as well as raising the costs of clearing (by making the labor more expensive). A good (if not fully replicable) example of this situation is in Puerto Rico, which actually has a net negative deforestation rate, since many abandoned farms and pastures are regenerating into forest (Birdsey and Weaver 1987). This has occurred despite Puerto Rico's typically strong, Latin tradition of extensive cattle ranching.

The details of what types of policies can best promote alternative employment opportunities for the rural poor are beyond the scope of this paper. However, policies which promote economic diversification, the creation of agricultural processing industries or other value-added activities, the use of more labor-intensive agricultural technologies and crops, and the development of cottage industries should be strongly encouraged to create alternative employment opportunities. Conversely, policies which reduce local employment should be avoided. For example, the subsidization of agricultural machinery can displace agricultural labor, thereby promoting deforestation because some of the displaced peasants then settle at the forest frontier. For example, Wilson et al. (1989) describe how mechanized soybean production has displaced many small farmers in Brazil and Paraguay, thereby encouraging them to settle forested frontier areas.

Population Policy

Human population densities in most Latin American countries are still relatively low, particularly when compared with those of Asia. Furthermore, it can be argued that extensive cattle ranching is a social response to low population densities, because it enables a relatively few people to settle and occupy relatively huge tracts of land. Nonetheless, policies to reduce population growth rates (and, ideally, to promote stabilization of population size) are still important for forest conservation, particularly over the long term. This is especially true with respect to the size of the pool of potential forest settlers, since each new colonist family at the forest frontier may clear hundreds of hectares in one generation (particularly if they raise cattle).

Conclusion

This chapter has stressed the need for livestock and complementary policies in Latin America to go in a new direction — one that is not blind to the extraordinarily high environmental and other social costs of extensive cattle raising on induced tropical pastures. Those policy makers concerned with deforestation need to recognize that this problem will not be solved unless the problem of cattle pasture expansion is solved. Government officials and international development advisers also need to realize that more than enough forested land has already been cleared for cattle pastures, and that any further forest-to-pasture transformation should be strongly discouraged.

Many of the policy reforms recommended in this paper are likely to encounter strong political resistance; in some cases, the proposed reforms represent a 180-degree departure from existing policies. Pro-cattle ranching interests and incentives are undeniably powerful. There is a strong "cattle culture" in most of the region (a legacy of Spanish and Portugese settlement), so that cattle ranching has high social prestige (Myers and Tucker 1987, Ledec 1985). The very extensiveness of cattle ranching (which makes it so destructive from a social and environmental standpoint) is typically a benefit from a private standpoint, since it often enables a family to claim or hold as much land as possible, with a minimum of labor or other inputs. Many politicians and other community leaders in Latin America own cattle ranches. Moreover, many well-intentioned but misguided development planners, in governments and in international agencies, continue to believe that "what is good for cattle is good for the country."

Notwithstanding these and other political constraints, major environmental reforms of livestock and related policies in Latin America are long overdue. Many socially desirable policies are very unpopular with certain segments of society; this in no way reduces the need to advocate such policies. Moreover, advocates of livestock policy reform in Latin America can work to build political coalitions (including environmentalists, land reform advocates, Indian representatives, foresters, and watershed managers) to help counter the political influence of the cattle ranching interests. International development agencies, once enlightened, can condition further grants or loans in the agricultural sector on environmentally-based livestock policy reforms.

It is fair to say that most (honest) government officials base their policy decisions on some combination of what they believe to be right and what is politically popular. There is thus an urgent need to inform Latin American officials of the true social costs of pasture expansion. These policy makers should not be basing their views of what is right on the dangerously misleading advice that has been provided by many livestock policy specialists to date. Whatever the political popularity of cattle ranching on induced tropical pastures may be, its high environmental and other social costs clearly show the need for new directions for livestock policy.

Notes

1. Deforestation pressure in Belize, while historically rather light, may be rapidly increasing because of the recent influx of Salvadoran and Guatemalan immigrants.
2. Some coffee is grown under the canopy shade of existing forest trees. It can therefore be argued that this type of coffee cultivation represents significant forest modification, rather than actual deforestation.

3. A major "side effect" of such pro-consumption beef pricing policies is often to depress production (Jarvis 1986). This side effect is viewed as undesirable by most development planners (who have overlooked the high social costs of beef production on induced tropical pastures).

References Cited

Alvarado, L.A. 1985. *Sedimentation in Madden reservoir*. Balboa, Panama: Panama Canal Commission, Meteorological and Hydrographic Branch

Arias S., O. 1987. *Decreto de emergencia forestal.* San Jose, C.R.: Presidencia de la Republica (18 September).

Baum, W.C. and S. M. Tolbert. 1985. *Investing in development: Lessons of World Bank experience*. New York: Oxford University Press.

Birdsey, R.A. and P. L. Weaver. 1987. *Forest area trends in Puerto Rico*. Southern Forest Experiment Station, *Research Note SO-331*. New Orleans: U.S. Forest Service.

Boza, M.A..1986. *Parques nacionales: Costa Rica*. San Jose, C.R.: Fundacion de Parques Nacionales.

Browder, J.O. 1988. The social costs of rain forest destruction: A critique and analysis of the hamburger debate. *Interciencia* 13(3):115-120.

Caufield, C. 1982. *Tropical moist forests*. London: International Institute for Environment and Development.

Costa Rica, Government of. 1986a. *Ley forestal*. San Jose, C.R.: *La Gaceta, diario oficial* (85):1-6.

____ 1986b. Reglamento de la Ley Forestal. San Jose, C.R.: *La Gaceta*, Diario Oficial (85):10-19.

Davis, S.H. 1977. *Victims of the miracle: Development and the Indians of Brazil*. Cambridge, U.K.: Cambridge University Press.

Dourojeanni, M.J. 1980. *Renewable natural resources of Latin America and the Caribbean: Situation and trends*. Washington: World Wildlife Fund-U.S.

European Economic Bureau. 1982. *Deforestation and development*. Brussels (June).

Ehrenfeld, D. 1981. *The arrogance of humanism*. New York: Oxford University Press.

Ehrlich, P.R., D. S. Dobkin, and D. Wheye. 1988. *The birder's handbook: A field guide to the natural history of North American birds*. New York: Simon & Schuster.

Farnsworth, N. 1988. Screening plants for new medicines. In: *Biodiversity*. Edited by E. O. Wilson and F. M. Peters. Washington: National Academy Press.

Farvar, M.T. and J. Milton, eds. 1972. *The careless technology*. New York: Doubleday, Natural History Press.

Fearnside, P.M. 1980. The effects of cattle pasture on soil fertility in the Brazilian Amazon: Consequences for beef production sustainability. *Tropical Ecology* 21(1):125-137.

Fitter, R. 1986. *Wildlife for man: How and why we should conserve our species*. London: Collins.

Fundacion Neotropica. 1988. *Costa Rica: Assessment of the conservation of biological resources*. San Jose, Costa Rica: Fundacion Neotropica.

Goodland, R.J.A. 1980. Environmental ranking of Amazonian development projects in Brazil. *Environmental Conservation* 7(1):9-26.

_____ 1984. Brazil's environmental progress in Amazonian development. In: *Change in the Amazon Basin*. Edited by J. Hemming. Manchester, U.K.: Manchester University Press, 2 vols.

Goodland, R.J.A. and G. Ledec. 1987. Neoclassical economics and principles of sustainable development. *Ecological Modelling* 38:19-46.

Goodland, R.J.A., C. Watson, and G. Ledec. 1984. *Environmental management in tropical agriculture*. Boulder, Colorado: Westview Press.

Goulding, M. 1980. *The fishes and the forest: Explorations in Amazonian natural history*. Berkeley: University of California Press.

Hartshorn, G., L. Hartshorn, A. Atmella, L.D. Gomez, A. Mata, L. Mata, R. Morales, R. Ocampo, D. Pool, C. Quesada, C. Solera, R. Solorzano, G. Stiles, J. Tosi, A. Umana, C. Villalobos, and R. Wells. 1982. *Costa Rica country environmental profile: A field study*. San Jose, Costa Rica: Tropical Science Center.

Hecht, S. B. 1981. Deforestation in the Amazon Basin: Magnitude, dynamics, and social resource effects. *Studies in Third World Societies* 13:61-108.

_____ 1983. Cattle ranching in the eastern Amazon: Environmental and social implications. In: *The dilemma of amazonian development*. Edited by E. Moran. Boulder, Colorado: Westview Press.

Heckadon M.S. 1984. Panama's expanding cattle front: The Santeno campesinos and the colonization of the forests. Ph.D. diss., Dept. of Sociology, University of Essex, Colchester, U.K.

Heckadon M. S., ed. 1986. *La cuenca del canal de Panama: Actas de los seminarios-talleres*. Panama City: Ministerio de Planificacion y Politica Economica, Oficina de la Area Canalera.

Inter-American Development Bank. 1987. *Costa Rica forestry development pilot project: Project report*. Washington: Inter-American Development Bank.

Iltis, H.H. 1988. Serendipity in the exploration of biodiversity: What good are weedy tomatoes? In: *Biodiversity*. Edited by E. O. Wilson and C. M. Peters. Washington: National Academy Press.

ISA. 1986. *Plan Forestal para Chivor 1986-1995*. Medellin, Colombia: Interconexion Electrica S.A., Departamento Cuencas Hidrograficas, Documento ABRN-107.

International Union for Conservation of Nature and Natural Resources. 1980. *World conservation strategy*. Gland, Switzerland: International Union for Conservation of Nature and Natural Resources.

_____ 1985. *United Nations list of national parks and protected areas*. Gland, Switzerland: International Union for Conservation of Nature and Natural Resources.

Jarvis, L.S. 1986. *Livestock development in Latin America*. Washington: World Bank.

Joly, L.G. 1989. The conversion of rain forests to pastures in Panama. In: *The human ecology of tropical land settlement in Latin America*. Edited by D. A. Schumann and W. L. Partridge. Boulder, Colorado: Westview Press.

Jones, J.R. 1985. *Land colonization in Central America: Experiences in the settlement of humid tropical lands in Panama, Costa Rica, Nicaragua, Honduras, and Guatemala*. Turrialba, Costa Rica: Centro Agronomico Tropical de Investigacion y Enseñanza.

_____ 1989. Colonization in Central America. In: *The human ecology of tropical land settlement in Latin America*. Edited by D. A. Schumann and W. L. Partridge. Boulder, Colorado: Westview Press.

Kirchner, J.W., G. Ledec, R. J. A. Goodland, and J. M. Drake. 1985. Carrying capacity, population growth, and sustainable development. In: *Rapid population growth and human carrying capacity: Two perspectives*. Edited by D. J. Mahar. Washington: World Bank, Staff Working Paper No. 690.

Ledec, G. 1985. The political economy of tropical deforestation. In: *Divesting nature's capital: The political economy of environmental abuse in the third world*. Edited by H. J. Leonard. New York: Holmes and Meier.

_____ 1990. The role of bank credit for cattle ranching in financing deforestation: An economic study from Panama. Ph.D. diss., Dept. of Forestry and Resource Management, University of California, Berkeley.

Ledec, G. and R. J. A. Goodland. 1988. *Wildlands: Their protection and management in economic development*. Washington: World Bank.

_____ 1989. Epilogue: An environmental perspective on tropical land settlement. In: *The human ecology of tropical land settlement in Latin America*. Edited by D. A. Schumann and W. L. Partridge. Boulder, Colorado: Westview Press.

Leonard, H.J. 1987. *Natural resources and economic development in Central America: A regional environmental profile*. New Brunswick, New Jersey: Transaction Books.

Mahar, D.J. 1989. *Government policies and deforestation in Brazil's Amazon region*. Washington: World Bank.

Molofsky, J., C. A. S. Hall, and N. Myers. 1986. *A comparison of tropical forest surveys*. Springfield, Virginia: U.S. Department of Commerce, National Technical Information Service.

Myers, N. 1979. *The sinking ark: A new look at the problem of disappearing species*. New York: Pergamon Press.

_____ 1980. *Conversion of tropical moist forests*. Washington: U.S. National Academy of Sciences.

_____ 1983. *A wealth of wild species*. Boulder, Colorado: Westview Press.

_____ 1984. *The primary source*. New York: W.W. Norton & Co.

Myers, N. and R. Tucker, 1987. Deforestation in Central America: Spanish legacy and North American consumers. *Environmental Ethics* 9(1):55-71.

National Academy of Sciences (U.S.), 1980. *Research priorities in tropical biology*. Washington: U.S. National Academy of Sciences.

Nations, J.D. 1985. Bearing witness: The Lacandon Mayas' traditional culture survives in the images of Gertrude Blom. *Natural History* 3:51-58.

Nations, J.D. and D. I. Komer. 1983. Indians, immigrants, and beef exports: Deforestation in Central America. *Cultural Survival Quarterly* 6(2):8-12.

Ortega T. J. 1986. *Codigo nacional de los recursos naturales renovables y proteccion al medio ambiente*. Bogota: Editorial Temis.

Panama, Goverment of. 1986a. *Informe del grupo de trabajo sobre la cuenca del canal de Panama: Sumario ejecutivo*. Panama City: Ministerio de Planificacion y Politica Economica, Oficina de la Area Canalera.

_____ 1986b. *Panama now: Yearbook, portrait of the nation, commercial directory, and reference book*. Panama City: Focus Publications.

Plotkin, M.J. 1988. The outlook for new agricultural and industrial products from the tropics. In: *Biodiversity*. Edited by E. O. Wilson and C. M. Peters. Washington: National Academy Press.

Prance, G.T. and S. A. Mori. 1983. Dispersal and distribution of *Lecythidaceae* and *Chrysobalanaceae*. Sonderbd. *Naturwiss*. Ver. Hamburg (Germany) 7:163-186.

Prescott-Allen, R. and C. Prescott-Allen. 1983. *Genes from the wild: Using wild genetic resources for food and raw materials*. London: International Institute for Environment and Development, Earthscan Paperback.

Rainforest Action Network. 1988. *Tropical rainforest press brief*. San Francisco: Rainforest Action Network, briefing package.

Ridgley, R.S. 1976. *A guide to the birds of Panama*. Princeton, New Jersey: Princeton University Press.

Robinson, F.H. 1985. *A report on the Panama Canal rain forest*. Balboa, Panama: Panama Canal Commission, Meteorological and Hydrographic Branch.

Rolston, H. 1985. Duties to endangered species. *Bioscience* 35(11):718-726.

Special Commission on International Pollution. 1975. London.

Society of American Foresters. 1988. First Brazilian conference on forestry economics. Bethesda, Maryland: Society of American Foresters, *International Forestry Working Group Newsletter* (Summer):1-2.

Salati, E. and P.B. Vose. 1984. Amazon Basin: A system in equilibrium. *Science* 225:129-137.

Sayad, J. 1983. The impact of rural credit on production and income distribution in Brazil. In: *Rural financial markets in developing countries: their use and abuse*. Edited by J. D. Von Pischke. Baltimore: Johns Hopkins University Press.

Shaffer, M.L. and K.A. Saterson. 1987. The biological diversity program of the U.S. Agency for International Development. *Conservation Biology* 1(4):280-283.

Shane, D.R. 1986. *Hoofprints on the forest: Cattle ranching and the destruction of Latin America's tropical forests*. Philadelphia: Institute for the Study of Human Issues.

Skillings, R.F. and N.O. Tcheyan. 1980. *Economic development prospects of the Amazon region of Brazil*. Washington: Johns Hopkins University, School of Advanced International Studies.

Tosi Jr., J. A. 1988. *Background information and recommendations for a forestry and wildlands management: Project identification document*. San Jose, C. R.: Tropical Science Center.

_____ 1974. Los recursos forestales de Costa Rica. In: *Acta final del primer Congreso Nacional sobre conservacion de recursos naturales renovables*. April 22-26. San Jose, Costa Rica: Universidad de Costa Rica.

Uhl, C. and G. Parker. 1986. Our steak in the jungle. *BioScience* 36(10):642.

Uquillas, J.E. 1989. Social impacts of modernization and public policy and prospects for indigenous development in Ecuador's Amazonia. In: *The human ecology of tropical land settlement in Latin America*. Edited by D. A. Schumann and W. L. Partridge. Boulder, Colorado: Westview Press.

United Nations Environmental Program. 1982. *Global assessment of tropical forest resources*. Nairobi: United Nations Environment Program, GEMS Pac Information Series No. 3.

United States Agency for International Development. 1987. *Natural resource management in Costa Rica: A strategy for USAID*. San Jose, C. R.: United States Agency for International Development.

_____ 1988. *Project identification document: Forest resources for a stable environment (FORESTA)*. San Jose, Costa Rica: United States Agency for International Development.

United States Department of State. 1978. *Proceedings of the U.S. strategy conference on tropical deforestation*. Washington: U.S. Department of State.

Voelker, D. 1988. Panama Canal: Falling victim to deforestation and politics. San Francisco: *World Rivers Review* 3(1):3-14.

Wetterberg, G.B., G.T. Prance, and T. E. Lovejoy. 1981. Conservation progress in Amazonia: A structural review. *Parks* 6(2):5-10.

Wilson, E.O. 1985. The biological diversity crisis: A challenge to science. *Issues in Science Technology* 2(1):20-29.

Wilson, J.F., J. D. Hay, and M. L. Margolis. 1989. The bi-national frontier of eastern Paraguay. In: *The human ecology of tropical land settlement in Latin America*. Edited by D. A. Schumann and W. L. Partridge. Boulder, Colorado: Westview Press.

Windsor, D.M. and A. S. Rand. 1985. Cambios climaticos en los registros de lluvia en Panama y Costa Rica. In: *Agonia de la naturaleza: Ensayos sobre el costo ambiental del desarrollo Panameño*. Edited by S. Heckadon M. and J. Espinosa G. Panama City: Smithsonian Tropical Research Institute.

Wolf, E.C. 1987. *On the brink of extinction: Conserving the diversity of life*. Washington: Worldwatch Institute, Worldwatch Paper 78.

World Bank. 1982a. *Tribal peoples and economic development: Human ecologic considerations*. Washington: World Bank.

_____ 1982b. *Brazil: A review of agricultural policies*. Washington: World Bank.

_____ 1983. *The energy transition in developing countries*. Washington: World Bank.

_____ 1984. *Brazil: Financial systems review*. Washington: World Bank.

_____ 1985. *Panama: Structural change and growth prospects*. Washington: World Bank, Country Study.

_____ 1986. *Wildlands: Their protection and management in economic development — operational policy*. Washington: World Bank.

World Rivers Review. 1988. IDB and Central America: Deforestation threatens big hydro. *World Rivers Review* 3(1):1-5.

World Resources Institute. 1987. World resources 1987. Washington,D.C.: World Resources Institute.

World Wildlife Fund. 1982. *North American birds which migrate to the tropics.* Washington: World Wildlife Fund-U.S.

4

Bio-Economic Costs

Victor M. Toledo

The potential types of exploitation of tropical forest lands has recently been the subject of considerable discussion, especially when the use implies the simplification of these ecosystems by converting them to permanent grasslands. Conversion of tropical forests to pastures — which is the most common practice in the lowlands of Latin America — produces three main types of impact: changes in the local hydrologic cycles and global climate (by accelerating the greenhouse effect), soil resource deterioration, and loss of living organisms. Although still scarce, some literature exists on the effects of deforestation on climate (Dickinson 1981, Henderson-Sellers 1981, Prance 1987), hydrological regimes (Gentry and Lopez-Parodi 1980, Salati and Vose 1984, Salati, this volume) and soil resource degradation (Hecht 1981, Fearnside 1982, Sanchez 1981).

In contrast, except for some general treatments (see a review by Lugo 1988) no analysis exists on the number of biological species and individuals displaced per unit area during the conversion process from forests to pastures. Biotic resources are valuable in a double sense: by themselves as an expression of the world's biological diversity and product of the evolutionary process, and as actual or potential economic goods of a given political unit. Due to this, in practice, both biological and economic costs must be considered when living organisms are displaced during the process of deforestation. Based on data derived from various biological, botanical, and forestry inventories, this paper attempts to evaluate the biological and economic costs (per unit area) of transforming tropical forests to pastures in Latin America and discusses some aspects derived from this process.

The Biological Richness

All the data derived from recent inventories seem to suggest that the Latin America and the Caribbean region houses the highest biological richness of the world. The list of the six countries considered as containing the maximum world's biological diversity is headed by three Latin American countries: Brazil, Colombia, and Mexico (Mittermeier 1988). Likewise, the great floristic richness of Latin America (the neotropical realm in a broad sense) has been stressed by various authors. Raven (1976), for example, estimated the number of neotropical plant species at 90,000, a figure that Prance (1977) and other authors have generally accepted. Gentry (1982a) has added support to this estimate of 90,000 species by compiling a list of all the neotropical seed plant genera based on available regional floras and monographs. According to Gentry's calculation, the estimated number of species from the resulting list of over 4,200 neotropical *genera* reached 86,000. More recently, Toledo (1985, 1989) made a new calculation derived from the analysis of 116 floristic inventories carried out through the entire region. The results obtained in this last account showed that Latin America probably contains between 100,000 and 120,000 species of flowering plants, confirming this region as the floristically richest area of the world. So, in accordance with Gentry's (1982a) estimates for other regions of the world, the approximately 120,000 species to be found in Latin America is four times the number found in all of tropical Africa and Madagascar together, and is more than three times the estimate for tropical Australasia.

In the case of terrestrial vertebrates, the panorama seems to be the same (K. Creighton, pers. com, 1985). The neotropical mammals (over 700 species), reptiles and amphibians (ca 2000) are more diversified than their counterparts in tropical Africa and Australasia. On the other hand, the neotropics have a higher number of species of birds (ca 3500) than Africa; this figure is perhaps similar to that of tropical Asia. Despite the lack of reliable data of invertebrate animals to make regional comparisons, the same pattern is likely to be found if, as hypothesized by Erwin (1988), host specificity is a main feature of the lifestyle of neotropical canopy insects.

As pointed out by some authors as Gentry (1982b, 1986), the great extension and geographical variation of Latin American tropical forests are highly responsible for the global biological diversity of the region. So, the **megadiversity**, the regional and national biological richness, is paralleled at the community level (Table 4.1). Thus, the richest tropical forest sites of Latin America (to be found in the wettest areas of South America) are massively richer than any other vegetation in the world in herbs, shrubs, lianas and trees (Gentry 1986, Gentry and Dodson 1986).

The Remaining Natural Vegetation and Deforestation Rates

In order to evaluate the degree of habitat disruption in the region, two main factors must be reviewed: the extent of the remaining natural areas

TABLE 4.1 Number of species of flowering plants and terrestrial vertebrates in
Latin America

	Flowering plants	Mammals	Birds	Reptiles	Amphibians
Mexico	30,000	439	961	704	272
Belice	3,240	121	504	107	26
Guatemala	7,751	174	666	204	98
Salvador	?	129	432	93	38
Hondura	5,000	179	672	161	55
Nicaragua	5,000	177	610	162	59
Costa Rica	8,000	203	796	218	151
Panama	6,900	217	840	212	155
Bahamas	?	17	218	39	2
Cuba	5,785	39	286	100	39
Hispaniola	5,000	23	211	134	53
Jamaica	3,000	29	223	38	20
Lesser Antilles	?	37	193	94	15
Neth Antilles	?	9	171	22	2
Puerto Rico	2,809	17	220	46	25
Colombia	?	358	1,665	383	367
Venezuela	25,000	305	1,295	246	182
Guyana	?	198	728	137	105
Suriname	2,000	200	670	131	99
French Guyana	5,000	142	628	136	89
Ecuador	10-20,000	280	1,447	345	349
Peru	18,000	359	1,642	297	233
Brasil	?	394	1,567	467	485
Bolivia	?	267	1,177	180	95
Chile	4,758	90	393	82	38
Paraguay	7-8,000	157	630	110	69
Uruguay	2,300	77	367	66	37
Argentina	10,000	255	927	204	124

Sources: Data bank of the International Program of the Nature Conservancy.
Washington, D.C. and Toledo 1985

(areas covered with natural vegetation) and the current rates of deforestation. To accomplish this, we have relied, principally, on the FAO and UNEP (1981) study of the forest resources of the American tropics, and on a synthesis of these information organized by Lanly (1981, 1982, 1983). The FAO-UNEP study gives an idea of the rate of destruction of natural habitats nation-by-nation by showing the magnitude of each nation's territory still covered with natural vegetation and the area being deforested annually. Based on this study and other sources (Lugo, et al. 1981, Ojeda and Mares 1984, Toledo 1988, Bisbal 1988) the country-by-country analysis reveals some interesting patterns concerning remaining natural vegetation. It is possible to distinguish four well-defined groups of countries: (1) those with natural vegetation covering most of their land surface (more than 70%), (Guyana, Suriname, French Guiana, Bolivia, Paraguay, and Brazil); (2) those with less than half their total area covered by natural vegetation, (Mexico, Guatemala, Colombia, Perú, Ecuador, Venezuela, and Argentina); (3) those with only a third of their land surfaces covered (Nicaragua, Costa Rica, Jamaica); and (4) those showing a strong degree of ecological transformation (less than 33% remaining natural vegetation), El Salvador, Cuba, Haiti, the Dominican Republic, and Puerto Rico.

In general, the countries of the tropical part of South America show the highest percentages of remaining natural vegetation (an average of 72.8%). Mexico's position is intermediate, while Central America and the Caribbean countries show a high degree of ecological transformation, with an average of 44.5% and 15.0%, respectively, of their areas remaining in natural vegetation.

We turn now to the process of deforestation. Biological evolution made Latin America and the Caribbean the depositories of the largest number of living organisms in the world but, paradoxically, the joint forces of historical and socioeconomic processes have caused the biota of this region to suffer the world's highest rate of ecological depletion. In fact, the FAO-UNEP study shows that, of the 11 million hectares of land annually deforested in the tropical regions, 5.611 million hectares (or 51%) are located in Latin America and the Caribbean countries (Table 4.2). This means that each year the region loses forested areas equivalent to the territory of Costa Rica! That results from the deforestation of 4.030 million hectares of broadleaf forests, 0.309 million hectares of conifer forests, and 1.272 million hectares of open forests. This situation becomes even more dramatic when the rates of deforestation in the three main tropical regions are compared for "closed forests" alone (Table 4.2). In this case the tropical American countries lose almost 60% of the total (4.339 million hectares from a total of 7.496), leaving the remaining 40% to Africa and Asia together. According to Lanly (1981) the annual estimated rate of deforestation during 1981-1985 for broadleaf forests is 0.61%, and for open forests is 0.59%. The coniferous forests suffer a higher degree of deforestation, reaching 1.25% annually.

Notwithstanding how high they appear, the rates of deforestation reported for the region by the FAO-UNEP study ought to be considered, for various reasons, as conservative estimates of the ecological destruction. As Lanly (1983) indicates, the term "deforestation" as used by the FAO-

TABLE 4.2 Estimated annual deforestation of closed and open forests for
the tropical areas of the world, 1981-85

	Closed Forests				Open Forests		
	Broadleaves	Coniferous	Total	%	Total	%	Total
Tropical America	4,030	0.309	4,339	(0.64)	1,272	(0.59)	5,611
Tropical Africa	1,324	0.007	1,331	(0.61)	2,345	(0.48)	3,676
Tropical Asia	1,796	0.030	1,826	(0.60)	190	(0.61)	2,016
Total			7,496		3,807		11,303

Source: Adapted from Lanly 1983:312

UNEP study means the total clearing of natural tree formations (closed and open forests) for agriculture and other uses. This relatively narrow sense of deforestation contrasts with concepts of conversion, disruption, and depletion used in many other studies to indicate any change brought about in a forest ecosystem, whether it is complete clearing or any selective felling (by logging), or any form of degradation (by overgrazing or repeated burning). Logging in particular is often assimilated with deforestation, while in the FAO-UNEP study it has been accounted for separately. Further, more recent studies employing satellite imagery reveal higher rates of deforestation (Green 1984), and new data from national forestry inventories in Brazil, Mexico (Toledo 1988) and Venezuela (Bisbal 1988) record higher deforestation figures.

For a country-by-country analysis, it is necessary to distinguish between absolute and relative rates of deforestation. It is possible to distinguish a first group of countries where deforestation reaches more than 1% annually, including México, Central America (with the exceptions of Belize and Panama), Jamaica, Haiti, and only two South American countries: Colombia and Ecuador (Figure 4.1). The rest of the countries sustain, in relative terms, a lesser deforestation, with the exception of the three Guyanas, where deforestation is insignificant. On the other hand, the absolute values reveal that, leaving the Guyanas aside, the deforestation of the seven countries of tropical South America amounts to 78% (4.397 million hectares) of the annual regional total, and if Mexico is included, the figure rises to nearly 90%. The case of Brazil is, nevertheless, exceptional: 45% of the deforestation of the whole region takes place in its territory. Actually the whole world is watching the Amazonian region, which is the most threatened area of Brazil but not the most destroyed, and other portions of the country which are no less important are forgotten. The enormous size of Brazil (851 million hectares) masks the high levels of deforestation (only 25% of the country has lost its natural vegetation cover). According to the

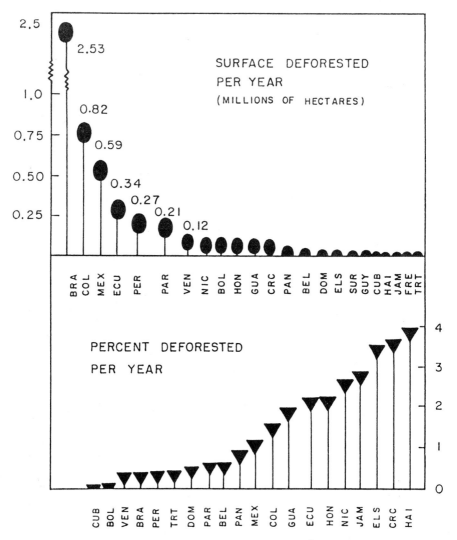

FIGURE 4.1 Surface deforested per year in millions of hectares and percentage of total territory for 20 Latin American and Caribbean countries

Source: FAO-UNEP 1981

meticulous analysis of the FAO-UNEP (1981), Brazil loses annually 2.53 million hectares of forest (1.36 million hectares of broadleaf forest, 0.12 million hectares of coniferous forest, and 1.05 million hectares of open forest). These figures could prove conservative if we take into account that for the Amazon region alone the last official figures (which are generally low) suggest that at present 2.3 million hectares of forest are being destroyed each year (Salati and Vose 1984). Even so, the total listed by the FAO-UNEP study is impressive. Each year Brazil loses an area equivalent to Belize or Haiti.

The same study shows that approximately half the deforestation is of the tropical forests and the other half coniferous and *cerrado* forests (the study does not give precise estimates for other vegetative formations like the *caatinga*). Similarly sized areas are being deforested within the tropical forests (which cover approximately 355 million hectares) and within the other open forests (which cover only 211 million hectares), leaving to the latter forests relatively higher rates of deforestation. This only confirms a clear process in Brazilian historic geography: the deforestation that began several centuries ago on the Atlantic coast (Dean 1983) is moving inland and today already touches the pristine Amazon. In this process the Atlantic tropical forests have practically disappeared (according to the FAO-UNEP only some 3 million hectares remain), the *caatinga* of the northeast has also been very degraded, and of the subtropical Atlantic coastal forests of the Southeast that once covered the states of Espirito Santo, Rio de Janeiro, Sao Paulo, and a third of Minas Gerais, only isolated fragments remain. The figures speak for themselves: the subtropical Atlantic forests covered 50 million hectares (Dean 1983), equivalent to a fourth of México and nearly all of Central America! Finally, the Araucaria forests of the south that once covered a good part of the states of Paraná, Santa Catarina, and Rio Grande do Sul, with a total area of 16-17 million hectares, today have been reduced to 1.2 million hectares, and are being deforested at a rate of 120,000 hectares per year.

To summarize, the largest areas being deforested in Latin America and the Caribbean are located in the countries of the tropical region of South America, given the large size of the countries and the sizable areas of natural vegetation that still exist (72.8% on the average). On the other hand, in relative terms, the percentages of annual deforestation in tropical South America are much less than in Central America, the Caribbean, or Mexico. From a national perspective the most difficult situation is taking place in Central America, where the small size of the countries and the moderate percentages of remaining natural vegetation (44.5% on the average) result in a 2.1% rate of deforestation annually. In the Caribbean where the areas of the countries are similar (Cuba, the Dominican Republic, and Haiti) or smaller than those of the Central America nations, and where the processes of severe deforestation took place in the last century (Lugo et al. 1981), the present annual rates of deforestation are smaller, perhaps because large level areas of natural vegetation are gone already, and only remnants on hillsides and inaccessible places have been left (Lanly 1981).

Cattle Ranching Expansion

A review of the region's recent statistics shows that parallel to human population, which grew from 216 millions to 410 millions between 1960 and 1980, two other "organisms" increased explosively in Latin America: cars, in the urban spaces, and cattle, in the rural areas. In fact, while the number of cars jumped from 2.77 millions to 19.84 millions between 1960 and 1980 (SALA 1983), cattle experienced an increase from 177 to 266 millions of head in a similar period (SALA, *op cit.*.) (Figure 4.2). It is interesting to note that from an ecological viewpoint, cars and cattle are two very inefficient examples of modern civilization, both in terms of overexploitation of natural resources (energy, water, food) and of the use of space.

As has been pointed out by some authors (Feder 1980, Shane 1986), the explosive increase of cattle in Latin America is a consequence of two world-scale phenomena: the consolidation of beef cattle as the primary protein source in the rich industrial nations and of national elites, and the displacement of England, by the United States, as the central axis of the international beef trade. As a result, this growing cattle population had a very negative ecological impact: the expansion of cattle raising areas from temperate grasslands and subtropical open forests, to tropical savannas (Parsons 1980) and, finally, tropical dry and humid forests. It is not accidental that from 1960 to 1980 Brazil (a tropical country) displaced Argentina (a temperate nation) as the first Latin American country in the number of cattle (Figure 4.2), and that large lowland regions of tropical Mexico, Central America and the Amazon basin became cattle raising areas.

Despite the voluminous literature available on cattle raising expansion in tropical Latin America (principally on Amazonia and Central America), statistics on the area regarding planted pasture are incomplete and unreliable. It is very difficult, therefore, to assess with accuracy what specific types of tropical forests (and their areas) are being transformed to pastures. Table 4.3 offers, however, a summary of the extension of tropical forest areas presumably converted to pastures in the three major cattle ranching zones of Latin America (Mexico, Central America and the Amazon Basin). This data indicates that over 30 million hectares of tropical forests had been converted to pastures by the end of the eighties in these three major areas alone. In contrast to the current idea that pasture lands transform

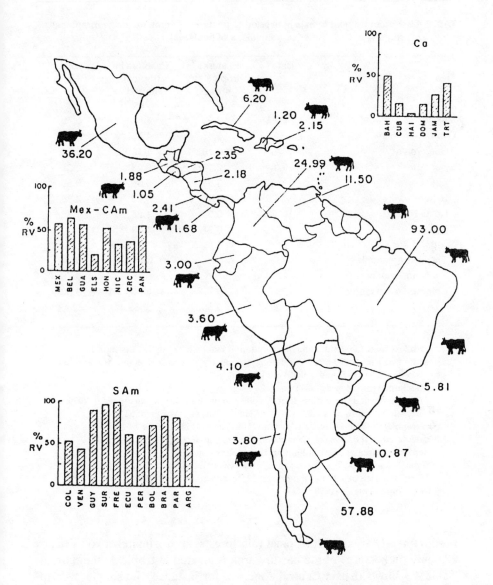

FIGURE 4.2 Number of cattle and percentage of total national territory remaining in natural vegetation in the Latin American and Caribbean countries, 1982

Source: SALA 1983, FAO 1982, 1983; FAO-UNEP 1981

TABLE 4.3 Area of tropical forests converted to pastures in three major geographical regions of Latin America (in millions of hectares)

Area	Date	Pastures in tropical dry areas[a]	Pastures in tropical humid areas[b]	Total
Mexico[c]	1980-1	2.93	3.82	6.75
Central America		6.87	4.30	11.17
Guatemala[d]	1978	0.78	1.19	1.97
Honduras[d]	1978	2.14	0.23	2.37
El Salvador[d]	1978	0.63	0.06	0.69
Nicaragua[e]	1978-9	2.45	0.43	2.88
Costa Rica[f]	1978	0.50	1.26	1.76
Panama[g]	1982	0.37	1.13	1.50
South America				
Brazilian Amazonia[h]	1980	-	10.75	10.75
Peruvian Amazonia [i]	1979	-	0.76	0.76
Colombian Amazonia[j]	1980	-	3.00	3.00
	Total	9.80	22.63	32.43

a. with less than 2,000 mm annual precipitation and/or more than 3 dry months
b. with more than 2,000 mm annual precipitation and/or no more than 3 dry months
c. after Toledo (1987) and Toledo et al. (1989)
d. calculated from Myers (1981)
e. calculated from information directly collected by the auhor in Nicaragua in 1979
f. calculated from figures 4.2 and 4.12 of Hall (1984) and Myers (1981)
g. extrapolated from Heckadon-Moreno (1985) and other sources
h. calculated as the 95% (cattle ranching area sensu Hecht (1981)) of a total deforested area of 11.31 million hectares (Hecht op. cit)
i. calculated as the 15% cattle ranching area sensu Hecht (op. cit) of a total deforested area of 5.12 million hectares (Dance and Ojeda 1979)
j. from Alarcon et al. (1980)

predominantly areas with tropical rain forests, approximately two thirds or 22.6 million hectares of the pasture area is located in tropical humid areas. Table 4.3 shows that in Central America, for instance, the simple overlapping of the areas dedicated to cattle ranching in every country (based on Parsons 1976 and other sources) with the respective national maps of vegetation, reveals that tropical dry forests have been more extensively affected (Honduras, El Salvador and Nicaragua) than forests of tropical humid areas (which are primarily modified by cattle ranching in only the cases of Costa Rica and Panama) (Table 4.3). Thus, the previously assumed idea that Central American rain forests are the more exposed vegetation to

cattle ranching expansion (Myers 1981, Nations and Komer 1984) is erroneous. In addition, the Mexican tropical dry forests have been affected by
cattle expansion almost in the same proportion as rain forests (Table 4.3),
and if agricultural areas are included the former appears more affected
with 29 percent of the total area (above 32.5 million of hectares) without
forests (Toledo et al. 1989). All of the above confirms the idea that tropical
dry forests are the most endangered major tropical ecosystem of
Mesoamerica (Janzen 1988). Finally, the Amazonian Basin, where in the
Brazilian portion alone there is an estimated pasture area of between 10
and 12 million hectares (Hecht 1981, Fearnside 1982,1985), is the Latin
American area with the highest amount of tropical rain forest converted to
pasture lands.

Gone with the Cattle

Biological Costs

The biological costs of transforming tropical forests to pastures can be
calculated by estimating the loss of biomass and the number of removed
organisms (species and individuals) in a given area. Based on the review of
numerous case studies carried out by Brown and Lugo (1982) it is possible
to conclude that one hectare of mature tropical (moist and wet) forest
stores 360 tons of organic matter (N = 20 sites). A similar figure was later
obtained by the same authors (Brown and Lugo 1984) in a calculation based
on the stemwood biomass: 384 tons per hectare (N = 9).

Given the present state of knowledge and the available information, the
number of displaced species and individuals can be estimated at two levels:
localities (involving areas of several hundreds of hectares) and **sites** (covering areas of one hectare or less). In the first case, the studies produce
species lists derived from long-term qualitative observations. Sites, on the
other hand, are inventoried through short or long-term quantitative cen-
suses of small study plots. While the former studies are more likely to
include the dynamic habitat mosaic of tropical forests (despite the fact that
such data permit only limited statistical analysis), the second level yields
more quantitative data, allowing calculation of species richness per unit
area.

Detailed efforts to record the number of species of every plant and
animal group living in specific tropical localities of Latin America have
been rare and only in very recent times have these types of inventories been
initiated. Table 4.4 summarizes information from several Latin America
localities where relatively complete biological inventories are available. The
table also suggests that between 800 and 1200 species of vascular plants can
be found in an area of about 1000 hectares of tropical (rain) forest, of which

TABLE 4.4 Number of species of vascular plants, trees and terrestrial vertebrates for selected tropical localities of Latin America

Localities	Area (ha)	Vascular plants	Trees	Mam- mals	Birds	Reptiles & Amphibians
Tropical Humid Areas						
Los Tuxtlas (MEX)	400	818	210	90	315	150
Uxpanapa (MEX)	1,200	870	230	34	> 150	?
La Selva (CRC)	730	1,860	460	100	388	119
Barro Colorado (PAN)	1,560	1,316	291	65	369	100
Rio Palenque (ECU)	170	1,033	154	?	?	?
Tropical Dry Areas						
Chamela(MEX)	1,600	758	?	-	-	-
Santa Rosa(CRC)	11,000	700	142	115	175	75

Sources: Los Tuxtlas:Ibarra and Sinaca (1987), Coates-Estrada and Estrada (1985), Estrada and Coates-Estrada (1983). Uxpanapa: Toledo et al. 1978. La Selva: Wilson (1983), Stiles (1983), Scott et al. (1983), Dirzo (per. comm.). Barro Colorado: Croat (1978),). Rio Palenque:Dodson and Gentry (1978). Chamela:Lott (1985). Santa Rosa: Janzen (1988)

between 160 and 240 should be trees (see Gentry 1986). Although more speculative, the number of mammal species to be found in a similar area could be between 60 and 100, of which 50-60% should be bats (Eisenberg and Redford 1979). Based on unpublished reports of M. Koepcke and J. O'Neill in Peruvian Amazonia and on his own records, Amadon (1973) concludes that one locality in Amazonia has 300 or more species of forest birds. This estimate is in accordance with studies carried out in extra-Amazonian sites such as Los Tuxtlas, Mexico (315 bird species), La Selva, Costa Rica (388 species) or Barro Colorado, Panama (310 species) (Table 4.4). Finally, based on Duellman (1978), it is possible to predict the richness of the herpetofauna of a tropical rain forest locality as between 100 and 200 species. According to this author a neotropical site without a strong dry season should contain the same proportion of amphibians (mostly anurans) and reptiles (mostly snakes), while in sites with a dry season, the number of reptiles would reach 65-68 percent of the herpetofauna because anurans are more dependent on equable moisture.

Samples of tropical forest sites (with areas of one hectare or less) have been carried out to inventory plants (principally trees) and some animal groups as birds, reptiles and amphibians. Based on the data reported by

TABLE 4.5 Number of tree species and individuals of different diameter at breast height (DBH) in one hectare as indicated by different botanical and forestry inventories

Site	Species	Individuals	Breast Height lower limit (cm)	Source
A. Huimanguillo (MEX)	101	530	5	Sarukhán 1968
B. Bonampak (MEX)	160	1,893	3.3	Meave del Castillo 1983
C. Acurizal (BRA)	36	274	15	Prance and Schaller 1982
D. Acurizal (BRA)	22	189	15	Prance and Schaller 1982
E. Manaus (BRA)	179	350	15	Prance et al. 1976
F. Belem (BRA)	87	423	10	Black et al. 1950
G. Mishana (PER)	281	842	10	Gentry 1986
H. Yanamomo (PER)	285	579	10	Gentry 1986
I. Beni (BOL)	94	649	10	Boom 1986

Note: Letters correspond to sites indicated in Figure 4.3

Lott, et al. (1987) and Gentry (1982b) who realized vegetational samples in various tropical plant communities of Latin America (see sites a to m in Figure 4.3) it is possible to conclude that a tropical forest site of 0.1 ha houses between 50 and 150 species of plants (2.5 cm DBH). More recently, Gentry (1986) based on data of 45 samples found a certain relationship between plant richness and precipitation. According to Gentry's assumptions the number of plant species to be found in an area of 0.1 ha between 50 and 100 in the **dry tropical forests** (Holdridge 1967), 100 and 150 in the **moist tropical forests**, 150 to 200 in the **wet tropical forests**, and from 200 to 250 in the **pluvial tropical forests**. Although there is evidence that the relationship of greater species diversity with increased precipitation does not necessarily hold when specific geographical areas are analyzed (see for example the comparative analysis of 16 tropical rain forest sites carried out by Toledo (1982) in Mexico and Figure 4.4), it seems that it constitutes a consistent general pattern. Unfortunately there is insufficient information to validate the above assumption when the vegetation sample is extended to a one ha area. So, the number of tree species oscillate broadly probably as a result of different environmental and historical factors (Table 4.5). Similarly, as indicated by the data of 54 samples carried out by several authors and summarized in Gentry (1982b) and Figure 4.3, the number of plant in-

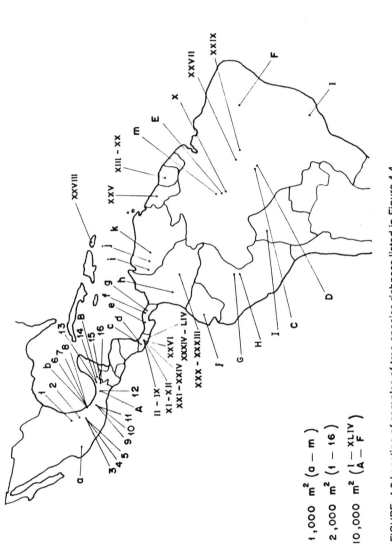

1,000 m² (a – m)
2,000 m² (1 – 16)
10,000 m² ($\begin{smallmatrix} I & - & XLIV \\ A & - & F \end{smallmatrix}$)

FIGURE 4.3 Location of samples of tree-species richness listed in Figure 4.4

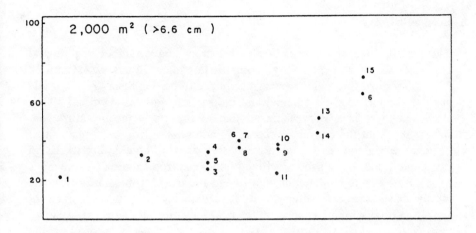

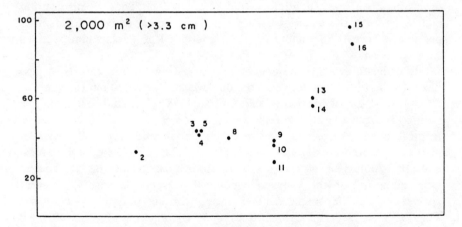

Numbers correspond to the sampled sites as indicated in Figure 4.3. 1. Huichihuayan (2146 mm of annual precipitation). 2. Misantla (2275 mm) 3,4, and 5 Tuxtepec (2822 mm). 6,7, and 8 Los Tuxtlas (4419mm), 9,10, and 11 Coatzacoalcos (2822 mm). 12, 13, and 14 Pichucalco (4037mm) 15 and 16 Lacandona (3405 mm). Source: Toledo, 1982

FIGURE 4.4 Number of tree species in samples of 2000 m² for 16 selected sites of tropical Mexico

dividuals range from averages of 350 to 550 per hectare in sites with 1200 to over 5000 mm of precipitation.

Economic Costs

The idea that tropical forests house an extraordinary number of potential resources has earned credibility during the last years (Myers 1984, Caufield 1982). Tropical forests have been recognized to be rich reservoirs of goods such as timber, foods, medicinal and industrial resources (Oldfield 1981). Although there is an increasing number of reports in the literature that inform us about the enormous economic potential of tropical forests, most of them are global and qualitative descriptions without utility to assign economic value to the products found in a given tropical area (Anonymous 1988). Based on the indigenous knowledge and use of tropical forests, some studies have started to offer quantitative data on the whole spectrum of useful materials found in specific tropical localities and sites (see below). This "ethnoecological approach" is perhaps the best way to disclose the promising economic potential of tropical ecosystems. Thus, by discovering and recognizing the traditional knowledge of tropical native cultures, it is possible to reveal the number of real or potential products embodied in a tropical forest.

In order to evaluate the economic cost of transforming forests to pastures, I will utilize data derived from our own study carried out ten years in a tropical region of Mexico (Toledo, et al. 1978). The study area was the region of Uxpanapa in Veracruz where a piece of about 1200 hectares of tropical rain forest (primary and secondary) contained over 1000 species of plants and vertebrate animals (see Table 4.4). Based on the ethnobotanical and ethnozoological information of 18 studies carried out in Mexico and Guatemala and on the knowledge of local peasants, the use(s) of every species living at Uxpanapa was inventoried (for methodological details see Toledo, et al. 1978 and Caballero, et al. 1978). The main findings derived from this study were:

- The great variety of products available from the tropical forest: 703 products from 332 useful species in a total of 1128 inventoried species (Figure 4.5). The above indicates a ratio of 0.62 products per inventoried species, and a total of products more than two times the number of useful species.
- The importance of tropical forests as a primary resource of three kinds of products: medicines (210 products or 30% of the total), foods (200 or 28.4%) and woods (lumber, fibers and others) (124 or 17.6%). The remaining 24% of products was distributed among

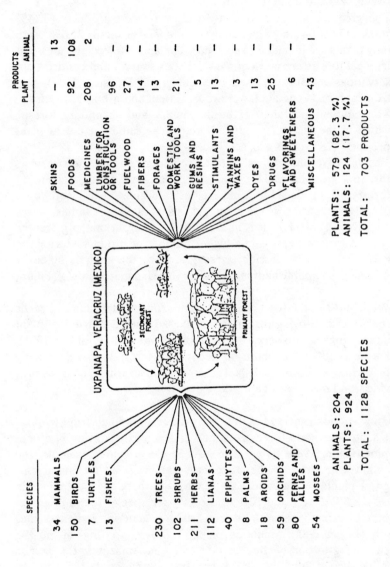

FIGURE 4.5 Number of plant and vertebrate species of a tropical rain forest locality in Mexico (Uxpanapa, Veracruz) and their economic potential as indicated by the number of obtained plant and animal products

Sources: Toledo, et al. 1978, Caballero, et al. 1978

UXPANAPA, VERACRUZ (MEXICO)

SPECIES

34	MAMMALS	
150	BIRDS	
7	TURTLES	
13	FISHES	
230	TREES	
102	SHRUBS	
211	HERBS	
112	LIANAS	
40	EPIPHYTES	
8	PALMS	
18	AROIDS	
59	ORCHIDS	
80	FERNS AND ALLIES	
54	MOSSES	

ANIMALS: 204
PLANTS: 924

TOTAL: 1128 SPECIES

PRODUCTS

	PLANT	ANIMAL
SKINS	–	13
FOODS	92	108
MEDICINES	208	2
LUMBER FOR CONSTRUCTION OR TOOLS	96	–
FUELWOOD	27	–
FIBERS	14	–
FORAGES	13	–
DOMESTIC AND WORK TOOLS	21	–
GUMS AND RESINS	5	–
STIMULANTS	13	–
TANNINS AND WAXES	3	–
DYES	13	–
DRUGS	25	–
FLAVORINGS AND SWEETENERS	6	–
MISCELLANEOUS	43	1

PLANTS: 579 (82.3 %)
ANIMALS: 124 (17.7 %)

TOTAL: 703 PRODUCTS

fuelwood (3.9%), drugs (3.6%), stimulants (1.8%), forages (1.8%) and other goods such as resins, dyes, gums, tannins, flavorings, sweeteners and domestic tools.

- The great importance of non-wood over wood products (82.4% versus 17.6% in the whole analysis, and 77.4% versus 22.6% when only plants are included (Table 4.6). The above rejects the idea that tropical forests are predominantly timber sources and confirms observations recently stressed by Gentry and Dodson (1987), that tropical forests contain fewer arboreal than non-arboreal species.
- The equal importance of both primary and secondary forests, which in the analysis produced almost the same amount of plant products (283 versus 296, see Table 4.6).
- The selective importance of primary and secondary forests: while the first provide mainly wood materials and foods, secondary forests also produce foods but are basically an extensive storehouse of substances such as medicines, drugs, stimulants, tannins, waxes and dyes (Table 4.6). It is interesting to point out that, apparently, secondary forests provide a higher number of products during the early stages of succession, as suggested by the analysis made by Caballero (unpublished paper) using the Uxpanapa 's data (Figure 4.6).
- While most of the food products come from edible fruits and seeds (63%), thus proving that humans take advantage of tropical plant adaptations to dispersal by vertebrate animals (Oldfield 1981), leaves (and entire plants of secondary forests) provide mainly medicines and other substances as, of course, trunks of trees provide wood materials (Table 4.6) .

Very few studies provide data on the products obtained from tropical forests at a site level, and these are concentrated on trees living in a one-hectare plot (Boom 1985, Balee 1986). As in the previous example, the method followed in these studies take as a starting point the indigenous knowledge of plants (ethnobotany approach). So, the Chacobo Indians in Bolivia use the 38%, 24% and 20% of the 117 tree species found in a one-hectare plot of rain forest as food, construction material and medicines respectively (Boom 1985). Similarly, Balee (1986) reports that of the 138 tree species living in one hectare of rain forest in Amazonia, the Tembe Indians utilize 35 as food (25%), 52 as construction material (38%) and 16 as remedies (12%). In both cases, more than half of the tree individuals had one or more uses.

The market value of the biological resources obtainable from a given area in a natural tropical forest has been calculated only once (Peters et al.

TABLE 4.6 Plant products of primary and secondary forests in a locality of tropical Mexico (Uxpanapa, Veracruz)

Uses	Root	Stem	Trunk	Exudate	Bark	Spine	Leaf	Flowers	Fruits	Seeds	Buds	All plant	Primary	Second.
Foods	0/6	6/1	-	2/0	-	-	2/6	5/1	29/18	5/6	2/1	0/2	51	41
Medicines	11/18	3/8	6/1	7/11	7/12	1/0	21/42	4/5	6/10	6/3	1/1	4/20	77	131
Woods	-	1/2	57/13	-	0/1	-	0/1	-	-	-	-	0/1	58	18
Tools	-	2/0	11/7	-	-	-	-	-	1/0	-	-	-	14	7
Lumber	-	-	15/5	-	-	-	-	-	-	-	-	-	15	5
Fuelwood	-	-	12/14	-	0/1	-	-	-	-	-	-	-	12	15
Domestic tools	3/0	5/1	5/0	1/0	3/0	-	3/9	2/0	2/4	2/1	-	1/1	27	16
Forages	-	1/0	-	-	-	-	3/4	-	0/1	-	-	0/4	4	9
Gums and resins	-	-	-	4/1	-	-	-	-	-	-	-	-	4	1
Fibers	-	0/1	-	-	3/8	-	-	-	2/0	-	-	-	5	9
Tannins Waxes	-	-	-	-	0/1	-	-	-	-	-	-	-	0	3
Oils	0/1	0/2	1/0	-	-	-	0/1	-	0/1	1/0	-	-	3	10
Stimulants	0/2	0/2	-	2/1	-	-	1/3	0/1	0/4	1/1	-	-	4	9
Flavorings Sweeteners	0/1	-	-	-	-	-	2/0	1/0	2/0	-	-	-	5	1
Drugs	0/1	1/3	1/0	-	1/1	-	0/2	-	1/10	0/2	-	0/2	4	21
TOTAL	43	39	148	29	38	1	101	19	93	28	5	35	283	296

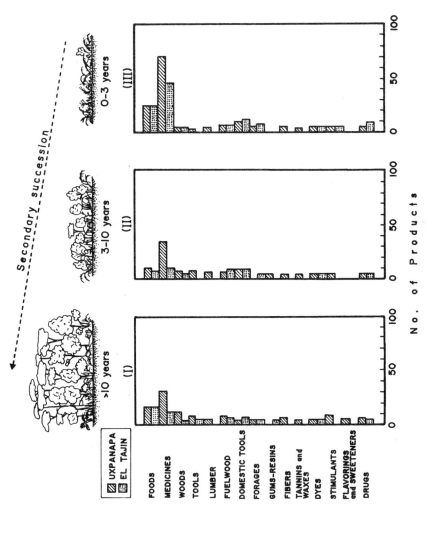

FIGURE 4.6 Number of plant products obtained from secondary forests of three different ages in Uxpanapa and El Tajin, Mexico

1988) and then only for plant (tree) products. The study estimated the net present value of the forest products in a one-hectare plot of the Mishana forest in the Peruvian Amazonia. The systematic inventory of the single hectare of forest showed 275 species and 842 individual trees of 10 cms DBH of which 72 species (26.2%) and 350 individuals (41.6%) yielded products which have an actual market value. The useful species include timber species (60), edible fruit species (11) and rubber species (2). It is interesting that 88% of the present net value of the forest of approximately $9,000 US came from fruit and latex products. The study of Peters and collaborators is an excellent example of the type of research that should be carried out in order to get a better estimate of the economic value of tropical forests products.

Conclusions

The review of the biological and economic value of tropical forests carried out on a double spatial scale *(localities and sites)* in the previous sections provides convincing evidence about the irrationality of transforming these complex ecosystems into pastures. In fact, the great biological richness of tropical forests when translated into economic values seems to demonstrate that natural forest utilization is economically competitive with other forms of ecologically disruptive land use, such as cattle pastures, and even plant agriculture or forestry plantations. So, the net present value (NPV) of approximately US $9,000 obtained from the forest products in a one hectare stand by Peters et al. (1989) is higher than the NPV from an intensively managed plantation ($ 3184) or a fully-stocked cattle pasture ($2960) (Anonymous 1988). It is highly probable that this assumption will become more evident when economic comparisons can be extended to large areas (with several hectares) where the whole spectrum of useful forest materials is higher. As a counterpoint, some recent studies suggest that beef cattle ranching in the tropical humid areas may be profitable only with fiscal incentives, low interest loans, tax benefits and land speculation (Hecht, et al. 1988, Browder 1988). It seems to me that the current idea that tropical forest is a low profitable natural resource will be seriously challenged by research in the near future. Since each society masters a particular set of cultural values and modes of production, a given ecosystem can be perceived and identified both as an invaluable natural resource or as an obstacle for economic transactions. In the modern, industrialized and technocratic societies, where a market oriented economy is the predominant mode of production, the high biological diversity of tropical forest and its economic potential tend to be overlooked by a rationality engaged in generating, compulsively, a great amount of a single (or a few) successful product (the commodities). In summary, the challenge seems to be the creation of modern forms of direct exploitation of tropical forests, ecologically sound, capable of overcoming the enormous temptation of transforming them into simplified ecosystems, as a reaction to the powerful and unmerciful forces of the market.

Notes

1. I wish to acknowledge the assistance of the following colleagues for providing information and unpublished materials: Ariel Lugo, Oscar Flores, Emily Lott, Alejandro Estrada, Susanna Hecht, Nils Svanquist, Javier Caballero and Benjamin Ortiz. For critical reviews I am also indebted to R. Dirzo, A. Gentry, and A. Challenger. The illustrations were prepared by Felipe Villegas, and I received invaluable technical assistance from Ana Irene Batis.

References Cited

Alarcón, E., M. Brochero, P. Buritica, et al. 1980. *Sector agropecuario Colombiano: Diagnóstico tecnológico.* ICA. Bogota.

Amadon, D. 1973. Birds of the Congo and Amazon forests: a comparison. In: *Tropical forest ecosystems in Africa and South America.* Edited by B.J. Meggers, E.S. Ayensu and W. D. Duckworth. Washington: Smithsonian Institution Press.

Anonymous 1988. *The case for multiple-use management of tropical hardwood forests.* A study prepared by the Harvard Institute for International Development for the International Tropical Timber organization. Yokohama, Japan.

Balee, W. 1986. Analise preliminar de inventario florestal e a ethnobotânica Ka'apor (MA). *Bol. Mus. Par. Emilio Goeldi,* Ser. Bot 36:18-45.

Black, G.A., T. Dobzhansky and C. Pavan. 1950. Some attempts to estimate species diversity and population density of tress in Amazonian forest. *Botany* 111:413-425.

Bisbal, F.J. 1988. Impacto humano sobre los habitat de Venezuela. *Interciencia* 13 (5): 226-232.

Boom, B.M. 1985. "Advocacy Botany" for the Neotropics. *Garden* 9 (3): 24-28.

____ 1986. A forest inventory in Amazonian Bolivia. *Biotropica* 18 (4): 287-294.

Browder, J.O. 1988. The social costs of rain forest destruction: A critique and economic analysis of the "hamburger debate". *Interciencia* 13: 115-120.

Brown, S., and A.E. Lugo. 1982. The storage and production of organic matter in tropical forests and their role in the global carbon cycle. *Biotrópica* 14 (3): 161-187.

____ 1984. Biomass of tropical forests: A new estimate based on forest volumes. *Science* 223: 1290-1293.

Caballero, J. , V.M. Toledo, A. Argueta, et al. 1978. Flora util o el uso tradicional de las plantas. *Biotica* 3:103-144.

Caufield, C. 1982. *Tropical moist forests: The resource, the people, the threat.* International Institute for Environment and Development.

Coates-Estrada, R., and A. Estrada. 1985. *Lista de las aves de la Estación de Biología Los Tuxtlas.* Instituto de Biología, UNAM.

Creighton, K. 1985. Personal communication.

Croat, T.B. 1978. *Flora of Barro Colorado Island.* Palo Alto: Stanford University Press.

Dance, J., and W. Ojeda. 1979. *Evaluación de los recursos forestales del trópico peruano.* Lima, UNA. Departamento de Manejo Forestal.

Dean, W. 1983. Deforestation in Southeastern Brazil. In: *Global deforestation and the nineteenth century world economy.* Edited by C. Tuckers and R. Richards. Duke Press.

Dickinson, R.E. 1981. Effects of tropical deforestation on climate. In: *Blowing in the wind: Deforestation and long-range implications.* Studies in Third World Societies. Publication No.14.

Dirzo, Rodolfo. 1988. Personal communication.

Dodson, C.H., and A.H. Gentry. 1978. *Flora of the Rio Palenque Science Center, Los Rios Province, Ecuador.* Selvyana 4 : 1-628.

Duellman, W.E. 1978. *The biology of an equatorial herpetofauna in Amazonian Ecuador.* Univ. of Kansas, Mus. Nat. Hist., Miscellaneous Publication 65.

Eisenberg, J.F. and K. Redford. 1979. A biogeographic analysis of the mammalian fauna of Venezuela. In: *Vertebrate ecology in the northern neotropics.* Edited by J. F. Eisenberg. Washington: Smithsonian Institution Press.

Erwin, T.L. 1988. The tropical forest canopy. The heart of biotic diversity. In: *Biodiversity.* Edited by E. O. Wilson and F. M. Peters. Washington: National Academy Press.

Estrada, A., and R.M. Coates-Estrada. 1983. Rain forest in Mexico: Research and conservation at Los Tuxtlas. *Oryx* 17:210-214.

FAO-UNEP. 1981. Tropical forest resources assessment project. Vol.1. Los Recursos Forestales de la América Tropical. Rome.

____ 1983. *Yearbook: Production 1982.* Rome.

Fearnside, P.M. 1982. Deforestation in the Brazilian Amazon: How fast is it ocurring? *Interciencia* 7 (2): 82-88.

_____ 1985. Deforestation and decision-making in the development of Brazilian Amazonia. *Interciencia* 10 (5): 243-247.

Feder, E. 1980. The odious competition between man and animal over agricultural resources in the underdeveloped countries. *Research* 3: 463-500.

Gentry, A.H. 1982a. Neotropical floristic diversity:Phytogeographical connections between Central and South America. Pleistocene climatic fluctuations, or an accident of the Andean Orogeny? *Ann. Missouri Bot. Gard.* 69 : 557-593.

_____ 1982b. Patterns of neotropical plant species diversity. *Evolutionary Biology.* 15 : 1-84.

_____ 1986. Sumario de patrones fitogeograficos neotropicales y sus implicaciones para el desarrollo del Amazonia. *Revista Academia Colombiana de Ciencias Exactas, Fisicas y Naturales* 16: 101-116.

Gentry, A.H., and J. López-Parodi. 1980. Deforestation and decreased flooding in the upper Amazon. *Science* 210:1354-1356.

Gentry, A.H., and C. Dodson. 1986. Diversity and biogeography of neotropical vascular epiphytes. *Ann. Missouri Bot. Gard.* 74:126-137.

Green, K.M. 1984. Using landsat to monitor tropical forest ecosystems: Realistic expectations of digital processing technology. In: *Tropical rain forest: Ecology and management*: Edited by S. L. Sutton et al. Blackwell Science Publications.

Hall, C. 1984. *Costa Rica: Una interpretacion geografica con perspectiva historica.* Editorial Costa Rica, San Jose.

Hecht, S.B. 1981. Deforestation in the Amazon Basin: Magnitude, dynamics and soil resource effects. In: *Where have all the flowers gone? deforestation in the third world.* Studies in Third World Societies. Publication No.13.

Hecht, S., R. B. Norgaard, and G. Possio. 1988. The economics of cattle ranching in eastern Amazonia. *Interciencia* 13(5):233-240.

Heckadon-Moreno, S. 1985. La ganadería extensiva y la deforestación: Los costos de una alternativa de desarrollo. In: *Agonía de la naturaleza.* Edited by S. Heckadon-Moreno and J. Espinosa-Gonzalez. Inst. Inv. Agropecuarias. Panama: Smithsonian Tropical Research. Institute.

Henderson-Sellers, A. 1981. The effects of land clearance and agricultural practices on climate. In: *Blowing in the wind: Deforestation and long-range implications.* Studies in Third World Societies. Publication No.14.

Holdridge, L.R. 1967. *Life zone ecology.* San Jose, Costa Rica: Tropical Science Center.

Ibarra, G., and S. Sinaca. 1987. *Listados florísticos de México. VII. Estación de Biología Tropical Los Tuxtlas, Veracruz.* Instituto de Biología, UNAM, México.

Janzen, D.H. 1988. Tropical dry forests. The most endangered major tropical ecosystem. In: *Biodiversity.* Edited by E. O. Wilson and F. M. Peters. Washington: National Academy Press.

Kelly, I. and A. Palerm. 1952. *The Tajin Totonac.* Part I. Washington: Smithsonian Institution

Lanly, J.P. 1981. Síntesis regional. In: *Tropical forest resources assesment project. Vol.1. Los recursos forestales de la América Tropical*: Roma.

_____ 1982. *Los recursos forestales tropicales.* Estudio FAO-MONTES No.30. Roma.

_____ 1983. Assesment of the forest resources in the tropics. *Forestry Abstracts* 44 (6): 287-318.

Lott, E.J. 1985. *Listados florísticos de México. III. La estación de biología Chamela, Jalisco.* Instituto de Biología, UNAM.

Lott, E.J., S.H. Bullock and A. Solis-Magallanes. 1987. Floristic diversity and structure of upland and arroyo forests of coastal Jalisco. *Biotropica* 19:228-235.

Lugo, A.E., R. Schmidt and S. Brown. 1981. Tropical forests in the Caribbean. *Ambio* 10 (6): 318-324.

Lugo, A.E. 1988. Estimating reductions in the diversity of tropical forest species. In: *Biodiversity.* Edited by E. O. Wilson and F. M. Peter. Washington: National Academy Press.

Meave del Castillo, J. 1983. Estructura y composicion de la selva alta perennifolia de Bonampak, Chiapas. Tesis Biológo, Facultad de Ciencias, UNAM, Mexico.

Mittermeier, R.A. 1988. Primate diversity and the tropical forest. Case studies from Brazil and Madagascar and the importance of the megadiversity countries. In: *Biodiversity.* Edited by E. O. Wilson and F. M. Peter. Washington: National Academy Press.

Myers, N. 1981. The hamburger connection: How Central America's forests become north America's hamburgers. *Ambio.*

_____ 1984. *The primary source: Tropical forests and our future.* New York. W.W. Norton.

Myers, R. and S. Rand. 1969. Vertebrates of Barro Colorado, Panama. Publication of Museum of Michigan State University Biological Serices. 1:101-127.

Nations, J.D., and D.I. Komer. 1984. Chewing up. Beef production is decimating Central America's forests. *International Wildlife* 14 (5): 14-16.

Oldfield, M.L. 1981. Tropical deforestation and genetic resources conservation. In: *Blowing in the wind: Deforestation and long-range implications*. Studies in Third World Societies. Publication No.14.

Ojeda, R.A., and M.A. Mares. 1984. La degradación de los recursos naturales y la fauna silvestre en Argentina. *Interciencia* 9 (1): 21-26.

Parsons, J.J. 1976. Forest to pasture: Development or destruction? *Rev. Biol. Trop.* 24 (supl.1): 121-138.

_____ 1980. Europeanization of the savanna lands of northern south America. In: *Human ecology in savanna environments*. Edited by D. R. Harris. London: Academic Press.

Peters, C.M., A. Gentry and R. Mendelsohn. 1989. Valuation of a tropical forest in Peruvian Amazonia. *Nature* 339:655-650.

Prance, G.T. 1977. Floristic inventory of the tropics: Where do we stand? *Ann. Missouri Bot. Gard.* 64 : 659-684.

_____ (Ed). 1987. *Tropical rainforest and climate*. Boulder: Westview Press.

Prance, G.T., and G.B. Schaller. 1982. A preliminary study of some vegetation types of the pantanal, Matto Grosso, Brazil. *Brittonia* 34: 115-130.

Prance, G.T. et al. 1976. Inventario florestal de un hectare de mata de terra firme Km 30 da Estrada Manaus-Itacoatiara. *Acta Amazonica* 6 (1): 9-35.

Raven, H. 1976. Ethics and attitudes. In: *Conservation of threatened plants*. Edited by J. Simmons *et al*. New York: Plenum Press.

SALA (Statistical Abstract of Latin America). 1983. Vol. 22. Latin America Studies Center, University of California at Los Angeles.

Salati, E., and P.B. Vose. 1984. Amazon Basin: A system in equilibrium. *Science* 225 : 129-137.

Sánchez, P.A. 1981. Soils of the humid tropics. In: *Blowing in the wind: Deforestation and long range implications*. Studies in Third World Societies. Publication No.14.

Sarukhán, J. 1968. Estudio sinecologico de las selvas de Terminalia Amazonia en la planicie costera del Golfo de Mexico. Masters thesis, Colegio de Postgraduados, Chapingo, Mexico.

Scott, N.J., J.M. Savage and D.C. Robinson. 1983. Checklist of reptiles and amphibians. In: *Costa Rica natural history*. Edited by D. H. Janzen. Chicago: Univ. of Chicago Press.

Shane, D.R. 1986. *Hoofprints on the forest: Cattle ranching and destruction of Latin America's tropical forests*. Institute for the Study of Human Values. Philadelphia.

Stiles, G.F. 1983. Checklist of birds. In: *Costa Rica natural history*. Edited by D. H. Janzen. Chicago: University of Chicago Press.

Toledo, V.M. 1982. Pleistocene changes of vegetation in tropical México. In: *Biological diversification in the tropics*. Edited by G. T. Prance. New York: Columbia Univ. Press, N.Y. pp. 93-111.

_____ 1985. *A critical evaluation of the floristic knowledge in Latin America and the Caribbean*. A report presented to The Nature Conservancy International Program. Washington, D.C.

_____ 1987. Vacas, cerdos, pollos y ecosistemas: Ecología y ganadería en México. *Ecología, Política/Cultura* 3: 36-49.

_____ 1988. La diversidad biológica de Mexico. *Ciencia y Desarrollo* 81: 17-30.

_____ 1989. The floristic richness of Latin America and the Caribbean as indicated by botanical inventories. Submitted to the *Annals of Missouri Bot. Garden*.

Toledo, V.M., J. Caballero, A. Argueta, et al. 1978. El uso múltiple de la selva basado en el conocimiento tradicional. *Biótica* 3: 85-101.

Toledo, V.M., J. Carabias, C. Toledo and C. Gonzalez-Pacheco. 1989. *La produccion rural de Mexico: Alternativas ecologicas*. Mexico, D. F.: Editorial Universo Veintiuno.

Wilson, D.E. 1983. Checklist of mammals. In: *Costa Rica natural history*. Edited by D. H. Janzen. Chicago: Univ. of Chicago Press.

5

Livestock Economy and Forest Destruction

**Carlos Seré
Lovell S. Jarvis**

The continuing destruction of humid forests is of major concern because of the ecological damage it implies. In most of the areas of Latin America where humid forests have been destroyed, significant parts of the cleared land have been planted in pastures which are grazed by livestock. As a result, many observers have assumed that livestock production, *per se,* has been a primary cause of forest destruction and have called for policies to curb such production.

There is surely some truth to the view that livestock production has contributed to forest destruction, although we believe the causal relationship is often exaggerated. Regardless, the policy problem is serious and requires additional research into the causes of forest clearing and, particularly, the role of livestock in it. Research is also needed into possible means of alleviating the damage caused by forest clearing. We believe that agricultural technologies — in which cattle constitute one element of the farming system — may be identified and developed which could lead to stabilized land systems which cause significantly less ecological damage. Technologies also may be identified to permit the economic recuperation of cleared areas which have already been degraded. Such recuperation might also significantly slow the clearing of new areas.

In this chapter we first briefly outline the structure of the ruminant livestock sector in the Latin American tropics. This basically means cattle. Beef and milk production are based on pastures in this region. Production has grown primarily in response to changes in domestic demand. Exports are now important in Brazil and Central America. In the latter area, the demand for meat and milk appears to have stimulated sufficient growth of the cattle herd to make it a significant issue in forest clearing.

Next, we show that livestock plays an important role in the economy of marginal areas in the Latin American humid tropics mainly because they are among the few activities offering the productive use of such areas. In Brazil, for example, where large areas are being cleared, land clearance is motivated primarily by fiscal and credit incentives. Were such government incentives not available — and they have been recently scaled back — neither clearing nor livestock production would take place in most tropical forest areas. In other humid forest regions, livestock form only part of the farming system in use on lands which have been cleared of forest. In cases where tree crops or annual crops are grown, livestock provide a relatively small proportion of farm income and we believe, again, are not the major force behind forest destruction.

Finally, from a pragmatic viewpoint, we believe that it may be politically impossible to stop the occupation of forests. If so, the development of improved technologies would permit improved use. However, it is a difficult judgment whether developing improved technologies for use of forests is better or worse. Though it is economically appealing, it could also encourage increased clearing. This issue must be rigorously analyzed.

Demand for Livestock Products

Among developing regions of the world, Latin America is clearly in a more favorable situation than the rest. Table 5.1 gives selected indicators of relevance for understanding livestock product demand. The ample land-man ratio of tropical Latin America, its colonizers' preferences, and the land tenure system adopted led to an ample supply of livestock products. This supply is reflected in the high number of cattle per inhabitant and the comparatively high levels of per capita consumption of beef (14 kg) and milk (96 kg) (Table 5.2). These levels, nevertheless, show considerable variability across countries and regions.

Very high levels of consumption are observed in temperate South America followed by tropical South America and finally Central America and the Caribbean. Particularly low levels of consumption prevail in Peru, Guyana, Haiti and El Salvador. Within countries, demand is by no means homogeneous. In general, urban areas have higher levels of beef consumption than rural areas.

A similar but not so marked consumption pattern is evident for milk. The consumption of beef and milk clearly depends on incomes, and income elasticities are relatively high (Rubinstein and Nores 1980, Jarvis 1986, Sanint et al. 1985). Nevertheless, empirical studies have shown that even the lowest income strata of the Latin American population spend about 25% of their food expenditure budget on beef and milk (Table 5.3).

TABLE 5.1 Macroeconomic indicators for major developing regions [a]

Indicator	Latin America	Africa	Near East	Far East
Population (1984):				
Inhabitants (millions)	397.1	435.2	233.0	1351
Density (inhabitants per km^2)	19.7	18.7	19.4	162.4
Growth rate (1970-84)(%)	2.4	2.8	2.8	2.2
Urbanization (%)	68.4	35.6	48.0	38.2
Per capita indicators				
GDP per capita (US$ 1985)	1673	469	2090	451
Protein consumption (gms/day)[c]	67.2	55.3	78.0	51.1
Animal protein (%)	41.2	20.7	24.1	15.4
Caloric intake (calories/day)[c]	2634	2367	2849	2164
Milk and dairy production consumption (kg/year)[bcd]	102.1	30.7	72.9	33.7
Head of cattle per inhabitant (1984)	0.79	0.32	0.24	0.20
Self sufficiency in milk and dairy products (%)[b c]	90.6	61.7	80.9	84.4

a. Country groupings follow FAO classification
b. Average weight by population
c. Average 1979/81
d. Fluid milk equivalent

Sources: FAO 1984a, FAO 1984b, IBRD 1986

Thus beef and milk are important staple foods in Latin America. Their role as wage goods is key to understanding the efforts by governments to control the level of their prices and to stabilize them (Jarvis 1986).

During the 1970s, rapid economic growth led to a rapid increase in demand for beef and milk. The low short-term supply response of each product led to an increase in domestic prices (Figure 5.1) and in many cases reduced exports or increased imports. Simultaneously, technological changes in the poultry industry and overvalued currencies, which reduced the domestic price of imported grain, fostered a rapid reduction of the real

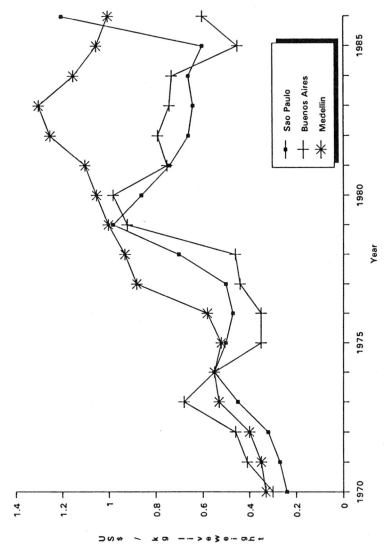

FIGURE 5.1 Domestic beef prices in select Latin American cities, 1970 - 86
Source: CIAT 1988

TABLE 5.2 Beef and milk: production, productivity, and consumption in Latin America

Country and region	Beef cattle distribution of stock and production (% of 1986 total)		Annual cattle productivity (average 1978/85)		Annual growth rate in production (%)				Consumption (kg/capita/yr)		Self sufficiency index	
	Stock	Production	Kg beef/head	Kg milk/head	Beef 71/78	Beef 79/86	Milk 71/78	Milk 79/86	Beef 79/86	Milk 79/86	Beef 76/86	Milk 79/86
Tropical Latin America	78.3	60.3	21.1	857.2	3.1	1.5	4.4	2.0	14.0	96.2	104.7	88.3
Bolivia	2.0	1.4	18.7	1402.3	5.5	5.7	5.5	5.4	16.8	23.4	99.4	57.9
Brazil	42.2	23.1	18.6	714.3	3.0	-0.4	5.7	1.7	14.8	94.6	114.0	96.8
Colombia	7.7	8.1	25.2	968.2	4.3	0.9	-2.2	5.9	22.1	97.6	101.9	96.5
Ecuador	1.2	1.2	28.8	1409.7	6.2	-0.3	2.7	1.4	10.4	114.7	99.8	96.1
Mexico	10.2	12.4	21.0	948.7	4.5	9.0[a]	6.6	1.7	10.2	112.5	99.7	86.4
Paraguay	2.3	1.5	18.0	1906.9	-2.0	0.4	7.8	2.2	29.0	53.0	110.1	95.1
Peru	1.2	1.1	23.8	1137.1	-1.3	2.7	-0.6	0.2	5.9	55.4	88.4	77.7
Venezuela	4.1	4.1	29.6	1165.7	5.4	-0.8	3.4	3.2	20.9	132.3	97.1	67.5
Central America	4.0	4.2	29.3	862.7	4.3	-1.3	4.5	-0.3	12.3	81.9	124.8	82.7
Costa Rica	0.8	1.3	34.0	1148.7	8.8	3.2	6.5	3.7	22.2	146.0	149.6	95.8
El Salvador	0.3	0.3	24.4	907.1	5.2	-5.4	7.2	-0.4	5.5	68.4	93.0	77.2
Guatemala	0.8	0.6	36.3	866.2	2.1	-9.0	1.9	2.4	6.4	55.6	142.0	80.7
Honduras	0.9	0.8	24.6	679.0	3.4	-0.6	3.7	-0.7	9.7	78.9	139.2	84.1
Nicaragua	0.7	0.6	23.9	710.0	3.7	-5.8	4.2	-11.0	13.8	70.7	127.0	76.1
Panama	0.5	0.7	34.2	989.1	2.6	6.1	3.4	1.1	27.1	60.0	90.7	76.4
Caribbean	3.4	3.2	25.3	1419.3	-2.8	1.9	2.6	1.6	13.6	90.2	69.4	68.9
Cuba	2.1	1.9	24.6	1483.2	-5.3	0.5	3.4	0.9	24.9	145.4	60.7	75.5
Dom. Republic	0.7	0.8	26.8	1815.9	3.0	4.5	1.5	3.0	8.6	91.8	107.9	85.0
Guyana	0.1	0.0	12.3	751.0	-4.4	0.1	-4.8	8.3	2.3	51.8	99.7	33.9
Temperate Latin America	21.7	39.7	47.9	1751.2	6.3	-1.2	1.1	1.5	62.7	171.6	118.2	98.9
Argentina	17.3	34.1	50.5	1843.9	6.7	-1.4	1.0	1.7	79.6	189.3	116.7	100.3
Chile	1.1	2.2	49.8	1456.8	6.1	1.2	1.8	-0.1	16.3	98.7	96.8	90.0
Uruguay	3.3	3.5	33.7	1620.4	2.9	-0.3	1.1	2.0	76.5	281.8	151.7	102.0
Latin America	100.0	100.0	27.4	959.8	4.4	0.4	3.6	1.9	19.6	104.3	109.7	90.4

a. Due to correction of FAO Series
Source: CIAT 1988

TABLE 5.3 Expenditure share and income elasticities of beef and milk demand
of the lowest income quartile of selected Latin American cities

Country	City	Expenditure share (percentage of food expenditure)		Income elasticity	
		Beef	Milk	Beef	Milk
Colombia	Bogota	18.6	9.6	1.09	0.91
	Cali	24.2	7.0	1.28	1.02
Chile	Santiago	14.1	6.9	0.90	1.16
Ecuador	Quito	12.9	8.7	1.28	0.87
Paraguay	Asuncion	26.0	11.2	0.80	1.02
Peru	Lima	18.6	11.7	0.92	na
Venezuela	Caracas	12.4	13.1	0.80	1.06

Source: Rubinstein and Nores 1980

price of poultry and a process of substitution in consumption from beef to poultry (Rivas et al. 1988). Table 5.4 shows the magnitude of such substitution for Colombia, Brazil and Mexico. Per capita consumption of beef dropped during the eighties as economic recession reduced incomes, compounded by the further reduction in price of the poultry substitute.

Future beef consumption levels will depend on the evolution of per capita incomes and the relative prices of poultry and beef. Further price reductions in poultry can be expected. Their magnitude will be heavily influenced by movements in international grain prices, as well as trade and foreign exchange policies of individual countries.

Supply

Production of beef and milk in tropical America is almost exclusively pasture-based. The region has an ample supply of land of limited cropping potential. In some regions cattle are being run on better soils due to tenurial problems (e.g. large holdings and a legal framework not conducive to renting or share-cropping). In 1986, tropical Latin America had about 240 million head of cattle (19% of the world's stock) which produced 5 million metric tons of beef (carcass weight), corresponding to 10.5% of world output (CIAT 1988).

Cattle have a peculiar attribute. They are a capital good when alive (producing beef, milk, or calves) and a consumption good when slaughtered (yielding beef and hides) (Jarvis 1969). This dual attribute causes the supply of beef to exhibit unusual dynamic behavior. A beef price increase leads producers to retain breeding animals to expand the herd, but such retention

TABLE 5.4 Extent of substitution of beef by poultry in selected Latin American countries

Country	Relative consumer price poultry/beef		Observed beef consumption kg/capita		Estimated beef consumption	Beef substituted kg per capita	Beef substituted as % of observed consumption
	Initial year [a]	Final year	Initial year	Final year	Final year [b]	Final year	Final year
Brazil	1.80	0.49	18.8	16.5	24.3	7.8	47.3
Colombia	1.20	0.70	22.7	25.4	32.3	6.9	27.2
Mexico	0.67	0.47	8.9	8.6	10.5	1.9	22.1

a. Brazil 1960-1982, Colombia 1960-1984, and Mexico 1966-1982
b. At poultry prices of the initial year

reduces the supply of beef in the short run. The supply elasticity usually remains negative for one or two years. Subsequently, the increased cattle herd leads to expanded beef supply. The long run supply elasticity is positive and frequently above one (Barros 1973, Yver 1972, Lattimore 1974, Jarvis 1969). These features lead to cyclical patterns of output and prices observable in most cattle producing regions. The opposite nature of short and long run price response implies that short-term trends can be misleading.

Production growth rates of beef, milk and other animal protein products in the tropical zone were all above the growth rates of population during the 1970s (Table 5.2). During the 1980s all these production rates dropped markedly and both beef and milk fell to levels below the growth rate of population. Self sufficiency indices decreased for beef and milk between the periods 1971/78 and 1979/86 (CIAT 1988).

The decline in production growth rates is clearly due to the reduction of consumer incomes, and thus, in price incentives for producers. Production growth was mainly achieved by horizontal expansion, i.e. incorporating additional heads of cattle. This is documented by the virtual growth stagnation in the rate of production per head in stock over the period 1971-86. In the tropical region, it remained at about 20 kg/head/per annum which is about half of the 1971-86 output per head achieved in temperate South America (CIAT 1988). Nevertheless, these levels of productivity were maintained despite a continuing movement of cattle production towards increasingly marginal soils in the tropical region.

The drop in growth rates of beef production was particularly impressive in Central America and Panama (from 4.3% per annum in 1971/78 to -1.3% per annum in 1979/86). The already low per capita consumption dropped slightly, but net exports fell from 83,000 to 66,000 metric tons during the same periods, reflecting both the political unrest in the region and the decline of export prices.

Trade

International beef trade is small in relation to world production. Given the existence of cattle cycles and the policies of developed countries to buffer their markets from this volatility and export it, the international market is a residual market of high volatility. It is additionally divided into two segments: the trade is fresh beef between countries with sporadic outbreaks of foot-and-mouth disease (FMD) and the trade between countries free from it. South American exporters except Chile, belong to the FMD circuit which receives lower prices than Central America, Australia, New Zealand which are free of FMD. Processed beef is not subject to FMD restrictions, but faces a strongly competitive market.

TABLE 5.5 Net exports of beef in tropical Latin America
            (averages 1970/77 and 1978/8 in MT)

Country and Region	Fresh, chilled, or frozen bovine meat		Canned meat [a]		Total	
	1970/77	1978/85	1970/77	1978/85	1970/77	1978/85
Tropical Latin America	165	82	30.0	135.0	195.0	217.0
Brazil	46	7	105.0	253.0	151.0	260.0
Central America	81	78	2.5	7.5	83.5	85.5
Caribbean	-4	-12	-92.5	-107.5	-96.5	-119.5
LATIN AMERICA	495	385	272.5	387.5	767.5	772.5

a. Carcass weight equivalent

The agricultural protection policies of developed countries have depressed international beef prices through the maintenance of high domestic prices and the subsidized export of surpluses. Valdés and Zietz (1980) have estimated that international beef prices could increase by about 20% if all countries liberalized beef trade.

Beef trade patterns between regions have remained relatively constant (Table 5.5). The averages, nevertheless, mask very wide variations between individual years. Tropical Latin America has remained a net beef exporting region of about 200,000 MT per annum. This is due to increasing Brazilian exports being to some extent offset by increasing imports in the Caribbean region. The value of the net exports dropped in spite of roughly constant volumes due to a substantial decline in international beef prices during the eighties.

The type of beef exported by tropical Latin America has changed over time (Table 5.5). Initially, all regions exported mainly chilled and frozen beef, in carcass and quarters. Central America, which is free of FMD, has quotas assigned for the US market. It still exports mainly fresh, chilled and frozen beef. Brazil, on the other hand, exports both fresh and processed beef. It has pursued an aggressive strategy of exporting processed beef to gain access to FMD free markets to increase the value added of its exports.

TABLE 5.6 Dry milk: net exports in Latin America (000 MT)

Country and Region	1970/77	1978/85	Annual growth rate (%) 70/77-78/85
Tropical Latin America	245	378	5.6
Brazil	25	22	-1.6
Mexico	52	111	9.9
Cuba	52	36	-4.5
Venezuela	38	90	11.4
Central America	12	32	13.0
Caribbean	76	75	-0.2
Latin America	252	389	5.6

Source: CIAT 1988

Net imports in dry milk powder increased substantially during recent years (Table 5.6), due to low international prices, the ample availability of dry milk food aid, and the ease of introducing powdered milk into the domestic market. This contrasts with the structural protection of the domestic beef markets, due to the lack of facilities to handle and distribute highly perishable imported meats.

Production Systems

Beef is produced in both large scale specialized ranching operations and in medium to small farms and is frequently combined with crop production or as a joint product in dual purpose (beef-milk) farms. Additionally, many countries of tropical America have specialized dairy production systems in the highlands, where temperate climate breeds and technologies can be used to a large extent. Detailed descriptions of such production systems are available (Von Oven 1971, Vera and Seré 1985, Seré 1983, Seré and Vaccaro 1985).

Livestock in Tropical Forest Ecosystems

Since colonial times forests have been cleared in Latin America both for crop and livestock production. Forests cleared were generally on drier, more fertile soils with good access to markets. Recent controversy centers mainly around the clearing of the more humid forests having low fertility soils and very fragile ecologies.

On a continental scale, the cattle inventory in the humid tropics is small (about 8% of total herds in tropical South America). In Central America the proportion is substantially higher due to the more limited land resources (e.g., 30% in Costa Rica). In Mexico about 10% of the stock is found in the humid tropics (CIAT estimates). Pressure on the humid forest is exacerbated by the fact that beef prices are higher in Central America than in South America, resulting from easier access to the US market and lower transportation costs.

Why Do We Find Cattle in the Humid Tropics?

Present livestock systems in the humid tropics are widely considered to be unstable and ecologically damaging. To improve this situation, whether by reducing the use of pasture-based systems (and thereby, forest destruction) or by developing more ecologically sound forms of livestock production in the humid forest, it is necessary to better understand the determinants of livestock uses in existing livestock systems. We shall discuss two sets of causes for the observed inclusion of cattle in existing rainforest use systems: sectoral and macroeconomic reasons on the one hand and microeconomic and farming-systems-type reasons on the other.

Macro and Sectoral Reasons

As discussed above, the Latin American tropical region has an elastic market for beef and milk. Brazil and Central America are already net exporters of beef, having humid tropic regions close to a developed export infrastructure. The Andean countries are essentially self sufficient (Colombia, Ecuador) or net importers of beef (Peru) and all are net importers of milk. In addition, the humid tropics region has a significant urban population.

The limited number of alternative land uses for low fertility soils, led policy makers interested in occupation of the Brazilian Amazon to foster the establishment of large-scale ranching operations. Tax incentives and subsidized credit were the main instruments used. This process was driven more by the geopolitical desire to achieve effective habitation of the land, but with limited public sector involvement, than by considerations of economic growth and welfare.

The same lack of viable alternatives contributed to the expansion of cattle production in Central America and the Andean countries. Particularly in the latter, settlement in the humid tropics was envisaged as an alternative to agrarian reform on more fertile lands. Promotion of pastures and livestock in this region largely occurred by default due to the absence of specific policies to either ban settlement or offer production alternatives with competitive returns to resources allocated.

Micro or Farming Systems Reasons

Clearing is a major investment in these production systems. Grasses have lower soil fertility requirements than most crops, thus extending the period of effective utilization of areas cleared.

Livestock are extremely well adapted to using frontier resources when infrastructure for transport, storage or marketing is lacking. Cattle can be walked over long distances and sale can be delayed without major losses. The high unit value often makes it economic to produce cattle even at locations with high transport costs.

Cattle are a liquid investment, making them an efficient way to store wealth and to overcome future cash flow problems.

The marginal cost of establishing pastures with or after crops is very low for small-holders, involving only some planting material and labor. There is no opportunity cost for the land when the fertility level has dropped below the critical value for economic crop production.

Livestock production offers a relatively high labor productivity and low risk when compared to other crops, particularly those with uncertain market prospects.

Established pastures improve the tenancy status and increases the value of the property allowing settlers to build "sweat" equity by converting labor into capital.

Western Amazon Case Studies

The role of the attributes discussed can be better understood as determinants of the existence of pastures in the humid tropics by comparing the role of cattle in different concrete scenarios. These cases used were selected to provide a sense of the contrasts available within the Western Amazon region. These are: (1) *Robusta* coffee/cattle systems in Napo, Ecuador (Estrada et al. 1988), (2) beef/mixed cropping systems in Pucallpa, Peru (Riesco et al. 1986) and (3) dual-purpose (beef-milk) systems in Caquetá, Colombia (Ramirez and Seré 1988). Table 5.7 presents the mean land use patterns and cattle inventories of the three farming systems.

TABLE 5.7 Settler farming systems in the Western Amazon

	Location		
	Napo, Ecuador 1986	Caquetá, Colombia 1987	Pucallpa, Peru 1981
Farming System	lowland cattle/coffee	dual purpose beef-milk	beef mixed cropping
Number of holdings surveyed	107.0	118	70
Rainfall (mm p.a.)	>3100.0	3500.0	1700-3800
Land Use (ha)			
Total farm size	46.0	130.5	59.2
Area cleared	15.8	121.4	40.8
Crops	6.5	3.7	6.3[a]
- coffee	5.1	na	na
- cacao	0.2	0.7 [b]	na
- corn	0.5	1.6	na
- subsistence	0.7	1.4	na
Pastures	6.6	95.3	24.8
Brachiaria spp.	3.2	25.9	4.2
Pennisetum purpureume)	2.4	0.8	na
Panicum maximum	0.4	0.7	na
Axonopus scoparius (gramalote)	0.3	na	na
Echinochloa polistachya (alemán)	0.3	1.3	na
Pueraria phaseoloides	na	na	8.8
Native and naturalized pastures [c]	na	61.9	9.2
Other	na	4.7	2.6
Secondary forest	2.7	22.4	9.8
Cattle	6.5	121.2	24.6
-cows	2.4	48.5	11.3

Notes a, b, and c: see endnotes
Sources: Estrada et al. 1988, Ramirez and Seré 1988, Riesco et al. 1986

Lowland Coffee/Cattle Systems in Napo, Ecuador

Settlement of this region was driven by the discovery of oil and the construction of roads into the region. Oil companies brought in labor, created local demand for food, and provided an income source for settlers developing their properties. Soils are extremely variable but include fertile areas partly being used by a few large scale oil-palm plantations and by settlers growing cocoa.

Over time the settlers' farming system evolved from mainly subsistence crops (corn, cassava, plantains) to a market oriented system based on perennial crops (coffee, cocoa), pastures and trees for the timber industry. Given the limited extent of the more fertile soils, settlers have increasingly occupied more marginal soils unsuitable for cocoa. Coffee, which grows on lower fertility soils, has become the mainstay of the economy. It uses about 60% of the total labor employed on farms and generates 84% of the average gross income.

Settlement policy allocates each settler a plot of 50 ha irrespective of land quality or production potential. Given the limited access to hired labor, farmers usually allocate available labor to the coffee crop and farm the rest of the land extensively via pastures and cattle, or simply exploit wood from the primary forest. The labor scarcity is documented by the fact that the cattle are seldom milked and that the major reason given by farmers for planting aggressive grasses of the *Brachiaria* genus is the reduced labor input required for weeding.

In this farming system cattle play mainly a role of wealth accumulation and a buffer for the highly variable income obtained from coffee.

Beef/Mixed Cropping Systems of Pucallpa, Peru

Settlement in this region stretches along the side of the highway linking the Ucayali River district to the Sierra and Coastal regions of Peru. The settlement process is relatively old, having gained momentum through the wood processing industry and the trade from Lima to Iquitos which fostered the growth of the city of Pucallpa, which today is an important local market.

The Sierra and the Coastal regions have limited potential for expanded agricultural production. This limitation has led Peruvian policy makers to emphasize the development of viable farming systems in the humid tropics. Several policies were put in place to this end, such as the official purchase of grains (corn, rice) at the same price in the whole country, giving a strong incentive to produce such crops in the Amazon.

Current land use patterns which include a relatively large annual crop-ping component, reflect the effect of the incentives offered. At the same time the limited resource base for pasture production in Peru has led to relatively high beef prices, particularly compared to milk which is imported commercially or as concessionary aid. Consumption patterns of the Peruvian humid tropics population traditionally have included very low amounts of milk and dairy products. Incentives for the development of a dairy industry have been very limited in spite of the fact that milk can be collected easily along the main highway and the small herd size could be expected to make milking an efficient use of farm labor.

In this farming system the contribution of cattle to farm labor use is higher than in the Napo case. Pasture establishment is more labor-produc-tive because the lower rainfall allows easier burning of the forest. Annual cropping is also more feasible, explaining the lower importance of perennial tree crops in this context.

Here again the land-man ratio was formally fixed by settlement agen-cies, leading to theoretical plot sizes of 50 ha, which are more than what a family can manage in crops with the existing technology and capital endow-ment. Here cattle on pastures again are a labor productive way of using additional land resources.

Dual-purpose (beef-milk) Systems in Caquetá, Colombia

The Andean Piedmont of Southeastern Colombia was colonized after the construction of roads into the region. These roads were built mainly for geopolitical reasons, i.e. border conflicts with Peru. The main settlement push occurred in the 1950s as people fled from the violence occurring in the more developed regions of Colombia. This settlement process was not or-ganized, but in the 1960s the government invested in infrastructure development (mainly roads) and supplied development credit to settlers.

The farming systems utilized went through a series of boom and bust cycles linked to rubber, marihuana and recently coca. Both a lack of good road linkage to the major population centers and also the distance to them have caused high transport costs. Colombia also has other regions which can produce the basic staples at lower cost and which are closer to the markets. Thus, Caquetá settlers have few alternatives besides cattle. This is reflected by the farm size and land use pattern (Table 5.7). Average farm sizes and, particularly, the areas cleared per farm are larger than in the two previous cases. This is associated with a low productivity of degraded pas-tures and a lack of cropping alternatives. Crops are basically grown for subsistence only. The availability of labor has led to the development of more intensive livestock systems, including milking. Originally milk was used for very extensive on-farm cheese production. In the 1970s, after local road infrastructure was improved, a dairy plant started to operate in the regional capital. Two thirds of the water in the milk was evaporated locally. This product was then transported to a full dairy plant in the Cauca Valley (several hundred kilometers away) to produce dairy products. A growing milk demand has led the gradual intensification and expansion of milk production. Livestock play the most important economic role in this system, being the only competitive enterprise given the distance to markets and the competitive position of the region vis-a-vis other producing regions (low pasture establishment costs, low beef prices, limited alternative uses of labor, etc.).

Conclusions

Almost by default, livestock and pastures have come to be an important part of farming in humid tropics. Livestock allow human beings to make a living on these marginal soils even when public sector support is absent. Given the fact that banning land use is generally not a feasible alternative in most regions, more ecologically attractive alternatives will have to be offered to farmers. These may comprise alternatives for more sustainable forms of pastoral land use, perennial crops or combinations thereof.

In the traditional systems, pastures degrade rapidly from initial high productivity levels to a situation where either a low level equilibrium is achieved (e.g. *criaderos* in Caquetá, Colombia) or where weed pressure is such that land use is abandoned and allowed to return to secondary forest. The cycle can then start again after a variable number of years. Research results support the hypothesis that sustainable legume grass pastures can be developed which will efficiently recycle nutrients and allow substantially higher stocking rates and productivity (see this volume, Serrao and Toledo, Chapter 15).

Such technologies lead to several options to achieve stable systems:

- Immediate establishment of sustainable pastures on cleared forest. This approach is technically and financially attractive because it reduces the weed problem and achieves higher fertility at low cost (burning). This approach implies additional clearing and thus increased negative environmental externalities and requires additional infrastructure investments.
- Establishment of sustainable pastures after secondary forest clearing. This option has lower ecological costs and permits better use of existing infrastructure. The major drawback is the need to wait several years for the fertility to build up, meanwhile leaving costly

infrastructure and land unused. However, such lack of use does not represent a major drawback as substantial areas of fallows (in secondary forest) can be found in many humid tropics land-use systems.

- Establishment of sustainable pastures by directly reclaiming degraded pastures using purchased fertilizers and tractors to establish favorable conditions for the legume-grass pastures. The high cash costs may be reduced by the establishment of a companion crop such as corn or rice. The major advantage would be the immediate use of the land having an existing associated infrastructure and the direct reduction of degraded areas in the region. The higher carrying capacity of such a strategy might allow farmers to turn other areas of the farm into fallow to establish pastures after secondary forest (option 2).

Clearly these different options will differ in terms of their ecological impacts and economics. A critical issue is the extent to which such technologies will increase deforestation by making it more attractive in financial terms. Short term technologies which will increase stocking rates 2-3 fold ought to reduce the pressure for deforestation, as the stock growth within the region is low. The issue is the supply elasticity of cattle from other regions. Transport costs are an important factor in many situations particularly in the Andean countries but are relatively low in Brazil. If the supply elasticity of cattle is low, or can be maintained low through appropriate policies, the introduction of improved pasture technology might reduce the need to clear forests for a number of years. Thus research in this area might buy time for the ecosystem as a whole.

We propose an iterative research approach integrating: (a) the technical feasibility of stable land-use systems including cattle, (b) assessments of the negative ecological externalities, (c) economic analyses of alternative strategies to move from existing systems based on degrading pastures to the envisaged more stable systems, and (d) studies of the impact of alternative policies on these development paths.

Given the demand by the human population in the Amazon for food and productive use of their labor as well as the stock of degraded pastures, we consider that research on these issues is vitally needed to allow the formulation of appropriate land-use policies for this fragile ecosystem.

Notes

1. Notes to Table 5.7. (a) Includes 4.2 ha of annual crops (mainly corn, rice, cassava, and plantain) and 2.1 ha of perennial crops (rubber, citrus, and others), (b) includes small areas of sugar cane, and rubber, and (c) "Torour-co" in Peru, "criaderos" in Colombia mainly composed of *Paspalum conjugatum, Axonopus compresus,* and *Homolepsis aturensis.*

References Cited

Barros M., C. 1973. *Respuesta de la producción bovina ante cambios de precios: un enfoque econométrico.* Santiago de Chile: Universidad Católica de Chile, PPA, Serie A, Trabajos de Investigación No.8. November.

Centro Internacional de Agricultura Tropical. 1988. *Trends in CIAT Commodities.* Internal Document Economics 1(13), May.

Estrada, R. D., C. Seré and H. Luzuriaga. 1988. *Sistemas de producción agrosilvopastoriles en la selva baja de la Provincia del Napo, Ecuador.* Cali, Colombia: Centro Internacional de Agricultura Tropical (CIAT).

Food and Agricultural Organization 1984a. *1983 Production yearbook.* Rome: Food and Agricultural Organization.

_____ 1984b. *Food balance sheets. 1979-81* Average. Rome.

International Bank for Reconstruction and Development. 1986. *Informe sobre el desarrollo mundial 1985.* Washington, D.C.

Jarvis, L. S. 1969. Supply response in the cattle industry, the Argentine case: 1937/38 - 1966/67. Ph.D. Thesis, Massachusetts Institute of Technology, August.

_____ 1986. *El desarrollo ganadero en América Latina.* Banco Mundial, Montevideo: Editorial Agropecuaria.

Lattimore, R. G. 1974. An econometric study of the Brazilian beef sector. Ph.D. Thesis, Purdue University, Ann Arbor: Xerox University Microfilms.

Ramirez, A. and C. Seré. 1988. *Brachiaria decumbens* en el Caquetá: Adopción y uso en ganaderías de doble propósito (in preparation).

Riesco, A., M. de la Torre, C. Reyes, G. Meini, H. Huaman, and M. Garcia. 1986. *Analisis exploratorio de los sistemas de fundo de pequeños productores en la Amazonia, Región de Pucallpa.* IVITA, Pucallpa, Peru: CIID.

Rivas, L., C. Seré, L. R. Sanint and J. L. Cordeu. 1988. *La situación de la demanda de carnes en países seleccionados de América Latina y El Caribe.* Proyecto Colaborativo FAO-RLAC/CIAT.

Rubinstein, E. M. and G. A. Nores. 1980. *Gasto en carne de res y productos lácteos por estrato de ingreso en doce ciudades de América Latina.* Segundo Borrador, July (mimeo). Cali, Colombia: Centro Internacional de Agricultura Tropical (CIAT).

Sanint, L. R., L. Rivas, M. C. Duque and C. Seré. 1985. *Analisis de los patrones de consumo de alimentos en Colombia a partir de la encuesta de hogares DANE/DRI de 1981*. Revista de Planeación y Desarrollo, Volumen 17 (3). Bogota, September.

Seré, C.. 1983. Primera aproximación a una clasificación de sistemas de producción lechera en el trópico Sudamericano. *Producción Animal Tropical* 8:110 -121.

Seré, C. and L. Vaccaro. 1985. Milk production from dual-purpose systems in tropical Latin America. In: *Milk production in developing countries*. Edited by A.J. Smith. University of Edinburgh, Centre for Tropical Veterinary Medicine.

Valdes, A. and J. Zietz. 1980. *Agricultural protection in OECD countries: Its cost to less developed countries*. Research Report No.21. Washington, D.C. International Food Policy Research Institute.

Vera, R. and C. Seré. 1985. *Sistemas de producción pecuaria extensiva: Brasil, Colombia, Venezuela*. Informe final del Proyecto ETES (Estudio Tecnico y Económico de Producción Pecuaria), 1978-1982. Cali, Colombia: Centro Internacional de Agricultura Tropical (CIAT).

von Oven, R. 1971. Produktionsstruktur und Entwicklungs- moeglichkeiten der Rindfleischerzeugung in Suedamerika. Dissertation, Goettingen.

Yver, R. 1972. El comportamiento de la inversión y la oferta de la industria ganadera en Argentina. Santiago:Universidad Católica de Chile, *Cuadernos de Economía* 21, Año 9, December.

PART TWO
FOREST USES

Throughout the world, forest management without a strong ethic leads to short-term exploitation philosophy, and forest harvesting under these conditions emphasizes the short-run economic maximization. Patterns of forest mismanagement can also be seen in many temperate forests, although the long-term ecological effects may be different. Given the proper incentives, most forest managers shift to longer cutting cycles and more aggressive reforesting efforts. Even the most ardent environmental foresters are not immune to political and economic forces. Too radical a departure from these principles will simply bring about the replacement of an environmentally oriented forester with one who is less environmentally oriented.

Some critics argue that the developed world's appetite for beef promotes tropical deforestation. Evidence presented in this book suggests, however, that the returns from land speculation appear to be greater than profits gained from livestock or timber harvesting. There are, however, regional variations.

Many developed countries have experienced processes that parallel the current practices in tropical nations. Not too many years ago, individuals in the United States could get title to tracts of land simply by harvesting the timber (the Timber Claims Act). This act is no longer in effect, but mining claims are still very much a part of the U.S. scene. Under mining law, one can gain title to land simply by continued development work. Supposedly there should be ore of economic value present on these claims, but the burden of proving that there is no valuable ore may fall to the government rather than on the miner. Some individuals will attempt to gain land title even if there is no economic incentive from the mining. The practice of timber cutting and grazing on tropical forests to gain land title is an exact parallel to the response of the U.S. mining law, and does not require a profitable livestock operation in order for these practices to be attractive to the individual.

— Donald A. Jameson

6

Tropical Forest Uses

Ariel E. Lugo

Tropical forests are a source of controversy among international and national sectors and in almost all parts of modern society. The positions assumed by the participants in discussions of the matter are divided and antagonistic. Some sectors do not acknowledge any value to tropical forests; others consider tropical forests so valuable that they should be protected and isolated from all and any human intervention. There are even other sectors that perceive tropical forests as unexplored areas which justify the exploitation of any timber, hydrological, wildlife, and mineral resources that may exist. However, many indigenous communities depend on these forests to satisfy their basic needs. For these communities, access to healthy forests is a matter of life or death. For the scientists who study the biota, the tropical forest is one of the most complex, least studied, and most fascinating ecosystem on the planet.

There is concern among the habitants of non-tropical countries about the consequences of the destruction of tropical forests, mainly regarding the possible climatic changes and the extinction of species. The destruction of tropical forests produces other consequences which directly and immediately affect the people of the tropics; however, these effects, i.e., the energy crisis, or the loss of soil fertility, do not have the international support that the aforementioned ones have.

It is interesting, though not surprising, that tropical forests cause so much distress on our planet. The main reason is that these forests constitute half of the forests of the world and they nest 70% of all the plant and animal species of the planet. Furthermore, due to the intensity of the biotic processes that take place in the tropics, any biogeochemical cycle considered at a global scale will be significantly affected by tropical forests. When human activity on our planet was less intense, the tropics captured the attention of only a small part of our society. At present, human activity affects our planet in ways that threaten the stability of it s biogeochemical cycles, its climate, and its species richness. In addition, human activity in the tropics has increased significantly and consequently its impact has become a matter of global concern.

Unfortunately, our knowledge of tropical systems and the number of scientists actively studying them are not proportional to the global concern about them. For example, a survey of the number of tropical foresters in Mexico, the United States, and Canada gave the following results: Mexico 31, Canada 65, and the United States 377 for a total of 474. Of these 474 foresters, only 126 had some research experience (USDA Forest Service and North American Forestry Commission, 1986). A census of tropical ecologists conducted in the latter part of the 1970s certified a total of 1832 scientists (few for such a large area), of which only 413 worked in Latin America (Yantko and Golley 1977). As a result, the dialogue regarding the use of tropical forests is generally full of myths and deceptive information which only sets back the important task of managing these systems for the benefit of all humans (Lugo and Brown 1981). A somber consequence of this situation is the polarization of the different sectors of society whom, in one way or another, are affected by the condition of tropical forests. It is imperative that myths be eliminated, knowledge be increased, the quality of dialogue improved, and that we search for viable alternatives for the use of tropical forests.

My objective is to present some facts on the status of tropical forests in Latin America, list the factors and conditions that affect the survival and quality of forest lands, present models of land-use and forest management, and point out action plans to implement the wise use of forest lands.

Area and Status of the Tropical Forests

In 1980, tropical Latin America (including Central and South America) had an area of 938 million ha of primary forests (21.7% of all the forests on the planet and 46.4% of the tropical forests, Tables 6.1 and 6.2). The great Amazon forest is the largest area of tropical forest in the world. It was recently demonstrated that the tropical forests in Latin America are as species-diverse as the Asian, which had been pointed out as the most species-rich (Gentry and Dodson 1987). The richness of species in forests is apparently dependent on climatic and edaphic factors (Gentry 1982, Lugo and Brown 1981), and not necessarily exclusively on biogeographic factors as had been stated (Whitmore 1975).

Primary forests in Latin America have been classified as open or closed, depending upon their canopy as depicted by aerial photos. Open forests permit light penetration through the canopy and as a result have

TABLE 6.1 Area and annual rates of gains and losses in Latin American and Caribbean tropical forests in 1980

	Conifers	Broadleaf forests			Total forests	Total under re-cuperation	Shrubs	Annual loss [a]	Annual gain [b]
		Closed	Open	Total					
Central America									
Belize	116	1,269	0	1,269	1,385	525	49	9	0
Costa Rica	11	1,653	0	1,653	1,664	120	120	60	0
Cuba	970	2,055	0	2,055	3,025	700	305	2	11
Dominican Republic	241	444	0	444	685	287	54	3	0
El Salvador	44	111	0	111	155	22	293	5	0
Guadalupe	0	0	68	68	68				
Guatemala	750	3,846	0	3,846	4,596	360	1,505	80	3
Haiti	12	46	0	46	58	43	53	2	0
Honduras	1,942	1,855	200	2,055	3,997	680	1,220	95	0
Jamaica	83	112	0	112	195	159	227	2	1
Martinique	0	0	28	28	28				1
Mexico	20,490	27,350		27,350	47,840	26,000	59,500	530	17
Nicaragua	338	4,170	0	4,170	4,508	1,370	210	111	0
Panama	35	4,169	0	4,169	4,204	124	0	31	1
Puerto Rico	6	150	148	298	304			1	1
Trinidad	60	308	0	308	368				1
Total	25,098	47,538	444	47,982	73,080	30,390	63,536	931	34

a. deforestation
b. natural regeneration or work done in population or repopulation

Source: FAO 1985

TABLE 6.1 Area and annual rates of gains and losses in Latin American and Caribbean tropical forest in 1980 — continued

| | Conifers | Broadleaf forests | | Total | Total forests | Total under re-cuperation | Shrubs | Annual loss[a] | Annual gain[b] |
		Closed	Open						
South America									
Bolivia	3	44,010	22,750	66,760	66,763	3,050	9000	65	0
Brazil	13,20	382,510	157,000	539,510	553,030	100,620	61,200	1,480	346
Colombia	607	46,744	5,300	52,044	52,651	8,900	5,500	800	8
Equador	107	14,572		14,572	14,679	2,350	1,050	300	4
French Guiana	2	8,903	70	8,973	8,975	75	7	1	
Guiana	12	18,475	25	18,500	15,512	200	115	3	0
Paraguay	18	4,082	26,260	30,342	30,360	5,650	0	160	
Peru	370	70,150	1,120	71,270	71,640	5,350	3,150	253	4
Suriname	85	14,830	690	15,520	15,605	270	200	3	
Venezuela	1,120	31,955		31,955	33,075	10,650	2,120	125	14
Total	15,844	636,231	213,215	849,446	865,290	137,115	82,342	3,190	376
Latin America	40,942	683.769	213,659	897,428	938,370	167,505	145,878	4,121	410
South America[c]	20,474	647,498	247,047	894,545	915,019	137,172	82,348	~3,171	470
World	1,463,562	1,827,486	1,029,455	2,856,941	4,320,503	406,738	623.732	~7,268	14,511

a . deforestation
b. natural regeneration or work done in population or repopulation
c. the whole continent
d. closed forests only (mostly tropical)

Source: FAO 1985

TABLE 6.2 Tropical forest biomass based on wood volume measurements

| | Closed forests | | | | | | | | Open Forests | | | Total |
| | Broadleaf | | | | Coniferous | | | | | | | |
	Matures and productives	Disturbed	Non-productives	Subtotal	Matures and productives	Disturbed	Non-productives	Subtotal	Productives	Non-productives	Subtotal	Total
Latin America												
Area (10⁶ ha)	452.98	53.50	147.45	678.66	1.53	13.64	9.56	92.48	142.89	74.11	217.00	895.66
Volume (m³)	71.07	6.37	13.21	92.48	0.27	0.93	0.63		6.17	1.33	7.50	99.98
Stem weight (10⁹ Mg)	43.92	3.94	8.19	56.90	0.13	0.43	0.29		3.81	0.82	4.63	61.53
Total biomass (10⁹ Mg)	70.28	6.31	13.10	91.60	0.21	0.69	0.47		11.02	2.47	13.49	104.55
Biomass per area (Mg/ha)	155.10	117.90	88.80	134.20	136.00	50.40	49.2		77.10	33.30	62.20	116.70
All tropics												
Area (10⁶ ha)	668.42	191.69	300.19	1,194.55	3/57	17.78	12.90	184.98	320.64	413.76	734.40	1,928.95
Volume (10⁹ m³)	122.35	24.48	35.01	184.98	0.62	1.47	1.05		11.26	5.44	16.70	201.68
Stem weight (10⁹ Mg)	73.41	14.32	20.69	109.94	0.31	0.71	0.50		6.75	3.20	9.95	119.89
Total biomass (10⁹ Mg)	117.46	22.92	33.10	175.93	0.50	1.14	0.81		19.52	9.60	29.12	205.05
Biomass per area (Mg/ha)	175.70	117.60	110.30	147.30	140.10	64.10	62.80		60.90	23.20	39.70	106.30

The classification and forest areas and volume data are taken from Lanly 1981
All terms are defined in Lanly (1981) and Brown and Lugo (1984)

grasses in their understory. The canopies of closed forests do not permit light penetration. Closed forests comprise 77.2% of the total area of tropical forests in Latin America and the remaining 22.8% is open forest (Table 6.1). The area of closed and productive (according to a forestry point of view) forests in Latin America represents 68% of all the closed and productive forests in the tropical area (Table 6.2).

In addition to these forested lands, in 1980, tropical Latin America had 167.5 million ha of secondary forests (fallow), which are located in zones which had been used unsuccessfully in the past for agriculture. The extension of these forests represents 41% of the total area of secondary forests in the planet (Table 6.1). Shrublands (primary and secondary) comprise an additional 145.9 million ha or 23% of the total area of these systems in the planet (Table 6.1).

The extension of secondary forests and shrublands in Latin America is impressive and merits special attention. These systems represent marginal lands that may have been mismanaged (with the exception of primary shrublands). Natural processes have re-established the forest at a slow pace. Planning policies and restoration strategies must be formalized to recuperate these lost values. In some cases, field research should commence immediately in order to assure the future restoration of the forest. Furthermore, these areas bear witness to the importance of implementing conservative policies in the use of certain lands and help avoid repeating past mistakes.

The diversity of tropical forests in South America has been described by Hueck (1978) and Morello (1985) and others. Life zone maps (*sensu* Holdridge 1967) for 16 countries in the region have been used to estimate forest biomass (Brown and Lugo 1982), the accumulation of carbon in the soil (Post et al. 1982, Brown and Lugo 1982) and the geographical changes that could occur and affect the world's climate (Emanuel et al. 1985). Recently, Matthews and Fung (1987) estimated the tropics contain 197.8 million ha of wetlands (38% of the wetlands in the world). Latin America has a high proportion of pluvial systems and wetlands in low and coastal lands.

The distribution of life zones in Latin America is important since the climate in these zones influences the type of forests you find there. Data show that when compared to the rest of the tropics, Latin America is more humid and has a predominance of tropical lowland systems (Table 6.3). There are hardly any dry areas in this region.

Recent biomass estimates from Latin American forests indicate that its closed forests accumulate less biomass per unit area than the average of all the tropics (Table 6.2). Its open forests, however, contain more biomass per

TABLE 6.3 Life zone distribution sensu Holdridge of forest lands of Latin Americain 10^6 ha

	Tropical			Subtotal			Total
	Wet	Moist	Dry	Wet	Moist	Dry	
Central America	5.1 (3)	7.0 (4)	1.3 (1)	21.0 (12)	55.7 (33)	80.4 (47)	169.5
South America	128.3 (10)	430.5 (35)	209.9 (17)	133.5 (11)	257.3 (21)	72.5 (6)	1,232.0
Latin America	133.4 (10)	437.5 (31)	211.2 (15)	156.5 (11)	313.0 (22)	152.9 (11)	1,401.5
All tropics	275.6 (7)	795.9 (19)	411.9 (10)	366.4 (9)	786.3 (19)	1,475.1 (36)	4,111.2

Values of deforested areas are included
Data for all topics are for reference
The percentage of total area is in parenthesis

Source: Holdridge 1967 and Brown and Lugo 1982

unit area than the average of all the tropics. Due to favorable humid conditions of the Latin American tropics, they account for half of the biomass found in all tropical forests (Tables 6.2 and 6.3).

Deforestation: Its Consequences and Reforestation

In 1980, the rate of deforestation in Latin America was 0.44% or 56.7% of the total deforestation on the planet (Table 6.1). Deforestation rates varied from country to country, depending upon the climate, and social and economic conditions. To uncover the causes of deforestation is very difficult, as it requires a careful and detailed analysis of each country (Porrás and Villareal 1986, Schmink 1987). It is obvious, however, that Latin America is losing its tropical forests faster than desired.

The destruction of tropical forests has potential global and regional consequences, such as changes in rain patterns (Salati et al. 1978) and loss of biological diversity (Lugo 1988a). However, the most devastating consequence may be the loss of the forest resource. Loss of forest affects the quality of life for citizens. Latin American tropical forests are used mainly to produce energy in the form of fuelwood or charcoal. Obviously, the destruction of tropical forests causes the energy crisis in rural and urban areas which depend on them to satisfy their energy demand. For example, FAO (1981) estimated that in 1980, Latin America had 161 million habitants suffering from the scarcity of fuelwood or charcoal and that by the year 2,000 this number would increase to 291.5 million (Table 6.4).

Without an effective erosion control program, significant changes in soil structure occur and tropical forest deterioration soon follows. These changes eventually have terrible economic consequences. The irreversible loss of soil fertility has similar effects. Massive movement of populations caused by the changes in land-use and natural resource management coupled with the deterioration of the environment, will eventually affect the health and economic welfare of vast regions.

The rate of natural regeneration and development of forest plantations in Latin America is low (Table 6.1). Only 2.8% of the global regeneration rate occurs in the forests of this region and for each hectare planted in 1980, ten hectares were deforested (Table 6.1). Even though these statistics are not conclusive, there is no doubt that in Latin America, the area and vigor of the tropical forests are in decline. This is due in part to the effort to provide survival alternatives and a better economical situation to a growing population. Such declination in forested areas is reasonable if the development that substitutes for it is sustainable. However, the uncontrollable destruction of these forests is unjustified if sustainable development does not take place. If wise use of the forest resource is not assured, future

TABLE 6.4 Latin American population that depends on tropical forests for energy
and the conditions of their supplies

Zone and conditon of supply	Population (millions)	
	1980	2000
Acute scarcity		
Andean highlands	2	3.5
Arid zones in Occident and densely populated zones	16	28
Deficit		
populated zones, semi-arid and Andean zones	143	260
Forecasted Deficit		
Less populated zones subtropical and temperate	30	50
Satisfactory		
forested zones	38	64

Source: FAO 1981

alternatives for growth and economic development are lost and the costs of development increase.

Threats to Tropical Forests

Latin American tropical forests are threatened by multiple factors. Population growth is one but not the only one, nor the most important one. Population increase brings increased demands for food, materials, and energy. Many authors assume that these increased demands are the fundamental causes for the destruction of tropical forests. However, studies in Costa Rica and Brazil (Porrás and Villareal 1986, Schmink 1987) have clearly demonstrated that the destruction of tropical forests is due to more complex factors such as politics, laws, and the social and economic conditions of tropical countries.

These social, economic, and cultural factors increase the tendency for destruction of forests, particularly when incentives are provided to convert forest lands to non-forest uses. These responses to economic need and the belief that forested areas do not have value cause tropical forests to be exploited or converted to other uses, i.e., mining, agriculture, or housing. In some instances, complex projects such as hydroelectric dams, highways, and flood prevention systems, also produce deleterious effects on the forested zones, even when this destruction is not necessary to satisfy human needs.

An even more fundamental concern is the extreme ignorance that exists regarding the value of tropical forests, their management alternatives, and their economic importance, particularly for regional and national economies. Because of this ignorance, tropical countries practice massive deforestation without even utilizing the resource. This action has a triple side effect since you lose: 1) the resource, and 2) the free services the resource was providing, while 3) operation costs increase since humans have to replace what was lost.

Deforestation is practiced in various ways. Mechanical devices are used to remove and burn forests on organic, nutrient rich soils which create poor conditions for forest regeneration. Because the real values of tropical forests are unknown, institutions are not committed to their protection and management. This perpetuates even more the attitude of abandonment and ignorance and explains why in the tropics, areas reserved for the conservation and preservation of wildlife are exploited without taking the necessary conservation precautions. Mares (1986) summarized the roots of the conservation problem in Latin America as being the following: 1) lack of information, 2) lack of personnel trained in conservation techniques, 3) lack of financial resources, 4) the absence of a long-term management plan, 5) weak economies, 6) short-term strategies, and 7) a feeling of panic among the population.

Ironically, tropical forests have values even if left alone. It is not necessary to list the values of the forest since this topic has been discussed extensively (Savage et al. 1982, Wilson and Peters 1988). However, it is necessary to point out that the forests in Latin America provide 8% of the total energy consumption of the region (Masson 1983), and provide sufficient products and services to maintain the economies of many small groups of the population.

Alternatives

Forests should form an integral part of Latin American regional economies. The protection and management of the tropical forests will be successful if society recognizes its value and its contribution to human welfare. If this is not achieved, it will be very difficult to prevent the uncontrolled destruction of the forests. It is unbelievable that the total wood exports of all tropical countries together only constitute 14.8% of the world's exports (FAO 1986). As a matter of fact, tropical countries import wood to satisfy their own needs for paper. In Latin America only 15 tree species are used for trade. It is clear that there is an urgent need to develop the tropical forestry sector in Latin America.

Development has multiple alternatives but as a minimum it should consider: 1) the satisfaction of human needs, including all sectors of the population (native, rural, and urban), while recognizing that the forest can provide wood, energy, posts, water, food, forage, and recreation; 2) that forestry is a vital sector of a sustained economy, and can contribute to short and long-term schemes for housing, food, energy, health, education, sustained industrial production, reducing financial deficits, generating foreign currency, environmental quality, protection of watersheds, wise use of the land, and recreation and generate employment for unskilled laborers; 3) the expansion of forestry to include non-traditional uses such as agroforestry (where the forest is integrated with agriculture); and 4) an increase in forest plantations and net production of forest lands through scientific management, including better species and wood product utilization (Lugo 1987).

However, how much area should be dedicated to forestry and how do you achieve this goal? There are various models which merit consideration. For example, in the Caribbean, where population densities are 10 to 100 times greater than other Latin American areas, forest area is an inverse function of population density and energy consumption because of human activity (Lugo et al. 1981). Islands which have lost their forests have confronted serious problems such as lack of water, agriculture collapse due to eroded soils, and poor economies (Lugo and Brown 1981). In humid islands which were once forested, water and wood are now imported.

On the other hand, in Puerto Rico the economic and social changes of the last 40 years have resulted in significant increase of forested lands from less than 5% in the 1940s to almost 35% in 1986 (Birdsey and Weaver 1987). This increase was due, however, to changes in 1) economic policies, which also changed land-use strategies (from agriculture to industrial and urban); 2) energy sources (from biomass or hydroelectric to oil); 3) self-sufficiency to dependency (the island is now totally dependent on imports and subsidies), and 4) extensive out migration of population.

The solution lies between the two extremes. You cannot protect the forests at the expense of local economies and completely depend on imports and subsidies, but you cannot destroy forests to the point where you again have to depend on imports and subsidies.

The model proposed by the Man and the Biosphere Program (MAB), seeks to integrate humans and their activities with natural systems to provide services and products for the human economy. Multiple services require suppressing the effects of human activity (i.e., through water quality control, air, soil, recreation, landscape, etc.). This can be achieved by designating areas for intensive human use and other areas for the preservation of natural values (Batisse 1986, Lugo 1989). Between these extremes of use, a gradient of human activity, will decrease in intensity as you approach the preservation area. Large areas of intensive urban use will require larger natural areas of protection.

This model recognizes that in order for people to look forward to a life with a high economic, spiritual, and environmental quality it is necessary to use natural resources. Otherwise it is impossible. In the long run, the important thing is not to determine a priori what is or is not satisfactory in terms of the ratio between natural and urban areas but of utmost importance is to recognize the interdependence between the two systems and take the necessary steps to maintain both systems. In an analysis of Brazil's development, Odum et al. (1986) indicated that in order to sustain the development of the Amazon watershed, it was necessary to maintain four land-use systems: 1) productive plantations, 2) secondary forests (for productivity restoration), 3) preservation of primary forests rich in species, and 4) urban uses of variable intensities distributed by hierarchy in the territory. These recommendations follow the model presented by MAB.

What to Do?

The steps to follow to assure proper forest land management in Latin America are well-known (Table 6.5). However, society and government support are imperative. This could be achieved through massive education, but also requires initiative and insight from government officials. This insight is necessary since those sectors who are in need do not have access to power and those in power do not always realize the relationship between the social and economic problems and the management of natural resources.

Assuming that the forestry sector obtains the support necessary to initiate its work in Latin America, they must develop multiple use programs for forest lands and start research programs to resolve the problems that will emerge with the establishment of plantations and the management of forests and watersheds (Table 6.5).

If the organizations in charge of the forests continue to falter, no progress will be achieved and the situation will deteriorate. In Latin America, where the most extensive area of productive tropical forests in the world exist, forest management programs only exist in Brazil, Peru, Colombia, Ecuador, Surinam, Costa Rica, and French Guyana (Schmidt 1987); however, all have failed but not due to technical reasons. In Colombia, the program failed due to lack of security. In Peru and Ecuador, it failed because of the invasion of farmers who took advantage of the roads to the

TABLE 6.5 Suggestions from various authors to assure the wise use of forested lands in Latin America

1. Convince the inhabitants of each region of the importance of forested areas.
2. Plant species appropriate to the region and of known origin.
3. Know what is going to be done with what is planted.
4. Obtain the resources and the will to start management projects and finish them.
5. Plan realistic operations in order to avoid financial failure.
6. Long term commitment.
7. Controlled government subsidies that cover the whole project.
8. Use lands adequate for forestry activity.
9. Start scientific research with emphasis on:
   * restoration of degraded lands
   * use of more species
   * adaptability studies, species improvement, and productivity studies
   * multiple use of species and lands
   * industrial development of agroforestry techniques
   * ecological studies of environmental impact of forestry activity
   * use of energy plantations
   * efficiency in the utilization of forest products
   * multiple use of plantations
   * techniques of economical optimizing of the forestry activity
   * social, economic, and cultural aspects of forestry activity
   * natural forest management techniques

Source: Zobel 1987, Whitmore 1987

forest which were made to facilitate management. In Brazil, the abundance of wood and government subsidy to deforest saturated the market and eliminated the commercial management of the forest. These examples illustrate the weakness of the governmental institutions that direct the forestry operations in Latin America.

Schmidt (1987) concluded that problems with the management of tropical forests do not exist because of the diversity of species or lack of knowledge of how the systems work, regarding forest regeneration, or response to silvicultural treatment. He believes that the problems are land-use policies, social and economic conditions, political realities, and incorrect evaluations of the value of the forest. Schmidt also suggests that the leaders of tropical countries should expand their horizons to be able to recognize future consequences of their current actions.

On the other hand, the academic and conservation sectors should also understand the problems faced by the tropical countries of Latin America. They should not ignore the magnitude of the human problem. It is necessary that all sectors of society work together. Preservation ideals have their place in the scheme of MAB and are the basis around which solutions are drawn (Lugo 1988). However, preservation has to allow for conservation and both ideas applied in realistic proportions can provide solutions to the problems of tropical forests.

References Cited

Batisse, M. 1986. Developing and focusing the biosphere reserve concept. *Nature and Resources* 22(3): 1-10.

Birdsey, R.A. and P.L. Weaver. 1987. Forest area trends in Puerto Rico. *Research Note* SO-331. Southern Forest Experiment Station, USDA Forest Service, New Orleans, Louisiana.

Brown, S. and A. E. Lugo. 1982. The storage and production of organic matter in tropical forests and their role in the global carbon cycle. *Biotropica* 14: 161-187.

Brown, S. and A. E. Lugo. 1984. Biomass of tropical forests: A new estimate based on forest volumes. *Science* 223: 1290-1293.

Emanuel, W.R., H.H. Shugart, and M.P. Stevenson. 1985. Climatic change and the broad scale distribution of terrestrial ecosystem complexes. *Climatic Change* 7: 29-43.

FAO (Food and Agriculture Organization). 1981. Mapa de la situación en materia de leña en los países en desarrollo. Organización de las Naciones Unidas para la Agricultura y la Alimentación. Roma.

_____ 1985. *Forest Resources 1980*. FAO, Rome.

_____ 1986. *Documentos de fondo para la 15ma Reunión de la Comisión Forestal Latinoamericana*. San José, Costa Rica.

Gentry, A.H. 1982. Patterns of neotropical plant-species diversity. *Evolutionary Biology* 15: 1-85.

Gentry, A.H. and C. Dodson. 1987. Contribution of non-trees to species richness of a tropical rain forest. *Biotropica* 19: 149- 156.

Holdridge, L.R. 1967. *Life zone ecology*. Tropical Science Center, San José, Costa Rica.

Hueck, K. 1978. *Los bosques de sudamérica*. Translation by R. Brun. Hoehl-Druck, Alemania.

Lanly, J.P. 1981. *Los recursos forestales de la América tropical*. Informe técnico 1; Forest resources of tropical Asia, Technical Report 2; Forest resources of tropical Africa, Parts 1 and 2, Technical Report 3. UN32/6.1301-78-04 FAO, Rome, Italy. Four volumes.

Lugo, A.E. 1987. Wood utilization research needs in the tropics in forest products laboratory. *Forest products research conference 1986: matching utilization research with the needs of timber managers.* Madison, Wisconsin: USDA Forest Service Forest Products Laboratory.

_____ 1988. Estimating reductions in the diversity of tropical forest species. pp. 53-70. In *Biodiversity.* Edited by E. O. Wilson and F.M. Peter. Washington, D.C.: National Academy Press.

_____ 1989. Biosphere reserves in the tropics: An opportunity for integrating wise use and preservation of biotic resources. Fourth Wilderness Congress, Symp. on Biosphere Reserves. U.S. MAB Program, Washington, D.C.

Lugo, A.E. and S. Brown. 1981. Tropical lands: Popular misconceptions. *Mazingira* 5(2): 10-19.

Lugo, A.E., R. Schmidt, and S. Brown. 1981. Tropical forests in the Caribbean. *Ambio* 10: 318-324.

Mares, M.A. 1986. Conservation in South America: Problems, consequences, and solutions. *Science* 233: 734-739.

Masson, J.L. 1983. *Management of tropical mixed forests. Preliminary assessment and present status.* FAO Miscellaneous Paper 83/17. FAO, Rome.

Matthews, E. and I. Fung. 1987. Methane emission from natural wetlands: Global distribution, area, and environmental characteristics of sources. *Global Biogeochemical Cycles* 1: 61- 86.

Morello, J.A. 1985. *Grandes ecosistemas de Sudamérica.* Fundación Bariloche, Bariloche, Argentina.

Odum, H.T., M.T. Brown, and R.A. Christianson. 1986. *Energy systems overview of the Amazon Basin.* Center for Wetlands Publications 86-1. University of Florida, Gainesville. .

Porrás, A. and B. Villareal. 1986. *Deforestación en Costa Rica.* Editorial Costa Rica, San José.

Post, W.M., W.R. Emanuel, P.J. Zinke, and A.G. Stangenberger. 1982. Soil carbon pools and world life zones. *Nature* 298: 156-159.

Salati, E., J. Márquez, and L.C.B. Molion. 1978. Origen e distribuicao das chuvas na Amazonia. *Interciencia* 3: 200-205.

Savage, J.M., C.R. Goldman, D.P. Janos, A.E. Lugo, P.H. Raven, P.A. Sánchez, and H. Garrison. 1982. *Ecological aspects of development in the humid tropics.* National Academy Press, Washington, D.C.

Schmidt, R. 1987. Tropical rain forest management: A status report. *Unasylva* 39(156): 2-17.

Schmink, M. 1987. The rationality of forest destruction. In: *Management of forests of tropical America: Prospects and technologies.* Edited by J.C. Figueroa, F.H. Wadsworth, and S. Branham. Río Piedras, P.R.: Institute of Tropical Forestry.

USDA Forest Service and North American Forestry Commission. 1986. *Directory of tropical silviculturists*. USDA Forest Service Timber Management Research, Washington, D.C.

Whitmore, J. L. 1987. Plantation forestry in the tropics of Latin America: A research agenda. *Unasylva* 39(156): 36-41.

Whitmore, T.C. 1975. *Tropical forests of the Far East*. Clarendon Press. Oxford. .

Wilson, E.O., and F.M. Peters. 1988. *Biodiversity*. National Academy Press, Washington, D.C. .

Yantko, J.A. and F.B. Golley, eds. 1977. *Censo mundial de ecólogos tropicales*. *Institute of Ecology*. The University of Georgia, Athens.

Zobel, B. 1987. El sector forestal en los países en desarrollo, una opinion general. *Venezuela Forestal* 3(2): 17-20.

Translated by Helen Nunci from: Uso de las zonas boscosas de America Latina tropical, *Interciencia*, vol.13. no.6 Nov-December 1988.

7

Forest Economies: Transition and Ambiguity

Jan G. Laarman

In Latin America as elsewhere, the livestock industries and timber-using industries share a number of structural and behavioral characteristics. Most importantly in the present context, both are land-extensive sectors. For a variety of complex and interrelated reasons, each is alleged to generally use resource inputs — forage and timber — much less intensively than is technologically feasible and socially desirable (Jarvis 1986, Buschbacher 1987, Leonard 1987). Each sector has been expanding output less through improved productivity per hectare than through penetration and timber cutting on new forest land. At least, this is the tenet which sounds the alarm on deforestation.

Thus the main links between livestock industries and timber-using industries are the markets and institutions governing the tenancy and use of forestland. Other connections can be hypothesized, e.g., in terms of competing for political favor, government subsidies, technical assistance, and investment capital. Not all relationships are competitive, as when some proportion of logs produced in pasture-making are extracted and processed by timber-using industries. Moreover, the two sectors sometimes share roads and other infrastructure. The dimensions of complementarity vs. competition are not critical for present purposes. Here it will be sufficient to claim that the sectors affect each other's growth and development, without requiring a detailed assessment of the interdependencies.

The objective of this analysis is to briefly describe and interpret recent patterns in production and trade of forest products. Trends in expansion or contraction, by subregion and type of industry, imply shifts in the sector's derived demand for industrial timber. Changing demand for industrial timber, in turn, affects the growth prospects of livestock industries through the supply and demand for forest land.

Macroeconomic Context

In Latin America, the economic perspective for forestry and forest industries is determined by the struggle for macroeconomic recovery. Thus the economic health of forest-based sectors is closely linked with movements in world petroleum prices, movements of local currencies against major world currencies, international terms of trade for imports and exports, policies on debt servicing, management of monetary inflation, and negotiations with the International Monetary Fund. Developments at the sectoral level also mirror social and economic policies of a large number of new governments. Virtually all such governments are under enormous pressure to find new solutions to chronic problems.

Although partial economic recovery began in some countries in 1984, improvements have not been evenly distributed. Moreover, the recovery process is fragile and highly vulnerable to reversals (Iglesias 1984, Restrepo 1985). In view of the macroeconomic upheaval, forestry (like other sectors) is undergoing structural adjustments not yet reported or even clearly visible by the late 1980s (Laarman 1987b). This increases the risks of faulty extrapolations from outdated information.

Recent Sectoral Performance

Production Trends

Figure 7.1 presents production levels (1974-1985) for the four main classes of forest products aggregated for all of Latin America. Production in all groups reached a first peak about 1980-81, declined, and subsequently rose to new highs by 1985. Movements in production are heavily influenced by Brazil, which accounts for half or more of all output in each product group except paper and paperboard. Recovery since 1980 was most pronounced in wood pulp, paper, and paperboard.

Table 7.1 shows production trends in more detail, disaggregating by subproduct and by main producing countries. Growth rates prior to 1980 are compared with those in the subsequent period. In 31 categories, output growth since 1980 was less than it had been during the late 1970s. Only seven categories showed more rapid output growth since 1980 than in the previous period: Mexico's coniferous sawnwood; Ecuador's non-coniferous sawnwood; Mexico's mechanical pulp; Brazil's semi-chemical pulp; Argentina's chemical pulp; Brazil's dissolving pulp; and Brazil's newsprint.

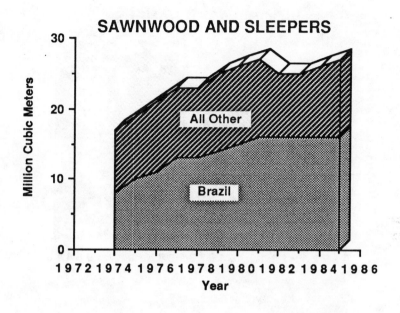

SAWNWOOD AND SLEEPERS

Million Cubic Meters (y-axis: 0, 10, 20, 30)

All Other

Brazil

Year (x-axis: 1972 1974 1976 1978 1980 1982 1984 1986)

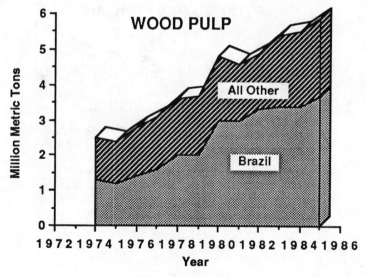

WOOD PULP

Million Metric Tons (y-axis: 0, 1, 2, 3, 4, 5, 6)

All Other

Brazil

Year (x-axis: 1972 1974 1976 1978 1980 1982 1984 1986)

FIGURE 7.1 Production trends in Latin American forest products, 1974 - 1985

Source: FAO, Yearbook of Forest Products.

continues

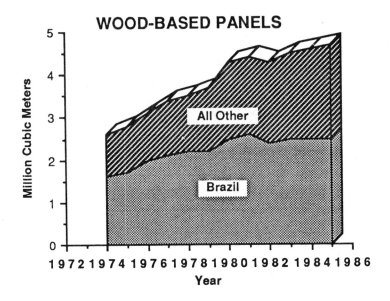

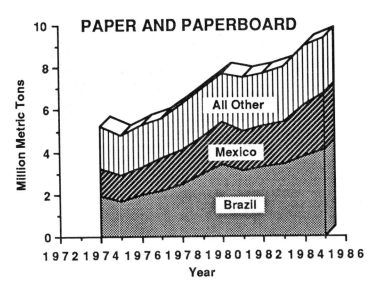

Figure 7.1 Production trends in Latin American forest products, 1974-75, continued

Source: FAO Yearbook of Forest Products

TABLE 7.1 Growth rates of forest products output in Latin America
1974-80 and 1980-85

Industries[a]	Period	
	1974-1980	1980-85
	(growth rates, simple %)	
Sawnwood and Sleepers (cu.m.)	53.9	3.4
Coniferous	51.4	5.6
Brazil	94.6	4.8
Chilel	64.9	2.2
Mexico	-7.7	18.7
Honduras	-5.3	-24.1
Non-coniferous	56.0	2.6
Brazil	94.5	8.3
Ecuador	8.4	34.4
Argentina	233.3	24.3
Paraguay	103.1	15.4
Colombia	0.0	-24.4
Wood-based Panels (cu.m)	64.1	8.4
Veneer Sheets	68.2	0.0
Brazil	22.2	4.5
Plywood	34.5	2.7
Brazil	17.1	9.3
Mexico	128.8	6.3
Particle board	88.5	20.4
Brazil	83.3	0.0
Mexico	236.2	34.5
Argentina	34.0	-10.1
Fiberboard, compressed	89.7	4.1
Brazil	111.7	-9.1
Fiberboard, not compressed	94.4	-4.9
Brazil	66.7	0.0
Wood pulp (metric ton)	88.9	23.0
Mechanical	50.0	29.2
Brazil	145.5	20.0
Chile	120.0	20.6
Mexico	20.7	123.9
Semi-chemical	8.3	15.4
Agentina	78.8	31.4
Brazil	-30.3	15.2
Chemical	115.1	22.2

Table continues on next page.

TABLE 7.1 Growth rates of forest products output in Latin America,
1974-80 and 1980-85 , continued

Industries[a]	Period	
	1974-1980	1980-85
	(growth rates, simple %)	
Wood pulp (m.t.)..continued		
Chemical	115.1	22.2
Brazil	175.3	19.5
Chile	101.3	7.4
Mexico	30.6	18.6
Argentina	-1.8	142.1
Dissolving	-56.1	36.2
Brazil	-62.0	57.9
Paper and Paperboard (m.t.)	48.7	22.0
Newsprint	77.8	75.0
Mexico	190.0	124.1
Brazil	-7.1	98.1
Printing and writing	76.4	35.3
Brazil	97.8	33.8
Mexico	176.8	48.9
Household and sanitary	97.2	35.2
Mexico	84.0	66.8
Brazil	139.2	22.0
Venezuela	87.3	16.5
Wrapping and packaging	49.8	10.9
Brazil	86.0	12.9
Mexico	40.0	16.3
Argentina	4.7	1.3
Other	-10.7	7.9
Brazil	61.1	6.9
Argentina	-79.8	-45.8

a. Within industries, largest producers in 1985 are shown in descending order
Source: FAO Yearbook of Forest Products (1974-1985)

The truly outstanding growth leaders since 1980 (subjectively weighted by
economic importance for Latin America) are Argentina in chemical pulp,
and Mexico and Brazil in newsprint. Chile, while not exhibiting output
growth comparable to that of the late 1970s, managed modest gains in wood
pulp.

TABLE 7.2 Growth rates in forest products exports from Latin America,
      1974-80 and 1980-85

	Period			
	1974-1980		1980-1985	
Industries[a]	Volume	Value	Volume	Value
		(growth rates, simple %)		
Sawnwood and sleepers	44	98	-32	-34
Chile	876	114	-45	-61
Brazil	14	66	-39	-42
Paraguay	42	149	24	25
Honduras	-45	-49	-14	50
Wood-based panels	136	210	5	-3
Brazil	85	155	41	9
Wood pulp	316	389	10	-18
Brazil	564	889	4	-24
Chile	131	153	21	-8
Paper and paperboard	72	180	93	33
Brazil	560	847	174	63
Chile	-23	20	54	30

a. Within industries, largest exporters in 1985 are shown in descending order
Source: FAO Yearbook of Forest Products (1974-85)

Impacts of these particular industries on lowlands tropical forests are minimal. Argentina and Chile normally are classified as temperate countries, even if forests in Misiones grade into subtropical. Brazil's pulp and newsprint are produced from timber increasingly harvested from plantations (U.S. Dept. of Commerce 1985, Stier 1987). Most of Mexico's commercial timber harvest is from softwoods growing above 2,500 meters elevation. Moreover, a large proportion of Mexico's fiber is supplied from wastepaper recycling and from imports (U.S. Dept. of Commerce 1987).

Exports and Imports

Figure 7.2 shows regional exports and imports by main product type. From very rapid growth in the late 1970s, exports subsequently flattened, dipped, and recovered. Imports peaked in 1981, falling sharply thereafter. The resulting sectoral trade balance registered its largest deficit in 1982, rebounding to a minimum deficit in 1984. Falling imports are largely explained by balance-of-payments problems in combination with import substitution strategies in some large countries (e.g., Brazil, Argentina, and Mexico).

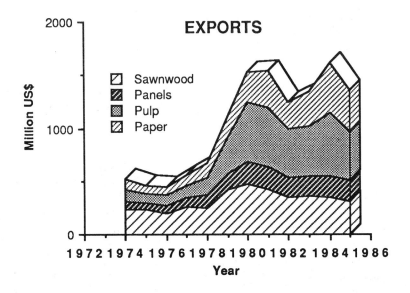

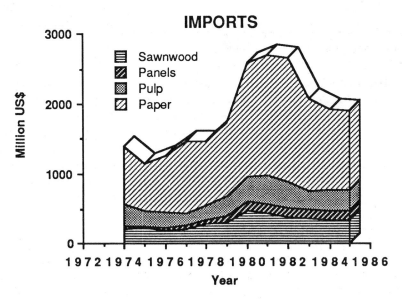

FIGURE 7.2 Forest products exports and imports in Latin America,
1974 - 1985

Source: FAO, Yearbook of forest products

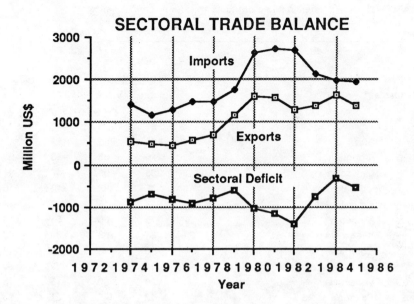

FIGURE 7.2 Forest products exports and imports in Latin America, 1974 - 1985

Source: FAO, Yearbook of forest products

TABLE 7.3 Growth rates in forest products imports by Latin America,
1974-80 and 1980-85

	Period			
	1974-1980		1980-1985	
Industries[a]	Volume	Value	Volume	Value
		(growth rates, simple %)		
Sawnwood and sleepers	61	126	-19	-25
Brazil	456	350	-23	-47
Argentina	26	65	-53	-69
Mexico	296	408	-47	-41
Wood-based panels	171	335	-10	-10
Wood pulp	-13	13	3	-19
Mexico	-15	26	53	8
Venezuela	81	168	31	49
Colombia	-10	13	19	4
Paper and paperboard	11	94	-29	-30
Venezuela	20	89	-13	10
Ecuador	-12	142	27	33
Mexico	111	405	-69	-65
Colombia	89	114	-11	-4
Brazil	-46	-24	-48	-43
Costa Rica	-31	19	34	24

a. Within industries, largest exporters in 1985 are shown in descending order
Source: FAO Yearbook of Forest Products (1985)

Tables 7.2 and 7.3 examine exports and imports, respectively, for the major trading countries. Whether measured in volume or value, export growth during 1974-80 was extremely buoyant. Honduras was the sole exception. Value growth outpaced volume growth, although value is not expressed in constant purchasing power.

For 1980-85, growth in export volume and value slowed or turned negative. The exception was paper and paperboard, whose exports continued strong. Since 1980, volume growth dominated value growth in all product categories, implying a softening of export prices.

Figure 7.3 portrays static or falling prices since 1980-81 for most of a variety of major exports and imports. Despite weak prices, forest products exports assumed increasing importance when compared with sharply declining or static meat exports in key subregions (Figure 7.4).

Table 7.3 indicates that the post-1980 slump in imports was widely spread across products and importing countries. Pulp was the only category

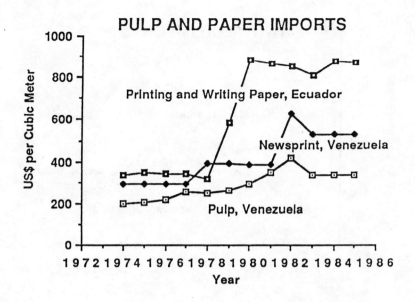

PULP AND PAPER IMPORTS

US$ per Cubic Meter

Printing and Writing Paper, Ecuador

Newsprint, Venezuela

Pulp, Venezuela

Year

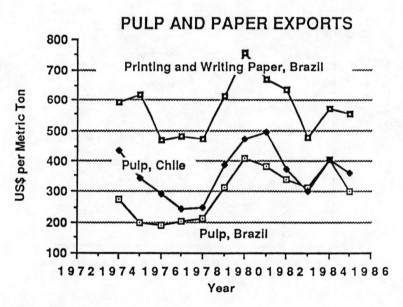

PULP AND PAPER EXPORTS

US$ per Metric Ton

Printing and Writing Paper, Brazil

Pulp, Chile

Pulp, Brazil

Year

FIGURE 7.3 Select price trends in Latin American forest products exports and imports, 1974 - 1985

Source: FAO, Yearbook of forest products.

continues

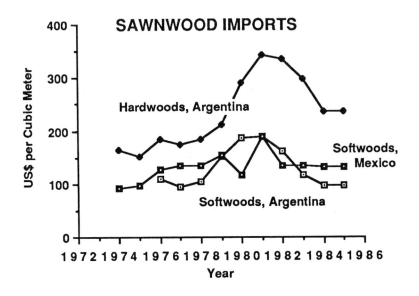

SAWNWOOD IMPORTS

Hardwoods, Argentina

Softwoods, Mexico

Softwoods, Argentina

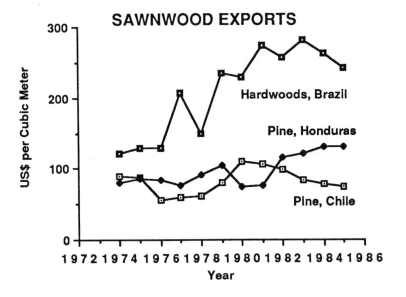

SAWNWOOD EXPORTS

Hardwoods, Brazil

Pine, Honduras

Pine, Chile

FIGURE 7.3 Select price trends in Latin American forest products exports and imports, 1974 - 1985, continued

Source: FAO, Yearbook of forest products

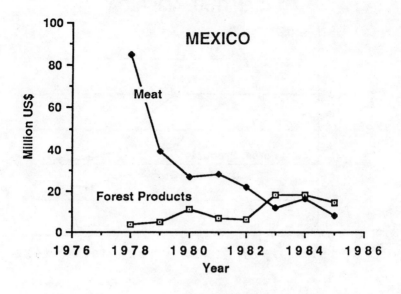

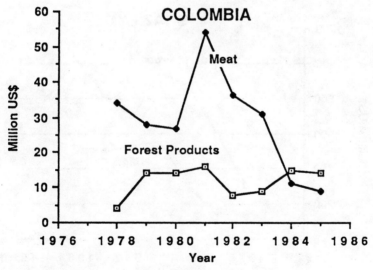

FIGURE 7.4 Comparison of forest products with meat exports
in selected regions of Latin America, 1974 - 1985

Source: FAO, Yearbook of forest products

continues

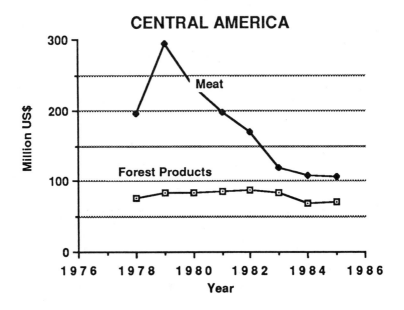

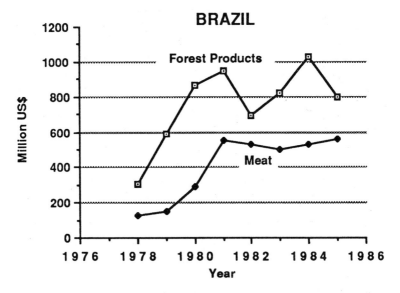

FIGURE 7.4 Comparison of forest products with meat exports in selected regions of Latin America, 1974 - 1985, continued

Source: FAO, Yearbook of forest products

to escape this slump. In terms of reduced total expenditures for imports, the largest decreases occurred for paper and paperboard. Of the six largest importers of paper and paperboard, only Ecuador and Costa Rica increased imports between 1980 and 1985.

Roundwood Production

The sum of production plus net exports (imports) generates the demand for roundwood production and consumption. Roundwood demand then drives the demand for timber cutting. The preceding subsections described depressed output, exports, and imports since 1980. General stagnation should be associated with low growth in the demand for industrial roundwood.

Figure 7.5 indicates flat demand since about 1980 for the entire region, the tropical countries (i.e., excluding the Southern Cone), and the largest single producer (Brazil). However, considerable variation characterizes production trends among individual countries (e.g., compare increases for Paraguay and Ecuador with decreases for Costa Rica and Honduras).

Table 7.4 shows roundwood production trends by country for the two periods before and after 1980. At face value, the statistics point to large increases in coniferous roundwood production in Argentina and Guatemala. Large decreases are indicated for Honduras, Colombia, and Uruguay. Many figures strain credibility, particularly those which indicate major changes in only five or six years.

The more interesting trends for present purposes concern industrial timber removals from non-coniferous forests. In aggregate, non-coniferous removals remained essentially constant between 1980 and 1985. This result is heavily weighted by minimal change reported for Brazil. Since 1980 the only increases were for Argentina, Paraguay, Ecuador, Chile and Mexico. This compares with 16 countries in which change was zero or negative.

Implications and Discussion

The data reviewed here tentatively suggest that the forest industries of Latin America are making few appreciable increased demands on tropical natural forests. Rather, commercial cutting in the natural forests would appear to be leveling or even declining in comparison with the pace of extraction in the 1970s. This is cautiously presented as a hypothesis requiring considerable testing. Admittedly, the data are inadequate and inconsistent across countries. Furthermore, the aggregates mask timber cutting pressures at subnational and local levels (Myers 1980). For example,

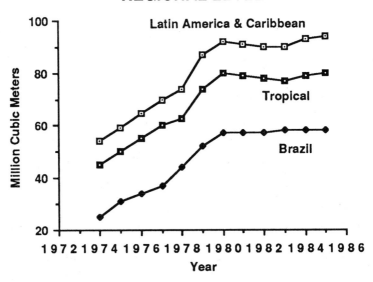

REGIONAL LEVEL

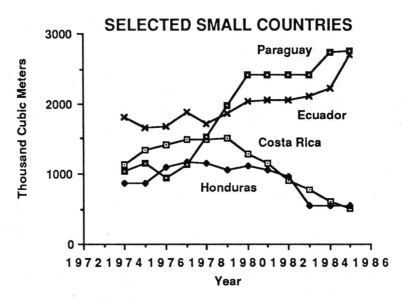

SELECTED SMALL COUNTRIES

FIGURE 7.5 Industrial roundwood production in Latin America, 1974-1985

Source: FAO, Yearbook of forest products

TABLE 7.4 Growth rates in industrial roundwood production in Latin America,
1974-80 and 1980-85

	Period	
	1974-1980	1980-1985
	(growth rates, simple %)	
Coniferous[a]	74	5
1. Brazil	129	1
2. Chile	69	15
3. Mexico	3	17
4. Argentina	25	66
5. Honduras	26	-50
6. Nicaragua	6	0
7. Guatemala	-60	41
8. Colombia	231	-45
9. El Salvador	483	-14
10. Uruguay	-26	-52
11. Belize	0	10
Non-Coniferous[a]	72	-1
1. Brazil	133	1
2. Argentina	6	11
3. Paraguay	132	14
4. Ecuador	12	33
5. Colombia	-1	-10
6. Peru	41	-39
7. Chile	3	11
8. Mexico	-7	29
9. Venezuela	-7	0
10. Nicaragua	10	0
11. Costa Rica	13	-60
12. Panama	178	0
13. Suriname	60	-38
14. French Guiana	408	0
15. Uruguay	23	0
16. Guyana	-26	-10
17. Bolivia	18	-66
18. El Salvador	-11	-17
19. Guatemala	-69	-12
20. Belize	-2	-36
21. Honduras	43	-90

a. Countries are shown in descending order of roundwood production in 1985.

Source: FAO, Yearbook of Forest Products

the data are too crude to reveal the post-1980 boom in Brazil's production of mahogany lumber (Browder 1987).

Yet it appears that the most dynamic industrial growth is occurring (1) in the temperate zones of Argentina and Chile, and (2) on the basis of forest plantations. Either development alone, and especially both together, imply a shift away from tropical natural forests. The main questions concern the extent and time rate of this shift, together with interregional differences in its significance.

Other factors shaping the future include the potential shift of tropical timber-based enterprise from Southeast Asia to Latin America; changes in the climate for foreign investment; the prospects for policy reforms in the forestry sector; and the impact of environmental pressures. Each of these is briefly reviewed.

Plantation Forestry

The Inter-American Development Bank projected that wood production from industrial plantations will increase by a factor of four between 1980 and the year 2000. By 2000, about 50 percent of total industrial wood is expected to be harvested from plantations (compared with 30 percent in 1980). Most of this plantation harvest will take place in Brazil and the Southern Cone, with regions like Central America and Mexico largely left out of this transition (McGaughey and Gregersen 1983). Data recently assembled by the government of Chile (INFOR 1987) affirm large projected increases in harvests of plantation-grown wood during the 1990s for countries like Brazil, Argentina, and Venezuela.

Although data to support the point are lacking, foresters have been claiming that plantations are established primarily on cerrados, savannas, and wastelands rather than by displacement of natural forests (Kellison 1988). However, it is widely recognized that pre-1980 plantation efforts in countries like Brazil led to substantial forest clearing (Beattie 1975). The widely publicized case of Jari Florestal illustrates this perfectly. Even now, Costa Rica's incentives for forest plantations are encouraging some landowners to deforest significant tracts. Examples undoubtedly could be reported for other countries if systematic information were available.

Forest Depletion in Southeast Asia?

Will continued timber cutting in Indonesia and Malaysia shift timber enterprise to Brazil and the rest of Latin America? A recent simulation model by Grainger (1987) forecasts a dramatic shift from Southeast Asia to Latin America as the chief supply source for exports of tropical hardwoods.

Exports from Latin America are projected to peak around the year 2005 before falling precipitously because of forest depletion and rising domestic consumption (Figure 7.6).

The model is driven by population growth, agricultural development, timber drain/growth projections, costs of timber extraction, and supply-demand relations. Plantation production in Grainger's model is unable to compensate for cutting in natural forests. The forecast indicates that Latin America will export more tropical hardwood than Southeast Asia as early as the mid 1990s. To the extent that the Grainger hypothesis is accurate, it casts serious doubts on prospects for plantation substitution. Moreover, the forecast of an imminent timber boom in Latin America — stimulated mainly by foreign demand — is not easily reconciled with data suggesting that current roundwood demand is static or even declining. Because of the model's enormous implications, Grainger's methodology and assumptions merit careful assessment.

Climate for Foreign Investment

The collapse of economies and the reduced inflow of capital have helped soften positions critical of foreign investment in many quarters of Latin America. Strict regulations put on foreign investment in 1969 by the five countries of the Andean Pact have been relaxed in an intensive and highly competitive search for foreign investment. For ideological and political reasons, some of these countries have been more cautious than others in welcoming foreign investment, but all have moved in that direction. Even Mexico, normally wary of foreign (mainly U.S.) capital, has been more receptive to foreign participation than at any time in recent history (Gilbreath 1986).

However, the liberalization policy may not be succeeding. A survey in 1986 found that foreign investment was treated no better in that year than before 1982 (Council of the Americas 1987). One explanation is that governments feel they must continue to steer their economies through the prolonged debt crisis. Foreign companies report that interventionist tendencies are as pervasive now as before the onset of the major problems.

The factors favoring increased foreign investment are impressive biological productivity of forest plantations, the strong purchasing power of foreign currencies, and outward tendencies toward a liberalized investment climate. Barriers to investment are weak and poorly conceived investment strategies, lack of an investment orientation by foresters and government forestry officials in many Latin American countries, and the business turbulence sweeping both the region and the rest of the world (Laarman 1987a).

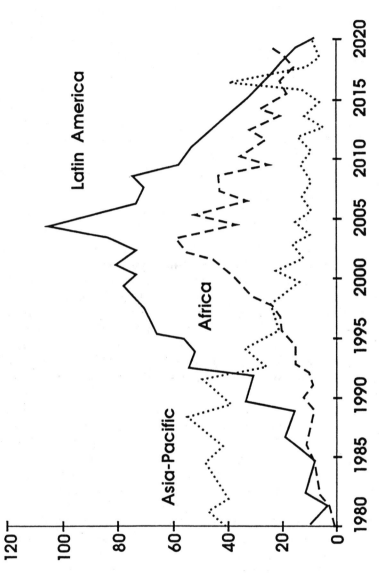

FIGURE 7.6 Projections of tropical hardwood exports in different macro-regions (millions of cubic meters), 1980-2020

Source: Grainger (1987)

Policy Reforms in the Forestry Sector

Much current thinking emphasizes macroeconomic and sectoral policy reforms, with the forestry sector a prime target for many proposals (Repetto 1988). At issue are questions on forestation subsidies, timber concession policies, and privatization of many activities currently managed by public agencies. In forestry, a possible package of proposals might include: (1) attempts to augment current timber concessions to generate more near-term revenue; (2) transfers of government-owned forest land to private owners; (3) divestiture of government assets such as processing plants and forestry nurseries, accompanied by a shift towards privatization of these assets; (4) reduction of government participation and regulation in commodity marketing and exporting; (5) elimination or reduction of subsidies for forestry investments; (6) orientation of forestry curricula in the universities and technical schools to include more emphasis on business training; and (7) increases in prices of seedlings, timber, and other publicly provided products and services to levels commensurate with costs of production and replacement (Laarman 1986).

At present, the "privatization" philosophy does not seem to be widely accepted in Latin American forestry circles. A possible exception is Chile. Additionally, Costa Rica is studying the creation of an "Oficina Forestal" to be oriented to objectives of private forest industries, with policy and programs largely determined by representatives of these industries. The outgoing government of Febres Cordero in Ecuador agreed to turn the country's main forest products laboratory and training center over to the private sector. The government of Mexico has attempted to sell a number of wood-processing plants to private hands, but without success due to the poor condition and revenue loss of these plants. The government of Honduras apparently has agreed to work towards turning the export marketing of forest products over to private ownership. Guyana may be obligat ed to do the same. Hence a few nascent attempts to move toward private ownership can be cited. For the most part, however, these are isolated examples which often lack integration with the mainstream of forest policy and management.

Privatization issues cause consternation for decision makers in public agencies, many of whom logically resent being asked to reduce their influence. The ideological bias may be repugnant to many. The emphasis on markets and enterprises is troublesome for forestry, a sector with an abundance of extra-market goods and services. Moreover, most traditional forestry agencies have taken a technical and biological approach to forest management, not an approach which emphasizes investment and returns (McGaughey and Gregersen 1983).

Yet, compelling budgetary and political pressures suggest that forestry in Latin America cannot remain totally insulated from the voices arguing for reforms. To the extent that reforms materialize in predicted directions, tropical timber sold by governments to private buyers should become far more costly in the future. Simultaneously, private commercial interests are likely to press for far greater participation in forestry policy making. Will these two prospects offset each other in terms of impact on timber cutting? The overall effect for rates and patterns of timber cutting is difficult to predict.

Impact of Environmental Pressures

The breadth and depth of environmental concerns related to cutting of tropical forests cannot be stated with any confidence. However, there should be relatively little disagreement that: (1) the fate of the tropical forests ranks high on the agenda of a large part of Latin America's intelligentsia; (2) the number of non-governmental organizations oriented to conservation in and for Latin America has been expanding rapidly; and (3) protection of the environment is increasingly accepted as a legitimate political issue in Latin America.

What economic impact would a powerful environmental movement have on forestry and forest industries? Conceivably, private firms would be obligated to submit forest management plans and to demonstrate successful reforestation to an extent not yet observed in practice. Timber harvesting would be restricted from more and more forests zoned for watershed protection and maintenance of biodiversity. Pulp mills and other processing establishments would be required to meet environmental standards far more stringent than they face presently. Environmental impact statements would be required for all significant projects which build roads, harvest timber, and process wood. Each of these scenarios increases production costs, reduces product supply, and ultimately reduces timber cutting.

Importantly, legislation motivated by environmental concerns sometimes leads to perverse results. For example, a recent emergency decree in Costa Rica was to have prohibited all logging everywhere in the country. Advance notice of the impending decree accelerated both the volume and pace of logging as private sawmills hurried to stockpile logs. The case illustrates the mistakes that are bound to occur as public agencies and private industries wrestle with each other in new contests for position and advantage.

Summary and Conclusions

The forest economies of Latin America were severely set back by the macroeconomic crisis of the early 1980s. This was manifested through reductions in sectoral output, exports, and imports. Aggregate production and consumption of industrial timber were essentially static between 1980 and 1985. Exceptions were most notable outside of the tropics, as well as for production of pulp and paper dependent on plantation wood and imported pulp.

Did the post-1980 economic shock fundamentally flatten the demand for tropical wood? Are the data sufficiently trustworthy to answer the question? Is the apparent leveling due to factors other than the macroeconomic shock? Is the slowing of demand merely a short-term downturn on a long-term growth trend? What new observations on production and trade should be added since 1985? These define some of the principal empirical issues.

The future is clouded by a number of possibilities which sometimes contradict each other. On the one hand is the almost certain prospect that harvests from forest plantations will increase substantially in the very near future. On the other is reasonable doubt that plantation harvests will reduce extractions from tropical natural forests, particularly if a significant volume of enterprise shifts from Southeast Asia to Latin America. On the one hand, conditions are attractive for increased foreign investment in Latin America's forest industries. On the other, current superficial warming of the investment climate does not disguise fundamental wariness and mistrust at a deeper level.

On the one hand, the forestry sector is ripe for far-reaching policy changes, particularly those encouraging privatization and market approaches. On the other, steps towards privatization are few, isolated, and perhaps not truly acceptable to those in positions of public authority. On the one hand, the rise of environmentalism seems certain to constrain the level and methods of cutting tropical timber in Latin America. On the other, examples can be cited which illustrate dismal failure of environmental policies and actions.

In conclusion, Latin America's forest economies are struggling to overcome recent setbacks while facing immense uncertainties ahead. Projections of future developments should explicitly recognize and contend with the full measure of ambiguity.

References Cited

Beattie, W.D. 1975. An economic analysis of the Brazilian fiscal incentives for reforestation. Ph.D. diss., Purdue University, West Lafayette, Indiana.

Browder, J.O. 1987. Brazil's export promotion policy (1980-1984): Impacts on the Amazon's industrial wood sector. *Journal of Developing Areas* 21:285-304.

Buschbacher, R.J. 1987. Ecological analysis of natural forest management in the humid tropics. In: *Application of ecology to enhancing economic development in the humid tropics.* American Institute of Biological Sciences, Aug. 12.

Council of the Americas. 1987. *Coping with crisis: U.S. investment and Latin America's continuing economic problems.* Council of the Americas, New York.

Food and Agriculture Organization. 1986. Yearbook of forest products. FAO, Rome.

Gilbreath, K. 1986. A businessman's guide to the Mexican economy. *Columbia Journal of World Business* 21:3-14.

Grainger, A. 1987. Tropform: A model of future tropical hardwood supplies. In: *Center for international trade in forest products symposium on forest sector and trade models.* University of Washington, Seattle. November 3-4.

Iglesias, E.V. 1984. Latin America: Crisis and development options. CEPAL Review 23:7-28.

INFOR (Instituto Forestal, Chile). 1987. Las plantaciones forestales de America Latina. Santiago, Chile. Informe Tecnico no. 102.

Jarvis, L.S. 1986. Livestock development in Latin America. World Bank, Washington, D.C.

Kellison, R.C. 1988. The changing quality of the Latin American timber resource. International Union of Forest Research Organizations, Forest Products Conference, Sao Paulo, Brazil. May 15-20.

Laarman, J.G. 1986. A perspective on private enterprise and development aid for forestry. *Commonwealth Forestry Review* 65:315-320.

_____ 1987a. Investing in timber and timberland in Latin America. In: *A clear look at timberland investment.* Forest Products Research Society, Milwaukee, Wisconsin. April 27.

_____ 1987b. The economic outlook for forestry in tropical America: A hazardous period for projections. In: *Management of the forests of tropical America: prospects and technologies.* Edited by J.C. Figueroa C., F.H. Wadsworth, and S. Branham, U.S. Agency for International Development, U.S. Dept. of Agriculture Forest Service, and U.S. Office of International Cooperation and Development. Institute of Tropical Forestry, San Juan, Puerto Rico. September 22-27, 1986.

Leonard, H.J. 1987. *Natural resources and economic development in Central America.* Washington, D.C. International Institute for Environment and Development.

McGaughey, S.E., and H.M. Gregersen. 1983. Forest-based development in Latin America. Inter-American Development Bank, Washington, D.C.

Myers, N. 1980. Conversion of tropical moist forests. National Academy of Sciences, Washington, D.C.

Repetto, R. 1988. The forest for the trees? Government policies and the misuse of forest resources. World Resources Institute, Washington, D.C.

Restrepo, J.L. 1985. Latin America: An assessment of the past and a search for the future. *Inter-American Economic Affairs* 39:3-26.

Stier, J.C. 1987. *A* review of the world eucapulp industry and its impact on the northern U.S. pulp and paper industry. Department of Forestry, University of Wisconsin, Madison.

U.S. Department of Commerce. 1985. *Developing competitive markets in forest products: Brazil.* International Trade Administration, Washington, D.C.

_____ 1987. Developing paper products markets in Mexico and the Caribbean. International Trade Administration, Washington, D.C.

8

Social Dimensions of Forest Utilization In Mexico: Implications for Intervention

Vanessa Halhead

The conversion of tropical forests to cattle ranching is but one manifestation of the approach taken to development in Mexico during the post-war years. It demonstrates many of the features of the Mexican socio-political situation which have shaped resource use in the country, and which must be well understood before considering future planning or intervention. Previous attempts to conserve natural resources have often failed because of their limited perspective on the social and political systems which underlie the use of those resources.

It was this view which prompted me, in 1980, to begin an extensive investigation into the socio-political context of forest utilization in Mexico (Halhead 1984). The results are of direct relevance to the problems underlying the conversion of tropical forest into pastures. Through a case study of Mexico, I demonstrate some major social factors limiting the sustainable use of forest resources and promoting forest conversion.

Superficially, two main, inextricably linked factors are associated with forest conversion:

- Agricultural expansion in the form of colonization, both spontaneous and planned, and agricultural development projects aimed at import substitution or the export market.
- Lack of development of the forestry sector and most importantly, the exclusion of local communities from the activities of the sector.

Underlying both factors are more fundamental characteristics of Mexican society and its development, which determine the avenues through which change may be pursued.

Characteristics of Mexican Forests

Mexico has an extensive and valuable forest resource, equal in area to those of some major timber producing countries. The 1978 National Forest Inventory estimated that 22% of the country was forested, (SARH/SFF 1978)[1] compared with only 15% suitable for agriculture. Over much of the rest of the country, where forests have been cleared for agriculture, it is estimated that timber production would be a more profitable use for the land than agriculture.

The utilization of the forests bears little relationship to their potential value. Although the forest resource has the capacity to meet most of Mexico's timber needs, timber imports currently account for over 10% of the national trade deficit[2]. An estimated annual rate of deforestation of 400,000 hectares is rapidly diminishing the extent of the forest area, while poor management practices are reducing it's quality and diversity (SARH/SFF 1980).

Turning to the social context, local people derive little or no financial benefit from the forest resource other than the extraction of fuelwood. The current pattern of land tenure in the forests is 7% state owned, 23% privately owned, and 70% held by ejidos and indigenous communities (SEP 1981). The majority of the 10 million people estimated to be living in the forest areas depend on subsistence agriculture for a living (PRI 1982). At the same time it was estimated that only 70,000 people were employed in the extraction sector of the forest industry, very few of whom were the actual land holders, and the average annual family income in the forest communities was approximately 500 US dollars (PRI 1982).

For example, the state of Chiapas is a major forest area and is one of the states most directly affected by conversion to cattle ranching. It has extensive forests (8.5 million hectares) covering nearly half of the state and the greatest volume of standing timber of any Mexican state, including 1.4 million hectares of high evergreen rainforest, yet timber production contributes only 2% of the total production of the primary sector of the state (Pacheco 1983; SARH/SFF 1979).[3] Chiapas also has the highest rate of deforestation of any Mexican state, 20,000 ha per annum.

In social terms, it is clear that current practices of commercial forestry contributes very little to the welfare of the Mexican population, either in employment or revenue, and of the revenue which is generated a very low percentage actually accrues to the owners of the forests themselves. Out of a state's total population of 2 million (SARH 1982), 9000 are employed in the forestry sector (UUEGCSC 1981). Some 77% of the forest areas are under the ownership of indigenous and ejido communities, 90% of which have little commericial involvement in forests. These figures do not reflect the apparent wealth of the natural resource base. The poor development of the forest industry and its failure to contribute to the development of local communities undoubtedly leads to the undervaluing of the resource and to the rapid rate of deforestation. At least five factors contribute to this situation:

- **Domination of large private and state run extraction companies.** Chiapas has a long history of large private timber companies, initially foreign companies extracting tropical hardwoods and more recently owned by local ladino families. These companies continue to dominate the forest sector, accounting for 80% of all authorized felling permits. In the rainforest, large state owned companies carry out 98% of the authorized timber work (SARH/SFF 1982).

- **Capital intensive production geared to an industrial market.** Since the 1940's forestry has been developed to reduce the import shortfalls in timber products. This was achieved with the aid of foreign capital and technology and has resulted in a large scale, capital intensive industry requiring a secure supply of raw material. In order to satisfy this demand, a system of long-term concessions over extensive areas of forests developed. Consideration of the local population or the rural development potential of the industry has largely been confined to rhetoric. The reality is that current forest practice is increasing social and economic duality and is biased towards the needs of the urban society.

- **Lack of awareness of land holders of the value of their timber resources.** As the local communties have been excluded from the timber production process, there is no tradition of silviculture and little awareness of the commercial value of forests. The revenue to land holders takes the form of "stumpage duty" which is set by the state or through negotiations with the contractor. As the land holders generally have little knowledge of the value of the timber, they are vulnerable to contractors and in reality receive a fraction of the real value.[4,5] In addition, most of the processing (and the consequent revenue) takes place outside the area. This produces an almost complete lack of interest on the part of land holders in the management and sustainability of the forest.

- **Lack of legalized land titles.** Land holders who do decide to work their forests typically run into problems from the lack of full title deeds to the land. In a long term, high risk industry like forestry, a fundamental requirement is security of tenure. In Mexico, the agrarian reform measures introduced after the Revolution have never been completed and only 25% of cultivatable land has regularized land titles. In more remote forest areas, especially in the south, the situation is much worse. This not only reduces the confidence of land holders, but also limits the availability of vital credit for forestry work.

- **Insufficient investment in the rural development potential of forestry.** Despite the obvious contribution that forestry and forest products could make to the local economy, little effort has been put into developing community forestry models. Rather, national emphasis has been focused on industrial forestry. The result is that involvement of indigenous communities and ejidos has been largely unsuccessful.

Development Trends in Agriculture

The problems inherent in the forestry sector are mirrored in the trends of agricultural development:

- **Agricultural modernization.** Agricultural modernization programs have channeled investment into limited "growth pole" areas and agricultural production, which was initially designed to reduce dependency on imported foodstuffs. This sector has rapidly evolved towards the lucrative export market, mostly in the US. This process has been supported by international aid and is a pattern witnessed throughout Latin America.
- **Unequal distribution of land.** Despite the agrarian reforms of the Revolution, population distribution in rural areas does not coincide with the productive potential of land. Patterns of settlement established during the colonial period still persist in many areas, with overcrowding and subsistence agriculture on the poor soils, often within the forest areas, while the fertile areas are farmed in extensive units, largely for the production of export crops, a major one of which is cattle.
- **Lack of investment in the traditional agricultural sector.** With government investment channeled into industrial development and the limited modernized agricultural sector, the bulk of the rural areas have been left to evolve without aid or planning.[6] This has produced a situation of extreme economic duality in agriculture.

Colonization

Traditional forms of subsistence agriculture have been unable to sustain the massive population increase experienced since the war (3.5% per

annum) and marginal rural communities have been forced to look elsewhere for a livelihood. This has resulted in two phenomena, massive rural to
urban migration and the colonization of previously unsettled lands.

In Chiapas, the combination of these factors has lead to increasing
colonization of the lowland rainforests, especially the Selva Lacandona
where the population has increased from a few hundred to over 300,000
since 1950[6]. This began as a spontaneous movement from the highlands and
has increased with the construction of roads for logging and oil extraction.
Colonization is also encouraged by the government as a safety valve for the
overcrowded areas and for the explicit strategic purpose of settling the
uninhabited border regions of the country (Revel-Mouroz 1980:99).

From this form of colonization, the inevitable pattern of forest conversion to subsistence milpa agriculture has occurred, followed rapidly by loss
of soil fertility and succession to poor quality cattle pastures. In the larger
colonization schemes, cattle ranching receives government and international support (Feder 1979), in other cases it is practiced in an opportunistic
fashion by campesinos. As the ability of the land to support cattle declines,
there is a trend towards the accumulation of land into larger and larger
units, many of which are run from Mexico City. By this process both the
profits and the biomass are removed from the area. By 1978, in Chiapas
alone, 2.1 million hectares had already been converted in this way (Pacheco
1983).

General Development Trends

The features just described reflect the broader trends of Mexican
society. These have a direct bearing on the whole question of forest utilization and must be taken into account when considering future action. In
common with many other countries, Mexican development during the last
50 years has been characterized by emphasis on rapid economic growth,
achieved through industrialization and agricultural modernization supported by massive injections of foreign aid. This produced economic growth
rates in excess of 6% and a crippling foreign debt.

Implicit in this development model is the idea that spin-off effects are
felt throughout the society — the trickle-down or diffusion theory. Accordingly, no effort was put into associated social development measures apart
from the modernized sector. The results have been increasing economic
disparity, with wealth accumulating in a limited sector of the community,
and duality between the traditional and modernized sectors (Navarrette
1980).

In the agrarian sector, modernization coupled with lack of rural
development aid, population increases and limited availability of land have

lead to enforced migration and increasing pressures on marginal land (Tirado de Ruiz 1971). Neither the modernized agricultural nor industrial sectors, resulting from their capital intensive technology, have generated sufficient employment to absorb the excess rural population, producing enormous unemployment rates (Trejo Reyes 1973). In accordance with this development model, natural resources have been used simply to support rapid economic expansion, without consideration for sustainability or rural development potential.

Political System

The control of the PRI is absolute and extends to all sectors of the society. The country is controlled by a strong elite, who run both the major industries and the governing party. Power is maintained by a top-down system in which power seekers at every level in the community must consult the wishes of their superiors and not of the electorate. This is reinforced by government control of trade unions, which are the only permitted labor organizations, and the sexenial change of leadership. Related to this is the ever present feature of corruption, which serves to reinforce top-down control.

There is, accordingly, no effective mechanism for representing the wishes of the poor, especially in rural areas. As Hansen (1971) points out, "a government in which the demands of organized labor and the campesinos were effectively represented could neither have designed nor implemented the development strategy that has characterized Mexico's recent economic growth."

The potential for rural unrest is recognized but to date this has been diffused. Despite the obvious inequalities, campesinos have few expectations of the system and have an ingrained distrust of it. There are two main ways by which government gains support of this sector. First, through land allocations, the land reforms of the Revolution were never completed and many areas are without title deeds. By showing that it is attempting to carry on the aims of the Revolution by distributing land titles, the government provides a climate of hope. Colonization and land allocations are used as safety valves for discontentment among the rural population. The second tool is more direct, and involves the suppression of campesino leaders (Amnesty International 1982) and thereby the emergence of any real grass roots involvement in the development process. These factors have a powerful influence on the bureaucracy of the country. The centralization of power, the *sexenial* upheavals and the extensive corruption dilute and confuse policies and reduce their effective implementation at the level of the community. Government agencies are also often used as social control mechanisms, rather than to encourage local development.

The implications for the development of rural Mexico are profound. The political system clearly drives the development model of the country and strongly reinforces the disparities it produces. It is difficult in fact to envisage any other development model emerging from the current political system.

There are, however, elements of the Mexican system which make it potentially more open to change than many. These stem from the reforms of the Revolution. Even today, the PRI maintains its credibility among the poor by extensive use of revolutionary rhetoric and reference to the reforms stated in the Constitution. This provides a potential basis for social and political evolution sympathetic with appropriate rural development and resource conservation.

Discussion

The conversion of forest to pasture is a feature of development trends which have their roots in an international economic system outside the control of any one country. The theoretical basis of this development model is becoming discredited, but the forces it has promoted are strongly ingrained in countries like Mexico. The effects have been to increase economic duality within developing countries and to seriously erode the sustainability of the natural resource base. As a consequence, the people who stand to suffer most from the process are the rural poor, who in the case of Mexico constitute a major sector of the community.

Native rural communities are often the tools in the process of forest conversion, as for example in the enforced colonization of virgin forests. In this vulnerable position, they are often blamed for the resulting erosion of the environment. In reality they are as much the victims of this corporate mismanagement as is the environment itself.

It is essential that in any sustainable program of rural development, the local people are placed at the forefront of decision making and their needs should form the primary condition for the management of the resource base. This is difficult to envisage in the context of Mexico; and substantial pressures, both internally and externally, will be required to achieve such a change of direction. Most importantly, there must be attention given to altering the power structures within the country towards a system which is a more open to the electorate and permits grass-roots involvement. Completion and updating of agrarian reform measures, to legalize holdings and where possible to create holdings of an economic size, is an important prerequisite for sustainable use of the resource base. The kind of economic duality found in Mexico makes effective rural development measures very difficult to apply. To achieve any kind of policy control it will be necessary to integrate the traditional and modernized sectors more comprehensively. It is also important to break down the sectoral divisions between disciplines and government agencies as these make effective integration extremely difficult to achieve.

It is the responsibility of the international community to assist as fully as possible in providing the right climate, both political and economic, for the emergence of a basic needs rural development program in which the sustainability of the resource base is a priority. This has major implications for the future development trends of Western nations, but ultimately will be as essential for their own survival as for the countries of the Third World.

In the context of the social and economic climate of countries like Mexico, site protection and the use of reserves for the purposes of conservation are inappropriate and ineffective tools. As one forester in Oaxaca pointed out - "we do not, at this time, have the right to pass laws which prohibit the use of resources." Most attempts to do this have failed. Prohibition of any kind, especially in the face of economic deprivation, is perceived as a threat and will induce the hostility of the local communities whose cooperation is essential. In turn this may lead to exploitation and misuse of the reserve in the face of competing local interests. It is impossible to adequately police a reserve and the costs of management will be unacceptably high. Success will require strong political commitment over a long period, this is most unlikely in a country undergoing rapid change. It is more likely that the reserve will be used as a cloak for other forms of government intervention, for instance, strategic control over areas as in the case of the reserves in the Selva Lacandona.

It is apparent that under the extreme social and economic pressures evident in Mexico today, the most important factor favoring the long-term sustainability of the forest will be its potential to generate income and employment. As traditional forms of agriculture break down under population pressure, local communities must diversify their resource base and find options for entering into the national economy in a way which will permit the retention of their lifestyles and culture. Within the forested regions, the most obvious option is through the economic utilization of the forest resources.

To enable local communities to embrace this option it will be necessary to develop a concerted program of community forestry based on the principles of sustainability and integration. There are some essential characteristics of community forestry, which have been well documented (UN/FAO 1978); most importantly though, it requires the commitment of the government to rural development. The Mexican system so far does not reveal such a commitment and it will be necessary to identify ways in which incentives for this may be provided. A more important question may be whether the time scales involved in introducing the rural communities to this type of production, given the problems of "cultural lag" (Fromm and Maccoby 1970), are in excess of the capacity of the resource to withstand current trends.

Finally, it is crucially important that knowledge and information is transmitted to the people on the ground, that they may use this knowledge to press for change. Local people must speak out in defense of *their* resources and in opposition to the kind of external forces which threaten both the resource base and the community, because inevitably the two go hand in hand. To do this they need to have the facts. Equally, we must be able to listen to the wisdom of the traditional rural people, who have a more complete understanding of the potentialities and vulnerabilities of their natural resources than do most policy makers.

Notes

1. Approximately 70% of these areas consist of temperate coniferous and broadleaved forests, and 30% are tropical lowland forests (*selvas*).
2. In 1980 the potential annual harvest was estimated at 23 million m^3 (sustainable yield). At that time, the annual harvest was in the region of 9 m^3, and timber imports were estimated at 4.9 million m^3. Exports at the same time amounted to 166,000 m^3.
3. 491,000,000 million m^3.
4. Derecho de Monte estimated by subtracting the cost of harvesting, transportation and processing from the market value of the final product.
5. It has been estimated that land holders receive approximately 20% of the real value for conifers and 8% for tropical hardwoods (UUEGCSC 1981).
6. In a study of the state of Oaxaca, where 80% of the population have an annual income of less than $200 US and 73% are rural dwelling, it was found that only 10% of federal investment in the state went into rural development projects (Wall 1982).
7. The cities now absorb 60% of the rural population increase, producing a 5% rate of urban population increase.
8. The Selva Lacandona is an extension of the Guatemalan rain forests. It's an area of about 1,400,000 hectares and is the most important area of evergreen rainforest remaining in Mexico. During the height of the Maya civilization, the area supported an extensive population but between the collapse of the Maya (800 - 900 A.D.) and the end of the 19th Century the area was practically uninhabited. Between 1863-1975 it was exploited by foreign timber companies for hardwood and chicle.

References Cited

Amnesty International, 1982. *Historical context of land disputes in Mexico.* Internal Report. AMR 41/16/82.

Feder, E. 1979. Lean cows - fat ranchers - the international ramifications of Mexico's beef cattle industry. *America Latina* 21-24.

Fromm, E. and M. Fromm. 1970. *Social character in a Mexican village - a socio-psychoanalytic study.* New Jersey:Prentice-Hall.

Halhead, A.V. 1984. The forests of Mexico, the resource and the politics of utilization. Unpublished thesis. University of Edinburgh, Scotland.

Navarrete, I. M. 1980. La distribucion del ingresso en Mexico: Tendencias y perspectivas. In: *El perfil de Mexico en 1980.* Mexico: Siglo XXI.

Pacheco, G. C. 1978. Entrevistas sobre la problematica de los bosques. Problemas de Desarrollo. No.35. Año IX. Mexico.

___ 1982. *Consulta popular sobre la silvicultura.* Mexico.

___ 1983. *Capital extranjero en la selva de Chiapas* 1863 - 1982. Mexico, D.F. Instituto de Investigaciones Economicas, UNAM.

Revel-Mouroz, J. 1980. *Aprovechamiento y colonizacion del tropical humedo Mexicano.* Mexico City: Fondo de Cultura Economica.

SARH - Secretaria de Agricultura y Recursos Hidraulicos/SFF 1972-82. *Plan forestal de Chiapas.* Tuxtla Gutierrez, Chiapas.

___ 1978a. *La actividad forestal en Chiapas.* Departamento de Divulgacion Forestal y de la Fauna. Mexico, D.F.

___ 1978b. *Estadisticas del recurso forestal de la Republica Mexicana.* Direccion General del Inventorio Forestal. Mexico, D.F.

___ 1979. *Informacion basica, sector agropequario y forestal - Chiapas.* Tuxtla Gutierrez, Mexico.

___ 1980a. *Programa nacional de desarrollo forestal.* Departamento de Divulgacion Forestal y de la Fauna, Mexico, D.F.

___ 1980. *Cifras estadisticas de la produccion forestal.* Departamento de Divulgacion Forestal y de la Fauna, Mexico, D.F.

SEP - Secretaria de Educacion Publica. 1981. Guia de planeacion y control de las actividades forestales. Mexico, D.F.

Tirado de Ruiz, R.M. 1971. Desarrollo Historico de la Poliiica Agraria sobre Tenencia de la Tierra - 1910-1970. In: *Bienestar campesino y desarrollo economica.* Edited by Ifigenia M. de Navarete. Mexico: Fondo de Cultura Economica.

Trejo Reyes, S. 1973. *Industrializacion y empleo en Mexico.* Mexico City: Fondo de Cultura Economica.

Union de Uniones Ejidales y Grupos Campesinas Solidarios de Chiapas (UUEGCSC). 1981. *Documentacion sobre problemas de uso de la tierra - Chiapas.* Unpublished. Mexico.

UN/FAO Forestry Papers 1978. *Forestry for local community development.* Rome:Food and Agriculture Organization.

Wall, M P. 1982. Integrated rural development in Mexico: Case study of the Mixteca Alta. University of Edinburgh, Scotland. Unpublished Thesis.

PART THREE
ENVIRONMENTAL IMPACTS

The public shares the scientific community's concern for the possible deleterious environmental consequences of tropical deforestation. Popular scientific reports have convinced many that a localized, environmental problem may have global impacts. Salati and Nations synthesize the preliminary data on environmental problems and suggest relevant regional or global trends. Piecing together fragmentary micro- and meso-climatic data, Salati builds a general model of the water balance of the Amazon river basin, revealing the importance of the forest itself as a generator of regional rainfall. Using this model, he attempts to determine land and ecosystem management techniques that might minimize the negative climatic impacts associated with deforestation.

Nations reviews the terrestrial impacts of deforestation from another perspective: that of the losses of biological diversity. His analysis is sensitive to the human dimension of the environmental problems. Listen to his somber warning: until the citizens of both the developed and underdeveloped world recognize their common interests are being threatened, solutions will not be forthcoming.

— *Carmen Garcia-Downing*

9

Possible Climatological Impacts

Eneas Salati

Conversion of tropical forests into pastures inevitably entails major changes in the ecosystem. There appears to be a consensus that this conversion changes the flora, the aquatic and land fauna and the physico-chemical and biological characteristics of the soils and surface waters. There also appears to be agreement that qualitative and quantitative changes are brought about in the biogeochemical cycles.

However, the question becomes controversial when analyzing the climatic aspects of the conversion of tropical rain forests into pastures. This is due to the difficulty of quantifying the components of the energy and water balances in the two ecosystems, and the difficulty of developing climate models at regional levels that permit reliable forecasting of the changes. It has been generally accepted that the flora is a consequence of the climatic conditions, the characteristics of the soil and the geomorphology. Therefore, it has been assumed that conversion of one type of ground cover to another should not induce climatic changes. However, studies are producing evidence that, for some ecosystems, the present dynamic equilibrium of the atmosphere depends on the vegetation, and the present climate is the consequence of the interaction between the biosphere and the atmosphere (Salati 1985). While discussions on the subject proceed and the efforts to improve the measurements and develop more suitable models continue, settlers steadily press deeper into the tropical forests or what remains thereof throughout the world (Setzer et al. 1988, Malingrau and Tucker 1988, Repetto 1988). Technical specialists and administrators did not expect that changes in these ecosystems would have the profoundly negative economic and environmental consequences that they did. Establishment of extensive pastures have not always been economically successful.

This chapter assembles some available information for the humid tropics regarding known data about microclimates and the climate at a regional level. Based on these data, it attempts to determine what land and ecosystem management techniques could minimize the impacts, especially the changes in the water and energy cycles. Although the chapter focuses on the Amazon region, many of the concepts herein are applicable to other regions.

Some Microclimatic Data

For the purpose of subsequent comparisons, the microclimatic data obtained in the Ducke Reserve (INPA), near Manaus, in the Brazilian Amazon, will be analyzed. Research was carried out in a joint program by Brazilian (INPE and INPA) and British (British Council Institute of Hydrology) researchers, beginning in 1983. The results were published by Shuttleworth et al. (1984a, 1984b, 1985) and summarized by Mollion (1987).

The research area is covered by dense forest with trees measuring about 35 meters, with branches sometimes reaching 40 meters. The observation tower is 45 meters high. Figures 9.1, 9.2, and 9.3 show the above and below-canopy fluxes of radiation. The energy reaching the ground averages only 1.2% of that reaching the tree tops. The average albedo for this forest was 12%, varying with the solar zenith angle.

By measuring the vertical temperature and humidity profiles it was possible to conclude that 75% of the energy available goes into evaporating water and the remaining 25% is used to heat the air. For a daily average of 4.96 mm water equivalent of radiation, 3.70 mm evaporated into the air.

Parameters connected with wind structure were as follows: zero-plane displacement (d) equal to 25.3 + 0.6 m; roughness length (Zo) equal to 5.0 + 0.4 mm and friction velocity (u•) equal to 0.79 + 0.13 m. Reifsnyder (1987) commenting on Molion's study (1987) concludes that:

> Perhaps the most significant finding of the work of the joint Brazilian-British research team of which Molion was a member, is that the tropical rain forest studied behaves pretty much as one might have expected based on experience in other forests, both temperate and tropical. That is, the dense canopy allows only about 1-2% of incident sunlight to reach the forest floor; that the variability of below-canopy solar radiation is greater than the above-canopy flux; that the mean albedo of the canopy is about 12%, with highest albedos at low solar angles (although the lowest albedo was measured at solar altitudes of about 55°); that the roughness length is about 5 m; that the ratio of evaporation flux to net radiation is about 0.7; and that precipitation is distributed about one quarter to direct evaporation of leaf-intercepted water, about one half has returned to the atmosphere by transpiration, and the remaining quarter to runoff and groundwater. These figures compare closely with those for mature hardwood forests in temperate zones and with the few measurements in other moist tropical forests.

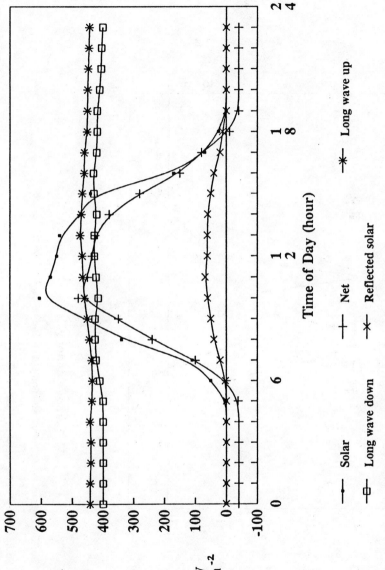

FIGURE 9.1 Radiation components above an Amazon rain forest (mean value)

Source: adapted from Molion 1987

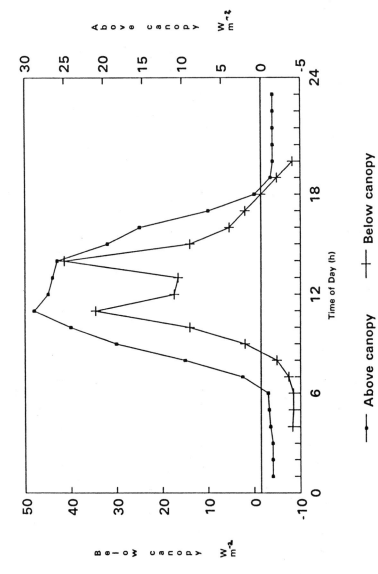

FIGURE 9.2 Mean values of net radiation above and below Amazon rainforest

Source: Adapted from Molion 1987

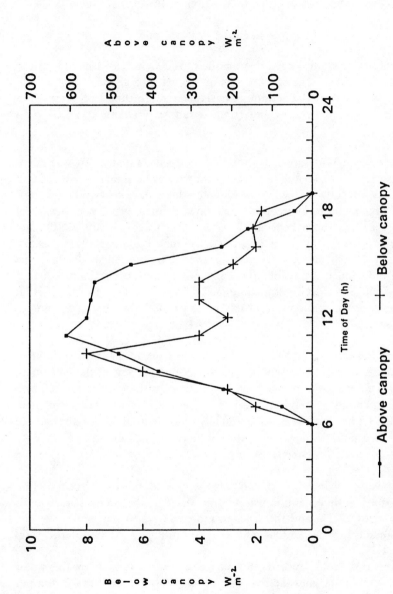

FIGURE 9.3 Mean solar radiation above and below the Amazon rainforest

Source: Adapted from Molion 1987

For established pastures with 60 cm high grasses the values for albedo range from 19% when the grass is green to 25% during the dry season.

Balance in Small Watersheds

A number of studies have been made in the vicinity of Manaus, in the Amazon, to determine the components of the water balance in a watershed. Readings obtained on a continuous basis over more than two years were published in various papers and summarized by Franken and Leopoldo (1984).

Model Basin Watershed. Located 80 km from Manaus, this watershed measures approximately 23.5 km^2 and is covered mainly with dense primary forest, with trees up to 40 meters high, on a heavy yellow latosol soil. Precipitation, interception and flow of forest waterways (*igarapés*) was measured from February 2, 1980 through February 10, 1981. Total precipitation during the period was 2,089 mm; the interception was 534 mm or 25.6% and the runoff was 541 mm or 25.9%. From these measurements it is possible to calculate that the transpiration is equal to 1,014 mm, and the evaporation equals 534 mm or 25.6%. This means that the evapotranspiration was 74.1% of the precipitation, corresponding to 1,548 mm.

Barro Branco Watershed. Located 26 km from Manaus, in the INPA, Ducke Ecological Forest Reserve. Ninety-five percent of the catchment area is covered with primary dry land rain forest (dense forest), 3% with experimental forest and 2% has been clear cut. The size of the catchment area is 1.3 km^2 and the soils are mainly yellow latosol. The water balance was measured during two different periods: September 29, 1976 to September 22, 1977 and from July 1, 1981 to June 30, 1982.

The average values for the two periods studied indicate a precipitation of 2,293 mm; the interception was 429 mm or 18%; the runoff corresponds to 635 mm or 27.7% and the transpiration was 1,229 mm or 63.6%. The evapotranspiration was 1,658 mm, corresponding to 72.3% of the total precipitation.

In the two areas studied, the measurements obtained for the water balance were similar and the real evapotranspiration averaged 4.3 mm per day. Ribeiro et al. (1979), using Thornthwaite and Mather method and the data for 1965-73, arrived at results 1,536 mm y[1] for potential evapotranspiration and 1,075 mm y[1] for real evapotranspiration. These readings agree with those obtained by Franken and Leopoldo (1984).

Water Balance of the Amazon Basin

The water balance is difficult to determine due to the lack of basic data systematically obtained over time and space. However, utilizing existing data and through successive approximations it was possible to establish a quantification of the fluxes involved.

Figure 9.4 shows values for the fluxes, based on published data obtained according to methods described below.

Radio Sounding

Daily radio sounding data were obtained from the stations in years 1972-75. Based on these data it was possible to determine the vertical wind structure, the precipitable water vapor, and the water vapor fluxes. For more details see Salati et al. 1984a, 1984b; Marques et al. 1979a, 1979b, 1980a, 1980b; and Kagano 1979.

From data obtained it was possible to conclude that:

- On the Atlantic coast and in the center of the Amazon region winds are predominantly from the East. Primary vapor reaches the region coming from the Atlantic coast.
- Water vapor flux decreases from East to West.
- Precipitable water vapor in the region averages 35 mm with a seasonal variation of 10 mm. Therefore, the average water volume stored in the atmosphere above the Amazon Basin is 0.21×10^{12} tons. This mass of water vapor is largely responsible for the isothermy observed in the region (daily low temperature).
- Divergence of the water vapor flux studied month by month corresponds to the flow of the Amazon River with a lag of approximately three months which indicates water residency time.
- Quantitative readings of water vapor fluxes on the Atlantic coast are insufficient to explain the values of precipitation observed in the region.
- There are no data on the atmospheric interactions for the boundering western region between the Orinoco and Amazon basins.
- More recent data (Nobre 1988) indicate that the vapor flux values used by Salati et al. (1984a) overestimate the water vapor flux for April-May in Belem.

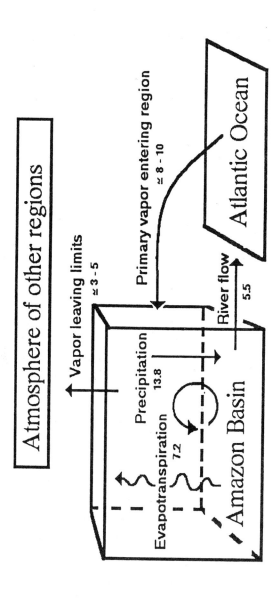

FIGURE 9.4 Water balance of the Amazon Basin

Approximately 50-60% of the rain results from recycling of water vapor in the basin. The fluxes are x 10^{12} m^3/ year.

- Primary water vapor flux for the Amazon region should be about 8-10 x $10^{12}m^3$/year. This is the parameter of greatest uncertainty in the water balance shown in Figure 9.4.
- At the southern boundaries of the Amazon region the direction of water vapor fluxes is north-south for virtually the entire year. This indicates that water vapor from the Amazon region can influence water vapor concentration in the atmosphere above the Brazilian central plateau.

Precipitation

Precipitation is abundant throughout the Amazon region, with values exceeding 1,700 mm/year. In general precipitation is heavy along the coast averaging 3,000 mm, but decreasing southeast of Belem. In the center Manaus region, precipitation exceeds 2,000 mm. The highest readings were registered in the regions influenced by the Andes, where precipitation in excess of 5,000 mm were observed.

There is also a noticeable seasonal variation with maximum rainfalls in the northern hemisphere during July-August and in the southern hemisphere during February-March (Salati and Marques 1984). The total precipitation for the Amazon has been estimated by various authors ranging from 2,000 mm to 2,379 mm. For the water balance, a rate of 2,300 mm/y was used, which corresponds to a total of 13.8 x 10^{12} m^3/year (Figure 9.4).

Evapotranspiration

Readings for actual evapotranspiration for the various ecosystems forming the Amazon region will only be known in the future. What can be presently obtained are estimates based on: (a) water balance calculations for model basins; (b) micro climate measurements; (c) isotopic dilution; (d) calculations based on the Thornthwaite and Penman methods. The estimates obtained by various authors are shown in Table 9.1.

By using different methods convergent values between 1,542 mm and 1,675 mm, representing 74% to 81% of precipitation were obtained from studies in dense dryland forests. For the Amazon Basin as a whole, values ranging from 1,146 mm to 1,260 mm corresponding to 48-54% of the precipitation were obtained. In the water balance shown in Figure 9.4, evapotranspiration of 1,200 mm/year was used corresponding to an annual flux of 7.2 x 10^{12} m^3.

TABLE 9.1 Summary of different researcher's results on the hydrological cycle of the Amazon Region

Research	Rainfall mm	Transpiration mm	%	mm/%mm	Evapotranspiration mm	%	mm/day	Runoff mm	%
	2328 [a]	-	-	-	1260[f]	54.2	3.5	1068	45.8
	2328 [b]	-	-	-	1000[f]	43.0	2.7	1328	57.0
	2328 [c]	-	-	-	1330[P]	57.1	3.6	998	42.9
Villa Nova et al. 1976	2000 [d]	-	-	-	1460[P]	73.0	4.0	540	27.0
		-	-	-	1168[f]	58.4	3.2	832	41.6
		-	-	-	1569[P]	73.4	4.3	532	26.6
Molion 1975	2101 [e]	-	-	-	1146[f]	48.2	3.1	1233	51.8
Ribeiro et al. 1979	2379 [f]	-	-	-	1536[P]	62.0	4.2	942	38.0
	2478 [g]	.	-	-	1508[f]	60.8	4.1	970	39.2
Ipean 1972	2179 [h]	-	-	-	1475[f]	67.5	4.0	704	34.5
		-	-	-	1320[f]	60.6	3.6	859	39.4
Dmet 1978	2207 [i]	-	-	-	1452[P]	65.8	4.0	755	34.2
		-	-	-	1306[f]	59.2	3.6	901	40.8
Jordan et al. 1981	3664 [i]	1722	47.0	4.7	1905[f]	52.0	5.2	1759	48.0
Leopoldo et al. 1981	2089 [j]	1014	48.5	2.7	1542[f]	74.1	4.1	541	25.9
Leopoldo et al. 1982	2075 [k]	1287	62.0	3.5	1675[f]	80.7	4.6	400	19.3

Observations: (a) acrological method, applied for all Amazon Basin, period 1972/75; (b) idem. for the region between Belem and Manaus; (c) idem. for the region between Belem and Manaus; (d) Penman method, mean for the period 1931/60; (e) idem. for Manaus Region; (f) climatonomic method, for all Amazon Region, mean for period 1931/60; (g) water balance by Thornthwaite and Mather method for the Ducke Forest Reserve, mean for the period 1965/1973; (h) Thornthwaite method for all Amazon Region and estimated for period over 10 years; (i) idem. for various periods; (j) water balance, with transpiration estimated by class A pan-evaporation for San Carlos Region; (k) "Model Basin" water balance and (k) "Barro-Branco" water balance (Ducke Forest Reserve).

Recycling of Water Vapor

In view of the results found for water vapor fluxes and precipitation it was concluded that vapor generated by evapotranspiration must recirculate in the region. This conclusion was evidenced by the distribution of isotopes (O^{18} and D) of rain waters of different areas of the Amazon (Salati et al. 1979). Using current existing data it is estimated that 50-60% of rains result from the re-circulation of water vapor.

Models

The models for forecasting climatic alterations resulting from changes in land-use, such as the conversion of tropical forests into pastures, are still inadequate tools for the purpose. Nevertheless, different authors made attempts in this direction. Their data and limitations were discussed by Henderson-Sellers (1987) and summarized in Table 9.2.

In an effort to better analyze the interactions and to improve the models, Dickinson and his associates (1988), sought to verify the importance of the vegetation canopy in determining the climate response to tropical deforestation. In summary:

In a 13 month integration that assumes that all of the Amazon tropical forest in South America is replaced by impoverished grassland, surface hydrological and temperature effects dominate the response. Reduced mixing and less interception and evaporation from canopy cause runoff to increase and surface temperatures to rise by 3-5°K. The period of driest soil is increased in the model from one month to several, but the possibility that this change is random cannot be excluded. Increased temperatures and drier soil could have a detrimental impact on survival of the remaining forest and on attempts at cultivation in deforested areas.

The land-surface model, driven in a stand-alone mode by prescribed atmospheric conditions and with an imposed seasonal cycle or rainfall, mimics the seasonal cycle of soil moisture and runoff found in the GCM (Global Circulation Model). Hence, it is used to estimate the relative contribution of the various changes imposed to simulate deforestation in the GCM with respect to the model's response at the surface. The change in surface roughness interacting with the canopy hydrology is evidently a major factor in determing the surface response to deforestation. However, the response to change in roughness is less pronounced for simpler models (Dickinson 1988).

TABLE 9.2 Comparison of results of climate model simulations of tropical deforestation

Model attributes	Throughout Humid Tropics		Amazonia Only	
	Potter et al. 1975	Wilson 1984	Lettau et al. 1979	Henderson-Sellers and Gornitz 1964
Features				
Areal Coverage	Global two-dimensional statistical dynamic model (tropical deforestation)	Global climate model (tropical land-type change)	Amazon Basin	Global climate model (deforestation in Amazonia)
Spatial resolution	10° latitude	2.5° latitude x 3.75° longitude	5° longitude	8° latitude x 10° longitude
Perturbation				
Albedo increase	0.18	0.08	0.03	0.06
Hydrological change	Dry case had increased runoff and evaporation	Soil moisture capacity reduced by 32, 20 and 12 cm for fine, medium and coarse textured soils	Evaporative flux from soil increased	Soil moisture capacity reduced from 200 to 30 cm and from 450 to 200 cm in upper and lower ground
Other changes	None	None	Infrared emissivity unchanged	Infrared emissivity Roughness length decreased
Results				
Atmospheric circulation	Weakened Hadley cell	No significant ($>2\sigma$) change detected	Assumed regional trade winds unchanged	Walker circulation showed no significant ($>1\%$) disturbance; no Hadley cell circulation change
Precipitation	Decrease 230 mm y⁻¹ in 5° N- 5°S zone	Decrease Amazonia 100-800 mm y⁻¹; Congo 200-600mm y⁻¹	Increase 75 mm y⁻¹ (Amazonia)	Decrease 220 mm y⁻¹ (Amazonia)
Surface temperature	Decrease 0.4° C in 5°N-5°S zone	No systematic change	Increase 0.55°C	No significant change

Possible Changes

The conversion of forested areas into pastures will bring about microclimatic changes which, when combined in large areas, will eventually cause regional climatic alterations. Depending on the scale of these alterations, they may result in changes at a global level.

Microclimatic

Changes may be introduced in albedo, and the energy and water balances. There will be a tendency toward less water infiltration and more runoff. The wind profile will be changed.

Mesoclimatic (regional)

The sum of these alterations may change the water balance and vapor transportation at a regional level with consequent changes in the energy balance. It is not possible at the present time to forecast these changes by means of models. The most probable tendency will be increased runoff and decreased evapo-transpiration. The consequence will be a decline in precipitable water vapor and higher temperature fluctuations resulting in more dramatic daily thermal amplitudes. These changes could affect the study area as well as surrounding regions.

Global

Tropical forests contribute in many ways to the maintenance of the present dynamic equilibrium of the atmosphere. Forests represent a carbon reservoir, both through their aerial and root systems as well as through organic water in the soil. Tropical rain forests possess a reserve of carbon equivalent to twice that of CO_2 reserves in the atmosphere. Therefore conversion of forests into pastures will release carbon dioxide from the biosphere into the atmosphere increasing the greenhouse effect.

Forest burning associated with the clearing process for conversion into pasture also releases great quantities of particles and compound gases into the atmosphere. Table 9.3 shows estimates of particles released in 1978 for the Amazon region. These particles cause changes in the atmosphere, especially in its chemical composition and energy balance. Satellite observations indicate that these clouds of gases and particles move toward the South Pole and may possibly contribute to the decrease of the concentration of ozone observed in that region (Setzer 1988).

Tropical rain forest areas also have a characteristic energy balance which contributes to the transportation of energy in the form of latent heat

TABLE 9.3 Gas Emissions from burnings in the Amazon region in 1978

Material	Estimation of Emission x 10^{12}g
CO_2	518(a)
CO	44
Particulate organic carbon	4
Elemental Carbon	1
NO_X	1
NH_3	0.5
ZSO	0.2
K	0.1
Total particulate matter	6.2
O_3	2.5
CH_4	4.7
CH_3C_1	0.01

(a) Emmisions of carbon as CO_2
Source: Setzer 1980

(water vapor) from the equatorial regions to those of higher latitudes. How these circulating cells and their alterations will affect the global climate still remains unknown.

Comments and Recommendations

Because of its equatorial location and geomorphology, the climate of the Amazon region is mainly hot and humid. The combination of these conditions and the characteristics of soils resulted in a kind of flora whose adaptations introduced changes in the environment, shaping biogeochemical cycles and the water and energy balances. The selection processes ultimately brought about a biota extremely rich in species with an exceptionally high primary production.

The present dynamic equilibrium of the ecosystem is the result of this long adaptive process. In the present dynamic equilibrium, a large part of the chemical nutrients associated with the biomass are subject to rapid recycling through different processes.

The processes depend partly on the ground cover, the water residence time, evaporation and transpiration rates, the rain/runoff ratio, energy balance, biogeochemical cycles and the associated fauna. To convert forests into pastures without causing alterations, it will be necessary for the new ground cover conditions to be formed in the present equilibrium. It is impossible to prevent alterations but what could be done is to minimize the impact through management techniques geared toward reproducing the natural process that maintains the water and energy balances. For conversion of forest to pasture not to introduce changes, it will be necessary that it:

1. Completely cover the ground,
2. Have the same albedo as the forest,
3. Have the same water infiltration into the soil,
4. Have the same interception and the same real transpiration,
5. Prevent erosion,
6. Maintain the biogeochemical cycles, and
7. Have the same wind profile.

For pastures to approximate the ideal conditions outlined above, some management techniques can be recommended:

1. Not to deforest or introduce pastures in areas of very poor soils or steep slopes;
2. Use richer soils for annual crops and pastures;
3. Use grass varieties which completely cover the ground;
4. Use soil conservation techniques to prevent erosion and decrease runoff and assure replenishment of the ground water;
5. Plan land-use taking into consideration micro catchment areas, leaving strips of original forest along waterways and in areas subject to flooding. Leave strips of forest totaling at least 50% of the forested area along the slopes.
6. Combine livestock activities with agroforestry, to obtain a system that is more sustainable over the long term, though with fewer animals per unit area. In some cases it may be preferable to develop semi-intensive livestock together with intensive agriculture for silo (fodder) production.

If for technical, economic or social reasons the above conditions cannot be met, conversion of tropical rain forests into pastures must be avoided.

References Cited

Franken, W., P. R. Leopoldo. 1984. Hydrology of catchment area of Central-Amazonian forest streams. In: *The Amazon: Limnology and landscape ecology of a mighty tropical river and its basin.* Edited by H. Sioli. Dordrecht, The Netherlands: W. Junk.

Henderson-Sellers, A. 1987. Effects of change in land-use on climate in the humid tropics. In: *The geophysiology of Amazonia*. Edited by R. E. Dickinson. New York: John Wiley and Sons.

Hutchinson, T. 1988. Global deforestation trends. Paper presented at the Interaction Council meeting. Lisbon. January.

Kagano, M.T., 1979. *Um estudo climatológico e sinótico utilizando dados de radiossondagens, 1968-1976, de Manaus e Belém*. INPE Report No. 1559-TDL/013, São José dos Campos, Brazil.

Malingrau, J.P. and C. J. Tucker. 1988. Large-scale deforestation in the Southern Amazon Basin of Brazil. *AMBIO*, XVII, No. 1, 49-5T.

Marques, J., J.M. Santos and E. Salati. 1979a. O armazenamen to atmosferico de vapor d'agua sobre a região Amazônica, *Acta Amazônica*. 9, 715-721.

_____ 1979b. O campo do fluxo de vapor d'água atmosferico sobre a região Amazonica, *Acta Amazônica*. 9, 701-713.

Marques, J., E. Salati, and J.M. Santos. 1980a. Calculo de evapotranspiração real na bacia Amazônica através do método aerológico. *Acta Amazônica*. 10, 357-361.

_____ 1980b. A divergencia do campo do fluxo do vapor d'agua e as chuvas na Região Amazônica. *Acta Amazônica*. 10, 133-140.

Molion, L.C.B., 1987. Micrometeorolgy of an Amazônian Rain Forest. In: *Geophysiology of Amazonia*. Edited by R.E. Dickinson. John Wiley and Sons.

Nobre, C., 1988. Spring American Geophysical Union Meeting. Baltimore, May.

Ribeiro, M.N.G. and N.A. Villa-Nova. 1979. Estudos climaticos da Reserva Ducke, Manaus, Am. 3. Evapotranspiração. *Acta Amazônica*. 9, 305-309.

Reifsnyder, R., 1987. Comments on Micrometeorology of an Amazonian Rain Forest. In: *The Geophysiology of Amazônia*. Edited by R.E. Dickinson. John Wiley and Sons.

Repetto, R. 1988. *The forest for the trees? Government policies and the misuse of forest resources*. Washington, D.C.: World Resources Institute.

Salati, E., 1985. The climatology and hydrology of Amazonia, In: *Amazonia*. Edited by G.T. Prance. Oxford: Pergammon.

Salati, E. and J. Marques., 1984a. Climatology of the Amazon region. In: *The Amazon:Limnology and landscape ecology of a mighty tropical river and its basin*. Edited by H. Sioli. The Netherlands: W. Junk, Dordrecht.

Salati, E. and P.B. Vose. 1984b. Amazon basin: A system in equilibrium, *Science* 225, 129-138.

Salati, E., A. Dall'Olio, E. Matsui, and J.R. Gat. 1979. Recycling of water in the Amazon basin: An isotopic study. *Water Resource. Res.* 15, 1250-1258.

Setzer, A. W., M.C. Pereira, A.C. Pereira Junior and S.A.O. Aleida. 1988. *Progress Report of the IBDF-INPE "SEQUE" project 1987.* Instituto de Pesquisas Espaciais. May 1988. INPE-45-34- RPE/565.

Shuttleworth, W.J., J.H.C. Gash, C.R. Lloyd, C.J. Moore, J. Roberts, A.O. Marques Filho, G. Fish, V.P. Silva Filho, M.N.G. Ribeiro, L.C.B. Molion, C.A. Nobre, L.D.A. Sá, O.M.R. Cabral, S.R. Patel, and J.C. Moraes. 1984a. Observation of radiation change above and below Amazon forest. *Quarterly Journal of the Royal Meteorological Society.* 110: 1163-1169.

_____ 1984b. Eddy correlation measurements of energy partition of Amazonian forest. *Quarterly Journal of the Royal Meteorological Society.* 110: 1143-1162.

_____ 1985. Daily variations of temperature and humidity within and above Amazonian Forest. *Weather* 40, 102-108.

10

Terrestrial Impacts in Mexico and Central America

James D. Nations

In 1592, a group of Spanish friars led by Bishop Diego de Landa gathered every sacred book that remained in Yucatan from the Classic and Postclassic Mayan civilization — a civilization that had flourished in Mexico and Central America for a thousand years. They declared the books works of the devil and placed them in a pile at the foot of a giant ceiba tree in the village of Mani, then set them on fire.

Years later, the Spaniards wrote that they were amazed when the Mayan priests who were forced to watch the event gnashed their teeth and pulled out their hair in anguish. The Maya knew that the books the Spaniards were sending up in smoke held the details of ten centuries of research and experience on astronomy, crop production, water control, mathematics, and wildlife management.

The only Mayan codices that survived were the three or four that had earlier been sent back to Europe as curiosities. Those curiosities are now prized museum pieces, and the scholars who study them get tantalizing clues to what the world lost in the bishop's bonfire in 1562.

Today, more than 400 years after the Mayan codices were burned in Yucatan, we are witnessing an analogous event taking place on a much larger scale and with far more serious consequences. This event is the destruction of the world's tropical forests, each plant and animal species a page in a priceless book we can never recreate if it is destroyed.

As conservationists, biologists, foresters, and government officials, our primary role is to put out the fires that are destroying the forest's genetic heritage and its unfulfilled future. To do so, we must understand what is happening and why.

How Serious a Problem?

The majority of conservation biologists will tell you that we are in the midst of a species extinction that compares with the massive dyings of the geological past (Wolf 1987). The difference is that, today, this extinction is not caused by dust clouds or climate changes, but by human beings. The primary cause of this massive eradication of species can be defined in one phrase — loss of habitat. In turn, that phrase can be narrowed down to one word, deforestation. In Latin America, the major cause of this deforestation is the conversion of tropical forests to pasture.

The reason this destruction is so serious is simple: tropical forests are the world's largest depositories of plant and animal species. They are home to at least one-half of all species on earth. The percentage may be even higher, for we continue to expand the number of discovered tropical species. Entomologist Terry Erwin, of the Smithsonian Institution in Washington, D.C., is carrying out research in Peru and Panama which indicates that as many as 30 million species of insects may live in tropical forests, mostly in the forest canopy (Erwin 1988).

The ironic thing about tropical deforestation is that we know so little about what we are destroying. The vast majority of tropical species have never been examined by scientists, much less analyzed for their potential benefit to human beings.

Our lack of information extends even to the rate of tropical forest destruction for Latin America and for the world at large. The best estimates indicate that, around the globe, human activities eliminate at least 100,000 square kilometers and degrade another 100,000 square kilometers of tropical forest each year (Melillo et al. 1985, Myers 1987, Myers 1988). Latin America is the most critically threatened tropical forest region in the world. There, human activities eradicate some 28,500 square kilometers of tropical forest every year (Melillo et al. 1985). A recent Brazilian study indicates that human activities have eliminated more than 200,000 square kilometers of tropical forest in the Amazon, 40,000 square kilometers since 1987 alone (INPA 1988, cited in Hecht and Schwartzman 1988).

Nowhere in Latin America is the problem of deforestation more evident than in Mexico and Central America. Two-thirds of the region's original tropical forest have already been eradicated, and another 4,000 square kilometers are cleared and burned each year. At current rates of clearing, much of the final third will fall during the next two decades, leaving forest remnants only in national parks and reserves. In Mexico and Central America, as well as in the Amazon, the driving force behind this destruction is cattle ranching (Nations and Komer 1983, Leonard 1988, Schmink 1987, Toledo 1988).

Ominously, the rate of forest clearing has increased during every decade since 1950 and shows no signs of slowing (Lanly et al. 1981). Nicaragua lost more than 1,000 square kilometers of its broad-leaved and coniferous forest each year during the 1970s and early 1980s. In Honduras and Guatemala, human activities destroy at least 900 square kilometers of forest each year. Panama annually loses 650 square kilometers and Costa Rica, 500 square kilometers. Only Belize, with its small population and low agricultural activity, has been spared this rapid destruction. Until recently, it lost only 90 square kilometers of forest per year. But Belize has opened up its forested countryside to 10,000 Salvadoran refugees, 6,000 Guatemalans, and an unknown number of Hondurans, most of whom are now engaged in slash-and-burn farming and cattle ranching. Belizean forests are falling more rapidly than ever (Nations and Komer 1983).

In El Salvador, forests are already a matter of history. The tropical forests that once covered more than 90 % of the country have been cleared for export crops, subsistence farms, pastures, and charcoal production, leaving one 20 square kilometer plot of cloud forest as the only relatively undegraded tract of forest in the country (Daugherty 1982). At least half of the territory of the State of Chiapas, Mexico has been transformed for agriculture, predominately for cattle ranching (Toledo 1988).

Patterns of Deforestation

Because the forests of Central America's western, Pacific plains were cleared long ago for export crops and subsistence agriculture, recent deforestation has been most severe in the lowland tropical moist forests of the Atlantic, or Caribbean, side of Central America. More than half of these forests have now been cleared and burned, mostly during the past 25 years.

In these lowland forests, deforestation usually follows a three-stage pattern. First, bulldozers clear new roads through the forest to take out timber, explore for oil, or establish military control in areas inhabited only by indigenous families. Down these new corridors come landless farm families from other regions of the country or sometimes from other countries. They clear the forest to plant subsistence crops such as maize, manioc, and rice, and cash crops such as coffee, chiles, and bananas (Sader and Joyce 1988).

Some of these pioneer farm families serve as professional deforesters for the benefit of those who follow behind. After one to three years of harvests, weeds, insects, and declining soil fertility reduce agricultural productivity. The farm families are prompted to clear additional forest land. But instead of allowing their harvested plots to revert to forest, they proved land" to cattlemen who follow in their wake, buying up the small plots to combine them into ranches to raise beef cattle or speculate in land.

Deforestation and Cattle

Land cleared from tropical forests will produce reasonable beef yields for an average of 7 to 10 years before erosion, weeds, and loss of fertility prompt the cattlemen to search for new pastures. In some places, cattlemen simply abandon the worn-out pastures and move elsewhere, much as geographer Susanna Hecht found that up to 80% of pasturelands cleared from tropical forest have been abandoned in some regions of the Brazilian Amazon (Hecht 1985).

In Mexico and Central America, cattlemen usually maintain the old pastures to keep title to the land. The land, not profits from beef production is what draws many of them into cattle ranching in the first place. But the yields on these degraded pastures plummet as erosion and nutrient-leaching take their toll.

Deforestation in Central America results from a series of interconnected trends in agriculture, land use, land speculation, and development policy. But if there is a symbol to point to, it probably has four legs and hooves. Joseph Tosi's charge has yet to be refuted: "The innocent-looking beef cow is at the center of a destructive ecologic cycle that is strangling Central America" (cited in Parsons 1988).

Urged on by United States beef imports, by financial incentives, and land speculation, cattlemen have pushed livestock production into the tropical forests of Mexico and Central America at an unrelenting pace. In human terms, as economist Robert Williams has written, "Life on the edge of the peasant system now consists of being chased toward an ever-vanishing frontier" (Williams 1986:117).

During the past 30 years, the transformation of tropical forest to pastureland for beef cattle has been the single most important cause of natural resource destruction in Central America. Livestock production consumes two-thirds of the agricultural land in Central America (Parsons 1976). In Costa Rica, where 71% of all new agricultural land is immediately devoted to pasture, ecologist Joseph Tosi notes that rapid deforestation stems not from the expansion of farmland, but from forest cleared for cattle production (Tosi 1972).

In the Selva Lacandona of Chiapas, Mexico, cattle ranchers burn forest to fulfill an unspoken national strategy that divides the nation into two distinct economic zones. In the north, cattlemen produce cattle for export to the lucrative beef import market of the United States. In the tropical lowlands of Veracruz, Tabasco, and Chiapas, small-scale cattlemen and peasant communities grow beef and corn for consumption in Mexico City and Villahermosa (Gonzales Pacheco 1983).

As recently as 1981, the Mexican press still carried stories saying that the selva Lacandona was being sacrificed to feed the nation's growing population and to achieve self-sufficiency in basic grains. But a 1981 study by Mexican anthropologist Rodolfo Lobato indicated that — although one-third of the Selva Lacandona has been destroyed — 80% of the cleared area was dedicated to cattle pasture (Lobato 1981).

The tropical forests of Mexico and Central America are not being sacrificed to grow food for the region's expanding populations. They are being destroyed, largely by cattle ranching, to produce profits and land titles for a small percentage of the region's citizens and to produce hamburgers and steak dinners for the urban elite in Mexico and Central America and the United States. There are few identifiable villains in this destruction because it is not a conspiracy but a complex process that revolves around foreign markets, financial incentives, land speculation, population growth, and unequal access to land and natural resources.

Identifying the victims of this destruction is much simpler. Among them are the peasant colonists who spend their lives clearing forest for cattlemen and the indigenous families who watch their forest home disappear into the smoke of burning pasture fires.

Researchers Christopher Uhl and Robert Buschbacher have described how the interactions of burning beef cattle pasture and selective logging can lead to uncontrolled forest fires in uncleared tropical forest. Logging roads and skidways cut through the forest to extract commercial hardwoods also open up corridors that are followed by fires from nearby pasture burns (Uhl and Buschbacher 1985). This pattern may have reached its peak in Central America during 1987 in Guatemala, where 1,450 square kilometers of the Petén tropical forest burned because of this "disturbing synergism" between logging and pasture fires (Billy 1987).

Despite the ravages that beef cattle production enacts on tropical forests and human populations, some governments and banks continue to promote its expansion. In 1984, the National Bipartisan Commission on Central America, headed by Henry Kissinger, pointed to the economic success of beef cattle production and recommended that the region's beef exports be expanded to help alleviate the social and economic crisis (Williams 1986). More recently, the government of Costa Rica announced US $10.8 million in subsidized loans to cattle ranchers as part of a two-year strategy, "to maintain normal exports to the United States and adequately supply its domestic market" (USDA 1988:2).

In reality, the conversion of tropical forests to pasturelands can eliminate the potential for sustainable economic development. In the tropical forest of the Guatemala Petén, for example, cattle pastures are gradually replacing a lucrative industry based on the extraction of renewable natural resources. Each year, Guatemalans harvest and sell US$4 million of Chamadorea palm leaves (*xate*), allspice, and *chicle* gum from the natural tropical forest, without destroying the resources. Conversion of the Petén tropical forest to pasture land destroys this lucrative, sustainable activity for the benefit of a handful of individuals.

If we define sustainable development as the process of generating economic and social benefits without depleting the natural resources those benefits are based on, you do not have to be an economist to realize that cattle production is not sustainable use of tropical soils, and not sustainable use of tropical forests.

Consequences

Loss of Biological Diversity

Don't let anyone tell you that it doesn't matter — that tropical forests have not provided important species in the past, or that we already have all the species we need from them. When we eat rice, chocolate, bananas, pineapples, or avocados, we are eating crops that originated in tropical forests. Without the tropical forests of Latin America, the Swiss would have no chocolate, the French would have no vanilla, and the Italians would have no tomato sauce. Tropical forests protect the germplasm for these crops' wild ancestors, and plant breeders use that wild germplasm to "top off" these crops to make them more productive or resistant to diseases (Iltis 1988).

In Mexico, researchers discovered a wild relative of corn that is resistant to seven major plant diseases. The world-wide benefits of that discovery may eventually be measured in billions of dollars a year (Iltis 1988). The value of all types of wild germplasm to agriculture in the United States is said to reach 700 million dollars each year.

We need tropical forests to sustain the productivity of modern agriculturè, and we need tropical forests to develop new crops to sustain the human food supply. New tropical forest plants do get introduced. A century ago, bananas were considered an exotic food in the western world. When they were introduced into the United States a hundred years ago, they were sold individually wrapped and cost two dollars each.

Twenty years ago, the average supermarket in the United States carried 65 kinds of fruits and vegetables. Today, many of them have at least 140 species of fruits and vegetables, and some of them have 250. One supermarket in Florida carries 400 different fruits and vegetables during the course of the year. Most of these new products came from the tropics; most of them are plants from the tropical forest (Plotkin 1988).

We have not even mentioned tropical forests as a source of new drugs and medicines. Seventy percent of the plants known to have anti-cancer properties come from tropical forests. Most of them were introduced to us by traditional peoples who lived in the tropical forest. According to the World Health Organization, 80% of the world's women, men, and children rely on traditional medicines for their primary health care, and 85% of these traditional medicines involve plant extracts, many of them originally from tropical forests (Farnsworth 1988). As the home of at least half of all the species on earth, tropical forests are the primary source of new species of use to human beings.

As well, Latin America's tropical forests are the winter home for dozens of kinds of birds that migrate south every year from the United States and Canada. Many of the birds that North Americans feed as back-yard residents — warblers, tanagers, thrushes, and orioles — spend much of each year in the tropical forests of Mexico and Central America. Of the 650 species of birds that breed in the United States, more than one-third pass their winters in the Latin American tropics (Steinhart 1984).

In places where pastureland replaces traditional tropical forest people and their agriculture, we also lose valuable land, varieties of food crops, most of them selected for their particular environment over hundreds of years of trial and error. Some researchers emphasize that maintenance of traditional agroecosystems is the only sensible strategy to preserve in situ crop germplasm (Altieri and Merrick 1988, Oldfield and Alcorn 1987). When cattle pastures replace the agroecosystems of traditional farmers, families lose the subsistence base for their society; the world loses the genetic variation of their food crops and the wild edible, medicinal, or industrially important plant species that go with them (Oldfield and Alcorn 1987).

Loss of Environmental Services

Geographer James J. Parsons reports that 80% of the soils of the humid tropics of the New World are acid and infertile (1988). Yet, some un-suspecting politicians continue to see the lowland tropical forest as the answer to their agricultural problems, mistaking the lush vegetation of the tropical forest as an indication of fertile soils and high crop potential. In reality, instead of absorbing nutrients from the soil, these forests live off their own debris, rapidly recycling nutrients that fall to the forest floor. Tropical forests are wearing almost everything they own. Ninety percent of

TABLE 10.1 Impact transmission mechanism for deforestation

Conversion of tropical forest to pasture causes
  loss in species diversity, which
    reduces genetic variability, which can lead to
      costly disease and insect outbreaks with reductions in land productivity
      lost abilities to develop new products
  erosion, which impacts on
    land values
    agricultural productivity
    livestock productivity
    forestry productivity
    water quality, which impacts on
      agricultural productivity
  sedimentation rates, which impact on
    hydroelectric power production
    recreation potential of bodies of water
  water quality impacts on
    health measured in higher health costs
    education and technology transfer, which can lead to
      use of better production techniques which impact land use productivity
    aesthetics, which determine
      recreation potential of body of water
    fishery productivity
  occurrence of floods, which cause
    loss of property and lives
  loss of aesthetic values, which affect
    real estate value
    tourism income
  climate changes, which affect
    agricultural productivity
    losses in biological diversity

After Rose 1988

the forest's nutrients are locked up in the vegetation. Clear and burn the forest and you have fertile soil only until the ash washes away with the rain. The nutrients are rapidly leached from the soil by continuously high temperatures and high rainfall (Parsons 1988).

Converting tropical forests to pasturelands also destroys the indirect benefits these forests provide (Table 10.1). Undisturbed tropical forests serve as a giant sponge, breaking the force of torrential tropical rains and allowing water to percolate slowly into the thin tropical soils. They absorb and then recycle the water that falls on them. Gradually, the forest releases this captured water into streams and rivers for the benefit of human beings and wildlife that live downstream (Myers 1988). When tropical forests are cleared, however, precipitation rushes off sloped land and causes downstream flooding and soil erosion. Erosion from bare soil can be 45 times higher than that from primary tropical forest (Myers 1988). Downstream, that lost topsoil becomes silt that can damage crops, wipe out fish populations, and have serious repercussions on people who live from farming or fishing. On a regional level, siltation caused by deforestation can cut the lifespan of hydroelectric dams in half by silting in the reservoirs that provide the water used to generate electricity.

How much deforestation and pastureland contribute to downstream flooding is a point of controversy. Some researchers suggest that deforestation intensifies rather than causes downstream flooding through declines in water infiltration, decreases of the soil's water storage capacity, and increases in water runoff. Obviously, the correlation between deforestation and downstream flooding depends on topography, geology, and soil types (Myers 1988; Hamilton and King 1983; Williams and Hamilton 1982).

The conversion of tropical forest to pasture may also lead to local and regional climatic changes (see Salati, this volume). Locally, deforestation causes more extreme fluctuations in surface temperature, making cleared areas hotter by day and colder by night. More seriously, forest clearing can also reduce regional precipitation. Studies in Panama and in the Brazilian Amazon show that almost half the rain that falls on a lowland tropical forest is water recycled by the forest itself through evapo-transpiration. Forest vegetation breathes out water vapor equivalent to thousands of gallons per hectare per day. That evaporated water combines with water vapor from the oceans to create rain. When the forest is cleared, this vast recycling system is destroyed, and regional rainfall may decline by as much as one-third of an inch every year, markedly altering regional climate (Salati et al. 1978). In central Panama, deforestation has caused a 17-inch drop in rainfall during the past 50 years. Because less water is rising into the air as vapor, less is returning to the land in the form of rain (Salati and Vose 1984).

Tropical forest destruction also adds to threats to the sustainability of human life on the planet. It is now certain that the level of carbon dioxide in the earth's atmosphere is increasing. A range of researchers claim that tropical deforestation carries part of the blame for this increase, because burning tropical forests, like burning fossil fuels, adds carbon dioxide to the atmosphere. Along with other gases, including methane from rice paddies, termites, and cattle, this carbon dioxide absorbs heat that would normally bounce back into space, and warms the surface of the earth in a process that meteorologists call "the greenhouse effect."

The serious consequences of the conversion of tropical forest to pasture, combined with Daniel Janzen's experiment in restoring dry tropical forest in Costa Rica, have people asking if the same can be done for humid tropical forest (Janzen 1988). The answer, in brief, is no, unless you are willing to wait 400 years. The humid tropical forest creates its own environment, and once cleared it does not easily re-establish itself (Parsons 1988:42). As Mexican researcher Arturo Gomez-Pompa and his colleagues stated almost two decades ago, clearing large patches of tropical forest almost precludes the restoration of tropical forests on that site again (Gomez-Pompa et al. 1972). More recently, Christopher Uhl has told us why tropical forests do not recolonize large areas cleared for pasture. When large sections of forest are transformed into pastureland, few seeds of forest trees are dispersed into the cleared area. Most seeds that do arrive are killed or eaten by predators, and most of the few seeds that do survive and germinate eventually die from the pasture's harsh environmental conditions (Uhl 1988).

Solutions

The long-term solutions to the problem of deforestation for pastureland in Mexico and Central America are not secrets. Land reform, a halt to subsidized credit for the conversion of forest and change laws that promote forest conservation rather than destruction would all be positive steps. But we will not see these solutions carried out until the citizens of both the developed world and the tropical world realize that it is in their own best interest to transform these potential solutions into realities.

Meanwhile, we are obligated to work on economic, utilitarian solutions to the problem, to educate politicians and financial decision makers, to demonstrate better uses of the living resources of tropical forests, and to remind the public of the unfulfilled potential of the genetic books the tropical forest holds — new food crops, new medicines, and new industrial products from germplasm still undiscovered. Most important, we must continue to protect the pages of the genetic books of the tropical forest from those who seek to burn them until the day when we can all sit down to decipher them together.

References Cited

Altieri, M. A. and L. C. Merrick. 1988. Agroecology and in situ conservation of native crop diversity in the third world. In: *Biodiversity*. Edited by E.O.

Wilson and F. M. Peter. Washington, D. C.: National Academy of Sciences Press.

Billy, S. 1987. *Reconocimientos aereos de las rozas (tala y quema de arboles) e incendios forestales arriba del paralelo 17° 10'*. Comisión Nacional del Medio Ambiente, Guatemala, Guatemala.

Daugherty, H. E. 1982. *The Conflict between accelerating economic demands and regional ecologic stability in coastal El Salvador*. Department of Geography and Institute of Ecology at the University of Georgia.

Erwin, T. L. 1988. The tropical forest canopy: The heart of biotic diversity. In: *Biodiversity*. Edited by E.O. Wilson and F. M. Peter. Washington, C. D.: National Academy of Sciences Press.

Farnsworth, N. R. 1988. Screening plants for new medicines. In: *Biodiversity*. Edited by E.O. Wilson and F. M. Peter. Washington, D.C.: National Academy of Sciences Press.

Gomez-Pompa, A., C. Vazquez, and S. Guevara. 1972. The tropical rain forest: A non-renewable resource. *Science* 177:762-765.

Gonzalez Pacheco, C. 1983. *Capital extranjero en la selva de Chiapas 1863-1982*. Instituto de Investigaciones Económicas, Universidad Nacional Autónoma de Mexico, Mexico, D.F.

Hamilton, L.S. and P.M. King. 1983 *Tropical forested watersheds: Hydrologic and soil response to major uses or conversions*. Boulder, Co. Westview Press.

Hecht, S. B. 1985. Environment, development and politics: Capital accumulation and the livestock sector in eastern Amazonia. *World Development* 13(6): 663-684.

Hecht, S. B. and S. Schwartzman. 1988. The good, the bad, and the ugly: Extraction, colonist agriculture and livestock in comparative economic perspective. Unpublished manuscript, Graduate School of Architecture and Urban Planning, University of California, Los Angeles, California.

Iltis, H. H. 1988. Serendipity in the exploration of biodiversity: What good are weedy tomatoes? In: *Biodiversity*. Edited by E.O. Wilson and F. M. Peter. Washington, D.C.: National Academy of Sciences Press.

Janzen, D. H. 1988. Tropical dry forests: The most endangered major tropical ecosystem. In: Biodiversity. Edited by E. O. Wilson and F. M. Peter. Washington, D.C.: National Academy of Sciences.

Lanly, J. P. et al. 1981. *Los recursos forestales de la América tropical*. Rome: United National Food and Agriculture Organization.

Leonard, H. J. 1987. *Natural resources and economic development in Central America: A regional environmental profile*. New Brunswick, New Jersey: International Institute for Environment and Development, Transaction Books. .

Lobato Gonzales, R. 1981. La reserva de la biosfera Montes Azules: Estado actual y perspectivas. In: *Alternativas para el uso del suelo en areas forestales del tropico humedo.* Publicación Especial No. 27, Estudios del Acuerdo sobre Planificación y Uso de Recursos Forestales Tropicales, Mexico-Alemania. Instituto Nacional de Investigaciones Forestales, Mexico, D.F.

Melillo, J.M., C.A. Palm, R.A. Houghton, G.M. Woodwell, and N. Myers. 1985. A comparison of recent estimates of disturbance in tropical forests. *Environmental Conservation* 12:37-40.

Myers, N. 1987. Tropical deforestation and remote sensing. *Forest Ecology and Management* 23:215-225.

_____ 1988. Tropical forests: Much more than stocks of wood. *Journal of Tropical Ecology* 4:209-221.

Nations, J. D. and D. I. Komer. 1983. Central America's tropical rainforests: Positive Steps for Survival. *Ambio* 12(5):232-238.

Oldfield, M. L. and J. B. Alcorn. 1987. Conservation of Traditional Agroecosystems. *BioScience* 37(3):199-208.

Parsons, James J. 1976. Forest to pasture: Development or destruction? *Revista de Biologia Tropical* 24 (Supl.1):121-138.

_____ 1988. The scourge of cows. *Whole Earth Review*, Spring 1988: 40-47.

Plotkin, M. J. 1988. The outlook for new agricultural and industrial products from the tropics. In: *Biodiversity.* Edited by E.O. Wilson and F. M. Peters. Washington, D. C.: National Academy of Sciences Press.

Rose, D. 1988. Economic assessment of biodiversity and tropical forests. background paper for guatemala biodiversity and tropical forest assessment project, Guatemala, Guatemala.

Sader, S. A. and A. T. Joyce. 1988. Deforestation rates and trends in Costa Rica 1940 to 1983. *Biotropica* 20(1):11-19.

Salati, E., J. Marques, and L.C.B. Molion. 1978. Origen e distribucion das chuvas na Amazonia. *Interciencia* 3:200-205.

Salati, E. and P.B. Vose. 1984. Amazon basin: A system in equilibrium. *Science* 225:129-138.

Schmink, M. 1987. The rationality of forest destruction. In: *Management of the forests of tropical America: Prospects and technologies.* Edited by Julio C. Figueroa Colon. Institute of Tropical Forestry, Southern Forest Experiment Station, United States Department of Agriculture Forest Service.

Steinhart, P. 1984. Trouble in the tropics. *National Wildlife* 22(1). Washington, D.C.: National Wildlife Federation.

Toledo, V. M. 1988. La guerra de las reses: Los impactos ecológicos de la ganaderia bovina en Mexico. In: *Medio Ambiente y Desarrollo en Mexico.* Edited by E. Leff. Mexico, D.F.

Tosi, J. 1972. *Los Recursos Forestales de Costa Rica.* Centro Cientifico Tropical, San José, Costa Rica.

Uhl, C. 1988. Restoration of degraded lands in the Amazon basin. In: *Biodiversity.* Edited by E. O. Wilson and F.M. Peter. Washington, D.C.: National Academy of Sciences.

Uhl, C. and R. Buschbacher. 1985. A disturbing synergism between cattle ranch burning practices and selective tree harvesting in the eastern Amazon. *BioTropica* 17(5):265-268.

United States Department of Agriculture. 1988. Costa Rica offers subsidized credit for beef cattle. World Production and Trade, Weekly Roundup WR 22-88, June 2, 1988. Foreign Agricultural Service. Washington, D.C.: United States Department of Agriculture.

Williams, R. G. 1986. *Export agriculture and the crisis in Central America.* Chapel Hill, North Carolina: University of North Carolina Press.

Williams, J. and L.S. Hamilton. 1982. *Watershed forest influences in the tropics and subtropics: A selected, annotated bibliography.* Honolulu, Hawaii: Environment and Policy Institute, The East-West Center,

Wolf, E. C. 1987. On the brink of extinction: Conserving the diversity of life. Worldwatch Paper 78. Washington, D.C.: Worldwatch Institute.

PART FOUR
SOCIAL IMPACTS

The extensive climatic, ecological, and bio-economic disruptions described in the preceding chapters have led to unanticipated social change. Restrepo suggests that the ecosystem of the tropics in Mexico is complex and the carrying capacity for humans is limited. Among the Quijos Indians, in the Equadorian Amazon, MacDonald discovers that the transformation of tropical forest to pastures has accelerated social evolution. Struggling to prevent destruction of their forest and culture, Indians initially reacted individualistically and defensively. Their communal organizations began to crack under the stress of individuals attracted by short-term, but ecologically disastrous opportunities. Assisted by dynamic leadership and external, non-governmental organizations, such as Cultural Survival Inc., the endangered groups began to shift from reaction to planning. Previously politically disarticulated communities began to link together and form regional federations. Comparable social transformations can be witnessed among the Mountain Zapotec Indians of southeastern Mexico (Chapters 21 and 22) and the Kuna in Panama.

Is social evolution creating the antidote to environmental threats posed by tropical deforestation, including its conversion to pasture? Or is the velocity of economic exploitation of forest and forest peoples so rapid that social institutions cannot reorganize fast enough to counteract irreversible losses of cultural and biological diversity?

Barkin opts for the latter, arguing for a direct linkage between pasture conversion and a decline in the economic status of forest peoples. Specifically, he focuses on the transformation of formerly self-sustaining, regional economies to ones heavily reliant on national economic systems. Native peoples enter this game with a permanent handicap. Regional development plans benefit the elites who are charged with implementing the programs. Deforestation simultaneously limits the capabilities of indigenous peoples to establish agricultural practices for sustainable grazing systems and shackles them to the lower rungs of the national economic ladder.

Allegretti is less pessimistic. She recognizes that many of the scientific and management techniques being proposed to limit deforestation are untested. Moreover, she is aware that the proposed "extractive" solution exemplified by Brazilian rubber tappers may be inapplicable in the long term and in other regions. She focuses on strategies for a regional model of sustainable development that might reconcile people's needs to the fragility of their habitat.

— *Theodore E. Downing*

11

Eating from the Tropics or Destroying It?

Ivan Restrepo

Every six years, during the presidential campaign, the Mexicans are reminded of the importance of their tropical areas. An example. During the campaign of Lic. Jose Lopez Portillo, he clearly expressed his position in that matter: " either we eat from the tropics or we eat up the tropics," he said in the tropical state of Tabasco. With this phrase, the President-elect joined those of us who have denounced the rapid, systematic destruction of the forest zones by traditional policies. In Latin America, traditional policies favor hurriedly and uncritically populating wealthy expanses of tropical zones into the national economy in hopes of recording short-term gains.

The old argument that some used to make is too simple: in the countryside great demographic pressures exist on the land, which prevents the full and rational use of labor and generates serious conflicts in the densely populated areas, above all in central and northern Mexico. In addition, the possibilities of meeting the food demands of campesinos with lands currently incorporated in production are ever more limited, and cannot be done without sacrificing the level of productivity and income of agriculture. Expanding the agricultural frontier to the humid tropics would be one of the most feasible alternatives for reducing the pressure from those asking for land, for generating a considerable part of agricultural and raw material production that the country requires, and giving employment to a very important number of campesinos families. It is calculated that considerable areas exist suitable for being opened to cultivation in Veracruz, Campeche, Yucatan, Chiapas, and Quintana Roo. The most optimistic insist that there are some 10 million hectares.

The uneasiness that for years has been expressed by various groups about the fate of the tropics are, therefore, more than justified, and every day less bound to certain strictly conservationist policies. It is a multi-faceted problem that cannot be treated with the lightness and irresponsibility of those whose thinking is limited to the immediate future. In fact, the tropics are the most complex and least studied ecosystem on earth. The policies traditionally designed for its development have been inspired by those used in temperate areas, which are adapted to totally different ecosystems. These have led to the total destruction of resources or the deficient use of their productive potential. For these reasons, specific projects and programs thus inspired resulted in the hoped for economic and social development. Neither have achived natural resource conservation, protecting the patrimony of present and future generations. It is a priority to seriously evaluate the policies adapted for such a promising region of the country and to evaluate their effects. We must design strategies that will allow the incorporation of such areas into the productive process of the country, and which will achieve both the rational utilization of resources and less environmental damage.

No studies calculate the capacity of absorption of tropical lands with certainty, or their most appropriate development, it is undeniable that the most important factor in the governmental action is the reduction of the high indices of unemployment, campesino underemployment, and a substantial increase in the productive capacity of Mexican agriculture. But a global plan that will make it possible to contribute to the achievement of those objectives is still lacking. This explains, in part, the absence of interdisciplinary research that should be the basis for the best alternatives for use and conservation of the resources that exist there. And so, as a result, many of the development systems have been transplanted from highly industrialized countries, but with ecological problems and economic interests very different from those of our areas of the southeast. As a result, the tropics are becoming a source of raw materials of the industrialized countries that have no interest in making a rational use of natural resources or they are under the control of a few large landholders.

A large group of specialists received with alarm a proposal from the Mexican Secretariat of Agrarian Reform which is responsible for the management of tropical lands. The Secretariat wants to foster the production of foods on the millions of hectares in forest and fallow to overcome the grain deficits from which we are suffering today. The danger exists that instead of the tropics becoming productive, it will be destroyed on the basis of certain measures to develop and test it. This would cause the contrary effect: we would be eating up the tropics. Perhaps the quickness in enunciating global policies aimed at transforming the tropics lies in the belief, very common in our countries, that the exuberance of the forest covers up a potential unsuspected timber wealth and that on those lands any crop is advantageous.

The truth is that in the tropical forest, the climate and edaphic conditions greatly limit the use of the soil for agriculture and livestock, as proposed. The degradation of the physical properties of the soils after the felling of the forest, and the decrease in porosity and aeration caused by the trampling of cattle drastically reduced productivity. This explains in part why, so many projects have not been successful, and why they have been so costly.

In spite of a history of failure, the destruction seems to reflect quite a well-defined policy at the regional level, which will aggravate even more the problems of the population seeking to continue in the countryside and it will alter the ecological balance. And although the various government legislation talks of the need to manage the forests with wisdom (regeneration, rational and long-term development, etc.), no government allocates the funds or the personnel required to meet these goals.

There is one more fact that influences the process of destruction of the forest: the image that forest, as such, has no and that it is an enemy of agricultural expansion and human employment. In recent proposals for colonization programs fostered by the State, the previous studies made by different governments agree that it is possible to transform the forest into economic enclaves with sustained production. However, some evaluations show, for example, that the usable wood potential that does exist is only being minimally utilized. The rest is destroyed.

The response to government guidelines for preventing degradation, regenerating forest, and achieving long-term resource conservation usually consists of hiring of specialized staff (forestry technicians) who do not hamper but rather support the policies of destruction. Agencies concerned with conservation do not have capital or power to create industries that optimally use the forest, benefit non-traditional species, or make basic studies for the best use of resources. Their powers are minimal for influencing colonization plans based on agricultural-forestry projects linked to capabilities of the soils and the socio-economic conditions of the tropical zones.

This last point is of great importance because in the countries of the region that have unoccupied tropical areas there is evermore interest in colonization. It means putting people in this agricultural frontier who have not had land in the traditional areas of cultivation. Those who migrate thus transfer the cultural standards that have been inculcated in them in the Andean regions, in the altiplano or northern Mexico or in the mountains of Central America. In addition, they enter into serious conflicts with the inhabitants of the zones that they come to occupy. It suffices to cite the numerous cases of massacres in the name of civilization that have been committed against the indigenous groups of the Amazon Basin and whom some consider subjects that should be exterminated as harmful obstacles to progress and civilization.

Thus, clothing, housing, food and agricultural practices are transferred indiscriminately to an unknown environment and enter into conflict with the cultural and economic standards prevailing in the areas to be 'conquered' with unfavorable results for those who come there in search of a piece of land that will allow them an escape from the disadvantageous situation in which they find themselves and without producing the foods and raw materials that they and the rest of society require. Instead of prosperity, more misery is produced among the traditional inhabitants of the tropics and among the new occupants; and in passing they destroy incalculable wealth.

This is what has happened in Mexico. The occupation of the Southeast has come about by overcoming numerous obstacles and at a high social and economic cost. In view of the purported need to expand the agricultural frontiers, policies encouraged not just at increasing agricultural activity but also "holding tank" for landless campesinos from the center and north of the country. At other times, demographic pressures from poor areas which border the tropics, slowly pushed those living there to penetrate it. On occassions, the forest is used for extraction of some useful wood species. Other times the forest is felled through slash-and-burn or with modern machinery; the lands thus opened up later are planted with corn or sugar cane or are used for pastures.

Unfortunately, the colonization process generally results to the repetition of traditional crops without making studies to allow the diversified use of those zones; the results in production have been discouraging. In the case of corn, not only are yields low, but often its cultivation must be abandoned in the short term because the land does not possess the hoped-for fertility and there is no way to control the weeds. The lands that at first it was thought could be developed for corn end up as immense pastures, with low use and and limited possibilities of regeneration.

The mistake has been made of extending the problems and vices derived from the exploitation of the land on the altiplano and in temperate or semi-desert areas to the most important natural reserve of the country. We think that in some official sectors the idea of turning the tropics into a large grain center and source of land, food and employment for thousands of peasants who exist in highly populated regions is beginning to fade. The colonization process that left peasants with very diverse histories and cultures at the mercy of the jungle are being abandoned. We hope that no longer will the large and criminal clearings of timber be made to benefit contractors related to influential officials. Even occupying the several hundred thousand hectares of tropical forests that the country is holding in reserve with the most appropriate agricultural methods will only satisfy a small proportion of landless population's demands.

Translated by Deanna Hammond
Congressional Research Services

12

From Reaction to Planning: An Indigenous Response to Deforestation and Cattle Raising

Theodore MacDonald

As the 15th Century closed, Spanish sailors hauled the first Old World livestock over the gunwales of their galleons and sloshed the animals ashore in the Antilles. By 1503 breeding stocks were sufficiently so large that no further imports were necessary from Spain or the Canary Islands (West and Augelli 1976). Subsequently herded throughout the Americas, cattle altered every social and physical landscape they entered. While their impact has varied across time and space, some issues arise regularly. As early as 1520, Indians of the Valley of Mexico lodged formal protests when Spaniards allowed their herds to graze on Indians' agricultural lands (Gibson 1964). One group from Xochimilco was said to have constructed, in only twenty four hours, an entire community to demonstrate its presence when Spanish colonists tried to establish a cattle ranch (Ibid.). Nearly 500 years later, in late 1987, Quichua Indians from the Ecuadorian Amazon cleared forest and built new houses at the edge of a road within a few weeks after that road was cut through Ecuador's northern Amazonian forest, again to demonstrate possession and prevent colonization. The Quichua's actions, the subject of this paper, illustrate a persistent concern over access and use of land, and a new response as cattle raising expands beyond rangelands to rain forests.

Cattle in Tropical Forests

Felling tropical rain forests for pastures is relatively new. Yet, the social and ecological impact has been immediate, extensive, and dramatic. Attention and concern for the future of these neotropical woodlands and their indigenous inhabitants has prompted protective national and international legislation. A nearly continuous series of meetings, publications, research, and other efforts now seek to maintain biodiversity and promote sustainable development.

Concern is warranted. However, many lump the flora, fauna, and forest residents together as "endangered species" and consider them equally as objects for protection or preservation. For some of the smaller, isolated Indian communities protection is essential for their survival. But to extend that response to all Amazonian indigenous forest residents overlooks a critical distinction between science and history — while all species continuously evolve, people do so socially and politically as well as physically. Beginning in the 1960's most of the larger Amazonian Indian groups, and many of the smaller ones as well, accelerated their socio-political evolution. Linking disparate communities and isolated groups into regional and national ethnic federations, forest residents shifted from reaction to planning and enabled assistance to replace protection in many areas.

Focusing on the contemporary Amazon basin, this chapter chronicles and analyzes Ecuador's Quijos Quichua Indians' response to cattle and pastures, and considers the case's implications for the region's social and biophysical future. The recent changes in that response illustrate the relationship between the Indians' land use patterns and that group's empowerment through mobilization. This suggests that ethnic federations are, or can become social mechanisms for extending sustainable land use systems over a broad social and geographical landscape.

Indians and Resource Management

Most observers agree that rainforest Indians can manage their natural resources in a sophisticated and sustainable manner (Posey and Balée 1989; Irvine 1985, 1989). But to end on that point suggests that Indians can oversee their lands and natural resources in some timeless manner, and ignores the Indians' own recognition of a current political reality. Most, if not all Indians face an expanding colonist frontier, a market economy, and a shrinking natural resource base. This has either reduced or eliminated their ability to subsist solely through traditional economic systems. They are also aware that lands which are not put to visible use are perceived or labeled as "idle" and become coveted targets for alternative claimants.

This led many to accept the colonists' economy — cattle raising. But, by and large, most Amazonian Indians are not enthusiastic about cattle raising. They, especially the women who do most of the herding, generally dislike the size, smell and appearance of the animals. Beef cattle rarely contribute to household income or subsistence; they are market commodities which usually enter and leave communities on the hoof. Income from cattle raising barely allows small-holders to meet interest payments on cattle loans let alone generate any significant surplus; average holdings are about 5 to 15 head and the animals often suffer high rates of accidental mortality. In the absence of economic incentives, why raise cattle? Rainforest Indians generally clear forests for pasture in reaction to external pressures rather than through any desire to shift their economies.

These external pressures build either from colonization and similar demographic change or from the policies and practices of national and regional institutions. Any shift away from cattle raising will result from new interplay of these influences. Some development and environmental planners, by contrast, suggest a broader stimulus for change, pointing first to the recent surge of international interest and concern for both forests and native peoples, and then to the subsequent increase in economic support for related research and development. This view presumes local support for broad environmental problems. At present, there is clearly *some* convergence of interests between long-term forest residents and those involved in environment and development planning. There is also potential for some future alliances. But links are still largely indirect and alliances quite fragile.

Mobilization is another response to inevitable social and environmental change. Such adaptation does not require total social or economic restructuring. On the contrary, it allows Indians and similarly unified groups to plan slowly rather than react suddenly. Consequently, many now seek to control the use of their resources. Resource management permits a combination of traditional production systems and new technologies adopted to improve or expand those practices.

Several current initiatives illustrate efforts to maintain sustainable resource management in the face of a reduced resource base (Chapin and Breslin 1984, Chapin 1985; Macdonald 1986; Macdonald and Chernela in press; Schwartzman 1981; Schwartzman and Allegretti in press; Chernela 1987). Similar concerns and directions are reflected in much of the planning underway among other groups (CRIC 1986, Shuar Federation 1988, FOIN 1988, CONFENIAE 1986, UNI 1988). The development and environmental implications of this trend are obvious, but for the Indians the work extends beyond the physical environment. Genuine convergence of interests and collaboration requires greater understanding and acceptance of the forest residents' broad social and economic concerns.

Ethnic Federations

Brazilian rubber tappers have fought to protect the rain forest upon which their economy depends. The rubber tappers' achievements, however recent, fragile and racked by violence, rest on their response to external threats. Encroachment spurred mobilization and organization of previously isolated and independent household production units. In a similar manner but on a larger scale, Indian communities throughout the Amazon basin have organized into local and regional ethnic federations, national pan-tribal units, and, most recently, international organizations (Cultural Survival Quarterly 1984; Smith 1984, 1985).

This socio-political evolution has strong economic and environmental implications. Previously, many Indians and similar forest residents had few options other than acceptance, and often participation in the conversion of their forest to pasture. Now their representative organizations have enabled a more active response to encroaching frontiers. First and foremost, the organizations seek local control of land and its use. Secured land tenure permits continuity of traditional, sustainable land use systems; it also encourages experimentation with new forest management technologies. However, ethnic federations know that technology is not the solution to their problems. Broader perceptions, concerns and objectives underlie recent indigenous social evolution.

Most Amazonian Indians and their organizations recognize that their land and its resources — their present and future capital — are at risk. For them "fragile lands" connote a political as well as physical environment. So they are wary of any form of "development" or "conservation." For good historical reasons, they ask "for whom?"

Indians and their organizations are fully aware of the implications of the Declaration on Environmental Policy and Procedures, and Procedures Affecting Economic Development, which was signed by 10 bilateral and multilateral development banks in 1979. While the document makes strong statements in support of environmental issues, Article 5 recognizes the right of governments to determine priorities and forms of national development. Few Indians ever participated in the government planning which most affects them. Consequently, their primary concern is not just the complex management of their land and its resources, but permanent and secure access to them. Since their capital base stands greater risk of loss than does their understanding of resource management, land tenure is awarded more public attention than its management. Indians' environment, therefore, is as much political as biological.

An effective means to defend this broad environment has developed over the past two decades; in every Latin American country, Indians have begun to consolidate their communities into regional and national organizations, or ethnic federations. Smith (1985:17) writes that by contrast to many other sectors of a national society, ethnic federations:

regard ethnic issues as a primary factor in their discourse with the national society. Issues of land and ethnic identity coalesced the ethnic federation. In each case a particular group felt its collective land base threatened by both state policies of colonization and integration, and by the expanding market economy.

Most federations maintain three primary concerns: 1) the defense of their member communities' rights to land and resources; 2) the expansion and strengthening of their organizations; and 3) the maintenance of their unique ethnic identity. These are linked to a single theme — empowerment.

Empowerment allows ethnic federations to expand the national political arena by including themselves within it. The Kuna of Panama, the Shuar of Ecuador, and Indians of the Regional Indian Council of Cauca in Colombia are now recognized social and political forces, and have thus created niches for themselves within plural national societies. Recognizing that they face common challenges, some federations have begun to organize internationally (Smith 1984). In regions or countries where ethnic federations have grown to become social sectors, they are positioned as the vehicles to lead their member communities toward broad, long-range social and economic change. They thus become the logical institutional link for work with development and environmental agencies. Yet few connections have been made. Most national or international development and environmental agencies do not approach the broad political concerns of such groups. But by neglecting these priorities they preclude fruitful collaboration in planning and decision-making.

The organizations now recognize the need for such assistance. Most ethnic federations initially focused on organizing member communities into ethnic and pan-ethnic federations at a local and regional level. Mobilization was an essential first step toward empowerment. Now, however, many indigenous communities are asking "now that we are organized, what comes next?" Activities such as pursuing land claims and providing technical assistance which serves to secure land tenure, enhances the status of the ethnic federations to the Indian communities they represent. Such work — institution building — is an essential organizational advancement for ethnic federations. Moreover, as these organizations continue to grow and link with one another, ethnic federations will become an unparalleled mechanism for the extension of resource management technology in the Amazon basin.

A Case Study — The FOIN Land Tenure and Resource Management Project

About 45,000 Quijos Quichua Indians live in the Ecuadorian Amazon's Napo province. Here during the mid-1970's, prior to the formation of any regional ethnic federation, the author conducted anthropological research on the cultural impact of cattle raising (Macdonald 1979, 1981).

Since 1982, Cultural Survival and OXFAM-UK provided core economic support for Indians to develop the Federation of Indian Organizations of Napo (FOIN), an ethnic federation which incorporates the Indian populations in the region where the earlier research was conducted. Beginning in March 1988, FOIN initiated a broad, regional resource management program in collaboration with Cultural Survival. Observations over this period allow longitudinal comparison and analysis of the role of ethnic federations in the development of land use programs.

Pastures — The 1960's and 1970's

Beginning in the 1960's and increasing in the late 1970's and early 1980's, many of Ecuador's tropical forest Indians cleared sectors of forest and filled the gaps with pastures. The physical and economic transformation was largely a series of individual reactions to perceived threats to community lands. In the early 1960's, Ecuador, like many Latin American countries, passed a sweeping set of agrarian reform laws, declaring the need to create equitable land ownership and increase agricultural production. However, again as with other Latin American nations, Martz (1972:173) writes:

> The history of agrarian reform in Ecuador stood as one of effusive public pronouncements but limited accomplishments. It had done little for the vast majority of the rural populace, land tenure practices were not greatly changed and overall agricultural productivity had not grown significantly.

However, land reform legislation directly and indirectly spurred colonization from the densely populated Andean highlands into the Amazonian forest. The region experienced the nations' greatest population growth — 135% from 1962 to 1974, as opposed to 40% nationwide (Uquillas 1983). Indians closest to the expanding frontier, fearing total dispossession, reacted to the influx by trying to join its ranks. They too asked the national agrarian reform agency (IERAC) to demarcate and provide them with title to a 50-hectare plot — the standard household allocation. Although IERAC actually granted few titles to Indians, local perceptions of "property" nonetheless began to shift from rights of usufruct on communal land to private holdings. But with no government pressure to demonstrate possession through production, traditional land use persisted and overshadowed the new juridical perceptions of the landscape.

After 1972, however, the lines transecting the new "cadastral map" suddenly became sharper. In June of that year Ecuador began to pump oil out of Napo Province and quickly became the continent's second largest oil producer. At the same time, agricultural production fell steadily short of domestic needs. The amount of land under cultivation increased only by 4.3% from 1964-1968 (Banco de Fomento 1974). Between 1965 and 1973 real per capita agricultural output declined by 14% (Zuvekas 1976). Outlays for agricultural imports rose from 1.9 to 3 million dollars between 1970 and 1973. Thus, while oil profits raised capital reserves sharply during the first few years of production, the bulk of the population faced food shortages and rising inflation.

In part, the dilemma of decreased production reflected a rejection of the 1964 agrarian reform legislation. While land tenure was precarious, large land owners with property in non-export agriculture did not seek credit to increase production. With the oil boom the situation worsened; investment turned toward urban construction rather then food production. Consequently, in April 1973, the government junta approved new agrarian reform laws (Ecuador − Ministerio de Agricultura y Ganaderia 1974). These laws stressed production rather than land equity. To encourage investment for modernization and other aspects of production, laws regarding expropriation were sharply limited. Land owners were told that, by and large, only idle lands were subject to expropriation.

The Indians of Napo province quickly learned of the priorities established by the 1973 *Ley de Reforma Agraria*. IERAC officials informed those with land titles that their land was liable for expropriation if they failed to cultivate or otherwise improve one-half of their holdings within five years. Individuals hoping to obtain land title realized that visible use of their claims was also essential. However, for an Indian family, ten hectares in various phases of rotation, were adequate for their subsistence swidden horticulture. So the Indians had to "improve" a significant portion of a fifty hectare plot in order to either secure existing tenure or exercise any future claims.

IERAC officials recommended that land not used for subsistence plots be converted to pasture for cattle. At the same time, low-interest credit for cattle became readily available to property owners. From 1973 to 1974 credit designated for pastures rose by 48%, and most of that (78%) was awarded to small holders. In brief, by the mid-1970's Amazonian Indians had been told that visible land use was essential to retain tenure, were encouraged to place cattle on the land, and were provided with relatively easy access to credit.

Cattle in the Upper Napo

Considerable research, experimentation, and debate now focuses on the environmental impact of converting tropical rain forests to pastures; much of it is reviewed and updated throughout this volume. Moist tropical rainforest cattle raisers, including those of the Upper Napo, work far from research stations and without any technical assistance. Their practices will continue to outpace research. Most specialists, whatever their opinion on the technical feasibility of cattle raising, agree that the predominant methods are ecologically and economically unsound.

As such pastures are hacked into the physical landscape of the Upper Napo, cattle raising often reshapes the area's social and cultural life as well. Indigenous reactions to cattle production in Napo province have been generally individual, spontaneous and uncoordinated. The socio-cultural impact during the 1970's and early 1980's has been detailed elsewhere (Descola 1982, 1988; Macdonald 1979, 1983) and will be reviewed briefly here.

First, although few Indians obtained land titles during the 1970's, their expectations were that individuals rather than communities received titles more readily. In addition, credit was more often extended to individual property owners. In order to gain access to both, many Indians began to etch out and lay claim to parcels of land within their communities.

The shift from communal toward private land ownership, whether actual or anticipated, provoked previously unknown sorts of land disputes. In all communities, "community land" rarely connoted random or open access; rights of usufruct included nearly continuous individual or family access to certain plots and hunting trails. However regular was such use of communal land and resources, there was a clear distinction between use and ownership. There were also means for debating, if not resolving, land use disputes. But as Indians either obtained or anticipated private holdings, no social mechanisms existed to resolve the new disputes. For example, swidden plots had been generally irregular in form and variable in size; suddenly, agricultural land required sharp definition and boundaries. Changes of shape or expansion of plots often resulted in charges of encroachment. Such problems provoked prolonged conflicts and tensions in many communities.

Similarly, to accommodate cattle or simply to plan for their arrival, required considerable individual decision making and entrepreneurship — e.g. planning property boundaries, dealing with agrarian reform agents, obtaining credit. Aware that such actions would lead to prolonged disputes, claimants often bypassed traditional authority figures; this not only created conflict but eliminated a common means to resolve it.

Another common manner of coping with conflict within a community was temporary or permanent departure. During this time usufruct lands remained with the community. Privatization, however, allowed individuals to consider leaving and selling land. This threatened the communities' physical as well as social continuity.

Similarly, viewed from the outside, privatization reduced the perceived physical parameters of a "community". Borders which previously were understood to encompass large communal territories later enclosed only a cluster of private plots for agriculture and animal husbandry. Peripheral areas previously regarded as a group's exclusive hunting and fishing territory, were opened to wider access. Most noticeably, unclear inter-community boundaries produced disputes when local hunters charged that outsiders were trespassing on communal lands.

Cattle also complicated subsistence economic activities. They often wandered into and destroyed agricultural plots. Also, animals pastured on converted forest lands — undulated and cut by streams and ravines — required their owners' daily attention. Adding cattle raising to subsistence horticulture thus demanded new work schedules. With both cattle and subsistence plots to tend, total labor allocated to the family lands increased; socially cohesive communal labor decreased. Time available for subsistence hunting and fishing decreased. Since such work often required travel far from the local community, adding hunting and fishing to a schedule which included cattle tending was quite difficult, often impossible.

In brief, as of the mid-1970's, cattle and pastures indirectly removed several of the threads which formed the fabric of indigenous society in Napo province; the cloth was not unraveled but was becoming difficult to manage. Communities, or segments of them, tried to adapt as groups, but the emergence of a cattle-based economy was making it increasingly difficult. The situation changed, however, when Indians began to organize into ethnic federations.

Ethnic Federations in the Ecuadorian Oriente

Ethnic federations first appeared in the southern Oriente during the early 1960's. In response to an influx of colonists into the relatively fertile Upano Valley, the Shuar Indians, aided by several progressive Salesian missionaries, first linked dispersed households through a central settlement and local organization referred to as a *centro*, or center. Several centers then joined to form associations (*asociaciones*) and in 1964 the associations united to form the Shuar Federation (*Federación de Centros Shuar* 1976).

The Shuar Federation spurred the formation of similar organizations among Quichua Indians in Napo province; the first among these was the Federation of Indian Organizations of the Napo (FOIN). Unlike the Shuar Federation, FOIN did not enjoy either economic or institutional support from the area's missionaries. On the contrary, both Catholic (Josefine) and Fundamental Protestant missionaries openly and vocally opposed the organization, as did many local political authorities and merchants who dominated the strong patron-client ties which characterized the area. Land tenure in Napo was also more precarious. While the Shuar were relatively successful in obtaining title to community lands, the national agrarian reform agency, IERAC, was notoriously slow to provide title to Quichua Indians in Napo province, either as communities or as individuals.

However, during the late 1970's and early 1980's, a progressive national government created two agencies which, despite small staffs and limited funds, provided assistance to the Indian organizations and communities. These were the Office of Indian Affairs (*Oficina de Asuntos Indígenas*) and the Fund for Development of the Urban and Rural Marginal Populations (FODERUMA). FODERUMA, a sector of the Central Bank, provided low interest loans and other forms of development assistance. The Office of Indian Affairs worked closely with the organizations and helped many of them obtain essential, corporate status (*personería jurídica*). Equally important, this office was empowered to grant communal titles to Indian lands, and was able to do so for several communities in Napo province.

Consequently, during this time, relations with the government were relatively cordial; the Indians regarded both agencies as service organizations which supported and strengthened the federations. The Indian organizations, previously aided almost exclusively by international non-governmental organizations (NGO) support agencies, began to work more closely with government institutions. This increased and expanded their sources of support and it drew them more closely into the national political arena, increasing their visibility and status within the country.

Newly enacted conservation legislation also supported Indian interests. In 1981, the Ecuadorian congress passed a set of forestry laws — *Ley Forestal y de Conservacion de Areas Naturales y Vida Silvestre.* These laws established forest management as a national priority and encouraged the development of forestry programs, especially among small farmers. More important, they declared exempt from the laws of agrarian reform protective forests, lands in permanent use for forest resources and those with established plans for reforestation. The new forestry legislation allowed land owners to substitute cattle and pastures with programs such as agroforestry and forest management (Macdonald 1983).

In brief, by 1982, Indians were positioned to consider alternatives to cattle raising. Independent Indian federations were part of the local and national political landscape. They increased their power and support base by working directly with government agencies. And new legislation enabled them to demonstrate land use by managing rather than clearing their forests.

Their situation, and public posture, changed dramatically in 1984 with the installation of a new government. Government leaders advocated unrestrained economic activities by the private sector, supported colonization in the Amazon and opposed popular organizations and agrarian reform. In May 1985, the previously benign and occasionally helpful *Oficina de Asuntos Indígenas* was elevated to the status of a directorate (Direccion Nacional de Poblaciones Indígenas del Ecuador) and was officially declared "the technical-operational agency in charge of defining and applying policy and executing programs and projects for the organization and integrated development of the indigenous populations of Ecuador" (Amanecer Indio 1985c).

Armed with such a broad mandate, the national directorate legally assumed the roles which the ethnic federations had been working to establish for themselves. Further diminishing the status of the independent ethnic federations, new organizations, often made up of only a handful of self-defined Indian leaders supportive of the government, suddenly appeared in many areas (Amanecer Indio 1985a). With the assistance and support of the new directorate, these pro-government organizations were quickly awarded *personería jurídica*. FODERUMA in turn, provided funds to the newly formed organizations, or otherwise weakened the federations' ties to the communities by funding communities directly. Seen as an effort to establish government hegemony over Indian communities, and thus weaken the power of the federations, the directorate's actions met with strong public rejection by the older, independent Indian organizations (Ibid.).

IERAC halted all communal land titling. Government-awarded concessions for African Palm plantations, however, increased and expanded rapidly, often on Indian lands (Hoy 1985a, 1985b, 1985c, Kirk 1986). By 1985, the expansion of African Palm plantations, and the tactics used to enable their growth, provoked another series of outcries from the regional and national Indian organizations (Amanecer Indio 1985b; CONFENIAE 1985a, 1985b; Latin American Weekly Report 1985).

This conflict also affected land use. The 1981 forestry laws were implemented by the National Forestry Directorate (DINAF), which like IERAC, was under the Ministry of Agriculture. Relationships between these institutions and the Indian communities had become adversarial. Indians regarded DINAF as an agency which primarily supported the interests of logging companies and forest concessionaires. They also felt that the Ministry of Agriculture had little interest in working with small land owners; its most recent attempt to work with this sector in the Amazonian Region had never reached a very wide audience (Macdonald and Chernela, in press).

In summary, from the mid-1960's to the early 1980's Ecuador's Indians had organized previously disparate communities into ethnic federations; these in turn united to form regional and national organizations. To an extent greater than any other Indians' response to colonization, resource extraction, and other external threats, was the mobilization of a new national political sector. Beginning in early 1984 the independent Indian organizations, particularly those of the Oriente, were forced by government policies into a consistently defensive posture with regard to such critical issues as land rights and their role as representatives of Indian communities.[2] Such issues dominated FOIN's activities.

Ethnic Federations and Resource Management — the 1980s

In the 1980's Ecuadorian public awareness of environmental issues rose sharply, pushed by NGO's such as Fundacion Natura and other environmental groups. Yet pastures remained the most visible form of land use in the Amazonian region, and thus the means to claim or retain land. From 1983 to 1985, lands used for pasture in Napo province increased by 62%. Credit too continued to be extended most readily for cattle and pastures. With the exception of an agroforestry program on the lower Napo, few government programs focused on forest management or sustainable resource development.

Nor did the ethnic federations; the broad political concerns mentioned earlier, dominate their agendas. Government agencies within the Ministry of Agriculture made few if any efforts to work with or through the 7 regional ethnic federations. The Indian organizations, in turn, did not support the few extension programs initiated by these agencies (see Macdonald and Chernela, in press). The dissonance stemmed from the government's failure to grant community land titles, its efforts to undermine Indian organizations, and its support of extractive enterprises. For the ethnic federations land use issues were secondary concerns.

Not so for the individual communities. While federations such as FOIN focused most of their attention on government policies and the activities of extractive and agribusiness industries (Amanecer Indio 1985), the communities began to question the utility of their organizations. As the federations reacted mainly to immediate political needs and local crisis, they provided little technical and economic support or assistance. Yet technical help was sorely needed. Facing a powerful expanding frontier and a shrinking resource base, many communities recognized that traditional economic practices could no longer guarantee subsistence, let alone permit participation in the market economy. FOIN's leadership acknowledged the legitimacy of the members' needs and the organization's failure to provide a response.

A natural disaster served, indirectly, to permit a restructuring of FOIN's activities. In March 1987 a powerful earthquake shook the Amazonian region and swept away a sector of the only road which connected eastern Napo province with the rest of the country. Consequently, a new road from the town of Loreto to the Hollin River, underway slowly for several years, was rapidly cut through relatively unmodified tropical forest dotted with Indian communities, most of which were members of FOIN. USAID provided several bridges essential for the Loreto-Hollin road. Complying with social and environmental regulations mandated by the U.S. congress, USAID conditioned its assistance on Ecuador's efforts to minimize social and environmental damage.

To meet these requirements the international donor and the Ecuadorian government had to act quickly. Any road penetrating tropical forest usually funnels colonists and land speculators into previously isolated areas. In Napo province, only 9 of the approximately 30 communities within the area opened by the road held land titles; 4 others had been demarcated but not titled. So the lands of approximately half the communities were at risk.

In anticipation of land grabbers, the area's scattered Indian households established residence alongside the road within a few weeks of its completion. To demonstrate their presence, they quickly cleared forest frontage and planted small patches of pasture. Previously, much of the felled timber would have been left to rot. But increased demands for hardwoods and pulp expanded the market for timber. Consequently, what for many began as a small demonstration of possession escalated to extensive logging. Individual purchasers and wood product companies spurred the work. They first bought up any logs and sawn wood visible from the roadside, and then sought formal timbering concessions for additional cutting in the communities. In several areas non-Indian lumber purchasers eased agreements by presenting permits to log Indian community lands obtained from regional DINAF officials.

Logging quickly produced internal disputes in several communities as Indians maneuvered against each other to get the cash from lumber sales, regardless of ridiculously low prices. In addition, while obtaining the logging permits from DINAF, the purchasers, rather than the communities, provided DINAF with the modest "deposit" designed to encourage reforestation. However, the high profits reaped from lumber sales, led the purchasers to simply regard the reforestation deposit as a tax or fee to DINAF. So there was no economic incentive for loggers to reforest. Nor were the communities obliged to do so.

In brief, the Indians' initial efforts to demonstrate "development" through modest land modification — cleared land, stumps and incipient pastures — fed into an expanding regional timber economy and produced denuded roadside landscapes in a number of areas. With no pressure to reforest, it appeared that pastures would be planted between the stumps. Alongside the grass the cattle-based economic and cultural patterns which emerged in the 1970's would simply reproduce themselves in the Indian households along the Loreto-Hollin road.

However, the situation produced an unanticipated and somewhat oblique convergence of interest between international donor agencies and the regional Indian organizations. USAID had to take actions to minimize the environmental and social damage. At the same time FOIN's leadership angrily discussed the loggers' exploitation of the Indians and the precarious land tenure which indirectly encouraged the Indians' actions.

While some Quichuas along the road sold off their timber and signed concessionaire agreements for more cutting, FOIN's directors recognized that added to the ridiculously low prices, extensive logging threatened these communities' future resource base. FOIN, rather than any outside organization, was positioned to dissuade Indians from their economically shortsighted decisions. But they could not simply tell people to give up an income-generating activity. There had to be an alternative. This presented FOIN with an opportunity to provide some of the services requested by its affiliates.

Project LETIMARIN

In March 1988, USAID agreed to fund the first phase of a three-stage project in which FOIN will eventually coordinate the design and implementation of a sustainable resource management program for the area affected by the road. Without disrupting or replacing subsistence agriculture, FOIN will help to introduce new technologies for natural forest management, agroforestry, and conservation.

Before testing or embracing any new technologies, FOIN's first concern was the political "sustainability" of the project. So the first phase focused largely on their principle concerns — land tenure and institution building. If the communities remained without secure tenure, FOIN argued, any development or conservation programs would generate income or raise the value of the area's resources, and thus draw more outside interest. This would further jeopardize the communities' precarious hold on the land. In addition, to strengthen FOIN's status in the eyes of outsiders and its value to the communities, the organization wished to assume a prominent role in the design and implementation of the project.

As a means to both ends FOIN established its first "technical staff" — 9 extension workers (*promotores*) and a coordinator. All were high school graduated, Quichua-speaking Indians and several had additional agricultural studies. They were thus prepared for advanced technical training and could serve as extension workers in the communities. The technical staff was to be a permanent work group; as such their work, though linked directly to the federation, would be interrupted by the bi-annual elections of FOIN's directorate. Previously, the directorate's short tenure in office made it difficult for officers to establish or maintain programs which could provide regular technical assistance to the member communities.

During initial training in March and April 1988, social scientists associated with Cultural Survival worked with the team for about two weeks to design, field test, and evaluate methods for gathering data on community land tenure status and current logging practices. Then over a four month period, two-person teams or *promotores* visited the *centros* and surveyed all 43 communities in the area. During July and August the team, again with technical assistance from Cultural Survival, correlated and coordinated the data collected in the field.

Initially, while undertaking the surveys and establishing the management program, the project coordinators hoped to establish a moratorium on logging. This proved to be an unrealistic expectation. Many of the communities were unwilling to wait and loggers continuously pressured them. So to stimulate control of logging during the research and training phases of the project, FOIN contracted an Ecuadorian forestry specialist to conduct a set of seminars in communities spaced along the road. The training focused on two themes — marketing economics of lumbering and logging techniques which were economically efficient and inflicted minimal environmental damage. The hope was that, with an understanding of the value of their resources and some training in efficient extraction, communities would realize that greater profits could be obtained under proper management. During this period, half of the communities canceled their contracts with logging companies. Others, mainly those which had accepted advanced payment, were unable to break their agreements.

In conjunction with the seminars and land tenure surveys, the teams met formally with each community to discuss the project's long range goals. This strengthened FOIN's role with regard to the communities; the *promotores* were providing economic services previously unavailable from the federation. The broad resource management program anticipated for the future would thus be understood as a logical extension of the organization's earlier research.

In October 1988, the results of FOIN's research, as well as a series of recommended actions, were presented to the national forestry directorate. In addition to detailing the precarious land tenure situation, the report's discussion of logging practices stated that, although DINAF was supposed to control logging in the area, its presence was minimal. In addition, the report questioned DINAF regional offices' criteria for issuing logging permits. The report also was presented to the national agrarian reform agency in early 1989. It included a formal request for land titles and a halt to additional road construction until a rational resource management program could be established. So the first phase of the project set two of FOIN's major goals into motion — land titling and institution building. The political as well as technical groundwork was thus established for further work.

In early 1989, the program moved into its second phase — training in resource management technologies. Since the region contained isolated untouched forest, utilizable forest made accessible by the road, and land already degraded by deforestation, a range of technologies was necessary. For this the technical team first had an opportunity to view on-going projects in agroforestry, natural forest management, and conservation. The projects selected for observation were ones linked to similar ethnic federations and ones which had received outside technical assistance.

The training began with general resource management planning and an introduction to conservation methods for extremely fragile lands. For this the Kuna Indians of Panama were among the best trained in the hemisphere. Staff members of their Project Pemasky had received extensive training in resource management and project planning at Costa Rica's (CATIE). They had also prepared a long-term management plan for their tropical rain forest reserve (*comarca*), established a program for locally-managed "scientific tourism", and were working to have the area designated as a UNESCO Biosphere Reserve. Equally important, they were willing and anxious to share their training with other Indian organizations.

So, following a brief visit in late 1988 to Project Pemasky by representatives of several Ecuadorian Indian organizations, FOIN, in collaboration with Cultural Survival, invited two of the Pemasky's indigenous staff members to train the staff of Project LETIMARIN. Following 2 weeks of local observations and meetings, the Kuna began 6 weeks of formal training sessions at FOIN's headquarters in Tena. The focus of the training ranged from general resource management concepts to specific techniques for planning and implementing such work. Although their training, particularly the planning exercises, could be applied to a wide range of projects, the

Kuna's primary training focus was on conservation and management of the extremely fragile forest lands.

To meet the needs of Ecuador's Jungle Quichua population, production systems were essential to generate income. For this they are undergoing training in natural forest management from members of the Yanesha Forestry Cooperative of Peru's Palcazu Valley. Since the mid-1980's, Yanesha (or Amuesha) Indians had received extensive training in sustainable production systems for relatively unmodified forest. The systems are designed for areas where that forest would, most likely have been removed for some other production system. The arrival of Sendero Luminoso in the area made it impossible for those of Project LETIMARIN to visit the Palcazu Valley. Consequently, when work with the Kuna ended, FOIN began work with indigenous staff members from the cooperative to visit and train in Ecuador for several months.

For training in other aspects of production systems, Project LETIMARIN will receive technical assistance in agroforestry technologies which have been the subject of experiments in other areas of Napo province for several years (Estrada, Sere and Luzuriaga 1988).

Additional training (e.g. land-use capacity studies) are being considered for project staff. The training outlined above will allow FOIN to create systems appropriate for a range of environments: extremely fragile forest lands which should remain as conservation areas; forest lands where some use system is likely and where natural forest management would be most appropriate; and lands which have already been deforested or otherwise degraded, and can be restored through agroforestry. This training will permit the third phase, implementation of a broad regional resource management program, and thus provide an alternative to the conversion of tropical forest to pasture.

This work can also begin to alter, even reverse some of the tendencies toward social and cultural atomization which, as mentioned earlier, occurred when Indians drifted toward cattle raising out of political necessity in the 1970's. They will no longer be obliged to adopt alien land use systems simply to secure their land tenure. The "new technologies" work within standing forests or expand on traditional agricultural systems. None of the technologies requires the division of communities into individual lots; most will function best using community-based concepts of land use. Some communities which subdivided in the 1970's have already reformed as clusters and are requesting IERAC to redefine their status. Also, the rise of ethnic federations has expanded the concept of "community" beyond a cluster of households to ethnic and pan-ethnic groups with increased political power. This has led naturally to increased ethnic pride and a sense that "Indianness" is not only acceptable but essential for a sustainable social and economic life.

Conclusion

The broad threats posed by tropical deforestation are now the subject of worldwide concern. National development and large scale development projects are recognized as primary stimuli. By contrast, small-scale grassroots development programs and "traditional" or ancient indigenous technologies have been promoted as examples or models for environmentally sound, sustainable development.

It would be tempting to place Project LETIMARIN among the small, the sound, and the sustainable. That however, would be premature. The technologies have not even been established let alone tested to the point where they can be evaluated. Also, if Project LETIMARIN leads to a sustainable and ecologically sound alternative to cattle raising, and avoids cattle's socio-cultural impact as well, its evolution is not easily replicated. The project was the indirect product of an earthquake and subsequent international assistance. USAID, often over governmental protests, applied its regulations with regard to social and environmental impact. Recognizing that poor relations existed between the Indians and those government agencies through whom USAID normally channeled its support, an Indian organization was able to design and implement its own program. In doing so they first brought their political priorities into the foreground.

The significance of this case is what it reveals about current attitudes and perceptions among long-term forest residents. The unusual circumstances which led the Quijos Quichua to shift from reaction to planning simply throw into high relief the views of a relatively new but widespread social sector in many Latin American countries — indigenous ethnic federations.

Many of them now find themselves in the same situation as those of the Ecuadorian Amazon. Energy and personnel have been concentrated on basic organization or conflicts arising from the expanding frontier or national development. They have had neither the time nor the training to establish technical staffs which enable the federations to provide essential development advice, assistance, and regular contact with the communities they represent. As they move to strengthen that arm of their work they will experiment with a series of land use systems. The earlier response to precarious tenure — joining the ranks of the cattle-raising colonists — thus becomes one amongst a variety of alternatives.

This provides an opportunity for those concerned with the environment and sustainable development to work directly with indigenous people. But that work is not simply to create technologies but to accept the conditions needed to apply them. The broad, indigenous socio-political movement has, at best, cautiously approached international environmental interests. Caution is warranted; Indians and other forest residents do not isolate technology, politics, and culture. Nor will they permit such separation from those who suggest a convergence of interests. Indians and other long-time forest residents have broad goals and priorities. These often conflict with more powerful interests. For many Indians, conservation and national development are analogous in terms of their claims on land and resources. Those who promote sustainable development must recognize the Indians' broad concerns and adapt to local priorities if they hope to be accepted.

The evolution from cattle raising toward Project LETIMARIN, even at this early stage, illustrates that environmental and developmental agencies must consider and work within a larger framework than the one which normally encases their activities. A new segment of the "private sector" has raised its head and is demanding attention, not simply as an object of research, largess, or sensitivity, but as legitimate actors on the national political landscape.

Notes

1. Compare the *Exposición de Motivos* from the 1964 *Ley de Reforma Agraria y Colonización*; this contained twenty-two pages of general statements proclaiming the need for equality in land distribution. In the 1973 Ley de Reforma Agraria, the second paragraph of a concise one-page introduction states:

> ....la Reforma Agraria propende a aprovechar adecuadamente los recursos naturales, lograr la plena ocupacion de la fuerza de trabajo en el medio rural y utilizar eficientemente los recursos financieros y tecnicos disponibles, con el proposito de alcanzar el crecimiento sostenido de la produccion y productividad del sector agropecuario, elevar y redistribuir los ingresos y, por consiguiente, alcanzar razonables niveles de vida (Ecuador – Ministerio de Agricultura y Ganaderia 1974:5).

2. In August 1988, a new, more progressive government took office. However at the time of this writing (January 1989), no new policies and programs with regard to Indians, colonization, land reform, or natural resources had been established, despite expressions of concern and sympathy for such matters. The Indian organizations, in expectation of improved relations, have withheld any judgment and assumed a wait-and-see attitude.

References Cited

Amanecer Indio (Quito, Ecuador). 1985a. Gobierno crea grupos divisionistas contra organizaciones indigenas. December 1985.
____ 1985b. Empresas y colonizacion causan violencia en la Amazonia. December 1985; p. 7
____ 1985c. Gobierno crea direccion de poblaciones indigenas. December 1985; p. 6
Banco de Fomento. (Ecuador). 1974. *El credito agricola en el Ecuador*. Ms. Quito, Ecuador.
Chapin, M. and P. Breslin. 1984. Conservation Kuna style. *Grassroots Development* 8(2):26-28.
Chapin, M. 1985. UDIRBI: An indigenous project in environmental conservation. In: *Native peoples and economic development: Six case studies from Latin America*. Edited by Theodore Macdonald Jr. Cultural Survival Occasional Paper #16.
Chernela, J. 1987. Environmental restoration in Southwestern Colombia. *Cultural Survival Quarterly* 11(4):71-73.
____ In press. Sustainable development and sustainable control: Political strategies of Indian organizations in a proposed binational reserve in Ecuador and Colombia. In: *Human Ecology in Amazonia*. Edited by Leslie E. Sponsel. Boulder, Colorado: Westview Press.
CONFENIAE. 1985a. *Palma Africana y etnocido*. Quito: CEDIS-CONFENIAE.
____ 1985b. Defendamos nuestra tierra! Defendamos nuestra tierra! Quito: CEDEP-CONFENIAE.
____ 1986. Proposal submitted to Cultural Survival.
CRIC (Regional Indian Council of Cauca, Colombia). 1986. Proposal submitted to Cultural Survival.
Cultural Survival Quarterly. 1984. Organizing to survive 8(4).
Descola, P. 1982. From scattered to nucleated settlement: A process of socioeconomic change among the Achuar. In: *Cultural transformations and ethnicity in modern Ecuador*. Edited by Norman E. Whitten. Urbana: University of Illinois Press.
____ 1988. *La selva culta*. Quito. Ediciones Abya Yala.
Ecuador — Ministerio de Agricultura y Ganaderia. 1974. *Reforma agraria: Ley y reglamento*. Quito: Cencotap.
Estrada, R. D., C. Sere, and H. Luzuriaga. 1988. *Sistemas de produccion agrosilvopastoriles en la selva baja de la Provincia del Napo, Ecuador*. Cali, Colombia: Centro Internacional de Agricultura Tropical (CIAT).
FOIN (Federation of Indian Organizations of Napo — Ecuador). 1988. Proposal submitted to Cultural Survival.

Gibson, C. 1964. *The Aztecs under Spanish rule*. Stanford: Stanford University Press.

Hoy. 1985a. Critican proyectos de palma Africana. 10 September, 1985.

_____ 1985b. Condenan invasion a comunidades. 9 October 1985.

_____ 1985c. Tierra de Indigenas esta amenazada. 20 October 1985.

Irvine, D. 1985. Resource management among the Runa of Ecuadorian Amazon. Unpublished ms.

_____ 1989. Succession management and resource distribution in an Amazonian rainforest. In: *Resource management in Amazonia: Indigenous and folk strategies*. Edited by D. A. Posey and W. Balée. Bronx, N.Y.: The New York Botanical Gardens. Advances in Economic Botany, Vol. 7.

Latin American Weekly Report. 1985. African palm and ethnocide. 8 November. (WR-85-44).

Macdonald, T. 1979. *Processes of change in Amazonian Ecuador: Quijos Quichua Indians become cattlemen*. Ann Arbor: University Microfilms.

_____ 1981. Indigenous response to an expanding frontier: Quijos Quichua economic conversion to cattle raising. In: *Cultural transformations and ethnicity in modern Ecuador*. Edited by Norman E. Whitten. Urbana: University of Illinois Press.

_____ 1983. Terrirorio indígena en el Ecuador: Un ejemplo de su delimitación. *America Indígena*, XLIII (3): 555-568.

_____ 1986. Anticipating colonos and cattle in Ecuador and Colombia. *Cultural Survival Quarterly* 10(2):33-36.

Macdonald, T. and J. Chernela. In press. Politics, development, and Indians: A comparison of two resource management projects in the Ecuadorian rain forest. In: *The social dynamics of deforestation in Latin America and its alternatives*. Edited by Susanna Hecht and James Nations. Ithaca, NY: Cornell University Press.

Martz, J.D. 1972. *Ecuador: Conflicting political culture and the quest for progress*. Boston: Allyn and Bacon.

Posey, D. and W. Balée (eds.). 1989. *Natural resource wanagement in Amazonia: Indigenous and folk strategies*. New York: The New York Botanical Gardens.

Schwartzman, S. 1981. Indigenists, environmentalists, and the multilateral development banks. *Cultural Survival Quarterly* 8(4):74-75.

Schwartzman, S. and M. Allegretti. In press. Extractive production and the Brazilian rubber tappers movement. In: *The social dynamics of deforestation in Latin America and its alternatives*. Edited by Susanna Hecht and James Nations. Ithaca, NY: Cornell University Press.

Shuar Federation — Ecuador. 1988. Proposal submitted to Cultural Survival.

Smith, R.C. 1984. Amazonian Indians participate at UN. *Cultural Survival Quarterly* 8(4): 29-31

____ 1985. Unity within diversity: Peasant unions, ethnic federations, and indianist movements in the Andean Republics. In: *Cultural Survival Quarterly* 8(4):6-13

UNI (National Indian Union — Brazil). 1988. Proposal submitted to Cultural Survival.

Uquillas, J. 1983. Indian land rights and natural resource management in the Ecuadorian Amazon. In: *Native peoples and economic development: Six case studies from Latin America.* Edited by Theodore Macdonald Jr. Cultural Survival Occasional Paper No.16.

West, R.C. and J.P. Augelli. 1976. *Middle America: Its lands and peoples*, 2nd edition. Englewood Cliffs, NJ: Prentice Hall.

Zuvekas, C. 1976. Agrarian reform in Ecuador's Guayas Basin. *Land Economics* 52(3): 341-329.

13

Rural Development Effects

David Barkin

The massive conversion of forest lands to livestock grazing is part of a broader transformation of agriculture from the production of basic food crops towards commercial crops for export or animal feed. This change involves not simply the switch from one crop to another but rather a change in the beneficiaries and the clients for the new products. It produces market driven modifications in cropping systems, marketing schemes, and trade patterns which diversify the diets and systematically enrich wealthier groups at the expense of the farmers and working classes in the producing nations.

In this article, we analyze the impact of the expansion of livestock raising into Latin America's forest areas on rural development. While it will be difficult to ignore the environmental and socio-economic impacts of this dramatic change in rural life, others have afforded a well-documented panorama of this distressing situation (see, for example, the extensive dossier on the Mexican situation and the bibliography prepared by Victor Manuel Toledo 1987). The questions that concern us involve the interaction between the destructive impact of the felling of vast areas of tropical rain forests and the displacement of indigenous groups with a consequent loss of knowledge about how to manage these complex ecosystems. This article builds on the literature that demonstrated that the conversion of forest land to pasture is the result of the pressures placed on resources by the demands of capitalist production (Feder 1982). This reorganization of the tropical rain forests is leading to a permanent loss of productive capacity in these regions as the fragile ecosystems are ravaged by the implantation of specialized production models, usually involving the extensive pasturing of livestock (Reig 1982).

Latin America's forests are viewed as a rich unexploited frontier. Population densities are low and social groups usually too poorly organized to be able to defend their social and pecuniary interests. Historically, these regions have been treated as targets of opportunity, ripe for increasing their contribution to national economic development, by placing their resources and productive potential at the disposition of new producers who can extract this wealth and reorganize production for their own benefit and that of the nation (see Barkin 1978b for an extensive analysis of impact of the denuding of the tropical rain forests in southern Mexico and the construction of drains to enable the implantation of new agricultural models). The urge to introduce specialized productive systems into these delicate ecosystems is similar to the imperative which leads governments to promote regional economic development in other parts of the hemisphere: the demand to accelerate economic growth by locating and incorporating new sources of natural resources into the national economy and promoting their extraction and/or exploitation. This internationalization of the Latin American economy has led to the local implantation of world wide patterns of capital accumulation which substitute profitability for usefulness as the principal criterion in the evaluation of productive investments (Rozo and Barkin 1983, Downing 1982, and Sanderson 1985 provide a further elaboration and application of the process to Latin America).

The conversion of Latin American forests to pastures, then, is a distinctive form of regional development. It is of special concern because of the particularly destructive impacts that it is having on fragile ecosystems. From the point of view of rural society, however, such transformations have predictably followed the patterns of capitalist development elsewhere: centralized control of productive resources, with deleterious effects on social organization, the environment, and the sustainability of the new productive systems which are implanted. Simultaneously, they offer limited numbers of new employment opportunities. Existing social systems are reorganized to preclude the active participation of affected populations in the economic or political opportunities created in the region. The literature amply traces the similarity of the effects of such development schemes on local populations and national economic structures throughout the world, regardless of the ecological settings within which they are implemented (Barkin 1973; Coraggio 1978, 1980). In the following pages I will review this general process as a prelude to examining the specifics of the forest regions.

The Unevenness of Regional Development

Development, whether on a national or regional level, is a dual process of enrichment and structural change. On the one hand, if successful, it raises incomes by using resources more intensively and accumulating additional resources to further increase production. On the other hand, it transforms productive structures, initially shifting resources from primary production to industrial transformation and then contributing to an explosion of the service (tertiary) sector. At its most incipient stages, development reorganizes production, substituting national markets and mass production for local and regional networks of exchange and social systems of self-sufficient subsistence.

This dual process has its counterpart in other dimensions of social and political organization. On a human level — a level all too often ignored by economists — development also involves enrichment and transformation. In this case, however, the structures which are modified are those of social class and the distribution of income. And on the physical plane, too, productive activity is rearranged spatially to make use of underutilized resources to accelerate the global process of capital accumulation, or economic growth.

One of the basic tenets of economic development applied to market economies is the desirability of the unfettered pursuit of higher incomes. Some analysts admit this struggle for individual enrichment will cause some deterioration in the distribution of income — greater concentration in the hands of a few — in the short run. Similarly, planners frequently operate on the assumption that part of the price to pay for successful development programs is the decline in the quality of the environment because of the misuse of natural resources along with the centralization of economic power and activity. There is an implicit faith, which is sometimes made explicit, that with the gradual solution of the basic problems of low income and inadequate growth rate for the nation as a whole, it will be easier to attack the distributive and ecological problems which the initial growth process exacerbated.

Regional development programs are frequently conceived as explicit instruments of state policy to correct some of the personal and spatial disequilibria which national policies have created or are expected to exacerbate; but at the same time they are usually based on an explicit program to intensify the use of the region's natural resources. They are often supposed to reduce income differentials among regions and people through a more "productive" employment of the region's potential. Such corrective approaches are required because capitalist development creates inequalities as part of its own internal dynamic.

Case studies of the historical development amply document the process of spatial and social centralization created by market forces, abetted by generous government subsidies to accelerate the rhythm of economic growth. These inequalities are the result of self-reinforcing patterns of economic growth which generate resources for reinvestment in existing or new ventures located near current centers of production. The reinvestment process is an important element in sustaining economic growth and helps explain the way in which incomes become increasingly concentrated on both a personal and regional level. Those with the initial capital, or access to it, are able to prosper by undertaking profitable ventures which generate greater surpluses for further reinvestment. These initial productive and/or financial resources, or political access to them through accepted or unconventional mechanisms, also accord to the bearer a privileged access to decision-making processes which allocate opportunities for further enrichment — conceived in political discourse as beneficial for both the individual entrepreneur and the political entity in which (s)he is located. Through the marketplace, the ubiquitous invisible hand of capitalism is expected to match the individual evaluation of the nation's productive needs with the collectively determined social requirements for the whole population.

State policies often reinforce this pattern of personal income concentration and spatial centralization by raising the profitability of existing investments and encouraging additional investment to accelerate economic growth. Economies of scale and agglomeration combine with cultural, political, and historical factors to favor the concentration of investments by an elite in a few rapidly growing urban centers; those few productive facilities which are not constructed in these areas are usually closely tied to particular natural resources or depend upon the availability of a specific type of labor not found in the traditional growth poles.

Regional development programs, then, respond to the need — often political— to deal with the problems of areas left in the backwash of economic growth. In order to stimulate national economic growth, they are usually conceived, on the one hand, to make fuller use of natural resources in the area and, on the other, to integrate isolated groups of people into the mainstream of economic life, transforming them into consumers and, most likely, into members of the already oversized "reserve army" of the unemployed. By mobilizing underutilized resources, such programs are expected to contribute to national growth while raising the incomes of regions that were previously left out of the growth process.

Regional development programs redistribute the benefits from this growth by diverting economic activity from existing production centers to the selected areas and incorporate new social groups into permanent productive activities. Because the potential benefits are so great and the competition for scarce investment resources so keen, the selection of a particular region for special attention will never, however, be the product of a strictly technical decision of productivity. The potential beneficiaries will not be limited to (or may not even include) the inhabitants of the favored zone. Rather, the public or private organizations charged with administering the investment budget, developing the resources, and taking advantage of the special incentives which are to be made available, will inevitably join in a struggle to attempt to determine not only the geographic placement of the project but also its allocation in sectorial and personal terms. It will be particularly difficult to ensure a privileged or even an equal access to the opportunities by marginal social groups who would have to benefit if the programs were to have favorable redistributive effects.

Furthermore, successful development requires a self-expanding process of economic growth. If the investments are concentrated in primary production activities, like agriculture and mining, then the possibilities of self-sustained growth are inherently limited; processing activities are also self-limiting, and unless a reinvestment process is undertaken to establish a growing productive base, the prospects for successful regional development are poor. To ensure the success of such a process, it is often essential for the government to provide special subsidies and infrastructure investments. This help is often not enough, however, and additional measures for protecting the initial high-cost production may have to be combined with more coercive policies concerning industrial location if a decentralization policy is to succeed.

Thus, even if successful in spatial terms, regional development programs do not necessarily facilitate or even permit a redistribution of personal income. Unless additional measures to provide financial resources to those who do not have them are combined with effective limitations on the participation of existing regional or national elites in the new ventures, new investment programs will merely provide further opportunities for the rich to broaden the scope of their activities. The control over potentially valuable natural resources may permit the owner to improve his economic condition, but only if the necessary complementary resources are available. In their absence, it is probable that effective control over the natural resources will pass to those with the financial resources needed to develop them; this is particularly true of large programs which would be a substantial embarrassment to government if they were not brought "on stream" as soon as possible. Regional development, therefore, requires much more than the (relatively) simple relocation of economic activity. It also requires an explicit mechanism to facilitate access to the productive opportunities by people who would otherwise be unable to take advantage of them.

On the social and ecological plane, the economic reorganization occasioned by the internationalization of capital is producing substantial displacements of traditional society. Peasant agriculture and craft goods turned out in artisan workshops give way to putting-out (contract) relations at the service of capitalist industrial and agricultural enterprise. In the process, society is reorganized towards specialized production while sacrificing inherited techniques for managing the environment and taking advantage of the plethora of wild flora and fauna as part of traditional production processes. Specialization advances rapidly as subsidies privilege commercial production benefiting a small national capitalist class and responding to the financial pressures of the international banking community; but this specialization is particularly destructive of social and resource bases. The universal victims are the social and natural environments which supported the domestic production of basic foods and other essential goods. Many basic products must be imported and distributed at either greatly increased prices or with substantial governmental subsidies — in either case, occasioning inflation with serious consequences for the living standards of the masses. The internationalization of capital, therefore, produces the paradoxical result of increasing society's productive potential while impoverishing its people and its environment.

Regional inequalities are particularly evident in the forest areas because of the perseverance of the cultural integrity of the ethnic groups who have survived. In these regions, many groups retain a regional and linguistic identity in defiance of demands for allegiance to the nation state. This manifestation of the national question is of considerable relevance to an understanding of regional development: in the forest areas of Latin America backward regions become coterminous with backward nationalities. Here regional development means appropriating resources from backward groups — however defined — for the benefit of advanced groups, which frequently combine ethnic and economic characteristics of power. An understanding of the interactions between social class, ethnicity, and development "could provide a useful antidote to the more mechanistic spatially oriented interpretations of regional backwardness" (Sobhan 1981: 20).

The uneven regional distribution of economic activity is a correlate, in space, of the concentration of personal income and economic power characteristic of capitalist development. It necessarily accompanies the national development process. Similarly, and just as intimately tied to the same process, is the pattern of differential sectoral growth which characteristically has left basic food production in the wake of national economic growth in much of the Third World. The destruction of the hemisphere's forests is an integral part of the blind search for profit and the erroneous assumption that nature can be reshaped to suit the interests of capital. The interrelationship between the different facets of national development — personal, sectoral, physical, spatial— cannot be sufficiently stressed. It is completely incorrect to conceive of the problem of disparities in any particular dimension as separable from those in any other. From this vantage point, then, regional underdevelopment cannot be understood, or much less attacked, if it is defined in terms of the physical inventory of natural resources which remain unutilized or underutilized, or in terms of the low levels of productivity of the natural and/or human resources already in production in the zone. Productive transformation and physical destruction, then, must be understood as complementary elements of a strategy devised by one powerful group to systematically wrest control from another weaker group.

Policy Responses to Underdevelopment

It is curious that policy makers seem convinced that while they are incapable of reversing the concentration of income, they can promote economic growth in backward regions. The usual array of tools to implement this redistributive function work through the market, influencing locational and sectoral decisions of private entrepreneurs by raising their profit rate. In many countries public enterprises complement private activity or even initiate the process.

This market approach to regional development provokes fundamental contradictions:

a) it enriches the already affluent entrepreneurs (either local or foreign) by improving the rate of return on their previously accumulated capital, thus heightening personal income inequalities;

b) it biases new investment and technological development in favor of additional investments in capital, by reducing the relative cost of capital and raising that of labor;

c) it makes the decision as to what goods to produce dependent on market signals, thus accelerating the trend away from the production of goods to satisfy the basic needs of the majority and towards the production of goods for the satisfaction of the demands of the economically privileged;

d) it penalizes a long-term approach to natural resource utilization by supporting high interest rates and failing to charge individual entrepreneurs the full social cost of their use of natural resources.

The cumulative experience reveals that regional development can lead to the effective integration of an isolated geographic area into the national market economy. But generally, in the process independent small farmers and craftspeople who managed to live at subsistence levels cannot maintain their independence. Paraphrasing an evaluation of one such experience, we find:

The new economic structure created by the regional development program requires capital, special technical skills, and access to political influence in order to thrive. Most of the ostensible beneficiaries of the program are not permitted access to these resources or to political power and they become dependent on a privileged group which is quite commonly composed of people who come from outside the region and were already integrated into the well-established financial, industrial, and political groups. As a result, the original inhabitants of the region often find themselves still living at subsistence — albeit at a somewhat higher material level consistent with the region's new status as a part of the national economy— but without their former independence, and without an ability to ensure their own well-being and that of their families because of the destruction of traditional productive organizations and social structures. Now they depend for their very survival on employment from the outside groups who gained effective control over the land and other productive resources created by the regional development program (Barkin 1975: 277-278).

Regional development programs may lead to a significant rise in production and, in some cases, a very substantial return on the resources invested in public works. The increased production is considered as an important contribution to "national" development, frequently contributing with key industrial inputs (steel, minerals) or scarce foreign exchange (export crops) which directly attack some of the key bottlenecks of national development. The programs may also attract people from other relatively overpopulated zones who might have migrated to one of the metropolitan areas and further heightened social tensions and overcrowding. But, in the ultimate analysis, most of the evaluations of regional development programs conclude by demonstrating that they do not provide a basis for promoting the self-sustained growth of the region and that the benefits from its initial integration into the national economy are systematically channeled into the vaults of the dominant economic groups.

Regional development, in this light, is a means for attacking inherited inequalities without changing them. It need not challenge fundamentally the existing distribution of wealth or power. By directly attacking the problems of geographic isolation, it provides an instrument for incorporating new resources and new social groups into the national (and international) market economy, to mobilize additional natural and human resources which might contribute to accumulation. It does this under the banner of redistribution, of equity, and even in the name of resource preservation. It therefore enjoys support from political currents which might otherwise offer resistance or mobilize foci of political opposition. But by defining the regional effort strictly in terms of accumulation in a specific area, such programs explicitly reject the possibility of achieving their self-proclaimed goals of promoting structural change and social justice; rather they sow the seeds of social and territorial destruction.

Herein lies the attraction of regional development. Since it can be used as a tool for political negotiation, as a mechanism for responding to national demands for a greater participation in development, as an instrument of redistribution, economic elites have found the approach of particular interest to promote change. But by focusing only on the increase in productive capacity, regional programs generally only serve to strengthen the power and consolidate the control over the nation's productive resources by these elites.

In this light, development schemes for forest areas are attractive tools for policy makers. They are often charged with accomplishing truly difficult redistributive tasks. Many ruling groups find them to be useful as an instrument for promoting economic change while not threatening the existing organization of society or the distribution of power and wealth.

As an ideological tool, rural development — regionalism — is a key element in the developmental scheme. It offers a framework within which the dominant classes can manipulate conflict and negotiation — generally centered in a country's urban centers. It is often a product of deliberate efforts to perpetuate the prevailing structure of domination. These efforts to stimulate rural growth can win the support of provincial bourgeoisies for national policies and prevent them from developing local class alliances which might undermine a centralist policy. Ironically, this support for regional demands has contributed to consolidating the support of the ruling classes throughout the region and in strengthening the prevailing spatial distribution of production and power (Salinas 1977; Moreno 1978).

There are very few, if any, instances in which a successful program really achieves its goal of benefiting a local group at the expense of the national dominant classes. In the Brazilian northeast, for example, the generous financial incentives, which were an essential building block in the regional development effort, induced a substantial flow of private investment; they "were offered because of the coincidence of needs with the national economic system" (Moreira 1978). Similarly,

> the Venezuelan commitment to regional development was only possible because of the importance of natural resources of Guayana for the basic industries which process them and for the national and international accumulation models of which they were a valuable input (Negrón 1978).

The examples abound, and because of their importance in national policy formulation and the popularity of regional development, it is useful to go into greater detail. Regional development, as a rural-oriented approach, assumes a sectoral character. The concept of "equity" or "social justice" has been relegated to an ideological level, the "benefit" which the peasant receives depends on his importance in stimulating growth and accumulation on a national level or as an agent in political protest. [In one particular project in the tropical rain forests, citing Barkin (1978a), it was precisely its local character which created opposition from Mexican political forces.] Financial support for the project was only restored once it was redesigned to directly respond to certain national requirements which reoriented it in line with the prevailing pattern of capitalist expansion (Lavell, Pírez and Unikel 1978). The local resource base and social organization were destroyed in the process.

Regional development can only succeed as part of an explicit national political commitment to redistribute resources spatially, sectorially, and interpersonally while restoring and defending the inherited resource base. To achieve this goal the role of agriculture within national life must be redefined. Much too often agriculture has become synonymous with regional underdevelopment and poverty. Any effective attempt to promote regional development must confront this problem directly and not simply sidestep the issue by focusing on natural resource exploitation or agroindustrial development.

The search for such examples is indeed frustrating. Thus, the study of the Cuban program is particularly rewarding because of the country's commitment to reduce the inherited socio-economic differentials, usually correlated with urbanization. Its rural development efforts include the reconstruction and strengthening of the rural resource base, by developing a thriving livestock sector based on an intensive use of land for feed needs which has permitted the rebuilding of tropical forest areas. Without going into the details of programs described elsewhere, or the possible problems with their implementation (Barkin 1978a; Pupo, Weinstein and Franco 1980), the original commitment of the Cuban leadership to the peasantry has been transformed into the cornerstone of a broader project to reduce the social and economic distance between the cities and the countryside. This is part of a substantial effort to modernize rural production, transforming and integrating the peasant family fully into the rest of the society. It seems significant that in the process of creating these changes, the Cubans have also been successful in opening channels of communication and increasing flexible administrative structures responsive to criticism. In this case, "regionalism" has found a solution in the concrete policies of the socialist government and clearly illustrates the socio-political character of economic and geographic concentration in other countries.

Conversion of Forest Lands

The conversion of forest lands for pasture in Latin America is another stratagem for the appropriation of nature to accelerate capital accumulation. It will proceed without regard for its impact on the sustainability of the carrying capacity of the resources as long as further areas can be appropriated in the future at lesser cost than protecting and strengthening the lands which are initially deforested. As such, it can be expected to have the same effects on rural areas as the other regional development schemes discussed above.

Historically, the human settlements in the forest areas have developed a diversified productive system which combines a variety of cultivation techniques with hunting and gathering to assure their livelihood. With the internationalization of the economy and their insertion into the circuits of commercial production, they have frequently also become part of one or more cash crop cycles. In this way, they have generally evolved a dynamic modus vivendi with their environment which permits their subsistence. It would be erroneous to exaggerate the precariousness of their living standards, because of the exploitative nature of the exchange relations in which they engage.

The transformation of forest lands contribute to the concentration of control over the land and the productive resources. Such a conversion requires capital or access to bank credits to finance the felling of the forests, the seeding of pastures, the purchase of the animals, and the period for the fattening of the cattle. This inevitably leads to a polarization of social groups, because of the differential access to the financial means and — more significantly — the familiarity with the technologies and the scale of operation implicit in this new form of production.

Forest conversion projects almost inevitably lead to the expulsion of existing social groups from the region. They destroy the resource base formerly used to sustain subsistence strategies and require fewer people to manage the new cattle grazing activities than were occupied in the communities. The livestock grazing alters the ecological balance, simplifying the environment and eliminating many species which were useful for equilibrium among varieties of flora and fauna as well as for the subsistence of native populations. From a social and ecological point of view, then, the forest conversion process must be understood as the "development of underdevelopment."

From the national point of view the conversion of forest lands to pasture is also questionable. The decision to encourage (or simply permit) livestock development in the forests is a continuation of the process of promoting the production of goods for the wealthy at the expense of the majority; such developments almost always enjoy political and material support from government to facilitate the reorganization of the land and resources as well as to dislodge the people from their settlements and their traditional use of the land. Furthermore, the livestock grazed on these lands is used to produce meat products which generally are part of the diets of the rich. Data from Mexico, which enjoys better nutritional standards than most countries in the region, suggest that even before the onset of the present crisis in 1982, less than one-third of the population regularly consumed any source of animal protein; of course these privileged few were not concentrated in the cattle producing areas carved out of the tropical rain forests. The situation has become even more critical since that time.

The question of forest development for livestock grazing is an integral part of the debate about the development strategy itself. Capitalist development will, if left unfettered, inexorably exclude the needs of the poor from its production agenda while trying to absorb what little purchasing they have through stratagems that would have them emulate the idealized patterns of the rich, as transmitted through commercial propaganda. In Latin America, the question of development strategies is the over-riding issue of the day: it involves the questions of what is to be produced, for whom, and how. These are social and political issues rather than questions of technological feasibility. A constructive response to the present trends towards the degradation of forests as a result of the pressure from pasturing, calls for a multifaceted approach to production aimed at the integral use of all resources.

References Cited

Barkin, D. 1973. A case study of the beneficiaries of regional development. *International Social Development Review* (United Nations) No. 4: 84-94.

_____ 1975. Regional development and interregional equity: A Mexican case study. In: *Urbanization and inequality: The political economy urban and rural development in Latin America*. Edited by W. Cornelius and F. Trueblood. Latin American Urban Research, Vol. 5. Beverly Hills, California: Sage Publications.

_____ 1978a. Confronting the separation of town and country in Cuba. In: *Marxism and the metropolis*. Edited by W. Tabb and L. Sawers. New York: Oxford University Press. First edition.

_____ 1978b. *Desarrollo regional y reorganizacion campesina*. Mexico City: Nuevo Imagen and Centro de Ecodesarrollo.

_____ 1982. The internationalization of capital and the spatial organization of agriculture in Mexico. In: *Regional analysis and the new international division of labor*. Edited by F. Moulaert and P. Salinas. Boston, Mass.:Kluwer-Nijhoff Publishing.

Coraggio, J. L. 1978. La problemática acerca de las desigualdades regionales. *Demografía y Economía* 12(2).

_____ 1980. Las bases teóricas de la planificación regional en América Latina. Demografía y Economía 14(2).

Downing, T. E. 1982. The internationalization of capital in agriculture. *Human Organization*, 41(3): 269-277.

Feder, E. 1980. The odious competition between man and animal over agricultural resources in underdeveloped countries. *Review* 3(3): 463-500.

Lavell, A., P. Pírez, and L. Unikel. 1978. El estado y la questión regional en México. Paper presented at the seminar on The Regional Question in Latin America. El Colegio de México, Mexico. (mimeo).

Moreno, O. M. 1978. La coyuntura política Argentina de 1966 a 1970 y los movimientos populares reivindicativos de carácter regional. Paper presented at the seminar on The Regional Question in Latin America. El Colegio de México, Mexico. (mimeo).

Negrón, M. 1978. El desarrollo y las políticas regionales en Venezuela: Experiencia y perspectivas. Paper presented at the seminar on The Regional Question in Latin America. El Colegio de México, Mexico. (mimeo).

Pupo, C., S. Weinstein, and X. Franco. 1980. Transformaciones revolucionarias en el campo Cubano y la urbanización del campo: Su efecto sobre el crecimiento urbano en Cuba. In: *Conflicto entre ciudad y campo en América Latina.* Edited by I. Restrepo. Mexico: Nueva Imagen.

Reig, N. 1982. El sistema ganadero industrial: su estructura y desarrollo 1960-1980. In: *El desarrollo agroindustrial y la ganadería en México.* Mexico: Secretaria de Agricultura y Recursos Hidraulicos, Documentos de trabajo para el desarrollo agroindustrial, No. 8.

Rozo, C. and D. Barkin. 1983. La producción de alimentos y la internacionalización del capital. *El Trimestre Economico*, 49:3 (No. 199): 1603-1626.

Salinas, P. W. 1977. Le developpemente regional et les limites d'une reforme: L'experience au Perou du gouvernemente militaire. *Revue Tiers-Monde* 18: 723-736.

Sanderson, S., ed. 1985. *The Americas in the new international division of labor.* New York: Holmes and Meier.

Sobhan, R. 1981. Public enterprise and regional development: The Asian experience. Paper presented to the Expert Group Meeting on the Role of Public Enterprises in Regional Development in Developing Countries, International Centre for Public Enterprises in Developing Countries, Ljubljana, Yugoslavia.

Toledo, V. M. 1987. Vacas, cerdos, pollos y ecosistemas: Ecología y ganadería en México. *Ecología: Política y Cultura* 3:36-49.

14

Reconciling People and Land: The Prospects for Sustainable Extraction in the Amazon

Mary Helena Allegretti

Recent data on deforestation in the Amazon announced by the Brazilian government indicate that about 8% of the forest has already been cut. In spite of the controversy about methods used to reach this figure, the indisputable fact is that between 8% and 10% of the rainforest has been destroyed. Alternatives to halt deforestation range from supervision and control of the migration process, to cutting of fiscal incentives, to taxation of agricultural activities and reforestation. The Brazilian government is expected to take stricter measures especially in the future because they are interested in presenting a positive image of their environmental administration to the rest of the world at a time when a major global environmental conference will be held in Brazil.

As the control of deforestation is the responsibility of the Brazilian government, the question to be asked now is, what should be the strategy for maintaining the remaining forest?

The most elaborate technical responses point to the sustainable management of timber because of the higher profitability of timber extraction and because reserves of valuable hardwoods are concentrated in areas belonging to the economically most powerful Brazilian and foreign groups. Therefore, it can be predicted that even with a decrease of deforestation for cattle ranching, the uncontrolled harvesting of wood will continue until the proposals for sustainable management become government policy.

If the point is the discussion of sustainable development — and by this I mean the sustainability of use of resources and distribution of social wealth — we are facing a total lack of available solutions. All current proposals — extractive reserves, biological agriculture, aggregation of value to forest products — are limited to a regional scope and their efficiency has not yet been satisfactorily proved. This situation results from the fact that those alternatives were suggested as some sort of "resistance" to the status quo, and as a form of concentrating the fight against deforestation. They are partial solutions for only certain sectors of the Amazonian regional society. The discussion of the relation between extractive reserves and regional development must be twofold. Limits must be considered first. The analysis of technical and political possibilities and requirements for new prospects of incorporation of common use resources to local policies should follow.

Limits of the Concept of Extractive Reserves

Extractive reserves were originally conceived as a way of addressing a social problem, specifically the expropriation of the customary lands of forest peoples by deforestation and ranching. The concept was powerful because it resulted from a social movement and became strong for the same reason. The original concept, however, has always been based on a specific social class and its scope limited to areas situated in the Amazon where populations exploit extractive resources in a traditional manner.

The extractive reserves began to be considered as an element of the question of regional development after two clearly defined events:

- Chico Mendes' death, because it revealed the existence of an extractive reality to both Brazil and the world;
- the intensification of research and debate on the intrinsic economic value of the forest compared to its use for farming activities and timber extraction.

Rubber tappers have always compared the advantages and disadvantages of living in the forest, to that of farms or outskirts of towns. They believe, and research seems to corroborate, that their real income was higher as forest dwellers. The result of this comparison was evident at the "*empates*" to protest against deforestation. Although the main aim of the first cooperative programs put into practice in Xapuri was not economic sustainability but political organization to defend the forest, they proved that the commercialization of forest products was profitable to those involved in extractive activities.

However, the analysis of the relationship between extractivism and regional development requires the consideration of other variables which have not yet been used by the rubber tappers' movement. First, the economic and social dynamics of extractivism should be better understood, both from the point of view of collection and processing of products and their commercialization and industrialization. Second, linkages should be established between extractive activities and other regional economic impacts should be more thoroughly understood.

All extractive products collected in the Amazon follow the same organizational rules: *aviamento*, the barter system. This means that the products are collected in the forest and exchanged for industrialized goods, in an operation which does not involve money. But one should understand that the barter system is a specific social relation which differs from all others existing in Brazilian rural areas such as wage-labor, share-cropping, and leasing. The main features of this barter system is that there is no prior definition of the prices on which the exchange will be based. In the case of wage-labor, for example, the worker knows in advance how much his hourly salary is and that he will receive the equivalent amount in goods. In the barter system, the rules of exchange are established a posteriori, which allows for dealers to easily manipulate prices. The main result of activities organized according to a barter system is indebtedness. The value of products extracted from the forest is neither low nor is extractivism unprofitable. It is the form of appropriation of the value generated by extractive activities through the barter system that impoverishes the extractive worker.

Another important aspect is the regional structure of land-use. In most cases, extraction takes place in large pieces of land owned by a few who exploit them through a leasing system which complements the barter system. This means that for each product there is a relation of dependence between the worker and the owner of the land who delivers subsistence goods in advance to obtain forest products and charges the worker rent for the right to exploit part of the forest.

Extractive reserves are primarily a solution for social problems inherent in extractivism. In this light, extractive reserves represent a major advance over traditional labor and social relations. The extractive reserve is also an adequate economic solution for extractive workers to the extent that rules are established for the access to land and to new forms of marketing of products and the consequent increase of income.

It is worth mentioning that even if the introduction of new technology means the aggregation of value to products extracted from the forest, it does not automatically imply an alternative for regional development. Whether or not extractive reserves are successful depends on how well they are linked to other regional policies. Such policies include the economic and ecological zoning of the region and the prevailing policy of technological development and industrialization.

In spite of existing constraints, the extractive reserve is still one of the most promising alternatives not only for the results it offers to extractive populations but also because they:

- are legitimate from the social point of view;
- deal simultaneously with social, economic and environmental aspects of land-use;
- establish concrete limits to deforestation;
- allow the establishment of forest reserve areas for future exploitation.

Within these limits, initiatives concerning the creation of extractive reserves should be provided with incentives and the concept could be expanded to situations outside of the Amazon, such as in the coastal mangrove areas.

Perhaps the direction of extractive reserve development can be seen in a cooperative program developed in late 1990 between the National Council of Rubber Tappers and the Institute for Amazonian Studies (IEA) with the Brazilian Environmental Institute (IBAMA). The program hopes to implement the National Program of Extractive Reserves emphasizing two main aspects: 1) the consolidation of existing reserves and 2) the creation of the largest possible number of extractive areas all over the Amazon within the shortest time possible. The most important consequence of the proposal for extractive reserves is the paradigm it establishes for local development: the economic valorization of the forest and the social benefit resulting from its exploitation. Although not originally devised as a local alternative, the extractive reserve presents the main parameters to be considered in a model of sustainable development for the Amazon in:

- use of the forest as a productive base,
- combination of social and economic aspects,
- and democratization of the structure of land-use.

A model for sustainable development does not yet exist, but the proposed model merits serious discussion.

Requirement for the Definition of a Regional Model of Sustainable Development

The definition of guidelines for sustainable development of the Amazon suggests that the method used by IEA in the preparation of the proposal for extractive reserves could be generalized to other areas and activities.

The Institute for Amazon Studies model proceeds from two general assumptions. First, there are separate realms of action. It is the responsibility of government to assure to its citizens the right to land, education, health, public goods and services, etc., and it is the people's duty to define how those needs will be translated into specific activities. The second assumption refers to the concept of social participation. In the formulation of public policy, IEA views its role to be that of a provider of certain skills in areas where less privileged social sectors do not have access. The most important of these areas is information, an essential requirement for decision making and a basic source of power. A relationship of exchange of different skills emerges among sectors of the civil society and/or between these sectors and the State. This competence is established to the extent that it is possible to gather key information to define public policies to meet social demand. Reconciling the needs of the Amazonian society with the future of regional development requires adequate information to be translated into new policies. However, the efficiency of these measures will depend on the strength of civil society involved in the process.

Basic Information

To advance any kind of social program for Amazon development along these lines a series of basic research and policy strategies must be addressed. These include:

- satellite-aided identification of the potential extractive areas in the Amazon.
- placing all potential extractive areas into extractive reserves to ensure that the necessary research eventually will be possible.
- map current and potential use of forests, including the precise features of prevailing social relations in the various regions of the Amazon.
- recovery of historical information about the volume, value, marketing and geographic distribution of all non-wood products exploited in the past or present.
- preform historical analysis of the structure of land-use comparing the present situation to the context before the incentive model of the occupation of the Amazon.
- define a scientific policy and stimulate the study of alternatives to sustainable exploitation of non-wood products, and
- define a regional industrialization model of forest products which includes other sectors of the Amazonian society.

The legal and institutional basis required to start this comprehensive program was prepared over the last six months by the IEA with the cooperation of the National Council of Rubber Tappers and the IBAMA and it resulted in Decree no. 98897 of the Executive Power dated 30 January 1990 dealing with the regulation of procedures involved in the creation of areas specially protected for sustainable extraction. The new aspect of this law is that large continuous areas can be assigned as extractive reserves regardless of their previous regularization concerning land-use. According to the Brazilian law, an area of environmental protection created by decree can only be altered by the National Congress. The creation of extractive reserves prevents local resources from being exploited in a non-sustainable way, which means that it imposes an absolute limit to deforestation and guarantees the rights of local people.

PART FIVE
PRODUCTION
ALTERNATIVES

There is a diversity of opinions on the causes of the conversion of forest to pasture. There is an even greater diversity of opinions held by agricultural production specialists on how to "solve" the problems. Production scientists view their challenge as that of developing and using technologies to meet livestock production goals while maintaining or improving the environment. This section presents three chapters that discuss production alternatives on areas formerly dominated by tropical forests and approach these from quite diverse perspectives.

Serrão and Toledo conclude that the major problem of cattle production in the tropics is pasture degradation. Vast forest resources of the humid tropics can be conserved by the use of sustainable production systems based on pastures. Venator, Glaeser, and Soto and others have determined that certain parts of the tropical forests in Mexico could be improved by planting agroforestry mixtures of crop plants, pasture plants, and low- and high-value trees. Restrepo suggests that the ecosystem of the tropics in Mexico is complex and the carrying capacity for humans is limited. Trujillo-Arriaga argues that social and economic constraints must be addressed to solve the problems of deforestation. Solutions to the problems associated with development of tropical forests involve the integration of political, social, economical, and technological factors for the benefit of the human race.

— Carlton H. Herbel

15

Sustaining Pasture-based Production Systems for the Humid Tropics

E. Adilson Serrão
Jose M. Toledo

Cattle ranching in Latin America has assumed a prominent role in occupation of frontier lands and has been regarded as one of the major contributors to deforestation of humid tropical areas in the region, fueled by socioeconomic and political forces operating in the different countries of the region. These forces include the high demands for beef and milk for rapidly increasing populations, a clear shift of the cattle industry from prime lands to marginal and frontier areas due to the expansion of crop production, migration of landless people from impoverished high-population density areas searching for a better way of living, and governmental fiscal incentives to cattle raising.

Reports from different countries in Latin America indicate that about 20 million hectares of humid tropical forest have been directly or indirectly converted to pasture. This represents about 3% of total humid forests in Latin America. Leading countries in that respect are Brazil with about 10 million hectares (Serrão and Conto, in press; Serrão and Kitamura 1988; Serrao and Toledo, in press), Mexico with 5.5 million hectares (Peralta and Ramos 1988), Colombia with 1.5 million hectares (Ramirez and Seré 1988), and Peru with 0.5 million hectares (Schaus 1987).

The dominant feature of cattle production systems replacing forests in the humid tropics of Latin America is pasture degradation, which is the main factor contributing to the low biological and economic efficiency of the production systems. The low biological and economic efficiency of cattle production systems, after converting tropical forest, is the result of the stage of development of the Latin American countries and the models of development adopted. These developing countries are forced to make use of their natural resources for economic growth. Large scale deforestation and pasture degradation in the region has been the result of poorly conceived policies which encourage large extensive ranching, threaten the fragility of the environment, and favor the utilization of poorly adapted forage germplasm and inappropriate technologies. In this paper, we analyze the productivity of pastures replacing forest with the available technology, discuss recent technological achievements, and suggest an integral approach to improve sustainability of pasture-based systems with emphasis on the acid, low-fertility soil areas of the humid tropics of Latin America.

The Problem: Pasture Degradation

Undoubtedly, the primary problem of cattle production in the humid tropics is pasture degradation, leading to unsustained and inefficient production systems. It is estimated that at least 50% of the pastures which have been planted are in some advanced stage of degradation (Serrão 1988; Serrão and Toledo, in press; Ramirez and Seré 1988; Schaus 1987; Ortega et al. 1988).

First-Cycle Pastures

Even though there has been a sharp reduction in the rate of deforestation for pasture during the last 10-15 years (Uhl and Buschbacher 1988), a considerable amount of new pasture lands in the region have been recently developed and are still in their first cycle. Besides, others will still probably be established, mainly in the Brazilian Amazon. The general pattern of the degradation process in this phase of pasture development has been widely described and illustrated (Toledo and Ara 1977; Serrão et al. 1979; Dias Filho and Serrão 1982; Toledo and Serrão 1982; Toledo 1986). In general, during the first three to four years after establishment, productivity in these pioneer pastures is good. However, after this period, there is a gradual, but fairly rapid decline in the productivity of the grasses planted, primarily commercially available "Guinea grass" (*Panicum maximum*) and "Jaragua" (*Hyparrhenia rufa*) and, in smaller scale, other less important grasses, including *Axonopus scoparius* and *A. micay*. This process of decline is accompanied by an increasing presence of weeds, the pastures reaching advanced stages of degradation after five to seven years on average. This pasture life period varies with prevailing biotic and management factors. Productivity has recently been extended with the advent of better adapted and more aggressive grasses such as *Brachiaria decumbens* (Serrão and Gondin 1966) and *B. humidicola* if severe biotic pressures (mainly insect pests) are not a limiting factor.

Second-Cycle Pastures

When first-cycle pastures reach degradation, ranchers either abandon degraded pastures to fallow for an indeterminate period or re-establish new pasture systems — the second-cycle pastures. Reclamation of degraded first cycle pastures (rather than continuing deforestation for new pasture lands) has been gradually coming into fashion because of (1) decreasing nearby availability of original forests; (2) pressure from society for deforestation reduction; (3) reduced fiscal incentives; and (4) the need for better utilization of ranching infrastructure already available. This has occurred mainly in Brazil in the last 10 years, where 700 to 800 thousand hectares of degraded pasture lands have been re-established with new pasture systems (Serrão 1988; Serrão and Toledo, in press).

Degraded pastures reclamation generally involves more intensive high-input practices such as mechanization for land preparation and planting, fertilization and pesticides for better pasture establishment and maintenance. *B. humidicola*, on the largest scale, guinea grass, on a smaller scale and, more recently — but increasingly — *B. brizantha* cv. Marandu and *Andropogon gayanus* cv. Planaltina have been the grasses used in this process. Due to the high costs involved (about US $200 per hectare), cash cropping, mainly with corn and rice, frequently has been used in the process of pasture establishment with satisfactory bio-socioeconomic results (Veiga 1986).

Even though the short and mid-term resulting pasture productivity and stability tend to be higher than those of first-cycle pastures, their long-term sustainability is questionable due to similar biotic and technological constraints of first-cycle pastures. Here again, although in smaller proportion, forage germplasm (grasses and legumes) is still the main limiting factor. The other limiting factor is the relatively high cost of the technology. Because of their poverty, this type of technology lies beyond the grasp of most Latin American agriculturalists.

Derived Grasslands

Under conditions of most other countries in Latin America, where cattle raising is carried out in much smaller holdings than those found in the Brazilian Amazon, several years of subsistence cropping practice elapse before pasture establishment, and pasture management (weeding, burning, grazing) is more intensive. Under this management, there is less chance for forest-like second-growth regeneration. After the planted grasses (*P. maximum, H. rufa, B. decumbens, Axonopus scoparius*, etc.) disappear due to edaphic, biotic and management factors, the area is dominated by a native herbaceous derived grassland "torourco" (*Axonopus compressus, Paspalum conjugatum*), or naturalized grasses. Although deriving from the pasture degradation process, these socio-economically important native grasslands, widespread in Latin America (except in Brazil), represent a relatively stable disclimax, which can carry up to 0.5 AU per hectare (1 AU = 450 kg of live weight). In spite of its relative stability, these derived pastures can also be further degraded due to mismanagement, primarily overgrazing, leading to soil compaction and biotic factors; for example, the soil worm *Eutheola* sp., can destroy considerable areas of the most palatable species (*A. compressus and P. conjugatum*), favoring the unpalatable *Homolepsis aturensis* (Toledo 1986, Ramirez and Seré 1988). Low stocking rates, and frequent fires in dryer environments, mainly in the Brazilian Amazon, degrade planted pastures into a derived grassland of *Imperata brasiliensis* and *Pteridium* spp. (Toledo 1986). Thus, there is a strong need for the development of pasture reclamation techniques for those low productivity degraded derived grasslands that exist throughout the humid tropics of Latin America.

Causes of Pasture Degradation

Degradation of pastures in the humid tropics is due to environmental, technological, and socioeconomic causes.

Environmental Factors

The generally poor resources of the humid tropical environment constitutes the main limiting force determining pasture productivity. Among environmental factors, most important is soil fertility. The initial pulse of soil fertility due to clearing and burning of the forest biomass (Falesi 1976; Seubert et al. 1977; Serrão et al. 1979), although bio-socioeconomically important, is ephemeral. Productivity decline of first-cycle pastures is directly related to the decline in soil fertility (Toledo and Ara 1977; Toledo and Morales 1982; Serrao et al. 1979; Toledo and Serrao, 1982; Serrão 1988). Phosphorus has been shown to be the most critical nutrient for pasture stability (Serrão et al. 1979; Falesi 1976; Rolim et al. 1979; Serrão et al. 1979; Dias Filho and Serrão 1987). The organic matter of the soil is able to maintain for some time a fairly acceptable supply of nitrogen for the grass growth. However, in time nitrogen availability is responsible for low productivity and lack of competitiveness of planted grasses.

The generally high humidity prevailing in humid tropical forest environments, favors the proliferation of pests and diseases which can undermine the stability of introduced pastures. Very important pests are the species of spittlebugs of the genera *Deois, Zulia, Mahanarva ("cigarrinha", "mion" "salivazo"*, other names), which have become the major limiting factor for *Digitaria* spp., *Cynodon* spp. and especially *Brachiaria* spp. pasture productivity (Silva and Magalhaes 1980; Calderón 1983; CIAT 1980-87). Also diseases by fungi of the genera *Colletotrichum* and *Rhizoctonia* have caused serious damages to commercial forage legumes of the genera *Stylosanthes* and *Centrosema*, respectively (CIAT 1980-87; Dias Filho and Serrão 1983). Similarly, Guinea grass seed fungal diseases caused by *Fusarium roseum* and *Tilleria airesii* (Freire et al. 1979) have been major degradants.

Excessive rainfall regions prevalent in the northwest of the Amazon basin (eastern Ecuador, northern Colombia, northern Peru and northwestern Brazil), Central America and southern Mexico are unfavorable environments for plant growth. The reduced radiation due to intensive cloudiness can negatively affect the growth rate of grasses and legumes (Pizarro 1985). The pastures under heavier saturated soils are prone to degradation by excessive trampling damage and resulting soil compaction under grazing.

The seasonal humid tropical climate that occurs in about 70% of the Amazon basin (southeastern Peru, northern Bolivia and southeastern Brazilian Amazon), and in large areas of Mexico and Central America have a distinct dry season. Prolonged dry spells frequently contribute to pastures degradation directly by drastically reducing forage growth and favor weed invasion, or indirectly by making pastures extremely susceptible to fire (Uhl and Kauffman, in press).

The native weed communities that sprout after pasture establishment, represent one of the greatest obstacles for maintaining pasture stability in the region (Hecht 1979; Uhl et al., in press). The question is, how much of the weed presence in pastures in the humid tropics is a consequence, and how much of it is a cause of pasture degradation.

Technological Factors

Although they can be, to a large extent, controlled by man, technological factors have been major constraints to pasture sustainability in the humid tropics of Latin America. The lack of adaptation of forage germplasm to the region's climatic, edaphic and biotic conditions is probably responsible for at least 50% of pasture degradation problems in Latin America, and an even higher proportion (90%) in poor acid soils. The past and most recent commercially available forages are either highly demanding of soil-fertility, such as guinea grass (Serrao et al. 1979; Italiano et al. 1982; Dias Filho and Serrão 1987), star grass (*Cynodon nlenfuensis*), and pangola grass (*Digitaria* spp.), or are susceptible to insect pests (spittlebug) such as *B. decumbens* (mainly), *B. humidicola* and *B. ruziziensis*. The legumes are susceptible to diseases, such as *Centrosema* spp. (*Rhizoctonia* and *Bacteriosis*) and *Stylosanthes* spp. (*Anthracnosis*), or either difficult to manage in association under grazing, such as *Pueraria phseoloides*).

These pastures based on limited adapted grass and legume species require management schemes based on high phosphorus fertilization (Serrão et al. 1979, Dias Filho and Serrão 1987, Veiga and Falesi 1986), nitrogen fertilization (Toledo and Morales 1979) and pesticides use (Serrão and Conto, in press; Ramirez and Sere 1988, Schaus 1987; Ortega et al., in press; Peralta and Ramos, in press; Prado et al. 1988). However, due to their high costs, these required management schemes have been replaced by cheap pasture management alternatives, such as pasture burning, which may also lead to pasture degradation (Uhl and Kauffman, in press). Other common types of pasture mismanagement are overstocking and insufficient livestock rotation in pastures, which lead to rapid degradation through excessive reduction in forage biomass, soil compaction and consequent weed dominance. The lack of tradition of using fertilizers is another important cause of pasture degradation.

The development of new adapted grasses and legumes is needed to reduce costs of management.

Socio-economic Factors

Although most times overlooked, the socioeconomic environment directly and indirectly play a very important role in pasture degradation in the region. The ratio of input/output prices is often politically determined by governments in their struggle for controlling inflation and solving the nutritional problems of an ever increasing urban poor population. Controlled prices of beef and dairy products, plus the generally high transportation costs of expensive agricultural inputs, have contributed to economic unfeasibility of adoption of capital requiring technologies for maintaining pasture productivity.

Government subsidies (SUDAM 1983) for investment in land clearing and cattle ranching in the Brazilian Amazon have resulted in the development of large-size ranches that, despite the possibilities of applying technologies, are extremely difficult to manage, given: a) that these large ranches often occupy big patches of land, which are cleared without planning for the best land use; b) the strong tendency of pastures to degrade and the weeds (secondary regrowth) to invade; and c) the extensive nature of the production systems, which unskilled managers are unable to control to minimize the complex degradation process.

On the other hand, farmers or medium size cattle raisers in Central America and the Andean countries are limited by the unavailability of integrated policies and relevant technologies to favor investment in appropriate technology and sustainable productivity.

Horizons for Sustainable Pasture-based Systems

Need for Intensification

Population density in developing frontiers determine, in high degree, the rural production systems, including farm size (production unit sizes). Figure 15.1 shows a model of the changes in intensification of land use and management of forest exploitation, productive trees, cropping and cattle production, as influenced by human population density.

In low population-density areas, where land prices are normally low, timber extraction is a major activity that co-exists with gathering of native tree and wild animal products, long-fallow shifting cultivation and extensive beef cattle ranching.

With intermediate population density, land prices are higher and the areas for timber exploitation tend to be reduced, and should be managed (Figure 15.1) together with reforestation. The use of multi-purpose trees and plantations grows in area and importance. Shifting cultivation is intensified, facing the problem of shorter fallow periods. Cattle ranches are subdivided and pasture management is intensified toward more efficient dual-purpose beef-and-milk production systems. This is the stage of agricultural development in which integrated farming systems (agro-silvopastoral or silvo-pastoral) become more relevant.

High population density leads to the highest land prices and to a situation of minimum native forest and expansion of tree plantations and high-input cropping to meet increased industrial and food demands. This expansion will occur together with specialization of production systems toward high levels of productivity. Dual-purpose pasture-based systems will also specialize in dairy production where pasture areas are reduced and managed intensively and supplemented by agricultural by-product concentrates. Beef production will continue in low population density areas within the region.

As population density grows, tree plantation and cropping will expand at the expense of native forest and pasture lands. High-population densities occur in localized areas around large cities throughout the humid tropics. An extreme situation of high population density occurs in Java, Indonesia. In the humid tropics of Latin America, in general there are contrasting

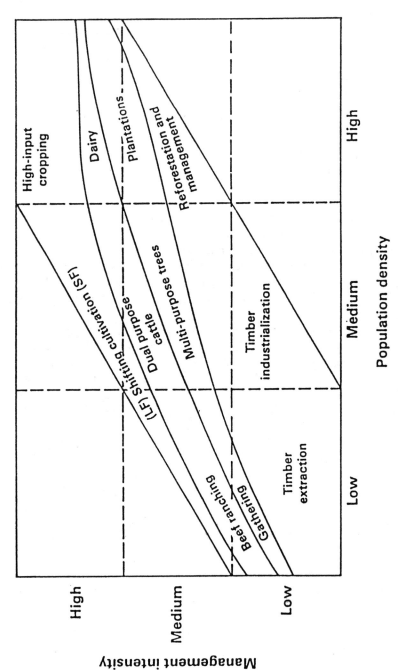

FIGURE 15.1 Model of land use and management intensity of different rural production systems in relation to population density
(LF = Long fallow, SF = Short fallow)

population densities ranging from low, in many areas of the Amazon basin, to intermediate in Central America and Mexico.

Cattle production in the humid tropics of Latin America is and will play an important role in rural development. It seems clear that intensification will have to occur naturally in presently extensive cattle ranching areas. More so, if the present consciousness for preservation of natural resources and for higher levels of socioeconomic benefits are to be realized at decison-making levels.

Recognizing the tendency toward intensification is particularly important for the large-size extensively managed ranches in the Brazilian Amazon and some extensive ranching areas in Central America. For the medium-to-small pasture-based farms that occur in the Andean Amazon, South Mexico and Central America, it is important to recognize that, despite the already reduced farm sizes, intensification of land use and management of resources are limited by socioeconomic conditions and the lack of appropriate technology for higher sustainability of the primary production system — the pasture.

Available Technology

Presently, technology for intensification of cattle ranching through reclamation of degraded first-cycle pastures using mechanization, fertilization and weed control is available. In the same way, technology for extending productivity of first-cycle pastures, including phosphorus fertilization, weed control and subdivision of paddocks for improved grazing management is also available. These technologies, resulting from years of research are, in some degree, being used in the Brazilian Amazon with varied degrees of success (Serrão and Homma 1982).

The limited success in the adoption of these high input technologies is due to: a) its economic feasibility is possible only under subsidized conditions, which infrequently occurs in developing countries. b) reclaimed pastures are based on forage species and cultivars of only limited adaptations to the naturally poor and acid soil conditions (as is the case of *Panicum maximum* cv. Coloniao and to a lesser extent, *Brachiaria brizantha* cv. Marandu) or to the prevailing biotic pressures (such as of spittlebugs on *Brachiaria humidicola*, and, especially on *B. decumbens*). Consequently, the reclaimed pastures, although generally more stable than first-cycle grass pastures, are still prone to degradation and their stability will eventually depend upon relatively high investments for maintenance, fertilization, and weed control.

Appropriate Technology

Considering the experience and knowledge previously gained regarding pasture development in the humid tropics, the following assumptions (hypotheses) should provide the foundation for the search for sustainability of pasture-based production systems in acid, low-fertility soils of the humid tropics:

- Adaptation of forage grasses and legumes to the prevailing environmental (soil-biotic-climatic) conditions is the basis for developing low-input, sustainable pasture systems for the humid tropics.
- Efficient nitrogen fixing and nutrient recycling is the basis for sustained pasture stability under low soil fertility conditions.
- Well established and well managed grass-legume based pastures can efficiently recycle the relatively small quantities of nutrients in the modified ecosystem.
- Intensification of pasture production using appropriate low-input pasture technology will increase pasture sustainability, thus reducing the pressure for more deforestation.
- In the medium and long-term basis, stable pasture-crop/pasture-tree systems are biologically and socioeconomically more efficient than pure open pastures.
- To be sustainable, pasture-based production system modules have to be within socioeconomically manageable sizes.

Intensification of pasture production systems on degrading and degraded pasture lands is, no doubt, a must to reduce deforestation. In summary, the appropriate pasture technology should be: a) based on well adapted germplasm; b) of low input requirements for establishment and maintenance; c) of high efficiency in nitrogen fixation and nutrient (P, K, Ca, Mg, S) recycling; and d) of high carrying capacity and quality of forage. In order to play additional roles in integrated pasture-based production systems, it should also have: a) the capability for improving physical and chemical soil conditions, and b) compatibility with crop and tree production.

Germplasm: The Foundation for Pasture Sustainability

Forage germplasm has been, to a large extent, the most important technological factor responsible for the success or the failure of pasture systems in the humid tropics.

The old generation pioneer pasture grasses such as "guinea grass," "Jaragua" and "molasses grass," accidentally introduced in the continent about 300 years ago with the slave trade (Parsons 1972), are now entitled to be referred to as "monuments" for the very important role they have played in the agricultural development in Latin America. However, they have proved to be far from the appropriate germplasm for the most limiting marginal environmental and socio-economic conditions of the humid tropics. They have largely been utilized for lack of better options, but gradually have been replaced by a more adapted generation of grasses.

Better adapted, less-demanding new generation of grasses which include *Brachiaria decumbens* and *B. humidicola,* along with the still-present, high-demand old grass generation. They presently make a major contribution to cattle production on pastures in the humid tropics of Latin America. Undoubtedly, this more recent grass germplasm is more appropriate for the environmental (mainly edaphic) and socio-economical conditions of the Latin American humid tropics. However, they suffer from lack of resistance to spittlebugs, the cause of some severe economic losses in *Brachiaria* spp. pastures throughout Latin America (Silva and Magalhaes 1980; Calderon 1983; Lapointe et al. 1988).

In spite of their potential contribution to pasture sustainability and quality, legumes in the past have rarely been used in Latin American pasture lands. Only in sporadic cases, legumes such as *P. phaseoloides, C. pubescens* and *S. guianensis* have been used in commercial pastures in the region, with little success due to lack of adaptability or management constraints of commercially available cultivars.

Due to the urgent need for appropriate germplasm for the development of low-cost, sustainable pastures for Latin America, the International Network for Evaluation of Tropical Pastures (RIEPT), coordinated by the Centro International de Agricultura Tropical (CIAT), and in close collaboration with national research institutions of the countries of the region, was initiated in 1979 (Toledo 1982). RIEPT's prime objective is to select new germplasm of grasses and legumes adapted to acid nutrient-poor soils, resistant to major prevailing pests and diseases, with high persistence and easy to establish.

This international regional forage selection effort is based mostly on important new generation collections of germplasm of the grass genera *Brachiaria, Panicum, Andropogon* and of the legume genera *Centrosema, Pueraria, Stylosanthes, Desmodium,* and in smaller scale, *Paspalum, Axonopus* (grasses) and *Leucaena, Calopogonium* and *Arachis* (legumes). About 800 new grass and 1200 legume accessions are now being tested in different sites in the Latin American humid tropics (CIAT 1986, 1987). Some species and accessions have shown considerable promise for low-input sustainable pasture production, and a few were released as cultivars and are already being utilized in pasture production systems in the region (Table 15.1). Such is the case of *A. gayanus* cv. Planaltina *(CIAT 621)* and *B. brizantha* cv. Marandu (Nunes et al. 1984), *B. dictyoneura* cv. Llanero (CIAT 6133), *and S. guianensis* cv. Pucallpa (CIAT 184), and *Centrosema acutifolium* cv. Vichada (CIAT 184).

Adapted germplasm is not a panacea. Adequate pasture establishment and post-establishment management are essential for the germplasm to be able to express its potential.

Low-input Establishment

Pasture establishment is critical for the future performance of the sward. The new grasses and legumes ought to be able to replace existing vegetation in degraded pasture lands, and advantageously compete with weeds in generally poor soil environment.

Efforts are underway to develop low-input techniques for pasture establishment in degraded lands in the humid tropics by EMBRAPA in Brazil, INIAA/IVITA/CIAT in Peru, Nestle/ICA/CIAT in Colombia; and INIFAP in southern Mexico. These research activities are mainly addressing the problems related to: (1) land clearing (native vegetation control) and soil preparation (upgrading physical and chemical soil properties) using low-cost systems for the efficient use of labor, mechanization, weed control and fertilization; (2) use of appropriate cash cropping to pay for upgrading of the environmental conditions for pasture reclamation; (3) making proper use of aggressive pasture species for initial weed competition and rapid establishment.

Low-input Management

The sustainability of pastures depends on the efficient nutrient cycling by adapted forage grasses and legumes with low fertility requirements. These species should be able to respond to higher fertility conditions and be compatible in association (grass-legume pasture) to produce an efficient nitrogen fixing pasture environment. These improved pastures should be of dense cover and sufficient aggressive enough to compete with weeds and minimize nutrient losses from the system. The new cultivars will tend to be highly stable.

Effective recycling and sustainable pastures will be possible with appropriate grazing management (Toledo and Serrão 1982; Spain and Salinas 1985; Spain 1988) to optimize utilization of available forage for high animal productivity, maintaining a good balance among the components of the

TABLE 15.1 Promising new cultivars and experimental germplasm of grasses and legumes for pastures in the humid tropics

Family - species	Name of cultivar	CIAT No.	Main attributes
Grasses			
Andropogon gayanus	Carimagua Planaltina San Martin	621	Resistance to spittlebug, low soil fertiliqy requirements, drought tolerance, medium quality
Brachiaria brizantha	Marandu	6780	High resistance to spittlebug, medium soil ferility requirements, medium to high quality
Brachiaria dictyoneura	Llanero	6133	Medium resistance to spittlebug, low soil fertility requirements, medium quality
Legumes			
Arachis pintoi [a]	-	17434	High compatibility with aggressive trailing grasses, medium to low soil fertility requirements
Centrosema acutifolium	Vichada	5277/5568	Resistant to Rhyzoctonia, low to medium soil fertility requirements, high quality
Centrosema macrocarpum	-	5452, 5713, 5887, 5735 CPATU/992	Resistance to Rhyzocton, low to medium soil fertility requirements, medium to high drought tolerance, compatible with medium aggressiveness grasses, high quality
Desmodium ovalifolium	-	13089	Resistance to stem nematoda and Synchitrium, compatible with aggressive trailing grasses, low soil fertility, low to medium quality
Stylosanthes quianensis	Pucallpa	184	Tolerance to anthracno, low soil fertility requirements, good seed yield, easy to establish, compatible with medium to low aggressive grasses, high quality

a. experimental, not commercially available as yet

pasture and enough reserve and leaf area index for high production longevity. Despite efficient recycling and nitrogen fixation, minimum mineral inputs of phosphorus, potassium, magnesium and sulfur may be required (to compensate for the small extraction of nutrients in the animal products). Similarly, strategic weed control may be required.

Up to the present, research on pasture recycling in the humid tropics is very limited and deals mainly with degrading and pure grass pastures. The data show that recycling efficiency depends on original soil fertility status and cattle mineralization in *B. decumbens* (Buschbacher 1984) and *B. humidicola* (Teixeira 1987) pastures. A study in Yurimaguas, Peru, showed that potassium is efficiently recycled in *B. humidicola* pastures. This is due to a profuse root system (7 tons/ha) and high K uptake capacity (luxury consumption) of this grass. (Ayarza 1988).

It is recognized that nitrogen is critical for pasture sustainability. Research on this is underway in Peru, where, after two years under grazing, a *B. decumbens* + *D. ovalifolium* pasture is fixing 450 kg of nitrogen per hectare per year, from which 175 kg have been transferred to the grass (Ara 1988).

These results clearly show the potential contribution of recycling and nitrogen fixation for the sustainability of humid tropical pastures.

Expected Pasture Productivity

Moderate to high levels of animal gains can be expected from this new emerging adapted germplasm-based pasture technology. Table 15.2 shows experimental results of research underway in different areas in the region, indicating that, with grass-legume associations of selected germplasm, it is possible to obtain average daily animal gains above 400 g and annual animal gains per hectare greater than 500 kg.

The Pasture-crop-tree Integration Approach

The agrosilvopastoral systems are potentially important land use possibilities in the humid tropics of Latin America. Several important papers by Hecht (1982) and Peck (1982) and, more recently, by Borel (1988), Estrada et al. (1988), Toledo y Torres (in press), review the state of knowledge, report case studies or explore the potential of integrated systems for the region.

Intensification of land use in Latin American humid tropics will spontaneously and unevenly occur in response to increasing population densities in different sites of the region, as discussed in Figure 15.1.

TABLE 15.2 Animal liveweight gains from grass-legume pastures in the humid tropics

Pasture	Years	Stocking rate	Weight gain Daily/animal	Weight gain Yearly/hectare
Paspalum notatum (Trensa)[1]	-	-	-	200
Andropogon gayanus[2]	2	2.1	0.443	340
Brachiaria humidicola[2]	2	2.5	0.380	351
Andropogon gayanus + Stylosanthes guianensis	5	4.4	0.412	660
Andropogon gayanus + Centrosema macrocarpum[3]	2	3.5	0.510	650
Brachiaria decumbens + Desmodium ovalifolium[4]	4	4.4	0.379	626
Brachiaria humidicola + Desmodium ovalifolium[4]	2	4.4	0.429	691
Brachiaria dictyoneura + Desmondium ovalifolium[3]	2	5.0	0.440	803

1. Santander de Quilichao, Colombia (Escobar et al. 1971)
2. Paragominas, Brazil (EMBRAPA 1988)
3. Santander de Quilichao, Colombia (CIAT 1987)
4. Yurimaguas, Peru (Dextre et al. 1987)

There is a need to reclaim degraded lands mostly resulting from shifting cultivation and unstable pastures. Efficient agricultural production systems of high productivity and sustainability ought to replace presently low productivity degraded areas in the ecosystem. The integration of annual crops (to pay for upgrading of the soil environment) with pastures that are established using residual crop fertilization (to further improve physical and chemical conditions of the soil through effective nitrogen fixation and recycling of nutrients), together with multipurpose trees (to pump nutrients to the upper soil layers, to fix nitrogen and provide supplemental animal feed, shade and extra income) seems to be the direction to follow.

Intensified pasture-based cattle production systems, together with crops and trees, can play an important ecological and economic role in the restoration of degraded lands of the region. These integrated systems may be extremely efficient in the use and conservation of natural resources (soil-water-radiation-animals) in the humid tropics. The proportion and dominance of the different components in the integrated production systems will depend on the:

- availability of agronomically reliable and economically attractive technologies for each component,
- market forces related to population densities, distance from high-density population centers, size of demand and value of the products, and
- policies for development at the governmental and regional level.

In agrosilvopastoral systems, efficiencies are expected to be gained in the management of the soil through:

- upgrading soil physical and chemical conditions through pioneer cash crops;
- effective nitrogen fixation and recycling of nutrients (mainly P-K-Mg-S) through grass-legume pastures and trees;
- protecting soil from erosion and leaching through high cover multistrata (pastures and trees) canopies.

Similarly, efficiencies are expected to be gained in managing the water resources through:

- reducing runoff by maintaining high cover of the vegetation and good structure and permeability of the soil through deep and profuse rooting of pastures and trees;

- increasing the potential evapotranspiration through high cover, deep rooted pasture-tree canopies, improving the hydrologic balance in the ecosystem, thereby minimizing water logging and flooding in the lower parts of the watershed, as well as tapping water deep in the profile during the dry season.

The trees will contribute to the reduction of temperature at the different strata of the system:

- at the soil level, enhancing micro and macrofauna for effective mineralization and turnover,
- above the soil, reducing air temperature to favor higher productivity of crossed cattle for dual purpose (beef-milk) production.

Efficiencies are also expected to be obtained at the economic level:

- Crop production will pay for soil upgrading for pasture establishment. Besides, after several years of good pasture-tree production, crops may benefit from the superior physical and chemical status of the soil, thus avoiding refertilization of the system and providing higher levels of profit. For example, in an integrated system, maintaining 10 to 20% of the area in crops and the rest of the area on pasture-tree fallow for five to ten years may be an economically interesting balance.
- Intensified pasture-tree production should be able to stock up to 2 AU/ha and generate daily income through milking and seasonal additional income from the selling of animals for beef or reproduction purposes. Cattle production on pasture also plays the important role of economic security for the producer, particularly in the inflationary and unpredictable economies of Latin America.
- The trees may also contribute economically as long-term return investment. They can be fruit trees, industrial trees and timber. They can also contribute economically as live fences and dry season feeding of cattle.

For effective integration into productive sustainable systems, the technological components (crops, trees and pastures) must be adapted to the environment, compatible among themselves and relevant to farmers' needs. Given the environmental constraints (poor and acid soils and high diseases and pest pressures) some promising pasture components are already available (commercially released or experimentally available) (Table 15.1). The agricultural components, such as rice and corn, need to be improved for adaptation to the environment and to the pasture-crop-tree systems. However, other crops with limited markets are well adapted such as cowpea, cassava and plantain. The tree components are perhaps the ones with greater difficulty in terms of adaptation (for example, Leucaena leucocephala-like trees for acid soils) and economic attractiveness. They normally are a long-term investment, with insecure revenue given the dynamic and reduced size of present markets. Research is needed for selection of multipurpose trees for acid poor soils and to develop the markets for well adapted humid tropical native timber and fruit trees.

Research on the pasture-crop-tree-animal interaction is very important for understanding and developing management principles to optimize productivity and sustainability of agrosilvopastoral systems.

Conclusion

Pastures have widely and somewhat unjustly been blamed as being the major threat to the humid forest ecosystems in Latin America. Pasture degradation has undoubtedly contributed to considerable deforestation in Latin America. The problems of degradation occurring in localized areas are, to a large extent, the result of political mistakes and socio-economic pressures for the utilization of forest areas. But there is enough room for optimism in the near future. In fact, with the emerging low-input appropriate technologies, pasture-based systems can certainly be a sustainable alternative for the intensification of land use in the humid tropics, thus reducing pressure for more deforestation. However, we have to bear in mind that the availability of improved pasture technology is not sufficient to solve the problem of degradation in the ecosystem. Favorable socio-economic conditions are required for the farmers adoption of the new technologies.

In order to properly induce land use intensification in general, and the use of new technologies for high productivity and sustainability, governments should:

- direct regional planning for agricultural development on suitable lands and the protection of fragile environments, inducing intensification of land use in already disturbed areas;
- reduce the fiscal incentives for large-size ranching and ownership in forest frontier lands in the humid tropics;
- invest in research and extension to apply reclamation technologies for utilization of already degraded lands with highly productive and sustainable systems, including pasture-based integrated systems;

- establish favorable mechanisms for production and commercialization of humid tropical plant products with present limited markets but with high potential to be used in integrated pasture-based systems.

Our challenge is to be realistic and pragmatic regarding pastures in the humid tropics. Cattle ranching based on pasture replacing large areas of rainforests, with its biological, cultural and socioeconomic impacts, is a reality, and may even continue to expand. One of the best approaches to conserve the still vast forest resources of the humid tropics of Latin America is to develop and induce farmers to use highly productive sustainable pasture-based production systems.

References Cited

Ara, M. 1988. Aporte de nitrogen de la leguminosa *Desmodium ovalifolium* en mezcla con *Brachiaria decumbens*. *Pasturas Tropicales*, CIAT.

Ayarza, M. 1988. Potassium dynamics in a humid tropical pasture. Ph.D. thesis. North Carolina State University, Raleigh, N.C.

Borel, R. 1988. Sistemas silvopastoriles para la producción animal en el trópico y uso de árboles forrajeros en alimentación animal. In: *VI encuentro nacional de zootecnia. Segunda conferencia nacional de producción y utilización de pastos y forrajes*. Edited by O. Sierra. Asociación de Zootecnistas del Valle de Cauca, AZOOVALLE, Palmira, Colombia.

Buschbacher, R.J. 1984. Changes in productivity and nutrient cycling follow conversion of Amazon forest to pasture. Ph.D. diss., Institute of Ecology, University of Georgia, Athens, Georgia.

_____ 1986. Tropical deforestation and pasture development. *Bioscience* 36(1): 22-28.

_____ 1987. Government-sponsored pastures in Venezuela, near the Brazilian border. In: *Amazonian rainforests: Ecosystem disturbance and recovery*. Edited by B.F. Jordan. *Ecological Studies*. no. 60. New York: Springer-Verlag.

Buschbacher, R.J., C. Uhl, and E.A.S. Serrao. 1987. Large-scale development in eastern Amazonia. Pasture management and environmental effects near Paragominas, Pará. In: *Amazonian rainforests: Ecosystem disturbance and recovery*. Edited by B.F. Jordan. Ecological Studies, no. 60. New York:Springer-Verlag.

Calderón, M. 1983. Insect pests of tropical forage plants in South America. In: *Proceedings of the XIV International Grassland Congress.* Edited by J.A. Smith and V.W. Hays, Lexington, Ky, June 15-24, 1981.

CIAT. 1980-87. Informe anual. Programa de pastos tropicales, CIAT, Cali, Colombia.

Dextre, R., M.A. Ayarza, and P.A. Sánchez. 1987. Legume-based pastures: Central Experiment. In: *TropSoils.* Technical Report 1985-86, North Carolina University.

Dias Filho, M.B. and E.A.S. Serrao. 1982. Recuperacao, melhoramento e manejo de pastagens na região de Paragominas, Pará. Documento No.5., Belém: Centro de Pesquisa Agropecuária do Trópico Umido (EMBRAPA/CPATU).

_____ 1983. Principais doencas associadas as gramineas e leguminosas em ecossistema de floresta na Amazonia oriental brasileira. EMBRAPA-CPATU. Comunicado No. 37, Belém.

_____ 1987. Limitacaos de fertilidade do solo na recuperacao de pastagem degradada de capim coloniao (*Panicum maximum* Jacq.) em Paragominas, na Amazonia oriental. *Boletim de Pesquisa* No.87. Belém. EMBRAPA-CPATU.

EMBRAPA. 1988. Recuperacao, melhoramento e manejo de pastagens nas regioes de Paragominas e Marajó, Estado do Pará. Belém. Research Project. Progress Report. EMBRAPA/CPATU, Projeto da Pesquisa. Form's 12 and 13).

Escobar, G.L., P.A. Ramirez, A. Michielin de Pieri and J.S. Gómez. 1971. Comportamiento de novillas Cebú en pastoreo continuo rotacional en pasto *Trenza.* ICA. Centro Nacional de Investigaciones Agropecuarias Palmira. *Boletin Técnico* No. 15.

Estrada, R.D., C. Seré, and H. Luzuriaga. 1988. Sistemas de producción agrosilvopastoriles en la selva baja de la provincia del Napo, Ecuador. Centro Internacional de Agricultura Tropical (CIAT), Cali, Colombia.

Falesi, I.C. 1976. Ecossistema de pastagem cultivada na Amazonia brasileira. Belém, EMBRAPA-CPATU. *Boletim Técnico* No.1.

Freire, F.C.O.. E.A.S. Serrao, and F.C. Albuquerque. 1979. Carie do sino, uma séria doenca de panicula de capim coloniao. *Fitopatologia Brasileira* 4(1): 111.

Hecht, S.B. 1979. Leguminosas espontáneas en praderas amazónicas y su potencial forrajero. In: *Producción de pastos en suelos acidos de los trópicos.* Edited by P.A. Sánchez, and L.E. Tergas. Centro Internacional de Agricultura Tropical (CIAT), Colombia.

_____ 1982a. Cattle ranching development in the eastern Amazon: Evaluation of development strategy. Ph.D. Dissertation. Berkeley, University of California.

_____ 1982b. Agroforestry in the Amazon Basin: Practice, theory and limits of promising land use. In: *Amazonia: Agriculture and land use research*. Edited by S. B. Hecht. Centro Internacional de Agricultura Tropical (CIAT), Cali, Colombia.

Italiano, E.C., E. Moraes, and A.C. Canto. 1982. Fertilizacao de pastagens de capim coloniao em degradacao. EMBRAPA-UEPAE Manaus. *Boletim Técnico* No. 31.

Lapointe, S.L., G. Arango and G. Sotelo. 1988. A methodology for evaluation of host plant resistant in *Brachiaria* spp. to spittlebug species (*Homoptera: Cercopidae*). XVI International Grassland Congress.

Nunes, S.G., A. Boock, M.I. de O. Penteado, and D.T. Gomes. 1984. *Brachiaria brizantha* cv. Marandu. Campo Grande, EMBRAPA/CNPGC. Documento 21.

Ortega, C.M., A.R. Delgado, J.J. Quill, D. Urriola, and P.J. Argel. 1988. Diagnóstico de la investigación pratense. Centro Internacional de Agricultura Tropical (CIAT). Cali, Colombia. .

Parsons, J.J. 1972. Spread of African pasture grasses to the American Tropics. *Range Management*. 25.5.

Peck, R.B. 1982. Forest research activities and the importance of multi-strata production systems in the Amazon (Humid Tropics). In: *Amazonia: Agriculture and land use research*. Edited by S.B. Hecht,Centro Internacional de Agricultura Tropical (CIAT), Cali, Colombia.

Peralta, A.M. and A.S. Ramos. 1988. Diagnóstico de los sistemas de producción bovina en el trópico de México. Centro Internacional de Agricultura Tropical (CIAT). Cali, Colombia.

Pizarro, E.A. 1985. *Red internacional de evaluación de pastos tropicales: Resultados 1982-1985*. Vols. I y II. III Reunión de la RIEPT. Octubre 21-24. Centro Internacional de Agricultura Tropical (CIAT) Cali, Colombia.

Prado, V.A., R.N. Rodriguez, and J.C. Vargas. In press. *Diagnóstico sobre la situación y avances de la investigación en pastos en Costa Rica*. Centro Internacional de Agricultura Tropical (CIAT), Cali, Colombia. .

Ramirez, A. and C. Seré. 1988. *Brachiaria decumbens* en el Caquetá: Adopción y uso en ganaderías de doble propósito. Documento Preliminar. Centro Internacional de Agricultura Tropical (CIAT), Cali, Colombia.

Rolim, F.A., H.W. Koster, E.J.A. Khan, and H.M. Saito. 1979. Alguns resultados de pesquisas agrostológicas na região de Paragominas, Pará e nordeste de Mato Grosso. Belém, SUDAM.

Schaus, R.A. 1987. El rol de investigación en pasturas en la Amazonia peruana. In: *La investigacion en pastos dentro del contexto cientifico y socioeconomico de los paises. V Reunion de Comite Asesor de la Red Internacional de Evaluacion de Pastos Tropicales (RIEPT)*. David, Chiriqui, Panama. May 11-16.

Serrão, E.A.S. 1988. Pasturas mejoradas en areas de bosque húmedo brasileño: Conocimientos actuales. In: *VI encuentro nacional de zootecnia. Segunda conferencia nacional de producción y utilización de pastos y forrajes*. Edited by O. Sierra. Asociacion de Zootecnistas del Valle de Cauca (AZOOVALLE), Palmira, Colombia.

Serrão, E.A.S. and A.J. Conto. In press. *Aspectos bio-socioeconómicos relacionados as pastagens do trópico úmido amazónico brasileiro*. Centro Internacional de Agricultura Tropical (CIAT), Cali, Colombia.

Serrão, E.A.S., I.C. Falesi, J.B. Veiga, and J.F. Teixeira Neto. 1979. Productivity of cultivated pastures in low fertility soils of the Amazon of Brazil. In: *Pasture production in acid soils of the tropics*. Edited by P.A. Sánchez and L.E. Tergas. Centro Internacional de Agricultura Tropical (CIAT), Cali, Colombia.

Serrão, E.A.S. and A.G. Gondin. 1966. *Capim braquiria*. Belém, IPEAN-DNPEA.

Serrão, E.A.S. and A.K.O. Homma. 1982. Recuperacao e melhoramento de pastagens cultivadas em area de floresta Amazonica. Documento No.17. Belém. Centro de Pesquisa Agropecuária do Trópico Umido. (EMBRAPA/CPATU).

Serrão, E.A.S. and P.C. Kitamura. 1988. Pecuária na Amazonia: Algumas implicacoes bio-socioeconómicas da implantacao e uso de pastagens no processo de desenvolvimento da pecuária. Resumo de Palestra apresentada no simpósio: Produtividade agroflorestal da Amazonia: Problemas e perspectivas. Faculdade de Ciencias Agrárias do Par (FCAP), Belém.

Serrão, E.A.S. and J.M. Toledo. In press. Search for sustainability in Amazonian pastures. In: *Alternatives to deforestation: Steps towards sustainable utilization of Amazonian forests*. Edited by A. Anderson. New York: Columbia University Press.

Seubert, C.E., P.A. Sánchez, and C. Valverde. 1977. Effects of land clearing methods on soil properties on an Ultisol and crop performance in the Amazon jungle of Peru. *Trop. Agric.* 54(4): 307-21.

Silva, A.B. and B.P. Magalhaes. 1980. Insectos nocivos as pastagens no Estado do Pará EMBRAPA-CPATU, *Boletim de Pesquisa* No.8. Belém.

Spain, J.M. 1988. The management of herbaceous legumes in tropical pastures. Paper presented at the Congresso Brasileiro da Pastagens. Piracicaba. Sao Paulo.

Spain, J.M. and J.G. Salinas. 1985. A reciclagem de nutrientes nas pastagens tropicais. In: *Reciclagem de nutrientes e agricultura de baixos insumos.* Edited by Rosand Cabala. Ilheus, CEPLAC/SBCS.

SUDAM. 1983. Controle estatístico dos incentivos ficais administrados pela SUDAM. Belém: Superintendencia para o Desenvolvimento da Amazonia (SUDAM).

Teixeira, L.B. 1987. Dinámica do ecossistema de pastagem cultivada em área de floresta na Amazonia Central. Tese de Doutorado. Manaus: Instituto Nacional de Pesquisas de Amazonia (INPA)/Fundacao Universidade da Amazonia (FUA).

Thomas, D., R.P. Andrade, W. Couto, C.M.C. Rocha, and P. Moore. 1981. *Andropogon gayanus* var. Bisquamulatus cv. Planaltina: Principais caracteristicas forrageiras. *Pesquisa Agropecuaria Brasileira* 16(3): 347-355.

Toledo, J.M. 1982. Objetivos y organización de la Red Internacional de Evaluación de pastos tropicales. In: *Manual para la evaluación agronómica.* Edited by J.M. Toledo. Red Internacional de Evaluación de Pastos Tropicales. Centro Internacional de Agricultura Tropical (CIAT), Cali, Colombia.

_____ 1986. Pasturas en trópico húmedo: Perspectiva global. In: *Anais del 1er simposio do trópico umido.* Vol.5., p.19- 36. (ISSN 0101-2835).

Toledo, J.M. and M. Ara. 1977. *Manejo de suelos para pastura en la selva amazónica.* Lima, Peru: FAO/SIDA..

Toledo, J.M. and V.A. Morales. 1982. Establishment and management of improved pastures in the Peruvian Amazon. In: *Pasture productivity in acid soils of the tropics.* Edited by P.A. Sánchez, and L.E. Tergas. Centro Internacional de Agricultura Tropical (CIAT), Colombia.

Toledo, J.M. and E.A.S. Serrão. 1982. Pasture and animal production in Amazonia. In: *Amazonia: Agriculture and land use research.* Edited by S.B. Hecht. Centro Internacional de Agricultura Tropical (CIAT), Cali, Colombia.

Toledo, J.M. and F. Torres. 1988. Potential of silvopastoral systems in the humid tropics. In: *Proceedings of the symposium on agroforestry land use systems.* AAAS/ASCS. Anaheim, Ca.

Uhl, C. and R. Buschbacher. 1988. Queimada: O corte que atrai. *Ciencia Hoje.* 7(160): 24-28.

Uhl, C., R.J. Buschbacher, and E.A.S. Serrao. In press. Abandoned pasture in eastern Amazonia: Patterns of plant succession. *Journal of Ecology.*

Uhl, C. and J.B. Kauffman. In press. Deforestation effects on fire susceptibility and the potential responses of tree species to fire in the rainforest of the eastern Amazon .

Veiga, J.B. 1986. Associacao de culturas de subsistencia com forrageiras na renovacao de pastagen degradada em áreas de floresta. In: *Anais del 1er simpósio do trópico umido*. Volume 5 (ISSN 0101-2835).

Veiga, J.B. and I.C. Falesi. 1986. Recomendacao e prática de abudacao de pastagens cultivadas na Amazonia brasileira. In: *Calagem e adubacao de pastagens*. Edited by H.B. Mattos, J.C. Werner, T. Yamada, and E. Malavolta. Piracicaba, S.P. Associacao Brasileira para Pesquisa de Potassa e de Fósforo.

16

A Silvopastoral Strategy

Charles R. Venator
Jurgen Glaeser
Reynaldo Soto

This chapter proposes a silvopasture system to permit reforestation with grazing as a system to recover degenerated secondary forest soils and increase economic returns for Latin American campesinos. There are diverse opinions, and often strong discussions about the value of grazing in forest plantations. Evans (1985) states that grazing of domestic animals has been and continues to be a most destructive agent for both natural and artificial regeneration in many of the semi-arid areas of the tropics. Although data cited by Evans is less oriented towards forests in the Latin American tropics, there are semi-arid areas in this region that are affected by grazing. On the other hand the Holistic Resource Management Group argues that intensive grazing combined with the trampling effect by animal hoofs during stampedes stimulates the growth of semiarid grasslands and combats desertification (Savory 1985). In his extensive review of general systems of agroforestry and silvopasture, Nair (1985) describes many variations in silvopasture systems throughout the world, each finely tuned to the local needs of the population and local resources.

Unquestionably there is a need to maintain a safe and sound environment. Moreover there is no doubt that increased population pressures are forcing campesinos to clear more and more forests in order to produce food for their survival. With this conflict in mind, agronomists and foresters must find solutions to maximize production and incomes for an ever increasing rural population. We believe that the open grazing silvopasture systems employed for centuries by rural groups should be replaced with a more successful silvopasture management practice and we propose some modifications which could be considered for the mountainous regions from Mexico to Chile.

Experiments in New Zealand show that a successful silvopasture program depends on: 1) tree species used; 2) initial growth of trees; 3) the type of cattle raised; 4) climate; 5) topography; 6) pasture quality; and 7) administration and experience techniques (Reid and Wilson 1985).

Furthermore, we recognize that there are many variables which must be considered and require individual solutions that are not necessarily global solutions.

The Silvopasture Unit Model

The silvopasture unit we propose is a management option designed to accommodate forest tree species, pastures and animals, according to the climate, soil, and slope of each site. This model emphasizes the optimum use of resources in each locality. We recommend that better management and organization of local resources be adopted in order to maximize the economic return from these. This model is designed to function within an ecological acceptable scheme. The management option that we propose should let the farmer receive an optimum economic return and fully use under-utilized pastures or abandoned secondary forest/pastures. The system is applicable for areas, ranging from humid tropics to the temperate mountain slopes. A schematic view of the evolution of a basic silvopasture unit (SU) is presented in Figure 16.1 .

The small forest block in each silvopasture unit is designed to allow pasture to grow without shade competition by the trees since each block has only 5 to 7 rows of seedlings at a 3 x 3.5 m spacing or 10.5 m^2 per tree. At this spacing the sun can penetrate under and between the seedlings, on all sides and from above since the seedlings are managed to avoid crown closing.

For the first 3 to 4 years the grass in the forest block will not be shaded, since the trees will be small. During this period the campesino will have to weed about 6 times per year, by machete, the pasture within each forest block. Between 5 and 7 years, 50 percent of trees will be removed leaving the remaining trees triangularly spaced at 3.5 x 7 m or 24.5 m^2 per tree. With this thinning, sufficient trees will be removed to avoid crown shading of the grass. At this period the forest block can be opened for grazing. Within 7 to 10 years an additional thinning, will be made for posts, chips and perhaps small poles. After 7 to 10 years the remaining 15 trees will be spaced with a configuration of 6 x 12.5 m or about 75 m^2 per tree which will permit good grass growth, due to the beneficial penetration of light.

Hence, it is important to prune throughout this period the lower branches of valuable trees. This pruning will also help permit an adequate penetration of sunlight for the pasture growth. The final thinning phase

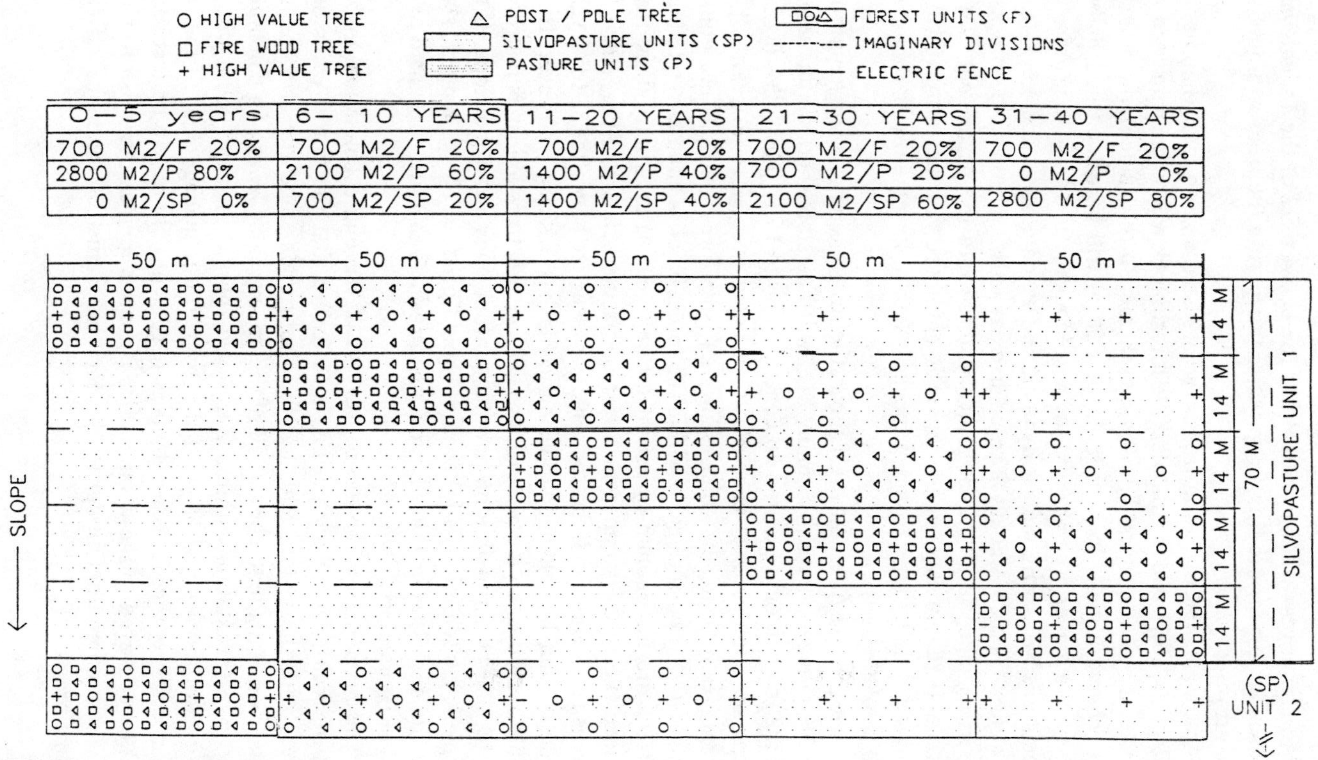

FIGURE 16.1 A silvopasture unit

after the tenth year will be gradual and the best 4 trees of the 15 high value trees will be left for the final crop. After this period the trees will have 225 m^2 of growing space.

As soon as the fuelwood trees are harvested and no later than harvest of the posts, chips and small poles, the forest block will be incorporated as a permanent pasture within the rotation scheme. At this stage in the management scheme a new block of trees 14 x 50 m will be established halfway between the harvested block and the next block further down the slope. The concept of silvopasture units is dynamic and we emphasize that a new forest block should be continually located halfway between other tree blocks as soon as an older forest block is incorporated into the permanent pasture rotation. If this management scheme is employed, all the pasture will be converted little by little to forest blocks which will eventually be thinned to leave valuable trees.

The silvopasture unit (SU) shows the progression of a single unit over time. In practice, several to many SUs will be established simultaneously with the forest blocks planted on contour (Figure 16.1). The following conditions are stipulated: 1) each SU is managed over 30 to 40 years, 2) the percentages indicate the changes in area from forest and pasture units to silvopasture, 3) pasture/grass within the forest block is hand harvested until the trees are big enough to permit grazing, and 4) imaginary divisions to visualize the progression from forest or pasture units to SUs. When this figure is read from top to bottom, one can visualize how after 31 to 40 years, the initial unit has changed. The basic SU has 3,500 m^2, however, this is flexible according to local conditions. The goal is to establish as many SUs side by side as is possible on parallel contour lines down the slope. If this scheme is conscientiously followed it should produce all the lumber, slabs, firewood and posts or other basic forest products that are consumed in the ejido or community.

The main reason for the conversion of the entire communal grazing land or area over a long period, is to assure that the entire community evolves with the system and that the youth understand the concept. If a crash effort is made to convert all of the open grazing lands of a community directly to this system within a 2 to 3 year period then the youth will not understand the process of gradual conversion or management of the land and most likely the necessary land management culture will be lost. What must be conveyed to the communities is that as long as they wish to maintain their communal integrity the members must adapt more efficient grazing practices.

Site Selection

In this presentation we will consider that ranchers wish to convert their secondary forest areas, or deteriorated pastures into an efficient silvopasture operation. We will not consider the option of converting primary forest into pasture. The target site may range from a transitional area of dry-moist to a moist climate site. The slope of these sites would vary from 15 to 35 percent. We recommend that slopes greater than 35 percent be permanently maintained in forest habitat. Areas with slopes of 15 percent or less should be used for intensive agricultural production, with appropriate terraces as necessary. In this hypothetical ranch we presume that there are few valuable trees. Given these situations we presume that the forest trees and pasture will be regenerated simultaneously.

Site Preparation

If the area is flat and the campesino has the necessary financial resources, the site can be prepared to establish trees and pasture by pulling a heavy chain between two bulldozers. On steep slopes, herbicides and manual labor are recommended methods for clearing. The small rancher may prefer to use a machete and fire to help establish the pasture. Once cleared the area should be simultaneously planted with forage and tree seedlings of the desired species.

Tree seedlings generally compete vigorously when planted simultaneously with pasture forage. However, it will be necessary to maintain a small area around the seedlings free of forage during the first 3 to 4 years. The forage could be hand cut with a machete and fed fresh or as hay to the animals.

Expected Tree Growth Rates

Growth rates (in height) expected for valuable species will vary between 1 and 2 m during the first 5 years. Trees with high commercial value would be harvested between 30 to 60 years according to the species, climate and soil. It will be necessary to use a strict pruning system for the valuable trees during the first 10 years to keep the first 8 m of the trunk free of large branches. Branches must be cut as soon as possible and no more than 40 percent of the crown should be pruned during this period. Where silvopasture activities are correctly realized, the valuable trees must be carefully pruned due to the tendency to produce large branches when they are grown in the open.

Many forest tree species are available for use in the silvopasture unit in the tropics. Some recommended trees for the system are: 1) species of fast growth, but low value such as casuarina, gmelina, eucalyptus, leucaena, etc.; 2) trees with fast growth rates and intermediate value, such as pine and terminalia, or 3) trees with slow growth and high commercial value such as mahogany, cedar, cordia, teak and walnut.

Slope Influence

For slopes of 15 percent or more, trees in the forest block should be planted in rows on the contour. When the silvopasture unit is established on slopes between 8 to 15 percent, planting on the contour is optional. Planting trees on the contour will help maintain the cattle concentration on the contour and reduce erosion. It is better to sacrifice pasture growth than to increase soil erosion. When the slope is less than 20 percent, cattle can be used in the system, but when the slope is greater, goats and sheep should be used. Slopes more than 35 to 40 percent should remain in forest and not grazed.

Subsistence Ranch Size

One of the most important problems is to determine the percentage of the farm to be planted in silvopasture units. Many campesinos are small landowners (with farms between 2 to 4 ha) and mainly produce subsistence food. They should plant their entire plot with a surrounding row of a mixture of firewood, posts, poles and high value trees. It is important that the rancher plant high value trees instead of live fence posts. Live fence posts should only be used when the tree is a multi-purpose species. We realize that it is easier to grow live fence posts, but these generally have less economic value and the campesino with little land has to make the maximum use of his available space. With a selective and intensive use of their resources campesinos could sell annually some fence row trees along with animals.

Small Ranches

For ranches between 5 to 15 ha the campesino should establish the silvopasture unit and manage these as shown in Figures 16.1 over several years. The owner of these ranches should establish forest blocks with 5 rows of trees. The silvopasture unit should be protected with solar powered electric fencing during the first 3 to 5 years to insure that the animals do not damage the trees (Droescher et al. 1987). The fence should be about a meter from the trees to avoid trampling the trees. The space between the trees will not be wasted since forage can be cut and given fresh to the animals or harvested as hay, to be consumed later. After 3 to 4 years the animals could be allowed to graze the forest areas.

The campesino must exploit his resource as completely as possible. He should develop an integrated production system of meat, milk, and skins from animals, lumber, poles, posts, chips, nuts, seeds, honey, from trees to allow maximum returns from the small ranch.

Intermediate Size Ranches

Owners of 16 to 50 ha ranches could combine tree plantations, according to their need to integrate the system described over several years. The owner should plant 5 rows of trees at an initial spacing of 3 x 3.5 m.

Each forest block will be 14 x 50 m and contain 65 trees, but it will be reduced in density to 4 trees after 30 to 60 years according to the species, site and desired rotation. The forest block will be planted on the contour as in the other conditions described in this model. The total area of the silvopasture unit will be surrounded by a row of trees. Each tree block will be adjacent to a 50 x 70 m block pasture. The silvopasture unit will permit the farmer to develop intensive grazing on his pasture or produce hay, for later use.

After the first 3 to 4 years, cattle can be grazed among the trees since they will be big enough to resist damage by the animals. Thus, the forest block will be an extension of the pastures. At the appropriate time a new block of trees will be established between the existing blocks. Solar powered electric fences could be used since most campesinos do not have electricity.

After 3 to 4 years, the basic grazing unit will consist of a block approximately of 50 x 84 m. Within this area the tree block of 14 x 50 m can be incorporated into the overall pasture scheme. The entire ranch should eventually be planted in a rotational scheme based on the silvopasture unit shown in Figure 16.1.

In this silvopasture unit management scheme, a firewood cut from the forest block will be the first income derived. Selected trees of the second thinning cut (between 5 to 10 years) will provide a supplementary income to that obtained from grazing. In this thinning, products obtained would be posts, poles, which are used by the owner or sold and chips. Only high value trees will be left for the third thinning. However, after 18 to 30 years, these trees could supply a small volume of lumber. If the campesino has carefully pruned the high value trees he will have optimized the commercial value of the timber.

If the campesino converts 3 ha to silvopasture units each year and carefully manages the small forest blocks, he will eventually develop a rotation system which will allow a forest harvest of 25 or more high value trees every few years. With appropriate management the silvopasture units will result in a rotation system that can be continued for generations.

Large Ranches

If the campesino owns hundreds of hectares, the silvopasture unit system can be organized on a large scale. Owners of such large ranches should plant predominately high value trees and only enough low value trees to provide fence post and pole needs. After 500 ha (or more) of silvopasture units are established, the owner would eventually obtain a high annual income from the perpetual harvest of valuable trees from the forest block.

Although we consider ejidal and communal farm systems as large ranches, these are frequently managed as small individual units. The system described for the large ranch owner is also recommended for these communal groups. However, individual communal groups will have to work out an acceptable interaction among themselves as long as they persist with their desire to live and work on communal property.

For ejidal and communal systems, the decision as to how to manage their forest resource can be a problem. Invariably, forest lands are harvested (most likely clear cut) to accommodate a growing population and develop more agricultural land. Thus, the administration of this land is probably dictated by social and political forces more than economic, ecological or biological impacts. Because of the wrong emphasis in management, optimum forest grazing systems such as the silvopasture unit based upon controlled grazing techniques with electric fences or barbed wire has not been widely employed in communal areas.

Silvopasture units for large ranches, ejidos and communities should have 7 rows of trees at an initial spacing of 3 x 3.5 m. This forest block will be 21 x 50 m and result in a larger harvest of valuable trees. We emphasize the importance of planting small forest blocks, because these will not cause a serious reduction in forage growth, but will provide lumber products and help combat soil erosion.

As in the previous section we recommend the entire silvopasture area be planted with a surrounding row of trees. When the slope is more than 20 percent we recommend that the width of pasture between forest tree blocks be no more than 42 m. In every case where blocks of trees are planted on a slope the trees should be planted in rows along the contour. In cases where the land is flat the trees should be oriented to provide protection from wind erosion. The selection of trees for a specific area should be done by local forest technicians. Agronomists should be consulted for the selection of cattle and pasture species.

It is important that the campesino is not frightened by the word *reforestation*. If he thinks that we are promoting mass reforestation, he will not respond to the silvopasture unit management concept. The main emphasis must be to provide: 1) protection for animals; 2) protection against erosion; 3) fuelwood, fence posts and poles; and 4) a future, but significant, income from trees harvested for lumber. It is also important to emphasize that trees will be the patrimony left for his children.

The Problem of Soil Erosion

Castaños (1988) emphasized that today the exaggerated and often clandestine harvest and frequent forest fires in Mexico are a result of the campesinos hunger for agricultural lands. These problems plus the lack of capital for reforestation has resulted in the conversion of forest land to subsistence agriculture. The farmer is often forced to sell his timber at a lower than market price in order to obtain scarce subsistence funds. The over harvest required to compensate for low stumpage prices has resulted in accelerated erosion. In the State of Jalisco, more than 100,000 ha of forest vocation land has been affected by erosion in this decade. The erosion problems are an example of what results when there is no strong program based on a rational use of land and where timber prices are so low that the farmer sees no value in maintaining a forest.

Unfortunately, but not unexpectedly, concepts of resource conservation are hard to promote among farmers living under subsistence conditions. Terraces are excellent for the recuperation of eroded agriculture lands, but are expensive to build and may require centuries to recuperate the investment. Silvopasture units managed as described in this publication will permit a better economical return for the indigenous populations living in the mountainous slopes of Mexico, Central America, and South America Andes.

The average subsistence and small farmer adopting the silvopasture unit management scheme should be able to increase his herd size by a factor of 5 to 8, depending upon climate, over a 6 year period. At the same time he would produce most of the wood he needs. This increase is at first sight impressive. However, it is doubtful that subsistence and small farmers will ever be able to further increase the economic return from the target figures that we project. Thus, it may be in the best interest for at least two of every three subsistence farmers to consider migrating to urban areas since even an eight fold increase in herd size will not provide an adequate income for most families. Once farmers migrate to cities, farm consolidation can occur. However, intermediate size, ejidal and communal farmers should be able to increase their herd size by a factor of 15 over a 10 year period since they have a greater land base. At this level of production they would have a viable economic farm operation.

However, indigenous communities with a small land base will always have a difficult time obtaining sufficient land to make any agriculture system profitable. Unfortunately because of overpopulation in many communal agriculture areas of Central and Latin America, migration to the cities may be the only long term viable alternative. The rural population needs to reach an equilibrium between 10 and 15 percent of the total population and/or the land per capita ratio for the farmer should be minimally 15 ha.

Current mismanagement of forest and pasture soils has resulted in a serious erosion problem in vast regions of Latin America. However, even on steep slopes, animals can be grazed if terraces are used. Thus, modern, rural indigenous and non-indigenous cultures can build more extensive terrace systems designed to endure centuries, such as was left by the Incas in Peru. The durability of the agriculture terraces of the Incas is perhaps one of the most important examples of indigenous patrimony left to the world.

The cost of terrace construction to recuperate eroded land will most likely originate from the urban population. This will be their contribution (tax) in return for a constant food supply. Consequently, the campesino will need to adopt agricultural practices that preserve soil and maintain agricultural productivity. The traditional, fierce independent nature of the farmer will probably clash with city dwellers who will insist on better soil management. At some point farmers will have to produce sufficient food to feed at least himself and probably 10 other individuals; failing to reach this goal will probably force them off the land.

The recuperation cost of eroded lands will be expensive, both in social and economic terms. But the need to abandon many traditional precepts, indigenous or not, to increase food production on steep slopes, will be the motivating force that will eventually require rural communities to work their farms with methodologies that reduce erosion. The present abuse of soil may require legal action such as erosion laws that obligate farmers to till their fields correctly or be severely fined.

The Problem of Tradition

Campesinos can grow trees and pastures of great value. Unfortunately, the majority of the farmers do not attempt to produce trees within their pasture. One approach to challenging the campesino philosophy is to convince them to plant trees that should leave a forest wealth for their children and think in terms of leaving an inheritance by increasing the value of their land.

The concept of the silvopasture unit implies that the campesino must change his work philosophy. In the proposed system, more labor and management is required. Animals will go from stable to pasture each day. Once animals are inside the fenced pasture the campesino will be free either to plant trees to establish a forest block or cut grass around the trees in this block for fresh forage or hay for later use. Adoption of specific changes in work philosophy is necessary to reforest land currently used in open grazing systems.

If campesinos were to adapt the silvopasture unit, they would be able to reforest, conserve the soil, increase their income and leave an inheritance for the children of their community.

Management Recommendations

Specific recommendations for campesinos :

- terminate the practice of unmanaged, open pasture grazing,
- use grazing management practices to prevent pasture deterioration and increase pasture productivity,
- prune trees to a height of 8 m properly and continuously for several years,
- plant high valued trees for the final rotation and use live fenceposts only when needed,
- establish high valued forage in the silvopasture scheme,
- within the tree block, hand harvest the forage and feed this as fresh forage or hay until the trees are large enough to resist trampling,
- use electric fencing to protect the trees and provide intensive grazing and consider solar powered fences as an option,
- seek technical assistance from forest, pasture and range specialists for intensive management suggestion,
- and avoid practices that increase soil erosion.

References Cited

Castaños, Leon Jorge. 1988. *El Excelsior*, August 8, 1988. Mexico City. pp. 3.

Droescher, P. S., S. D. Tesch and M. A. Castro. 1987. Livestock grazing: A silvocultural tool for plantation establishment. *Journal of Forestry* (10): 29-37.

Evans, J. 1985. *Plantation Forestry in the Tropics*. Oxford Science Publications. New York:Oxford University Press.

Nair, P. K. 1985. Classification of agroforestry systems. *Agroforestry Systems* 3: 97-128.

Reid, R. and G. Wilson. 1985. *Agroforestry in New Zealand*. Victoria, New Zealand:Goddard and Dobson.

Savory, A. 1985. The role of herding animals in brittle watersheds. *The Savory Letter* (April Issue).

17

Integrated Production Systems

Javier Trujillo-Arriaga

Agricultural resource management has been conducted under diverse criteria in both time and space throughout human history. During the initial periods of agricultural societies it appears there was a coevolutionary development between social systems and ecosystems. Then, nature was resilient enough to supply food and fiber for human societies without jeopardizing the continuity of agricultural output. However, harmony between these two systems has been diminished through time, as human populations have grown, and pressure for revenues has increased.

By the end of the nineteenth century, an industrial approach to agriculture began in Europe (Auge-Laribe 1979) with the widespread use of inorganic fertilizers. This approach lead to a novel paradigm of agricultural technology, one that subsidizes production with energy and nutrient inputs. It has had a remarkable acceptance and/or development in many countries. More recently, there have been frequent cases of resource management techniques that resemble mining. This book examines such a situation.

The process of agricultural modernization that most countries have followed, characterized by a neglect of ecological principles, has promoted important environmental imbalances such as: (a) the generation of technology-induced environmental diseases (Hodges and Scofield 1983); (b) the loss of native cultural knowledge which is a valuable collection of successful experiences over hundreds or even thousands of years (Leff 1986), and (c) the loss of a country's food self-sufficiency, since a significant proportion of their agricultural land has been devoted to the extremely inefficient use of meat production (Barkin and Suarez 1985).

For example, the Brazilian government could have acquired nearly four metric tons of foreign beef for the same cost it absorbed subsidizing the production of one metric ton of Amazonian beef (Browder 1988). In fact there is evidence documenting that the lack of harmony between socio-systems and ecosystems is partially responsible for the failure of a nation's economic development (Norgaard 1981). In the case of tropical forests an additional consequence, which is difficult to assess, is the extinction of numerous species of plant and animals (Myers 1980; Lewin 1986). The magnitude of this loss is practically impossible to determine using neoclassical economic models (Norgaard 1987).

The discussion on the roots of hunger in the world has many components that have been analyzed elsewhere (Lappe and Collins 1977); but aside from controversial standpoints, it can be accepted that the increasing demand for agricultural products will genuinely require the use of tropical forest land for agricultural production. Therefore, there is an urgent need for the development of an ecologically grounded paradigm of agricultural resource management in these ecosystems. This paper presents a conceptual view of some technological and sociological strategies that could be helpful in the design of ecologically rooted productive systems.

Criteria for Designing Successful Production Systems

The success of agricultural systems can no longer be measured by the single concept of productivity; Conway (1986) proposes four criteria needed to be considered simultaneously when evaluating agricultural performance: (1) productivity, (2) stability, (3) sustainability, and (4) equitability of benefits. In principle, it seems very likely that the simultaneous achievement of these four criteria would ensure a good compromise between conservation and management of natural resources.

Agroecology: A Methodology for Managing Agricultural Resources

Altieri (1989) advocates the concept of agroecology as a scientific approach for studying, diagnosing and proposing ecologically based management of agricultural resources. Thus, agroecology promotes efficient nutrient, water, and energy cycles and the stability of biological components. Some technologies that promote agroecological development are listed in Table 17.1.

Ecology provides the basic principles that agroecology uses for the design of environmentally robust productive systems; however, since ecology is a rather young science there is a lack of basic knowledge for most types of ecosystems. Its contributions for the design of sustainable agroecosystems are limited for the moment, in part due to the hesitation of most ecologists to apply their expertise to management.

An alternative source of principles for the development of ecological agriculture is the scientific study of traditional resource management. Typically traditional agriculture involves diverse ecological features that can be uncovered and integrated into modern cropping designs.

TABLE 17.1 Technologies to promote ecological agriculture

Efficiency of energy use:
    Improvement of plant architecture for better light interception
    (i.e. intercropping C3 and C4 plants)
    Use of genotypes with high leaf area index

Efficient planting patterns (orientation of rows)

Soil and plant nutrient management:
    Minimum or reduced tillage
    Use of manure, compost, cover crops, and green manures
    Use of biological nitrogen fixation
    Re-incorporation of crop residues

Stability of the biological community:
    Landscape diversification
    Plant mixtures to reduce pest and disease attacks
    (through camouflage of attacked crops or enhancement
    of entromophagous arthropod populations)

Biological Control:
    Trap crops

Peasants who have not been displaced from their settings during the agricultural and industrial modernization processes have empirically developed and updated technologies to manage their natural resources very efficiently. The features of traditional agriculture are supported by strategies that promote efficient land use, soil conservation, and reduction of pest damage. Traditional agricultural technologies enhance the capture of locally available resources (i.e. water and nutrients), whereas modern agricultural technology enhance only the response to purchased agrochemical inputs.

The studies on traditional resource management are rather scarce. Ruthenberg (1976) offered an extensive description of tropical farming systems. Alcorn (1984) work on forest management in the Huasteca region of Mexico revealed sophisticated knowledge of resource management on the part of indigenous people. Altieri (1987) has documented the properties of the Talunkebun, an agricultural system in Indonesia. This system appears to have been derived from shifting cultivation. Each of the different stages of plant succession in this system serve a different function. Wilken (1987) has made a collection of cases for the traditional agriculture in Mexico and Central America, showing that traditional farmers are more efficient than modern growers in their use of resources. Likewise, Rappaport (1971) details an Asian case of efficient use of farm resources.

A few modern annual agriculture systems have been generated which take advantage of traditional agriculture to design productive and stable production systems. For example, waste cycling has been a key feature of success in integrated crop-livestock-fish farming in the Republic of China (IRRI 1979). However, the cases of integrated production systems in the tropical forests are less common. Ewel (1986), and Harwood (1979) have proposed guidelines for agroecosystem design in tropical forests. An important strategy is to establish cropping systems similar to the natural secondary succession of the area. Forest production is characterized by its diversity, not by high productivity of a few species. From this perspective, specialized production systems such as the substitution of forest for pasture represents a strategy opposite that of nature's for resource management (Toledo et al. 1985).

An example of ecological design for the management of tropical forest is "alley cropping" (Wilson and Kang 1981) which is an improved bush fallow system using selected shrubs or tree species. Usually legumes, are planted in association with food crops to accelerate soil nutrient regeneration, thus shortening the fallow period while sustaining production stability.

Belshaw (1979) has emphasized the need for a serious consideration of traditional agriculture as a useful component of modernization. Similarly, Richards (1984) states that traditional knowledge is the only great resource not yet mobilized in the rural development enterprise.

Scientific work has at least three important roles to play in the development of successful production systems. First, it can focus on the formal surveying of farmers' production systems, such that conducted by Altieri et al. (1987). Secondly, it can provide an experimental evaluation of the ecological properties suggested by the survey (Trujillo and Altieri, in press). Lastly, it can be used to evaluate production systems proposed as result of agroecological guidelines. This evaluation needs to simultaneously consider ecological and economic features, as well as the degree of acceptance by the farmers with and for whom the agroecological technologies have been developed. The third stage has practically never been reached; one of the few examples is the Plan Sierra in the Dominican Republic (Lissette-Wozniak 1988).

Site-specific Agroecological Development

There is no unique strategy for the development of integrated management of forest agroecosystems. Each geographical region requires a unique set of solutions. The need of a particular agroecological planning for each geographic region cannot be overemphasized. Unfortunately, most world agricultural development programs have neglected the need for regionalization; instead, they have promoted the generalized use of technological packages exported from one region of the world to another. This tendency is related to the current profit-oriented socioeconomic framework that most Latin American countries follow, as a consequence of the multinational agrobusiness strategies (Levins and Lewontin 1985).

Generalized technological solutions are also inadequate since they ignore fundamental regionally specific economic and political problems. These problems must be addressed if a solution to tropical deforestation is to be found.

Sociological Strategies to Achieve Agricultural Sustainability

Social goals for agriculture may not be intentionally sought or desired by any farmer (Thompson 1986). A key factor for success in the rural development task is the reconciliation of individual goals and those of the nation. The lessons that modern societies can learn from peasants are not just ecological. Peasants have developed ways of social organization that protect the interests of each individual in the community (Shanin 1972); thus promoting general well-being. A new paradigm for rural development is needed that explicitly gives priority to the poorer part of rural population (Chambers 1983). The current political structures of many countries are concerned only with increased agricultural production, rejecting the importance of stability, sustainability, and equitability.

Very likely, a healthy social change will not come from the government; alternatively the work conducted through non-government organizations (NGO's), and other grassroot groups has been shown to be effective (Hirschman 1984; Page 1986). Thus, grassroots activities seem to be naturally associated with the success of agroecological designs, especially in countries where national goals reject environmental commitments. Universities can play an important role in this regard: for example the project "Alcozahuaca" promoted by the Universidad Nacional Autonoma de Mexico (Casas 1988), provides a successful integration of the diverse aspects of rural development guided by community needs, including political and social.

Financial Sources for Developing Integrated Production Systems

There are strong arguments that support ecologically sound production in tropical forests. Nevertheless, it seems clear that the main driving force for an alternative management of these ecosystems, relates more to the social monetary value that the proposed ecological management strategy represents; particularly after environmental degradation is estimated in dollars. A mining approach to production does not allow profit after the forests have been destroyed; consequently, no further forest destruction can possibly be endorsed as a means of economic growth.

Financial support policies need to consider the potential benefits that the entire society can obtain after local needs have been satisfied. The success of the Marshall plan encouraged a blind faith among academics and policy makers in the idea that development was possible for all socio-systems and ecosystems through central planning and capital and technology transfers (Norgaard 1981). Support for agroecological development in each region is needed. Development of a conspicuous body of agroecological knowledge requires resources to educate people, and to conduct appropriate research to propose ways of agricultural production suited for each ecological region, and each culture. Agroecology development and ecology merit definitive support from society and investment in this work should rank as a high priority.

Conclusions

The examples of integrated production systems in the tropical forests are still practically absent in Latin America. This is not surprising, taking into account that skewed concentration of political and economic power has placed a higher priority on profit than on conservation and sustainable approaches for resource management. The scientific expertise to generate ecologically efficient and economically viable agricultural production systems in the tropical forest needs much growth; however, it has been sufficiently developed to be useful.

The mere availability of ecologically sound, technological solutions may be useless. All the main causes of tropical forests destruction are ultimately explained by political and economic unbalances. Policy making must address the social and economic obstacles if there is to be a solution to deforestation. This argument was made 15 years ago (Janzen 1973), but it is still being ignored. It remains valid today. There is a fundamental need for social change (with concomitant economic policy evolution) as a requirement to achieve a wise management of tropical forests. Growth of agroecological knowledge, through allocation of social funds is expected to come along with a social organization paradigm that puts long-term social needs above today privileged groups' focus on short-term profit.

References Cited

Alcorn, J. B. 1984. Development policy, forests, and peasants farms: Reflections on Huastec-managed forests' contributions to commercial production and resource conservation. *Economic Botany* 38(4):389-406.

Altieri, M. A. 1989. Agroecology: A new research and development paradigm for world agriculture. *Agric. Ecosyst. and Environ.*

_____ 1987 *Agroecology. The scientific basis of alternative agriculture.* Boulder Colorado: Westview Press.

Altieri, M. A., J. Trujillo, and J. Farrell. 1987. Plant-insect interactions and soil fertility relations in agroforestry systems: Implications for the design of sustainable agroecosystems. In: *Agroforestry: Realities, possibilities and potentials.* Edited by H. L. Gholtz. Dordretcht: Matinus Nijhoff Publishers.

Auge-Laribe, M. 1979. *La revolucion agricola.* Mexico, D.F.: Union Tipografica y Editorial de Hispano America.

Barkin, D. and B. Suarez. 1985. *El fin de la autosuficiencia alimentaria.* Mexico, D.F.: Oceano/Centro de Ecodesarrollo.

Belshaw, D. G. 1979. Taking indigenous technology seriously: The case of intercropping techniques in East Africa. *IDS Bulletin* 10(2): 24-27.

Browder, J. O. 1988. The social costs of rain forest destruction: A critique and economic analysis of the "Hamburger debate." *Interciencia.* 13(3):115-120.

Casas, A. 1988. La montana de Guerrero. *Ciencias* 12:4-8.

Chambers, R. 1983. *Rural development. Putting the last first.* New York: Longman Inc.

Conway, G. R. 1986. *Agroecosystem analysis for research and development.* Bangkok, Thailand: Winrock International.

Esteva, G. 1985. El desafio: Detener el desarrollo rural. In: *Desarrollo agricola en Mexico: Presente, pasado y futuro.* Edited by M. A. Altieri and D. Nestel. Berkeley, California: Seminar Document Series. Program in Mexican Studies.

Ewel, J. J. 1986. Designing agricultural ecosystems for the humid tropics. *Ann. Rev. Ecol. Syst.* 17:245-71.

Harwood, R. R. 1979. *Small farmer development: Understanding and improving farming systems in the humid tropics.* Boulder, Colorado: Westview Press.

Hirschman, A. O. 1984. *Getting ahead collectively. Grassroots experiences in Latin America.* New York: Peragamon Press.

Hodges, R. D. and A. M. Scofield. 1983. Agricologenic disease: A review of the negative aspects of agricultural systems. *Biol. Agri. and Hort.* 1:269:325.

International Rice Research Institute. 1979. Integrated crop-livestock-fish farming. Proceedings from the synposium-workshop on integrated crop-livestock-fish farming. Los Banos: International Rice Research Institute.

Janzen, D. H. 1973. Tropical agroecosystems. *Science* 182(4118):1212-1219.

Lappe, F. M. and J. Collins. 1977. *Food first.* New York: Ballantine Books.

Leff, E. 1986. *Ecologia y capital. Hacia una perspectiva ambiental de desarrollo.* Mexico, D.F.: Universidad Nacional Autonomia de Mexico.

Levins, R. and R. Lewontin. 1985. *The dialectical biologist.* Cambridge: Harvard University Press.

Lewin, R. 1986. Damage to tropical forests, or why were there so many kinds of animals. *Science* 234:149 -150.

Lissette-Wozniak, M. 1988. Local organizations as participants in conservation: Reconciling social and ecological objectives in the Dominican Sierra. University of California at Berkeley: M.A. Thesis, Center for Latin American Studies.

Myers, N. 1980. *Conversion of tropical moist forest.* Washington, D.C. National Academy of Science.

Norgaard, R. 1981. Sociosystem and ecosystem coevolution in the Amazon. *Journal of Environmental Economics and Management* 8:238-254.

_____ 1987. The economics of biological diversity: Apologetic or theory? In: *Sustainable resource development in the Third World.* Edited by D. D. Southgate and J. F. Disinger. Boulder, Colorado: Westview Press.

Page, D. 1986. Growing hope in Santiago's urban growing gardens. *Grassroots Development* 10 (2):38-44.

Perelman, M. 1977. *Farming for profit in a hungry world.* Montclair, New Jersey:Allanheld, Osmun and Co.

Rappaport, R. A. 1971. The flow of energy in an agricultural society. Scientific American 224:117-132.

Richards, P. 1984. *Indigenous agricultural revolution.* Boulder, Colorado and London: Westview Press/Hutchinson.

Ruthenberg, H. 1976. *Farming systems in the tropics.* Oxford: Claredon Press.

Shanin, T. 1972. *The awkward class. Political sociology of peasantry in a developing society: Russia 1910-1925.* London: Oxford University Press.

Thompson, R. B. 1986. The social goals of agriculture. *Agriculture and Human Values.* III (4):32-42.

Toledo, V. M., J. Carabias, C. Mapes and C. Toledo. 1985. *Ecologia y autosuficiencia alimentaria.* Mexico, D.F.: Siglo XXI.

Trujillo, J. and M. A. Altieri. In press. An assessment of the aphidophagous community in corn monocultures and polycultures in central Mexico. Agric. *Ecosyst. and Environ*.

Wilken, G. C. 1987. *Good farmers. Traditional agricultural resource management in Mexico and Central America.* Berkeley: University of California Press.

Wilson, G. F. and B. T. Kang 1981. Developing stable and productive biological cropping systems for the humid tropics. In: *Biological Husbandry: A scientific approach to organic farming.* Edited by B. Stonehause. London : Butterworths.

PART SIX
DEVELOPERS'
AND
DONORS '
PERSPECTIVES

In the process of converting forests to grazing lands, several political, sociological and economic issues are identifiable. There is no simple solution to the problem, from the view of the governments currently developing the forested regions of the tropics. Conversion to livestock and farming creates short-term capital, provides large-scale employment and creates immediate, additional foreign exchange. Furthermore, highly technical skills are needed. These developmental decisions normally are made in the absence of a true understanding of the real value of the total timber and non-timber production capacity of the tropical forest and until very recently a clear understanding of the long-term effects on global change. The perspective from the developers in the chapters in this section identifies many issues and economic forces driving the conversion. It also identifies several "requirements" that must be met to enable developing tropical countries to halt the current developmental efforts and secure long-term timber production and protection of environmental values.

Moran's chapter critically reviews a novel concept, the debt- for-nature swap. Within the developing world, almost one trillion dollars of debt exist. Seven countries account for almost half of that debt, almost all with vast tropical timber resources. To have any one of these major debtors default on their loan would shake the foundations of the international banking system. The chapter on debt-for-nature offers a novel discussion about a possible avenue or a conceptual framework from which other mechanisms may evolve to reduce developing country debt load and, at the same time, fund the creation or preservation of tropical forest reserves.

— Gary R. Evans

18

Debt-for-Nature Swaps: A Response to Debt and Deforestation in Developing Countries?

Katy Moran

In 1984, Thomas E. Lovejoy, then vice-president for science at the World Wildlife Fund and deeply concerned about the accelerating rate of both debt and deforestation, first proposed that indebted developing countries be allowed to exchange their debt for protection of natural resources, particularly tropical forests (Lovejoy 1984). Less than seven years later, this visionary concept has become reality through over $100 million in debt-for-nature swaps. As the U.S. initiates the use of official debt to expand this concept, policy makers need to examine more thoroughly the benefits and constraints of this action, and clearly define options available for implementation.

Nature of the Debt

During the inflationary economic environment of the 1970s, the Third World borrowed heavily from three types of creditors — commercial banks, multilateral development banks (MDBs), and bilateral foreign assistance programs — that were eager to encourage economic development. However, oil price shocks in 1973 and 1979, and the U.S. recession starting in 1981, altered the economic conditions that affected debt payments. Rising interest rates, an appreciating dollar, and declining commodity price, soon made it difficult for developing countries to pay the interest on their debts (U.S. Joint Economic Committee 1986).

In August of 1982, the Mexican government revealed it could not service its $80 billion debt. The flood gates were opened. By the end of 1983, forty-two other countries were behind on their payments. They resorted to borrowing from the International Monetary Fund (IMF), which grants short-term loans to financially troubled countries if they submit to specific economic reform programs (Hino 1986).

The IMF ordered fiscal austerity and export programs to reform economic conditions in the over-borrowed countries that applied for funds to service their external debt. Austerity programs made imports more expensive to debtor countries by devaluating local currency, and made basic goods more expensive by eliminating subsidies. Currency devaluations increased import prices and stimulated a general inflation rate. For example, after three devaluations over a 13 month period, Philippine families paid 80% more for the same basket of groceries in 1984 than they did in 1983. Reduced government subsidies created a shortage in fertilizers and other agricultural inputs for small farmers, leading to food shortages and malnutrition in the rural poor. Wages of workers were frozen and government expenditures were reduced by eliminating social welfare programs which resulted in diminished education and health services (Debt Crisis Network 1985).

Since loan payments must be paid in U.S. dollars or another hard currency, the IMF also required debtor countries to increase their production of export commodities and develop non-traditional exports to trade for hard currency (Bird 1987).

Struggling to pay even the interest on their mounting debt, developing countries flooded export markets with primary commodities such as coffee, cocoa, clothing, coconuts, and copper. But world trade stagnated from 1980 through 1983, coinciding with IMF export programs, and prices were driven down. For example, world sugar prices remained at 5-6 cents a pound in early 1985, while production costs in the Philippines were at 12-14 cents a pound.

To promote exports, subsistence agriculture was substituted with monoculture for world markets. Staple food crops were less available to the poor, increasing malnutrition. A diverse and relatively balanced food producing system was replaced with ecologically unstable monocrops.

IMF austerity and export programs created greater hardships for the poor and environmental degradation in the already impoverished Third World, and did nothing to increase its creditworthiness. The World Development Report of 1988 (World Bank 1988) stated that resource transfers from industrial countries to developing countries shifted from a capital inflow of $147 billion between 1977 and 1982, to a capital outflow of $85 billion between 1982 and 1988. By 1991, more money was going out of developing countries for debt payments than is going into them for development.

Impact of Developing Country Debt on the US Economy

Debt creates crises for both creditor and borrower countries in many sectors, including trade, industry, banking, and farming. Since about one-third of U.S. trade is with the developing world, massive job losses in U.S. export-oriented industries occurred partly due to IMF import restriction in borrower countries. Wharton Economic Forecasting Associates testified before the Joint Economics Committee of the U.S. Congress in June of 1985 that in one year, the U.S. lost 800,000 jobs as a result of the debt crisis in Latin America alone.

In creditor nations, commercial banks that hold large portfolios of Third World debt are at risk. U.S. taxpayers have learned from the savings and loan crisis that they pay the cost when overexposed banks fail.

U.S. farmers also are affected negatively by IMF imposed export and import programs. While Third World imports of U.S. commodities are declining, increased Third World exports directly compete with the corn, rice, and soybeans produced by U.S. farmers. Markets are flooded and prices driven down, undermining the position of farmers everywhere. Farmers in the U.S. and in the Third World both suffer from the high and fluctuating interest rates generated by U.S. budget deficits and an unstable international economic system (Debt Crisis Network 1985).

Who Owes What to Whom

Seven countries account for almost half the $1.3 trillion Third World debt: Mexico, Brazil, Argentina and Venezuela in Latin America; and South Korea, Indonesia, and the Philippines in Asia. Each owes over $25 billion, mostly to commercial banks that hold short term loans with high interest rates. The default of one of these "Big Seven" debtor nations would shake the international financial system; their collective default could destroy it.

Middle-range debtors consist of two dozen African nations; Costa Rica, El Salvador, Guatemala, Honduras and Nicaragua in Central America; and Bolivia, Peru, Ecuador, and Chile in South America. These countries owe, to both commercial and official creditors, large debts in proportion to their domestic capacity to repay, but their default would not trigger a worldwide financial crisis.

The very poorest African countries are the third group of debtors. They owe official creditors, both multilateral and bilateral, which grant low interest rate loans with long term payment schedules. They do not have large debts because commercial banks regard them as poor credit risks, but they are seriously affected by the international financial system (Wertman 1986).

Today, most of the capital of developing nations is used to pay the almost $1.3 trillion external debt owed to developed nations. There is not only no money left for growth in the Third World, but economic policies, including the required IMF export emphasis, are depleting the natural resource base upon which the future growth of the developing world ultimately depends.

Social and Environmental Impacts of Debt and Deforestation

All resources are affected by the debt of the developing countries, but it is tropical forests, and the poorest of the poor who depend on them as their only resource that suffer worst and first from deforestation. Not only do forest peoples lose their homelands, but also humanity loses the indigenous knowledge on the use of forest resources that its inhabitants have accumulated over millennia. One-half of the worlds' population uses fuelwood as an energy source for cooking and heating, so it is the rural poor in developing countries who are the first to suffer from deforestation. Mathews (1989) writes that, "Traced through its effects on energy supply and water resources, tropical deforestation impoverishes about a billion people."

Socioeconomic pressures associated with deforestation are difficult to address and they intensify relentlessly each day. Poverty, overpopulation, inequitable land distribution, poor land use and land tenure policy, and inappropriate development leads to a vicious cycle of more poverty and more pressure on resources. National and international policies to generate hard currency for debt payments promote mining, logging, cash crop monocultures, and expanded cattle production. They are the leading reasons why tropical forests the size of a football field are being degraded or destroyed every second of every day. The urgency of tropical deforestation is sounded by an alarming report by the Food and Agriculture Organization and the World Resources Institute which states that roughly 50% more tropical forest is being cleared today than as little as one decade ago (Petesch 1990).

Deforestation also compromises future generations. Tropical forests are the habitat of almost half of the plant and animal species of the planet; deforestation erodes the biological diversity of life itself, as it accelerates the extinction of more than 100 species daily. Forests moderate climate. As forests are destroyed, they not only release carbon into the atmosphere, but diminish its capacity to absorb carbon emissions. Loss of forest cover exacerbates soil erosion and flooding, increases siltation in rivers and estuaries, impairs watersheds, and disrupts the hydrological cycle of large areas.

These links between debt and deforestation demonstrate that it is impossible to isolate economic, social and environmental problems. Solutions require recognition of their relationship to each other (Downing and Kushner 1988). In the past we feared the impact of economic growth on the environment, but today we must admit to the consequences of environmental stress — deforestation particularly — on future economic prospects worldwide.

Current Status of Debt-For-Nature Swaps

United States Commercial Bank Debt

Of the three types of debt, the "first generation" of debt-for-nature swaps (Sale With A Purpose) used commercial bank debt (Conservation International 1989). Because many commercial banks are collecting neither interest nor principal payments for Third World debt, a secondary market has developed where banks can trade or sell their foreign debt at a discounted rate to minimize their losses. Commercial debt has been sold or donated to environmental non-governmental organizations (NGO), and swaps have been small and country specific, but they illustrate how the debt-for-nature swap concept has developed.

In the first debt swap during July of 1987, Conservation International (CI), a U.S. based NGO, and the government of Bolivia announced a plan to manage almost 4 million acres of tropical forest in the Bolivian Amazon. Six-hundred and fifty thousand dollars worth of deeply discounted Bolivian debt was purchased for $100,000 (U.S.) on the secondary market by CI, which then canceled the debt in return for a tropical forest protection and management plan. CI is the first to acknowledge that its pioneer debt-for-nature swap was not without problems, but the swap laid a foundation for other conservation NGOs that soon followed its lead.

One lesson learned was the inflationary effect of a sudden increase in money supply in the host country's domestic economy. This would have limited the number of future swaps. To counter this effect, swap arrangements now routinely convert most of the debt title into local currency bonds, using the interest as stable and long-term financing for conservation programs.

Local NGOs such as Fundacion de Parques Nacionales in Costa Rica, Fundacion Natura in Ecuador, and the Haribon Foundation in the Philippines have facilitated nearly $100 million of U.S. debt retirement in their countries through swaps. Their U.S. based counterparts such as Conservation International, World Wildlife Fund, The Nature Conservancy and others have facilitated these swaps to finance a wide range of activities such as the training of local scientists and land managers, natural resource conservation, and management of buffer zones around critical natural areas (Cody 1990).

Each swap has been country-specific, but a generic swap procedure is as follows:

1. The impetus for a swap originates with a local NGO that enlists the help of a U.S. based NGO to raise funds to purchase a portion of its country's commercial bank debt.
2. A U.S. commercial bank either sells (through the secondary market), or donates to a U.S. based environmental NGO, a debt instrument that would sell at a deep discount on the secondary market.
3. The U.S. NGO negotiates with the borrower country on the terms of settlement and for the environmental activity suggested by the local NGO.
4. The borrower country typically agrees to pay some or all of the value of the loan in local currency long-term interest-bearing bonds to a local NGO working with its U.S. counterpart.

To date, debt swaps have been narrow in scope, creating a misconception of the purpose and potential of swaps. "Ecological imperialism" has been charged, criticizing swaps as an exchange of debt for ownership of sovereign territory. In fact, of the first generation of swaps, ownership of land has never, nor ever was intended, to change hands. Likewise, the impetus has emerged from the debtor country, and funds are managed by local organizations and structured to meet local conservation priorities (Bramble and Millikan 1990).

October 19, 1987 is remembered as Black Monday on the New York Stock Exchange. Coupled with the international economic instability of the time, Black Monday caused many large commercial banks to increase their loan loss reserves for developing country debt. This additional expense created an incentive for banks to donate or sell that debt for swaps. To encourage this, environmental NGOs lobbied for a measure that was adopted in the Continuing Resolution (CR) that passed in the U.S. Congress on December 22, 1987. The CR legislation requested the U.S. Treasury Department to report on initiatives to promote the "...purchase, at market discounts (such as the secondary market), developing country debt in exchange for domestic currency investments in conservation at the full par value of the purchased debt."

In response, the Treasury Department issued Revenue Ruling 87-124 that allows a commercial bank to take a deduction from taxable income to the full face value for a donation of debt to use in debt-for-nature swaps, even though the loan instrument would sell on the secondary market at a deep discount. Although Treasury views this as revenue neutral, to date, no commercial bank has attempted this transaction due to remaining tax and accounting uncertainties that have yet to be resolved.

Multilateral Development Bank Debt Owed to Creditor Nations

Congressman John Porter (R-IL) took the first legislative action to alleviate the debt and deforestation problem. Porter's Tropical Forest Protection Act (H.R. 3010 and H.R. 1704 during the 100th and 101st Congresses respectively) called on the U.S. Executive Director to the World Bank and other multilateral development banks (MDBs) to allow a country with MDB loans to convert part of its debt payments into local currency to use for environmental activities. The bill also carried important provisions to strengthen non-governmental organizations worldwide that are involved in grass-roots environmental protection and resource management in developing countries.

The World Bank responded to Porter's bill by stating that any form of debt rescheduling or restructuring would undermine its AAA credit rating, and that rescheduling is forbidden by its charter. However, under Article IV, Section 4 (c) of the Bretton Woods Conference, loan contracts can be made in accordance with the following contract provisions: "If a member suffers from an acute exchange stringency," it may apply to the Bank for a relaxation of the conditions of payment, and the Bank may accept service payments on the loan "... in the members currency, for periods not to exceed three years." Also the Bank may "... modify the terms of amortization or extend the life of the loan, or both" (International Bank for Reconstruction and Development Articles of Agreement 1945).

Many feel that debt-for-nature swaps offer an opportunity for the Bank to demonstrate concrete mechanisms to improve and mitigate admitted negative environmental consequences of past Bank funding. In 1988, Bank President Barber Conable publicly stated a commitment to improve the environmental quality of its loans, stating that "If the Bank has been part of the (environmental) problem in the past, I intend to make it a leader in finding solutions " (Holden 1988).

During the 101st Congress, Representative Porter's bill was rolled into H.R. 2494. The bill passed and was signed into law (PL 101-240) by President Bush on December 19, 1989, as The International Development and Finance Act of 1989. Current efforts to use multilateral bank debt for swaps are being promoted by international NGOs and by Executive Directors to MDBs in other creditor countries.

Bilateral Debt Owed to the United States

The possibility for a great increase in the scale of debt swaps occurred following the February 1990 summit meeting between President Bush and the presidents of Colombia, Peru, and Bolivia. The outcome was announced by Bush on June 27, 1990, as the Enterprise for the Americas Initiative (EAI). The purpose of the EAI is to forge an "economic partnership" within the Western Hemisphere through a plan that concerns trade, investment and debt. Under the EAI, if a Latin American or Caribbean country has demonstrated actions toward economic, trade and investment reform, the U.S. will reduce the country's official bilateral debt (Gibson 1990). These countries owe a total of nearly $12 billion to the U.S. in concessional debt which includes PL-480, or Food for Peace, and the United States Agency for International Development (USAID) loans, as well as market-rate debt that includes Export-Import Bank and Commodity Credit Corporation loans. Debt-equity swaps, which are also part of the EAI, will not be discussed in this paper since most of the environmental community have historically claimed that these transactions are an entirely different concept from debt-for-nature swaps.

To be eligible for EAI debt reduction, a debtor country must have plans to satisfy four conditions:

1. Economic reforms through the World Bank.
2. Economic reforms through the International Monetary Fund.
3. Investment reforms through the Inter-American Development Bank (IDB).
4. Debt reduction programs with commercial bank lenders.

If a debtor country has complied with the above conditions, its principal will be reduced by an average of 50%, and in some countries as much as 85%. The reduction will be determined on a case-by-case basis and the remaining principal must be paid in dollars over 20-30 years.

It must be emphasized that the debtor country will receive a reduction in what it owes, but not in the amount it currently pays. Its historical principal payments must continue so that the U.S. government will continue to receive the payments that the budget was constructed to receive. In this way, the process remains neutral to the U.S. budget and requires no new appropriation.

The debtor then pays a concessional interest rate (2.5%) on its reduced debt in its local currency, which will be placed in a local Environmental Fund for the country to use for environmental activities. Local currency interest payments will gradually decrease as principal diminishes.

Financial incentives for a debtor country to participate in the EAI are that its principal will be substantially reduced, that interest payments can be paid in local currency rather than dollars, and that the debtor will not continue to accumulate principal and interest arrears which lead to an ever mounting debt burden.

However, many Latin American and U.S. environmental NGOs criticize the EAI as having cross-purposes. They recognize that the EAI increases funding for environmental activities through debt-for-nature swaps. But they are concerned that the EAI conditions for economic reform make everything else secondary, including the environment. Legitimate doubts were raised after the World Bank completed an evaluation on the impact of its economic reform programs. The evaluation failed to include the environment as an indicator and it highlighted the need for a better understanding of the costs and benefits of its economic reform programs (Thomas et al. 1988).

More importantly, policies of the IMF, unlike those initiated by Conable for the World Bank, lack an institutional mandate to assess the environmental and social impacts of its actions. Many question whether unevaluated conditions for economic reform are consistent with the environmental objectives of the EAI and the process of sustainable development.

Nevertheless, intense lobbying by environmental NGOs eased some of the stringent conditions of the Bush administration's original bill and resulted in passage of a part of the EAI. At the close of the 101st Congress, the Farm Bill (S.2830, S. Rpt. 101-357, H. Rpt. 101-569, Conf. Rpt. 101-916) incorporated the PL-480 component of the EAI. It passed the Congress and was signed into law by President Bush on November 28, 1990. It authorizes $1.7 billion of the U.S. PL-480 debt in Latin America as eligible for debt reduction.

A Debt to Nature

In 1988, Thomas Lovejoy, now Assistant Secretary for External Affairs at the Smithsonian Institution, stated, "I am utterly convinced that most of the great environmental struggles will be either won or lost in the 1990s, and that by the next century it will be too late" (Lovejoy 1988). To finance solutions to these urgent struggles, bilateral, multilateral, and commercial bank debt now offers an enlarged scale of what can be called a "second generation" of debt-for-nature swaps (Conservation International 1989). This increase in scale more clearly defines some incentives and constraints associated with debt swaps, and raises other questions that remain unanswered.

Incentives: U.S. NGOs lobbied for a significant provision in the EAI that mandates local NGOs play a key role in implementing and managing programs funded by the Environmental Trust Funds. This incentive can dovetail macro and micro economic objectives of debt reduction at the national level, and employment in grass-roots environmental programs at the local level. It can decentralize funds, political power and personnel to those best placed to understand and manage local resource needs. Strengthening NGO institutions in developing countries can create potent results in Latin American countries with fragile new democracies.

Since 80% of Latin American debt is owed to commercial banks, the EAI can be the catalyst to move those debt negotiations forward. To help fulfill the fourth condition of the EAI and mobilize funding for swaps, the U.S. government could clarify revenue rulings and tax laws which may encourage commercial banks to donate their debt to NGOs for use in swaps.

As bilateral debt begins to play a major role in financing debt-for-nature swaps, the World Bank is recognized as the institution to even further increase the scale of future swaps. Debt restructuring in developing countries is sound policy as debt swaps offer both the long-term financial and the natural resource management benefits necessary for sustainable development.

Constraints: Some believe swaps "legitimize" debt which was created unjustly to benefit only the dictators who negotiated the loans in the past, and not the people who today struggle for democratic rule. They feel debt problems are so severe that debt forgiveness is the real issue, and that swaps distract from it. Proponents argue that swaps never were intended to solve the debt crisis, but to free funds for much needed conservation programs.

The EAI is also politically sensitive because debtor countries must liberalize trade and privatize investment to satisfy foreign interests rather than domestic ones. Critics doubt that governments will take the political risk of imposing stringent macroeconomic and trade reforms without immediate cash flow relief in their country.

Because second generation swaps will expand dramatically the scale of debt reduction, remaining commercial bank debt will have a higher value for "free riders." These are banks that have not participated in debt reduction, but will benefit because their remaining debt will become more valuable as it becomes more likely to be paid. The secondary market for commercial bank debt should reflect this change, and NGOs may lose the advantage of the large discount that gives them leverage for their contributions.

Unanswered questions that arose during congressional hearings on the EAI include: Are eligibility criteria too rigid and could the U.S., itself, meet them? Could this disqualify or discourage countries that merit help? By law, the President was given discretion to determine a country's eligibility. Does too much discretion vested in the President to waive conditionalities relinquish too much congressional control of the EAI process? How can eligibility conditions be harmonized with environmental protection? Does the EAI set unwanted precedents to forgive other debt? Have budget impacts been fully accounted for? Should the use of environmental funds be broadened to include development? Can, or should, criteria for the "representativeness" of an NGO be determined? Exactly what kind of environmental activities has first generation swaps accomplished, and what has been their impact on local people?

Conclusions

As the scale of debt swaps increases, so does the scale of their consequences. The Congress is likely to pursue further action on the EAI during the 102nd session, so a careful consideration of their consequences is required through a balanced discussion of social needs, economic growth, and the wise management of natural resources.

Two things are quite clear. Debt-for-nature swaps offer critical time to secure environmental protection of the larger ecosystem for the present and future global community. They also protect and promote the sustainable use of the natural resources that is necessary for the economic development of the Third World.

It is unrealistic to expect developing countries to halt deforestation for environmental reasons alone. Developed countries, the U.S. in particular, cannot muster the political will to accomplish this. Today, the immediate priority of developing countries is the debt crisis. Perhaps it should be called the "bad-lending crisis." Existence of the secondary market proves that many debts are not being serviced and will never be paid in full (Eberstadt 1988). Debt swaps offer something in return. Is not the conservation of natural resources a fair swap?

References Cited

Bird, G.R. 1987. *International financial policy and economic development: A disaggregated approach*. New York: St. Martin Press.

Bramble, Barbara J. and Brent H. Millikan. 1990. *External debt, democratization, and natural resources in developing countries: The case of Brazil*. Washington, DC: National Wildlife Federation.

Cody, Betsy. 1990. Debt-for-nature swaps in developing countries: An overview of recent conservation efforts. Congressional Research Service Report for Congress. 88-647 ENR. Washington DC: Library of Congress.

Conservation International. 1989. *Debt-for-nature exchange: A tool for international conservation.* Washington, DC: Conservation International.

Debt Crisis Network. 1985. *From debt to development.* Washington DC: Institute for Policy Studies.

Downing, T.E. and G. Kushner. 1988. *Human rights and anthropology.* Cambridge: Cultural Survival, Inc.

Eberstadt, N.N. 1988. How creditworthy is the World Bank? *New York Times,* March 1. p. A23.

Gibson, Gene. 1990. *Enterprise for the Americas offers innovative debt-for-environment program.* Washington DC: Natural Resources Defense Council.

Hino, H. 1988. IMF-World Bank collaboration. *Finance and development* 23. September.

Holden, Constance. 1988. The greening of the World Bank. *Science* 24. June.

International Bank for Reconstruction (IBRD). 1945. Articles of agreement of IBRD (as amended). TIAS 1503; 3 Bevans 1390; 16 U.S.T. 1942; TIAS 5929.

Lovejoy, Thomas E. 1988. Nothing, nothing at all? American Institute of Biological Sciences 39th Annual Meeting. University of California at Davis.

_____ 1984 Aid debtor nations' ecology. *New York Times.* Oct 4, A31.

Mathews, Jessica Tuchman. 1989. Redefining security. *Foreign Affairs,* Winter. P. 165.

Thomas, V. and A. Chhibber (eds.). 1988. A*djustment lending: How it has worked, how it can be improved.* Washington DC: World Bank.

Petesch, Patty. 1990. Tropical forests: Conservation with development? Overseas Development Council Policy Paper No. 4.

U.S. Congress, Joint Economics Committee, Subcommittee on Economic Goals and Intergovernmental Policy. 1986. Managing the debt problem. Hearing, 99th Congress, 2nd Session. Jan. 23. Washington DC: Government Publications Office.

Wertman, Patricia. 1986. *The international debt problem: Options for solution.* Washington, DC: Congressional Research Service, Library of Congress.

World Bank. 1988. *World development report.* New York: Oxford Press.

19

The Timber Industry Perspective

Nils H. Svanqvist

The indications with regard to the development that has been and is taking place in the tropical forests of Latin America and which are conveyed to the general public through reports and media channels are confusing and contradictory and much emotion has gone into the interpretation of available information. Factual knowledge of the situation may be available with agencies and institutions in the region, but has not been made fully public or has been buried in interpretations and reassessments which may not be correct or honest but have the advantage of better public and media appeal.

FAO/UNEP forecasted in 1981 that the deforestation of tropical Latin America would increase during the first half of the 1980's compared to the previous five year period.

Each satellite track over the Amazon region registers hundreds of fires, in primary and disturbed forests. Most of these fires are started to clear land for agriculture development. The Economist reports:

Satellite photographs show huge swathes of rain forests being cleared for ranching and mining. Some projections suggest that the entire state of Rondonia will be bare of forest by 1992. (Economist 1987)

In contrast, Dawnay notes:

Analysis of the first satellite pictures suggest that by 1979, even after the big road projects, only about 5 percent had been lost to man. While maybe another 5 percent has gone since, some scientists believe that the rate of destruction is declining as immigrants realize that much of the land is useless for farming (Dawnay 1988).

One receives the impression that FAO/UNEP's pessimistic 1981 forecasts are confirmed and verified but also contradicted. However, detailed evidence based on compatible sets of imagery data, verified by ground observations, are not available for two points of time and for the entire region. Therefore, the actual trend cannot be determined.

If the data were available they would certainly be subject to contradictory interpretations by agencies and organizations which want to utilize the interpretation results in support of their specific aims and of the message they want to convey.

Historical Perspective

What is happening in Latin America with regard to forest removal for agricultural development is an extension or continuation of what has happened in India and China over the last four thousand years, in Africa and Europe over the last three thousand years, in North America over the last three centuries and in Southeast Asia mainly in the last century. Forests have been and are regarded as obstacles to agricultural development and are therefore destroyed. The negative consequences of this had been recognized throughout history, but the lesson these consequences offer is repeatedly ignored. The restraint on expanding exploitation has, in the past, been more a consequence of the terrain than official control or pressure of public opinion.

Thus, Latin America is experiencing a development which has parallels, now and in the past, in Europe, Asia and Africa. If the deforestation continues, a stage will be reached where adverse ecological effects will become apparent and self-perpetuating. At that point it would be very difficult and tremendously costly to halt the adverse effects and restore the environment.

The early clearing of land provide increased food production, timber extraction, and fuelwood collection to meet local demands. The more recent large scale development in Southeast Asia and parts of Africa resulted in the replacement of the natural tropical forests with agricultural crops which cater to the international demand for such products as rubber, vegetable oil, cocoa and fruits.

Logging of timber and clearing for agriculture has become easier as a result of power saws, improved communication into the forests, and more convenient access through the use of outboard motors, light aircraft and helicopters. The information on where to go is also readily available through maps, satellite imageries and mass media.

Wildlife species which have a value for recreation and trade are normally managed with great care. On the other hand, species which have no commercial value and those that compete with economically valuable species are often closely controlled or destroyed just as weeds are removed to eliminate their competition with the economic crop. The economic reasons for this is accepted. For the same reasons, forests are removed to make room for economically more valuable production. That is what is now happening in Latin America.

The problem is that this forest removal, to a considerable extent, reflects a lack of understanding and knowledge of the total production of tropical forests. Forests are removed because their expected future timber production cannot compete with the expected value of cattle production. Their removal erodes the capacity of the vegetation to regulate water regimes, prevent floods and erosion, absorb carbon dioxide, provide acceptable environmental conditions for many species of animals and plants and reduce the genetic resources which could provide valuable materials for future plant breeding.

When the goods and services of the forests, which at present are not traded and therefore have no apparent market value, have been reduced so that they are in short supply, they become noticed and appreciated and, finally, appraised. At that point of time it may be difficult to stop or reverse the development.

Unlike forests in temperate zones, tropical forests do not have a nutrient reserve stored in humus and soil. Almost the entire nutrient capital is stored in the biomass itself. Litter which falls to the forest floor is rapidly broken down and absorbed by the plants and reincorporated into the growing biomass. An important aspect of this tropical nutrient cycling and storage mechanism is that it is easily disturbed by removal of wood and leaves and that the nutrient reserves are completely destroyed when the forests are cleared for agriculture. For this reason, the productive capacity often fades very quickly when the forest is removed, and can be restored only by supply of fertilizers.

Worldwatch Institute (1987) observes:

> Time is of the essence: species lost cannot be recreated. Soil washed away may take centuries, if not millennia, to replace even under careful husbandry. Once the Earth gets warmer there will be no practical way of cooling it.

Development Trends

Demand for timber and timber products is expected to expand along a rising trend as wood is increasingly substituted for steel, concrete, brick, glass and other materials derived from non-renewable resources. In addition, many industrial and developing countries have dramatically increased their use of fuelwood since the early 1970's when petroleum prices started their rapid climb.

It has been estimated that in the Latin American/Caribbean region over 30 million people will be unemployed in 1990, most relying on the forests and forest lands to provide them with the means for survival. By the year 2000, an additional 30 million hectares of land will be required for agricultural crops. And the 250 million people who use fuelwood as household fuel may double by the end of this century.

Weakening values of local currencies, growing international debts and shortages of foreign currency make increased exploitation of forests for export attractive, at the same time as they make it difficult for the wood based industry to obtain foreign exchange to invest in expansion and to maintain existing facilities.

The growing international demand for timber, vegetable oil, coffee, tea, cocoa, beef and other tropical products offers attractive export markets for the countries in the tropics. It can therefore be expected that the demand for land for agriculture development will continue. Financing for such development was, in the past, often provided by timber harvested in the conversion area and on adjacent land, and there is no reason to assume that this will change. Very little of the timber revenues have, on the other hand, been used for restoration or improvement of forests. Ironically, the forests have, to a considerable extent, financed its own destruction, and will most likely be relied upon to do so in the future; there are few indications that the revenues they earn will be used to secure their continued life.

There is a growing awareness, among countries in the tropics as well as among those countries importing the goods produced from the tropics, of the irreparable losses which may be encountered if the deforestation and degradation of the tropical forests continue.

Thus, there are indications that deforestation will continue, but there are also signs of growing forces interested in applying the brakes to this particular form of development. Present economic and financial pressure favors deforestation and heavy forest exploitation. Although the need for wise, sustainable use of the forests, and for conservation, are gaining ground, the immediate problem of providing a decent life for those living in the tropics, and the lure of instant wealth, is and will remain strong.

The World Commission on the Environment and Development reported on "Our Common Future" in April 1987. It focuses on poverty and calls for a new era of economic growth. The report points out that growth need not be environmentally destructive, but can instead generate capacity to solve environmental problems and can be made sustainable, that is, achieved in a manner "which meets the needs of the present without compromising the ability of future generations to meet their own needs."

The problem which faces the forest and forest industries sector is to develop the political will to affect changes in resource management policies and establish economic and financial incentives which will make protection and reinvestment in the forest resource and in the timber industry and trade, politically, economically and financially attractive.

Some Economic Features of Forestry

Investment into natural tropical forests management and development has several serious disadvantages compared to investments in other economic sectors. The three most serious of these relate to cash flow, product pricing and the vulnerable nature of the investment.

Post felling silvicultural treatment of a stand normally does not yield cash returns until after 20 - 60 years. Though the return at that time may be substantial and provide high return on the investment, the cash flow situation is very awkward, especially for a public investor who does not have the option to sell the investment if fresh cash is required to meet urgent requirements or take advantage of unforeseen opportunities.

The long gestation periods also make forestry a very inflexible business in that it commits the investor for a specific production at a point of time so far in the future that the market development cannot be predicted with any degree of certainty.

In an export oriented forest sector, which is one of many suppliers to the international market, the producers have little power to realize optimal prices. These prices are determined by the supply situation in the market area and are at present to the advantage of the processing industries in the importing countries, in a manner which effectively effects the expansion of processing in the producing areas.

Another feature which affects the prices is the fact that few of the producing countries have markets for products such as fiber boards, particle boards and paper, manufactured from residues of the primary log converting industries, large enough to support domestic production on an economic scale. Consequently, approximately half of the volume extracted from the forests have no market value.

Investments in the form of natural forests are often very difficult to protect, not only from natural calamities such as fire, storms and insect attacks, but also from unauthorized human action like unlicensed timber extraction, illegal agricultural development and fuel poaching. This is especially the case where the local communities have no direct economic interest in the forests or have not developed a generally accepted opinion on nature conservation and environment protection, particularly in areas where economic development has provided few opportunities for income earning employment.

Some Characteristics of the Timber Industry
and Trade

The timber industry and the timber trade have many features in common with other economic activities but have, at the same time, unique characteristics. These features stem from the fact that the raw material is collected from vastly extensive land areas under difficult climatic and terrain conditions, and that timber is not one product, it is a host of products with widely differing physical and aesthetical characteristics and which can be substitutes for each other to a limited extent only. The timber trade and industry, because of these features, react in unique ways to changes of the environment in which they are to perform.

If the outturn of timber increases drastically, above what established markets can absorb and established industries and market channels can handle, the prices will drop and the industries and the marketing agencies are bound to become selective. This will lead to waste of raw material, which under more stable and market adjusted production conditions would be of value to industry and trade. It would further create a false, unfavorable impression of what the real productive capacity of the forests is and give these forests, in the eyes of the investors and the policy makers, a less competitive image.

The selective attitude of the trade coupled with the depressed prices resulting from a situation of over-supply will make the industry hesitant to invest in increased production capacity to cater to an expanded export trade in processed wood. Visibly dwindling resources will give the added impression that the raw material supply will disappear, and that will further strengthen the hesitancy to invest. If, in addition, plans and policies for resource utilization are unknown or unclear, there is little incentive to establish more than the most basic primary production facilities.

Investment into wood processing facilities are long term and the intermediate and final products carry a rather large capital cost component. Timber processing is also a long and, in its primary stages, a geographically dispersed production process. The accumulation of stock, in various stages of processing, at various points of the production chain, is large in comparison with most other industries. In addition, the material accumulated in the early stages of the production chain has to be processed to avoid deterioration, loses and harm to the environment. This means that it takes a long time for the authority issuing concessions and the logging industry in the producing area to react to a change in market demand which is initially felt by the retail trade in the importing country. In a similar manner, but not to the same extent, the production chain is slow to react to sudden changes in primary supply. While signals of change travel along the production chain, manufacturing in the various links will continue along the trend indicated by the previous signal of change, creating over- or under-supply, as the case might be. In other words, the system has limited ability to absorb and adjust to sudden fluctuations in raw material supply and market demand without serious adverse economic effects in the industry. The reoccurring over- and under-supply situations also tend to generate wide fluctuations in prices, especially of primary timber products.

The timber-based industry and the timber trade do not necessarily need prospects of exceptional profits or assurances of specific market and cost environments, but it needs to be able to project market and raw material supply conditions for a minimum period of time and with reasonable certainty. It needs to know what the plans and policies for resource utilization are and to have confidence in the authorities' ability to implement the plans and desire to uphold the policies.

Examples of Actual Development

In 1978 the Brazilian Government established, in cooperation with FAO, a pilot project for natural forest management of the Tapajos National Forest in the Amazon basin. A pre-feasibility study indicated that very high internal rates of return could be achieved under normal cost and price conditions. Even in the projected least favorable financial environment, returns were not expected to go below 20 percent.

A review mission conducted by FAO/UNDP in 1982 observed that applied forest management had still not been started and that outside interference was a major obstacle to the full implementation of the project. The mills in the area were operating at capacity using logs from land clearing operations supported by Instituto Nacional de Colonizacao e Reforma Agraria. These logs were available free of charge, or nearly so, in return for clearing the land. The project remains operational though forest management for industrial production is still not implemented.

In 1971, three million hectares of undisturbed accessible forests which could form the basis for a sizable industrial development were identified in Ecuador. In the period 1971-1975 over 400,000 hectares of these forests were occupied by farmers who used petroleum industry roads as channels into the area. The 32 saw mills located in or near the forests could use only some 2 percent of the timber cut in the process of converting the land. In 1982, the FAO project ECU/77/005 concluded that the agricultural development was threatening the future of the entire forest industry in the area.

The forests of Peninsular Malaysia provided over a long period of time raw materials to a large log processing industry in Malaysia and Singapore, producing sawnwood, veneer and plywood for local consumption and export, and exported at the same time logs to other countries in and outside the region. The log production increased throughout the 1960's to stabilize around 9 million cubic meters per year in the 1970's. The increase in log outturn was to a considerable extent a result of massive efforts by the Government to expand agricultural production through conversion of forest lands into plantations of mainly rubber and oil palm.

The log export grew with the increase in log production and exceeded 2 million cubic meters per year in 1970-1971. In 1972 the Government introduced restriction on export of logs of some species groups. This restriction was gradually made more severe until, in 1980, log export, including that to Singapore, from the Peninsula was reduced to below 100 thousand cubic meters per year.

The processing industry in Peninsular Malaysia responded to the increased availability of logs by expanded production to a log intake of just below 9 million cubic meters in 1973 and then leveled off. The production expansion was realized partly through better utilization of established mills, but there were also a number of new mill units coming into production and a number of units increasing their capacity through modernization.

The conversion of forest land into agricultural uses has continued in Peninsular Malaysia, but at a decreasing pace. At the same time new policies for forest conservation and utilization have been developed and gained acceptance by the States, the outturn from logging concessions have been regulated so as to maintain a stable supply of industrial timber.

The International Tropical Timber Organization (ITTO) is carrying out a pre-project study on natural forest management in the three tropical regions of Asia/Pacific, Africa and Latin America/Caribbean. The preliminary results of this study indicate that the implementation of management measures in Asian/Pacific forests primarily depends on availability of technical means and financing. The political commitment is generally well established. On the other hand, in Latin America/Caribbean, with a few exceptions, the political commitment to natural forest management is just beginning to emerge and so far little public initiative in this field is evident. Africa represents a transitional stage between those of the two other regions.

Past and Projected Production

Disregarding short-term cyclical fluctuations, the world wood products market has been expanding along a rather slow but steady trend. This development has over the last two decades incorporated a gradual shift towards a greater reliance on tropical timber. The supply of tropical timber has until now been dominated by Southeast Asia. Latin America has played a very limited role as a timber supplier to countries outside that region.

World production of tropical hardwood logs grew by an average of 2.1 percent annually over the period 1974/76 - 1984/86. The Latin American/Caribbean region recorded the fastest growth among the tropical regions with 2.9 percent compared to 1.8-1.9 for Africa and Asia/Pacific and contributed over 20 percent of total world supply at the end of the period.

Production of hardwood timber can be expected to continue to grow at a rapid rate in the Latin American/Caribbean region. The major portion of the production will most certainly come from the Amazon basin where large development programs — oil exploration, mining, road construction, dam building, etc. — will continue to make new areas economically accessible for exploitation.

In the Amazon basin, Brazil has in the past played a leading role as hardwood timber producer and is expected to continue to increase production rapidly. Moreover, it will probably become a sizable exporter of hardwood logs, as restrictions on log export have been lifted for timber from areas to be cleared for agricultural, mining and cattle ranching projects. In 1987, export of logs from such areas amounted to over 50 thousand cubic meters and is expected to exceed 200 thousand cubic meters in 1988.

The policy of the Brazilian Government to remove restrictions on export of logs from land clearing areas reflects the non-sustainable nature of this supply and the hesitancy of the timber based industries to establish processing facilities for logs from a "disappearing" resource.

Forecasts by the World Bank for the period 1985-2000 put the expected growth in hardwood log production at 2.4 percent for tropical Latin America/Caribbean compared to 1.4 percent for all tropical countries.

These forecasts assume that production will be in approximate balance with demand. If the production in the Latin American/Caribbean region grows faster and results, as a consequence of clearing of new grazing areas, in increased supply of logs to the international market, the effects may be disturbances as described above in section "Some Characteristics of the Timber Industry and Trade."

Requirements for Change
Policy Development

If the value of the non-commercial goods and services of the forests at various levels of supply, that is at various stages of deforestation, had been known from the outset, a sensible land use plan for the tropics of Latin America could have been developed. This plan would have suited at least the immediate ranges of population density and per capita income. If this plan was based on hard economic facts, it would most certainly would have been politically acceptable. However, we have very limited insight into the functioning of the very complex ecosystem of the tropical forests, and we are far from capable of even describing all those goods and services produced by it, not to mention evaluating them.

The policy research issues which need attention are: the establishment of sound land use policies which take into account modern technology and are conducive to maximum financial production and optimal economic benefits from the use of the land; and which can guarantee the retention of an environment which does not threaten the sustainability of the productive capacity of the land and the protective capacity of the vegetation.

There are land use models which have worked for thousands of years, but with modern speed and scale of development these models can no longer be applied. Modern development has not derived any models or norms which have been tested and found feasible with regard to sustainability of production and environmental protection.

Clearing of land for agricultural uses is, in many cases, a first step in an effort to obtain the right to hold or possess the land. If taking and utilizing forest produce, and managing the forests would lead to securing tenure in the same way, some of the tropical forests of Latin America might be saved for sustained production of industrial raw material and environmental services, and important tropical ecosystems might be conserved for the future.

There is also a need for reviewing land tenure policies in order to achieve long term optimal land use development. Much of the knowledge of the value of goods and services produced by various short, intermediate, and long term forest and agriculture management alternatives which would be desired for this policy review may not be immediately available. However, enough is known for basic strategy decisions which can guide the initial stages of land use and research. As new knowledge becomes available, it will assist in refining these strategies and converting them into long term policies.

Research

The immediate research need would be to establish the extent of all production of the tropical forests including currently traded products, such as timber, and goods taken free of charge, mainly non-timber goods, and all the services, and assess their value at different levels of supply. The results of this research would form the basis for the policy development discussed above.

Nearly a century of research into tropical silviculture has not established the economic viability of tropical forest management and the competitiveness of timber production as a land use alternative. Earlier research focussed attention on and has provided substantial insight into the biological aspects of forest stand dynamics. Many of the management systems which have been developed, based on these research efforts, would go a long way in safeguarding environmental values, but because they are costly to apply or require harvesting techniques which are not readily available or not regarded as acceptable in the current situation of technological development, they have been applied in practical management only to a very limited extent.

On the other hand, the cultivators and the developers of cattle ranches carry with them knowledge and experience of crop and livestock production in other geographic areas which they believe are valid also in the new environment or, if they experience problems, can easily be adapted to the conditions they encounter.

What has been happening in the tropics of South and Southeast Asia, Africa and now in Latin America amounts to replacing something we know almost nothing about and believe we cannot afford with something we think we know at least a little about and which appears to offer reasonable economic security.

Immediate attention therefore has to be given to the performance of various tropical forest management systems, both with regard to their economical and financial viability and their ecological impact. Such research would contribute to the creation of a sound basis for the development of forest utilization and land use policies.

Although much research needs to be initiated without delay, the current lack of knowledge should not be taken as an obstacle to implementation of sustainable forest management. The research will be required to refine the systems, but existing insight into and knowledge of tropical forest growth dynamics form a sufficiently good base for designing and initiating management practices. The problem is not a lack of basic knowledge but one of political commitment, socioeconomic conditions and resource utilization policies.

Manpower Development

The disturbance which is acceptable in a wood removal operation and the treatment which is required to retain and enhance the value of forests production are basically site-specific. The forest manager must therefore be able to decide what combination of removal intensity, removal technique and post felling treatments are to be applied in any given situation. This skill or insight can, to some extent, be obtained through theoretical studies but, to a large extent, it comes from practical experience. It is therefore important that the professional and technical staff is available in sufficient number in the forest management authorities to allow a substantial portion of their time to be spent in the field and that logistics and funds for economic compensation for this are available to the staff.

Planning

The continued supply of timber and the sustainability of a healthy environment are issues of global concern which are attracting increasing attention worldwide. Though the sovereign right of individual countries to manage their own resources must be accepted, it must also be recognized that forest and environment management are becoming aspects of global economics and international relations, including international law. Such management issues are beginning to figure prominently in international assistance. This interdependence of nations, in the utilization of natural resources, calls for regional and global cooperation and coordination of planning and action in the fields of forest and environment management.

A mechanism for a broad, holistic approach to forest development planning exists in the Tropical Forestry Action Plan (TFAP) which is a new concept for international cooperation in tropical forest development (WRI 1985). Expertise and manpower for planning and implementation of plans are available with the large number of bilateral agencies which provide assistance in forestry and forest related activities, with the development banks, with UN agencies like FAO, UNLDO, UNEP and UNESCO and with ITTO, and of course with the various agencies and institutions in the tropical countries.

Financing

Increased knowledge of the total production of the forests and of the value of these goods and services must result in increased charges for the use of the resource, and these charges must grow relative to the increasing value of the remaining productive capacity of the resource. There is little else to resort to with regard to policy action if we want to introduce control and attempt to steer the development.

A taxation model must be found which will meet three criteria:

- it should correctly reflect the value of the goods removed and the reduction of other production which becomes a temporary or permanent consequence of that removal;
- it should provide funds and incentives for administrative control and reinvestment into the resource, and
- it should not be so high that it discourages sustainable use of the forest resource

If these criteria are met the result will be increased revenue to the forest owner from the forest. Of course, this in itself cannot guarantee that increased funds will be available for forest management and for investment into the forest resource. There must also be a desire to give this increased flow of revenue a long term nature by recycling a sufficiently large portion back into resource development to guarantee its continued productivity.

Summary

The conversion of forests into grazing areas for cattle, which is taking place in Latin America, is likely to have a disturbing effect on the global timber supply and may adversely influence the climate of the world by reducing the carbon dioxide absorbing capacity of the vegetation. Locally it may reduce the productive capacity of the land and, in the long term, reduce earnings of people living in the affected areas. On the other hand, clearing of the forests may, at least temporarily, provide high income earning employment and increased export revenues.

The main reasons for the preference for development of cattle farming rather than forest based activities are financial: long gestation periods of the investment in forestry, the inflexible nature of forest investment and the fact that most of the non-timber values produced by the forest cannot be converted into cash for the owner or manager.

Governments have different reasons for accepting the deforestation development: it provides immediate, large scale employment, it can provide immediate, additional foreign exchange revenues and it does not call for skills which are not available domestically.

The attitude of both the people and the administration is to a great extent the result of ignorance of the real value of the total timber and non-timber production of the forests and of the long term adverse effects of deforestation.

In order to halt the current development and secure long term timber production and protection of environmental values of the forests, several requirements have to be met:

- It is necessary to review and revise government policies so that the competitive strength of forest management corresponds to its importance in the national economy.
- Research has to be devoted to establishing the full value of all products and services produced by the forests.
- Training of all categories of forest and forest industry personnel needs to be intensified and geared toward developing insight into the dynamics of various types of tropical forest.
- International cooperation in planning and implementing activities in tropical forestry need to be strengthened.
- Systems of charges for the use of forests and forest land, which correctly reflect the cost to the society of such use, need to be designed and implemented.

References Cited

Dawnay, Ivo. 1988. "Brazilian corruption claims continue." *Financial Times*, February 20.

The Economist. 1987. *An Amazon Tragedy*. October 17, p. 52.

World Commission on the Environment and Development. 1987. *Food 2000: Global policies for sustainable agriculture. A report of the advisory panel on food, security, agriculture, forestry, and environment*. London: Zed Books.

World Resources Institute. 1985. *Tropical forests: "A call for action."* Report of the Task Force convened by the World Resources Institute and the United Nations Development Programme. Washington: World Resources Institute

Worldwatch Institute. 1987. *State of the world*. Washington, D.C.: Worldwatch Institute.

PART SEVEN
COMMUNITY
PERSPECTIVES

The preceding sections focused on the problem of forest destruction or development from the technical and theoretical point of view. In contrast, this section shows the problem from the perspective of the people in the forest communities, including their achievements and frustrations in managing their forest resources.

The chapter prepared by the Union of Forest Ejidos and Communities of Oaxaca should dispel any doubts that one might have that local communities are capable of managing their own resources. Their contribution demonstrates how communities can, through collective organization, work, and determination of its leaders, overcome bureaucratic, technical, economic obstacles and take control of their forest resources.

In a book on deforestation, it is tempting to ignore the fact that forest communities have multiple needs and resources beyond those of the forest industry. Eucario Martinez shows the need for governments to recognize that, at the community level, integrated resource management is the norm. He demonstrates how communities handle their development projects through a collective approach. Rather than a generalized, governmental program, he stresses the need to formulate development projects, policies, and regulations within the community, based on their needs and limitations.

Next, two Mexican peasants, Martinez and Matias, express their perception of the deforestation problem and possible solutions. They suggest alternatives to firewood consumption. They point out the need for the creation of alternative occupations for those who currently make a living out of the forest resources. Their frustration is evident when it comes to obtaining technical assistance for combating problems outside their local expertise such as beetle infestations or disease plagued trees and the cost that such disaster entails.

It is often difficult to realize the physical violence which too often accompanies the struggle between people who depend on the forest for their livelihood and those who use cattle to establish rights to land. The interview with Osmarino Amâncio Rodrigues, an Amazonian rubber tapper and organizer, provides a stunning glimpse of the front-line struggle to maintain sustained production from the tropical forest. What can foreigners do? Read his answer.

These chapters present an overview of the skepticism and optimistic spirit of cooperation that exist at the community level in the process of implementation of development or conservation works.

Carmen Garcia-Downing

20

Union of Forest Ejidos and Communities of Oaxaca

Javier Castañeda

A member of the Union of Forest Ejidos and Communities of Oaxaca recalls:

Who does not recall those long years which left us such sad memories? And our forests, dare one say how they treated them? And we know that some were treated worse than others. How much wood did they remove? Who knows! But in our forests most of the trees are missing.

Scarcities, poverty, humiliations of those years engrave our memory. Perhaps for that reason, non-conformism began to grow in those early years, although it was not yet known what to do and how to do it.

The *Union de Comunidades y Ejidos Forestales de Oaxaca, S.C.* (UCEFO), is an organization of Zapotec forest communities that seeks to improve the standard of living of their inhabitants by wisely using their natural and human resources. The communities that form part of what is today UCEFO S.C. are located in the Sierra Juarez, and the Northern, and Southern mountain ranges of Oaxaca. In this area, which includes the steepest slopes and highest elevations in the region, is found one of the best forest reserves in the country.

Historical and Political Context

Increasing erosion in some mountainous zones, added to the ruggedness of the terrain, abrupt slopes and a pronounced degree of isolation of many communities has fostered, in the last 50 years, a considerable decrease in the levels of productivity and self-sufficiency in food of the indigenous communities. As a result, the region has become more dependent on urban centers. In the 1930's, these regions began to experience heavy out-migration which, in turn, favored a reinforcement of the conditions of dependence and lower productivity as labor was siphoned away from the farm. These phenomena have grown more acute during the last decade in the great majority of the indigenous mountain villages.

The accelerated change during the last 50 years has been accompanied by a destabilization of local cultures. Individualism of the communities has been accentuated. Inter-community trade or exchange has been weakened, both in economic and socio-cultural terms. Expansion of Spanish in regional communication has accentuated the linguistic fragmentation and has limited the use of native languages to the community-family spaces.

At the economic level, the development policy of the national society of the last decades discovered an excellent source of raw forestry materials in the Oaxaca mountains. This led to a massive and irrational exploitation of the forest resources. For almost a half century, the region's forests were monopolized by private companies, the so-called "Industrial Units for Forestry." These companies were financed with private and state capital. Chief among these, over the last 30 years, has been the "Tuxtepec Paper Manufacturers, S.A." (a mixed capital company) and its affiliates.

Created in 1955 by presidential decree, Tuxtepec Paper Manufacturers obtained through a concession of the federal government, most of the forest area in the State of Oaxaca, and in particular, the forests in the Sierra Juarez and Southern Sierras. The company did not pay attention at all to the need to preserve and foster the forest resource, or to channel the economic profits generated toward the residents, the legitimate owners of the forests.

The strategy resulted in the deterioration of large parts of the forest (immoderate felling, erosion, fires, plague, infestations, poor roads, reduction of forested areas, climatic changes, etc.) and the progressive plundering of the communal patrimony of local populations...their forest. The erosion of the lands has also contributed to the decrease in agricultural productivity and consequently an increase in indigenous migration.

The urgent need to defend the forest resources and their use led to the creation of the first indigenous-peasant movements in the State of Oaxaca and organized at the inter-community level. The renewal of the industrial forest concession by presidential decree in 1982, accompanied by increasingly negative evaluations inside and outside of the government toward this type of company, generated a strong resistance movement in several mountain communities. The discontent culminated in a writ by the forest communities of the Juarez and Southern Sierras against the presidential decree, an action which nullified the decree and opened the door to direct negotiation between the communities and the timber industry.

From 1982 to 1985 many communities, from both regions of the Juarez and Southern Sierras, entered into discussions aimed at developing an organizational structure that would allow them to deal directly with the users of the forest. Around 25 community organizations arose with different names and forms, which were grouped together in a structure called "Community Forest Raw Material Productive Unit." In this first organizational stage, many communities, which did not succeed in a broader integration at the regional or state level, continued depending on the local industry because of a lack of financing, questions of political control and corruption of community authorities and because of pressures from private industrialists, Tuxtepec Paper Manufacturers and public officials, whose economic interests had been affected negatively in the new producer-industry community relationship. In contrast to these communities, the municipalities that today belong to UCEFO began a process of exchange and common identification of goals, their integration culminating in a productive organization of an inter-community nature. These mountain communities are the ones that historically have the broadest tradition of organization and struggle around the conquering and defense of their lands and community rights. Their experience and organizational ability, developed from the times of the Mexican Revolution, have been the essential premise toward the creation of a common organization. These characteristics, accompanied by the nature of forest use as a productive activity which must be profitable, requires a wider degree of community and economic organization than that of a single community. This ability has allowed these communities to achieve a level of integration unique in the history of the mountains of Oaxaca and of the country.

Forest Leases (1955-1982)

The exploitative situation continued until the forest leases expired in 1982 and new decrees were made that repeated the words of the old ones. The communities were fed up. They protested that the new decrees were unjust, arguing that their intent was to continue "leasing" the forests. They demanded a more equitable treatment. Some politicians tried to form a union of forest ejidos, but failed.

Taking advantage of the situation, some private companies offered to train the communities in some things. Moreover, they offered them personnel to administer their business and to train them little by little. For the communities that was an old story that nobody ever followed through.

Unhappy with the new decree, some communities sought legal advice and filed writs. They sought to publicize the problem and their opposition to the new decrees. They denounced the new decrees at the national level and in magazines, Mexico City newspapers, and in the state capital of Oaxaca. The communities were resolute. Their forests would never again be exploited in the same manner by means of government concessions. Their position affected the forest industries. Milling yards were empty and some companies began to bring logs from other regions of the country. Officials of government institutions and the lumber companies called assemblies in different communities. They gathered together. But nothing was resolved. They just wanted to go on controlling us. One thing was clear at that time: the indigenous communities no longer wanted to continue leasing their forests. But, they did not know what else to do either.

So the months passed until the example of some communities of the Sierra Juarez came forth. These mountain Zapotec Indians had accepted the proposal of a group of experts with experience in forestry use and development who managed to win their trust for a new proposal. That group proposed a solution: organize to make use of forest resources under the form of Forest Raw Material Producer Unit or UPMPF (Figure 20.1).

The communities had many doubts. Above all they doubted they had the ability to manage a forest enterprise, in the midst of a totally different community dynamic. Therefore, the communities decided to begin to work (a test) with 500 to 1000 m^3 of uncut timber. This was done with a double purpose. First, it would prove whether the community could, indeed, carry out that work. And second, they could determine whether or not working the forest was a good community business, something that until that time was reserved for industrialists and specialists.

Managing just one part of its volume was a big mistake, as stated many times and in different state and federal places by the industrialists. Sales contracts were too small. However, the communities believed this to be an appropriate action. They wished their members who did not have formal academic preparation to receive in depth training in all the areas of work (operation, accounting, marketing, etc.)

This approach was seriously criticized by the industrialists who considered the community residents incapable of carrying out all the necessary activities for forest development.

One aspect that turned out to be extremely important for achieving the organization of the communities was the constant communication. Such communication which was often conducted in a simple and graphic form to inform the assemblies about all of the activities that were going to be carried out and those already accomplished. This aspect was decisive. The communities could thus have confidence in their representatives and, in turn, they would learn and make group decisions on the operation of their forest enterprises.

Nevertheless, as the communities increased their timber volume, the amount of money being handled increased considerably, with the risk that the internal stability would break down. Some communities were still

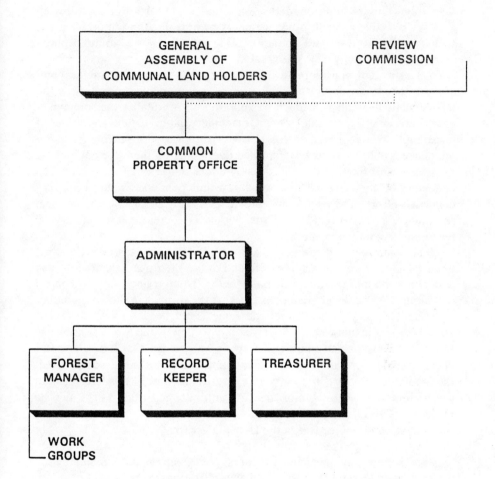

FIGURE 20.1 Organizational structure of the UPMPF

resentful over previous negative experiences. Therefore, a commission was formed to periodically evaluate the administration and accounting of the work. That commission was made up of group members of the same general assembly. This strengthened the community organization by allowing greater collective control. More members were trained in important areas such as administration and accounting. Through this work, an atmosphere of internal community trust was created.

An aspect of considerable importance was the decision of the communities not to divide up the profits of each community. According to the intermediate term plans made, it was important to capitalize the community companies in all aspects: equipment, machinery, labor, capital and wages of personnel. The real motive for that decision was the search for independence from the wood buyers, since depending on them for equipment, machinery and financing would directly affect the price of the wood. The communities correctly felt that to achieve independence would require a collective effort of several years, provided there was an internal political tranquility, a solid organization for work and a greater level of general forest culture of the assembly.

The communities continued to advance. In 1985, they needed to combat forest plagues. Five communities decided to use their own resources to pay community people (male and female youths) to be trained in pest control techniques. When the communities saw that the training in those techniques was possible, they deduced that the same could be done with the other areas of forest management which were controlled by the forest administration units. This was an important step. It was not an easy struggle. After considerable effort, in 1986, the communities had technical services. Although not always formal, they were operative. In view of this later goal, to get technical services, Union de Comunidades y Ejidos Forestales de Oaxaca (UCEFO, S.C.) was formed.

The statutory objectives of the UCEFO are to:

- support and participate in forest policy and the federal and state forest administrative decentralization, to the benefit of the peasant;
- create sources of work and improve the general well-being of the members of the communities;
- improve management of forest resources;
- protect the natural resources of each community;
- control production costs, improve the quality and value of natural resource products;
- improve the political, productive and technical organization of the communities;

- foster the exchange of experiences, mutual assistance and common effort among communities;
- harmonize and join efforts with the federal and state government and other communities.

Since 1985, UCEFO has been providing technical services to its communities. One of the characteristics of the organization has been its ability to train community experts in the different types of forestry work. Because of the internal growth of the organization in the communities, UCEFO stopped being a forest technical management organization and, instead, became an organization providing multiple services, including having its own projects, so that the communities could make better use of their forest resources, such as charcoal.

UCEFO and its growth have followed the needs of its communities; however, it is unable to keep up with all the needs, especially in non-forest activities such as agriculture, fructiculture, livestock, and floriculture.

One might think that from the forest production great profits are obtained. However, great investments are necessary in order to be able to preserve the forest and to meet basic needs such as health and education.

The UCEFO has shown that its development model has helped to raise the standard of living of the group members. Above all, it prevents the exodus of its people to cities and outside of the country. Its example is beginning to be followed in neighboring communities, so UCEFO is constantly meeting with those who seek its advice and guidance. UCEFO still has problems with some industrial companies, since they do not agree with the changes occurring in the forest sector in Oaxaca and they seek to return to the situation existing in earlier years, when they obtained the forest raw materials at very low prices.

All of the initial concerns cited were motives that led UCEFO to formulate their objectives. These objectives began to materialize over a three year period (Table 20.1).

Union Structure

Nine communities make up the organization: San Juan Bautista Atepec (ex-district of Ixtlan); San Miguel Alopan (ex-district of Ixtlan); Santa Catarina Ixtepeji (ex-district of Ixtlan); Pueblos Mancumunados (ex-district of Ixtlan); Santiago Textitlan (ex-district of Sola de Vega); Santiago Xochiltepec (ex-district of Sola de Vega); Santa Maria Zaniza (ex-district of Sola de Vega); San Pedro El Alto (ex-district of Zimatlan); and, San Andres El Alto (ex-district of Zimatlan).

Internally, the organization has an Assembly of Representatives, a Review Commission, an Executive Committee, a Commision on Planning

TABLE 20.1 Important dates for the consolidation of the Union of
Forest Ejidos and Communities of Oaxaca

1985	UCEFO S. C. was formally established
1986	New Forest Law was decreed
	Agreement signed with SARH for operating the forest technical services
1987	UCEFO S.C. was granted the National Forest Prize
1988	The formal granting of the forest technical services to UCEFO S.C.

and Agreements (Figure 20.2). The Assembly of Representatives is the highest authority of the organization and includes: the president of the Executive Committee, Advisory Council, the coordinator and delegates from each community. The Review Commission is made up of a delegate from each participating community. It annually reviews the budget of the organization and its implementation. The Executive Committee is made up of a president, secretary and treasurer. The Commission on Planning and Agreements is in charge of Operations, Support and Services. Operations is responsible for forest management, supply and industry, charcoal and saturation plant. Support and Services is responsible for accounting along with finances, communication and promotion of projects, staff and social security, and marketing.

Union Revenues

The organization funding comes from annual fees charged per cubic meter of wood. Each community contributes according to its forest permit. Funding is also derived from consulting that it provides to each community. The consulting fee increases if the community has an installed processing industry or processing shops.

Union Resources

The Union's human resources consist of 46 persons, 7 women and 39 men, forty of whom are specialized community experts. Two forest specialists, an economist, a lawyer, and an accountant assist the Union as outside advisors. Moreover, the Union has generated 1320 jobs. The Union owns equipment consisting of 10 vehicles, a crane, a computer, and a wood saturation plant.

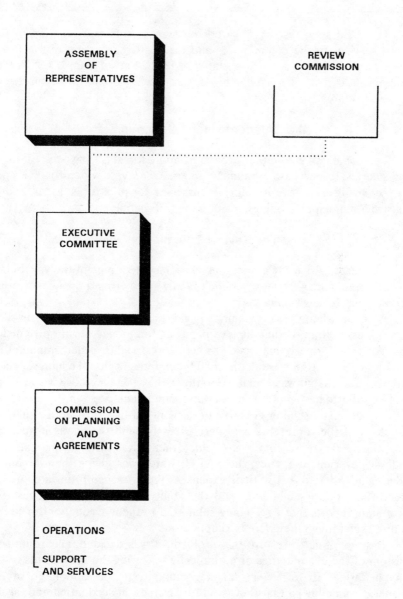

FIGURE 20.2 Organizational structure of the Union of Forest Ejidos and
Communities of Oaxaca

The legal specialist has insured the legal and formal granting of the forest services to the communities and the legal registration of the Company. The key natural resources consist of 186,824 m^3 of pine; 111,357 m^3 of oak; and 10,008 m^3 of oyamel, *Abies spp.,* covering a total forest surface of 161,000 hectares.

Use of Income in the Communities

The communities use the revenue from the forest for payment of wages and salaries, to purchase equipment and machinery, to widen roads, to pay for technical services, to install tree nurseries, for pilot forest areas, and to construct municipal buildings, local roads and schools.

The Review Commission

The term " Review Commission" has become a part of the vocabulary in our communities. By now, in each family some friend or a relative has served on a Review Commission.

By 1984, when the communities began to have a lot of activity in their operations, both in the handling of paper and in money, this in proportion to what they formerly managed through forest rights, other communities took note. Some who were not in the Union, thought that the name seemed strange. But when it was explained to them, they exclaimed "we wish we had that in order to have more peace in our community!"

In one of the Union communities, members began to notice that the expenses of the representatives were excessive and there was no control over them. The representatives shielded themselves through the staff of a federal government agency, the SARH, which was giving them technical advice, in order to justify their expenses. This was inappropriate. At the same time, the assemblies lacked the ability to analyze and discuss the economic reports that were being submitted to them accounting for use of funds, even though they were in simple terms.

In attempting to resolve this problem, it was decided, according to a custom of the communities of periodically reviewing the movements of the commissariats, to form a group of community people appointed by the General Assembly so that they would be trained in accounting and, at the same time examining or reviewing the administrator's performance.

This idea was accepted by the communities, so that a simple system was devised by which any community member who knew how to read, write and do a few numbers could participate in the work of a Review Commission.

Currently, the Review Commissions are not only trained to review the Union's operations, but they also prepare the accounting report and present it to the assembly.

So far, the communities that have a Review Commission for their unit have been able to continually work without internal problems. A great tranquillity exists with respect to the handling of funds and, above all, there is good participation in the assemblies when the budget or accounting report are submitted, since the community members know what will be discussed.

Functions in the Structure of UCEFO S.C.

The General Assembly, as already said, is the highest authority in the organization. All community members who are 18 years or older have the right to participate. The Review Commission named by the Assembly from among the groups takes office at the end of each fiscal year in order to review the state of the accounts. The Administrative Office of Communal Property is appointed by the Assembly. They form the top community authority after the Assembly itself. It is made up of the president of the Administrative Office of Communal Property, the Secretary, the Treasurer, and the President of the Advisory Council. The Assembly also appoints the Administrator, who is in charge of marketing, negotiating prices, and buying equipment, along with the President of the Administrative Office. The Assembly appoints the treasurer, who administers the money in joint bank accounts with the Administrator, conducts the accounting and submits the annual budget balance. The Assembly also appoints the Director of Forests who is in charge of production in the forest, handling of machinery, road construction, transportation, distribution of personnel and stocks of prepared products. The Documenter is appointed by the Assembly. He documents the products transported and prepares the payrolls.

Achievements

It is with this small and simple structure that something has been consolidated in the last five years and that now is irreversible because of the achievements attained thus far:

- For the first time, in 1983, profits from the use of the forest were obtained;
- The belief that peasants are incapable of administering has been disproved;

- It has also been shown that those possessing the resources are the only ones who can sufficiently protect and develop them;
- Profits have been divided among the community members who have participated;
- Machinery and equipment has been acquired;
- Workers have determined their salaries and increases;
- For the first time, workers have social benefits;
- Community members were trained in accounting, preparation of documentation, measuring the volume of wood, classification of products, fire fighting, and pest control in the forests;
- Community members were continously informed about the production costs of each of the products that they market;
- Members demonstrated their negotiation skills;
- They built works of social benefit: health clinics, places for child care, a government building and introduced potable water.

Translated by Deanna Hammond
Congressional Research Services

21

Integrated Resource Management: A Zapotec Community's Approach

Peasant Solidarity Group of Quiatoni and Eucario Angeles Martinez

The Quiatoni region is among the most isolated of places within Oaxaca, Mexico. Its small, scattered Zapotec Indian hamlets and ritual center of San Pedro are not known for their timber production or cattle. Clinging on the extreme margin of subsistence, Quiatoni's Indians survive by diversifying their productive strategies. To them, forestry and grazing are one of many forms of resources that they must carefully manage in order to <u>marginally</u> survive.

Eucario Martinez, a village native, describes his community's struggles to survive. Anyone proposing solutions or combating the deforestation problem in communities, such as Quiatoni, must consider the local forms of organizations and these poor people's undaunted will to survive. Above all, solutions would have to face the problem that neither Quiatoni nor most Latin American communities can, in fact, maximize a single resource such as timber or cattle and ignore their demands for other resources. Any plan brought to this community or any community like it, must be integrated within the community's complex, multi-family, multi-resource management activities. Impossible? Yes, if we attempted to "program" a solution from the outside. But chances for sustainable resource management improve if more faith and trust is placed in the abilities of these peoples to find their own solutions and if they are provided with the technical help to achieve their objectives. Fortunately, the community's objective of integrated resource management often matches that of many "outsiders" who want to see that the Quiatonis of this world prosper and protect their ecological and cultural diversity.

— T. E. Downing

Our community's problems are the same as that of other communities in the underdeveloped world: unemployment, migration, malnutrition, deficient education, discord, acculturation, and accelerated destruction of our cultural identity and our natural resources. This situation is exacerbated by the economic crisis that the country is experiencing. These problems are worsened by droughts, which grow year by year, causing greater problems in our fields. Our people believe these droughts are related to an increased clearing of our forest. That is why the peasants feel pressured to seek new forms of subsistence.

Quiatoni, our municipality, has about 13,000 Zapotec inhabitants, divided into two smaller political subdivisions or police agencies, two municipal agencies, and 32 other widely dispersed settlements scattered over 537 km^2 of land. The topography is so rough that all the work of planting is done by hand, with only a very small portion cultivated by teams of oxen. The municipality is between 800 and 2,800 meters above sea level. Lower altitudes are hot, dry and rocky; upper regions are scattered pine and oak forests. We have very little forest located on our higher mountain peak, perhaps about 72 km^2. Nonetheless, it is very important.

Our communally owned forest provides us with ritual and medicinal plants, construction materials for our homes and farm implements, and, above all, our only source of fuel — firewood. We consider the forest part of our shared patrimony.

Forms of Organization

Our ancestors had their traditional form of organization, which consisted of family gatherings (grandparents, children, grandchildren, nephews, godchildren and friends). They would meet on the main holidays, or celebrate some saint's day, or gathering of the harvest or some other occasion in order to thank their gods (nature, sun, mountain) for the benefits obtained. This gratitude consisted of sacrifices, ceremonies or religious acts. These gatherings were a combination of religious, political, economic and cultural meetings. They kept families in contact and in co-existence.

Currently we are trying to recover this form of organization in the Solidarity Group (*Grupo Solidario*) with the voluntary participation of its members, holding bimonthly meetings in order to discuss and analyze the progress of each project.

History and Development of Projects

For 10 years the cultivation of an ornamental flower (a large lily) was a very good source of work for almost everyone in the entire municipality. At all the small springs, small wells were carved out to water this flower. But cultivation failed due to a virus. With the intention of reviving this activity, we turned to the government for assistance. An analysis was ordered to identify the disease with the experts of the *Instituto National Indigenista* (INI) in Tlacolula, Mexico, through the *Secretaria de Agricultura y Recursos Hidraulicos* and the Center for Interdisciplinary Research for Integral Regional Development. As a result of the INI analysis, they recommended two types of chemical treatments which we tried but did not work. After almost two years of searching, we did not find a solution. We abandoned the crop. The collapse of this important and lucrative activity meant that we had to seek new economic alternatives.

Toward the end of 1983, work groups began to organize in order to analyze, discuss, and seek solutions to our problems. These groups were supported and, at times, were led by the few natives of Quiatoni who had moved to the cities and were conscious of the problems facing their rural community. The groups proposed specific projects: fruit trees, vegetable gardens, chicken farms, pigs, rabbits, bees, fish, and others.

Fish

The water problem continues and is magnified by the deforestation. The people feel that cutting our forest has decreased the amount of humidity kept by the soil which fed our brooks and wells. We had experience in the use of small wells for watering large lilies. At first it seemed advantageous to construct larger reservoirs, but after discussions, we decided to use existing wells and brooks for fish production. Therefore, with experience in reproducing small fish *(tripon)* in the wells and brooks, the aquaculture activity began. Aquaculture and fishing had been practiced traditionally in Quiatoni. Until eight years ago, fish could be found in two of its main brooks. In earlier years, members of the community could catch a great variety of fishes, such as trout, *barbel*, tilapia *(mojarra)*, and prawns in all the brooks. Currently, the increasingly serious drought has caused the total extinction of this activity as the waterways dried. The people relate this drought to the deforestation of the mountains which feed our small wells and brooks. The only new and viable possibility is breeding and fattening in reservoirs.

For the authorization of fish breeding, there were a lot of problems. The Mexican Secretariat of Fisheries, as a requirement, asked that the reservoirs must have 250 m^2 of surface area. This was an impossible requirement for us to meet because of our topographical situation. However, we built 25m^2 reservoirs, where, although with many problems, we managed to obtain tilapia nurseries which we spread throughout the warmer zones. In the cold zones we introduced Israeli carp, which we obtained after two years of paperwork.

Under optimal conditions, this system produced 25 to 45 kilograms per year for each 100 m^2 of surface water. However, the Secretariat of Fisheries reports lower yields (10 to 18 kg). We emphasize optimal conditions because currently due to drought problems in the zone, most of our small reservoirs are drying up, with a corresponding decrease in production. From this experience, some families made their own reservoirs. Six to eight small tanks were constructed, in addition to the 18 operated by the Solidarity Group.

Crops

A variety of pilot cropping experiments have been carried out in the different localities. In the communities of Lachibarra and Union Juarez, papayas, watermelons, and tomatoes were grown on a hectare of land, with irrigation from the reservoirs. There was also experimentation with growing onions, chiles, peanuts, and soya, and the adaptation of rustic beehives into modern boxes.

In Buena Vista, people experimented with peanuts, soya, and chiles. Currently there are about 150 different fruit trees in the region. Experiments are being carried out in grafting to improve fruit quality. They have planted sugar cane and are beginning to prepare coarse sugar, a traditional work abandoned years before. They have also adapted rustic beehives into modern boxes, with positive results. In Rio Minas and Piedra Tehuana, others have carried out the same experiments as well as handled rustic beehives, on an individual family basis.

In Centro Quiatoni, individual families have been experimenting with cochineal crop for natural dyes, a colonial crop abandoned here about 50 years ago.

Farms

In Union Juarez, groups are experimenting with 6 pigs to be fattened for slaughter, giving them balanced feed and corn in order to learn which feed is the most profitable for this activity. The community is also beginning to experiment with hens of the region for intensive production, both for meat and eggs. In Maconada, people are experimenting with 30 chickens for meat production. Unfortunately, in Rio Minas an experiment with eight rabbits for reproduction failed because of a lack of follow-up and medicines. Individual families in several settlements experimented with laying hens bought from the government in Oaxaca.

Apiculture

In 1985, 24 nucleuses of bees were financed by an INI loan. The bees arrived in the community in poor condition, diseased and very weak. According to the credit agreement, INI promised to give training and technical advice until the groups learned to handle the bees, but INI did not keep its commitment. Nevertheless, the groups, on their own and with assistance from other groups, received training and in two years expanded to 38 complete beehives with a harvest of approximately 250 liters of honey. With this experience in two communities (Unión Juárez and Buena Vista) we dared to request beehives for the other communities, an objective that we achieved in early 1988. Currently our harvests have stabilized. We are planning for 130 hives in five communities: Buena Vista, Centro Quiatoni, Piedra Tehuana, Rio Minas and Unión Juarez, with a harvest of 750 liters of honey this year. The problem of disease is more and more acute. This year we lost 20 hives. Because we lacked boxes for increasing the apiary of Buena Vista, 7 boxes were made. We also lacked adequate tools for making the boxes, which caused considerable delay.

Crafts

Craft projects were also initiated. An effort was made to recover the people's long abandoned weaving abilities. Miscellaneous goods, embroidered smocks, sashes, napkins, blankets and fish nets were made. Unfortunately, we were unable to create a market for these products. The effort was abandoned.

Events and Training

Theater works and different socio-cultural events at the municipal seat were used to promote these projects. Above all, these events were staged at the main village fiestas. Moreover, training was given in apiculture, crops, preparation and consumption of foods, and different forms of organization.

At the same time, we had regularly scheduled meetings to strengthen our organization as well as bimonthly meetings of representatives from the different communities. At these meetings, we discussed, reflected, analyzed the advances made in each project, and planned future work.

Problems: Groups that Withdrew

Our Solidarity Group of Quiatoni is now made up of six groups of communities with a total of 37 families (approximately 250 persons), directly involved in the projects. However, four Solidarity Groups have withdrawn (Agua Blanca, El Cargador, Cerro Costoche and Rio Lana). Reasons for withdrawal include family problems, illness, religious conflicts, exhaustion, and lack of time to attend project meetings. It should be noted that getting to and from these meetings often require participants to walk from two to seven hours over rough mountainous terrain. Others lacked the economic resources for carrying out profit-making projects. Despite all these problems with several of the projects, the fish reservoirs continue operating regularly in these communities, except in Agua Blanca.

Marketing

The dream of production for self-sufficency in 1983 is becoming a reality in 1986. But before achieving a production that supplied the needs of the people and of the group itself, it was necessary to take an intermediate step. This was the establishment of consumer cooperative stores. The first one was opened in Unión Juárez in 1986. It sells basic products at lower prices and had an initial capital of 1 million pesos. In 1986, another store opened in Rio Minas with an initial capital of 500,000 pesos; and in 1988, one was opened in La Mancornada with a capital of 250,000 pesos. These co-ops supply to around 13,000 inhabitants of the municipality and people from other neighboring areas. People walk up to a day and a half to get to our stores in order to buy corn, beans and sugar.

The three shops have increased their capital, with loans through some nongovernmental agencies. However, the available capital is insufficient to meet the demands of the municipality, since, in addition, an effort is being made to introduce tools for the peasants. An 8-ton truck is needed for transporting products to the regional market. To eliminate the middlemen, direct buying relationships with producers' organizations were established, but this requires readily available capital.

Progress

After five years of collective work, we have gradually increased the active participation of children and women. Women have always participated in different ways in the community, but they are often excluded from communal work. Unlike their parents, children normally do not appear to be concerned about the economic, political, social and cultural situation. Nonetheless, they suffer the consequences. From a very early age they realize that there is not enough food, alcoholism is a problem, their parent's argue, and their fathers leave home to work elsewhere for extended periods. Our groups are not, however, affliated with any religious organization our outside political organizations.

For that reason, we believed it important to have women and children directly involved in the different group tasks, both the physical and the reflective, so that we can achieve family integration in some communities of the *Grupo Solidario*. When we began in 1983, we hoped for community participation and to find solutions to our problems in general. We viewed our community as the family and sets of families. After five years of experience, this objective of integration has been achieved, which for us, is the most important aspect of any community project.

Our organization's concern now is to get the State to respect the peasant's work and schedules in order to successfully meet the project's objectives. We are concerned, since traditionally when some resource is requested for a project, it is scheduled or "calendarized" by the government according to its plans and programs, but the schedule is not always synchronized with that of the community.

Finally, the *Grupo Solidario* joint work is focusing on educating and making each of its members conscious of their full freedoms. The goal is to guarantee the advancement of all activities in their totality. This means that our work stands out in contrast to the methods used by the Rural Clinic of *Instituto Mexicano del Seguro Social* (IMSS) in its COPLAMAR community program. This program wants to carry out projects for vegetable gardens, farms, promotion of hygiene, construction of latrines, etc., by pressuring the peasants. If the people do not meet the requirements, they have no right to consultation or medicines. Such an approach leads to apathy or hatred toward the institution.

The indigenous communities, since pre-Columbian times, have worshiped Mother Nature, but, unfortunately, the alienation, the crisis, drought, and lack of better lands for cultivation, force them to make poor use of their natural resources. Through our work of group analysis and discussion, the people are recognizing the need to conserve their natural resources, in contrast to an emphasis on regulations established by the government institutions (SARH or SRA). Regulations without a local level concern for conservation create conflicts and injustices in the communities. Look at the consequences. Peasants are told that they cannot cut trees in order to build their houses. If they do, they are fined. However, it is widely known that private companies carry out improper felling of forests without being punished. This double-standard generates hatred toward the state.

Translated by Deanna Hammond
Congressional Research Services

22

Two Peasants Discuss Deforestation

Ismael Martinez
Fortino Matias

Two Oaxacan indian-peasants, Ismael Martinez and Fortino Matias, attended the Oaxaca workshop that was the precursor to this volume. A few months later, back in their village, they discussed the problem. Their conversation was taped as the two sat talking in the shade on Ismael's patio. Their ancient community located near Tlacolula, 25 miles southeast of Oaxaca City, was once covered with forest. By the late 19th Century, cattle, sheep and goats had overgrazed most of the lands nearby the community. As they chatted, they scanned the barren hillsides. Thousands of feet above, they could just see the edge of what remains of their community's pine-oak forest. What follows is a lightly edited transcript of their conversation. — T. E. Downing

Ismael:

Fifty years ago our community had a forest about two kilometers from the center of the village. Now, the forest is about 7 or 8 kilometers away. The deforestation of the nearby forest was due partly to our people's use of firewood for all household cooking and tortilla making. Now, firewood is far from the village and is also being used less because domestic gas is being utilized instead. Because firewood is less accessible, some people in the community feel it has become more economical to utilize domestic gas. To stop the current rate of exploitation of firewood, I believe that the government should subsidize the cost of propane tanks and domestic fuel at lower prices to all rural communities. If the government were to take this action, it is possible that someday fuelwood consumption would be reduced to around 10 percent of its current use in our community.

Fortino:

Well, I agree with you but I know quite well that the national and state government will never work through the local community. That is only wishful thinking. As you know, propane tanks are very expensive.

The gas itself is cheap, but not the tank. Unless the government promotes rural stoves or something similar, we will continue with the deforestation of the mountains because we have a lot of people who still depend on the use of firewood. Each week, they must climb the mountain and cut or gather up two or three donkey loads of firewood. And for those who can't afford to go to the mountains themselves, they must purchase a donkey load of firewood, which is very expensive.

And there is another cause of deforestation — the plague of the *gusano barrenador*. In our community, it has already killed our forests in several areas: *Cerro Iglesia*, near Santa Catarina, all the tract known as the *Alcatraces*. These areas used to be pristine. Now, we only have pristine forest in the area known as *Llano Cuartel*, on the other side of *Cerro Iglesia*. This is the only area where the pine has withstood the plague because, the variety differs from that which the *gusano barrenador* is killing in other areas. It is resistant to the plague. This is what has saved the forest on the Mitla side. The ecology in this area is pristine. It is good. It rains there all the time. You go there in February and March and it is raining. This is an area which man's hand has not touched.

Another cause is the government practice of granting concessions to timber companies. They are allowed to exploit and destroy the communities' forest resources in exchange for insignificant incentives, such as small amounts of money to the municipios. Therefore, there are a lot of things that we see that is killing the ecology of Mexico and of communities which in the past used to have pristine forests with a lot of vegetation, water and everything. For example, do you remember when we used to go for walks up into the mountain forests?

Ismael:

Yes.

Fortino:

At that time there were a lot of streams, the forest looked good. But in 1987 when we went up there, the *gusano barrenador* had attacked the pines and killed a lot of trees. The village authorities who were in charge at that time said that they did everything possible to obtain help to combat the blight. They went to the government, the *Secretaria de Agricultura y Recursos Hidraulicos* (SARH), the corresponding agency, but SARH people didn't pay any attention to them. The blight spread and killed about 180 hectares of pines. By now it has probably destroyed more than half of the hectares of the village's forest lands. Therefore, I see the need for our government to help combat plagues and to help insure that the forest is not over exploited for firewood or used for anything but the most essential household needs. This will help maintain the forest ecology and give us more live trees. Now, as we both know, people cut trees even before they reach some degree of maturity.

Ismael:

The municipal authorities, should formalize a way in which the consuming public is allowed to collect dead trees for firewood. They should categorically prohibit the cutting of standing trees. By putting in effect this system in the community, it will possibly preserve the trees that are still standing. But it must be given priority, it must be acted upon now. Otherwise, in the not too distant future, perhaps 10-15 years, there won't be any trees left. And we, the peasant people, won't have any irrigation water left.

Fifty years ago, even during drought periods, the river that passes through the village was constantly flowing, approximately 3-4 inches deep. It even had little fishes. Now, past the rainy season, the river bed is dry. This is because the trees are further away now and there is nothing nurturing the soil. The ecology is dying. That is why I think that the government should do something. I don't know why the agencies such as SARH exist. They are a disgrace! They don't do anything. They have trucks, resources, but have we ever seen them here showing some concern for our forest? They have never offered to evaluate the condition of the forest, or offered technical assistance to the villagers. They didn't tell us: "We will give you technical assistance and you do the cutting of the diseased trees so the blight won't spread."

The communities are left to the best of their own abilities as far as knowledge of forest resources are concerned. From our perspective as consumers of firewood, it is good that the trees die, because then we go and collect it for firewood. But, I don't think that is right.

Fortino:

During the first few years that we were in the Presidency of the village, a friend, Gabino Juan, came and reported that certain areas of our forest were being plagued. That was when Pedro Garcia and I tried to mobilize some response. An agronomist from far away Tuxtla Gutierrez came. He climbed all the way up to the forest, something that the employees from SARH or any of the other government agencies which are in charge of these resources will not do. The agronomist examined the tree bark and told us that the best and immediate action that could be taken under those circumstances was to burn the dead trees and bury the ashes to prevent the spread of the disease. Then, SARH or the agency who was in charge of the forest, went up there and afterwards told us that they didn't have any budget. Yet they had money to build a logging road into the forest area. What would it have cost them? The agronomist had told us that another way of halting the spread of the blight was to spray the area with an airplane, and that there were some institutions that could do the spraying. Spraying with airplanes required a lot of money. We didn't obtain any assistance from the government.

The municipal authorities called a public meeting of the entire community. At that meeting, several people said that it was better that the trees were dying so they could be cut for firewood, if they weren't going to be allowed to cut live trees. This way, the trees killed by the blight could be used to get firewood without killing live trees. I see that even among ourselves there is lack of awareness. There is no humanitarian desire for a green and fertile forest, something that will be the lungs of the village. Just look at the areas that are still forested. There is water. It rains. You know why? Because the ecology has not yet been disturbed. But the water from there flows into the Papaloapan Basin (*Atlantic watershed.* − ed.) towards the Mixe and Sierra. The Mixe and other Sierra communities cannot utilize this water for irrigation purposes because the rivers pass across these communities way at the bottom of their steep enclaves. At the most they are used for a fish or two or some other use but not for irrigation or other helpful uses, like in the drier Central Valleys where in good periods we get good harvests. Therefore, in order to solve these problems we need a lot of support from the government, community awareness, and more demanding local level leadership. Those who cut our community's firewood for sale to Tlacolula (*a nearby urban area of about 25,000 people* − ed.) must be made aware of other means of earning an income, such as bricklaying or other occupations. The selling price for firewood is meager. But there are people who are used to that type of occupation and are not aware of the damage that they are causing to the ecology and to the community. Apart from the streams drying up, there are other ecological damages that result from tree cutting.

Ismael:

Yes, the government needs to improve the condition of the peasant, because it is the peasant who is the main consumer of firewood. But if the government makes an effort, instead of pocketing the monies of the communities, they could use a portion of it to subsidize the cost of gas tanks and stoves for the people. The government doesn't have to subsidize the total cost, but at least 50%. If this approach doesn't eliminate the problem of deforestation, at least it will diminish the problem. Then, slowly, the process of deforestation will reverse itself, perhaps in a period of 10, 20 or 30 years. I think this might be the solution.

Fortino:

That will be the day when Mexico gets an effective government and leaders who know the purpose of money!

Ismael:

Leaders who think about the peasants. Not like now when in their discourses, the politicians tell us that they are giving millions and millions to the peasants but that is all it is... speeches!

Fortino:

Pure demagoguery! Those millions never reach the farmers!

Ismael:

A case in point: approximately three months ago, a villager went to the bank to inquire about a loan and the necessary requirements. In the past, to obtain a loan the bank required a land title and an application explaining the purpose of the loan. Now, they require two letters of recommendation from two business people, legalized land titles, tax receipts, bank appraisal, birth certificate, marriage certificate, photo identification, a land survey and other documents. What business person will be willing to provide a villager with a letter of recommendation? Maybe one or two villagers might be able to obtain letters of recommendation because they are constantly in touch with businessmen in Oaxaca. But imagine someone in the village with no business connections. Who will be willing to give them a recommendation?

Fortino:

It never ends....They trap you in such a way that it is impossible to obtain a loan.

Ismael:

How is it possible then? Politicians talk about the peasants, yet, they never pay them any attention.

Fortino:

Before the banks were nationalized, it was better. They gave credit when they were privately owned. Now that the banks have been nationalized, things have gotten worse. Instead of the banks benefiting the peasants, they benefit the bureaucrats. The same people who are in charge. We have the case of the pickup trucks, which were given supposedly for the support of the rural communities. The pickups are being driven or owned by the government representatives and their relatives. Certainly the peasants haven't seen them.

Ismael:

I put in my loan application at the bank for a pickup truck but in less than a month the money was gone. Now the only ones with the trucks are the big business people, seed dealers, and so on....but not the peasant people.

Fortino:

That's right. That's what I have seen. The representatives, their children, brothers and relatives are the ones who are driving those pickup trucks. The bureaucrats bought them for good prices, but not the peasant for whom the loan money was earmarked. The monopolization of the money by the bureaucrats infuriates me. They monopolize aid provided by the Americans or other organizations for the needy people to work with. But, frankly, when that aid gets here, the first people to benefit are the vultures who are in power. There it stays and you never see or hear from that money again.

Ismael:

Let me tell you a story. Sometime around September of 1982, I went to the bank in Oaxaca to apply for a loan (approximately 300,000 pesos — which at that time was a lot of money) because my son-in-law was buying a piece of land. I went, turned in my application, my papers and everything else but they told me that they weren't giving out any loans until the following January. They told me to stop by and check once in a while. That, perhaps, when the loan money arrived, someone might not want their loan after all. Then I could get it. One day, one Sunday, a van, a wagoneer, drove through and hit one of the pillars of my porch. The van belonged to BANCOFULANO. Immediately, a man got out of the car and apologized. He explained what had happened and promised to pay the damages. He told me to look for him at BANCOFULANO and gave me his card. He left. A week later I went to the bank and I saw him there. When he saw me, he told me not to worry that the van was insured and that the insurance company will pay me. I told him that I had not gone to the bank to collect but to make a loan. I told him about my loan application and what the loan representative had told me, that there wasn't anymore money for loans. He seemed surprised. He introduced me to someone and said, "My friend here wants a loan." They explained to him that they already had my papers. And he asked them why they hadn't given me the loan when there was 40 million pesos available. He ordered them to attend me right away. A week later, I had my loan. But, if that guy hadn't had the accident, I would never have gotten my loan.

......and conversation continues.

Translated by Carmen Garcia-Downing

23

A Rubber Tapper Speaks Out

Osmarino Amâncio Rodrigues

All through the Easter Week meeting in March, 1986 in Rio Branco, one of the most visible rubber tappers was an energetic and humorous young man called Osmarino Amâncio Rodrigues. He hails from Brasileia, a small town southwest from Rio Branco, almost on the Bolivian border. Osmarino is the secretary of the Rubber Tappers' Union. Schooled in organizing by the Catholic Church and a longtime associate of the late Chico Mendes, he is one of the most dynamic of the forest's activists. He talked to us the evening of Easter Sunday, as his bodyguards paced about somewhat unconvincingly in the shadows.

— *S. Hecht*

I was born in 1957 on a rubber estate called Hummingbird. At the time it was really a traditional *seringal,* where the rubber baron forced everyone to sell at a lousy price only to his middlemen, and to buy supplies from his agents. It's far back in the forest, and the guy would only send his middleman out once a year with merchandise, and rubber tappers would be out there starving, waiting for supplies and unable to sell or buy from anybody else. And we still had to pay rent on our holding! We were in debt slavery because no matter how much rubber you got, the supplies always cost more. So, when I was a teenager, the struggle began out there simply because it was impossible to live in such conditions.

In 1970, when Wanderley Dantas was Governor of Acre, he began a big propaganda campaign about how Acre should advance and have progress, and the only thing that would do that would be ranching. He arranged land concessions, bank financing and fiscal incentives of people from the south, all the things he never gave to the actual workers of his state. Ranchers began to come here, and after telling the poor guys out in the *seringal* that the Governor had sold them the land, they'd threaten rubber tappers or burn their houses and buildings. And then began the expulsions and the killings, as ranchers' gunmen — *jaguncos* — came into the rubber plantations and forced people to leave. They did this with thousands of people.

Right now there are 10,000 *brasilenos* living in Bolivia because they were forced out of Acre.

Well, this strategy of expulsion and killing worked up to a certain point, but only as long as people didn't realize that it was going on all over. They didn't yet know about the deaths in other places. We were all very isolated. In 1973 there began the organization of base communities by the Catholic Church, and this is where I really got going. I started to go to these church meetings. And there they talked of human liberation, of freeing oneself from slavery. Lots of people were interested in this, because the conditions were really awful and we had to do something.

In 1975 we began to work on union development. When I started to get involved, I went because I wanted to learn. I didn't realize then that I would be in this till the end. Anyway, in 1976 we started the first *empates*, the standoffs to the ranchers. These *empates* really gave us hope. Here's how it was done. The leader of the union in a place like Boca de Acre or Xapuri, Brasileia or Assis Brasil, would learn that tappers were being thrown off their land. A leader in, let's say, Boca de Acre would then get on the phone or radio to Xapuri or Brasileia and ask people there to travel so that these guys in Boca de Acre wouldn't be kicked off their lands. Truckloads of people would show up. It was really great.

The first *empate* occurred in Brasileia, where I'm from, on an *seringal* called Carme, which still is a standing rubber forest. The ranchers kicked everybody off, but we really battled it out. We had to face down the army, the police, but we had right on our side. After all, we were struggling for the land we had lived and worked on all our lives. State officials worked out a deal where they gave each tapper from 25 to 125 acres so that they wouldn't have to migrate to the city. This system didn't work out all that well, which was why we want to go with reserves.

Well, *empates* became a regular thing, and each year there were more, so rubber barons and ranchers began to go after the union leadership. I was getting involved more, especially after 1980, when they killed Wilson Pinheiro, then the Rubber Tappers' Union leader. The secretary of my union, who was Chico Mendes, had to go to Xapuri to organize the union there, and the few people who could work away from the *seringal* went from municipality to municipality trying to make sure that unions were in touch with each other. I didn't know how to read them, but I had to learn because I'd go to meetings and I'd come back and have to read things to people in my union. There I was, a director of a base community and a union leader, and I didn't know how to read. It was awful.

In 1985 we set up the first Rubber Tappers' Council meeting to get people organized on a national level, to get extractive reserves going and also to talk about the systematic murder of the union members and leaders.

From then until now it's only been this work. I don't even have time to play soccer. I used to like to go to parties, to dance, to bum around a bit. But all my time was taken. There were killings and killings and killings. They were murdering the lower leadership, but I told Chico at that time that they are going to keep killing until they get to us. They're breaking the legs of the union now, but they won't stop until they get to the heart. We have to prepare people so that when we're shot there will always be others to take our places.

Nobody believed that people lived in the forest. Even as recently as 1985 the Census Bureau said there were no people out here in spite of the fact that these forests are full of tappers, Indians and *ribeirinhos*. We may be illiterates isolated in the middle of the forest, but we do know what's going on. We know that livestock doesn't work here, and we know what other things will, but we don't have the technical ways of explaining it. So the authorities never give much importance to what we have to say. The only time they give us any credit is when they're crying crocodile tears after one of us has been shot.

In a seminar on the environment and development in 1988, things took on a different rhythm because we finally had some technical information that we could use to wrangle with the government officials. The government was more concerned, and began to have meetings with us. That was also when they declared the first extractive reserve at Sao Luis de Remanso.

Today we see that a lot of people are concerned with our struggle, but basically Brazilian justice doesn't give a shit about us. And we're worried; all this international attention doesn't make the Brazilian nation do anything about the systematic murders. Brazilian authorities have done nothing to calm this violence. I, for example, have about a 2 percent chance to get through this year. The same night they went to get Chico they also passed by my house in Brasileia. There's just no way I'm going to get through this alive. There are organized death plans, and everybody knows it. Out in the Jurua a rubber baron, Camili, says that there is no doubt that Macedo--who organized people not to pay rent − is going to die. He says, "I'm going to order it; I'm going to kill him." Meanwhile, in the judicial district of Brasileia there are more than 200 cases that haven't got a public prosecutor or even a police detective on them. The Governor doesn't appoint prosecutors, or people simply won't take these jobs on. Each year the University of Acre coughs out forty new lawyers, but you can't get a lawyer out here for public service or for rural workers' rights. If people kill and are never punished, they just keep on murdering.

Today, for example, I'm not permitted to carry a firearm, but every goddamn rancher out here is armed to the teeth, as are all their minions. They've circled my house various times, wrecked my house on some occasions. One time it was just luck that a car came by and they fled. We sent letters to the Governor, to the head of the federal police, Romeo Tuma. We've sent letters and telegrams about the nature of the organized violence, and the only thing that happens is yet another one of us gets blown away. We don't really have immense options. We have to think of ways to live a bit longer. I have those bodyguards over there from the government. The guns that they have mostly don't work.

I have to pay for those guards — travel, meals, lodgings, even their bullets. Look, I don't have any money. I sent a letter to the Justice Department explaining that I understood the importance of security, but I don't have any way to support four men. I live with my parents, I don't have the wherewithal to set up my own housekeeping. The government isn't interested in my safety. They want me to sign a document saying that I dismissed these guys. The thing is I simply can't pay for them. What will happen is that once the document is signed, the government will say, Look, we assigned guards to him, and he dismissed them; it's not our fault if he gets killed.

What are the things foreigners can do? They can do a lot. We need people who can help us evaluate natural resources, marketing the products, and who can get a better price, ways to get better cooperatives going. We know that rubber and other extractive products can sustain a community without destroying the forest. We need market development and basic economic infrastructure. We're not anti-development, you only need to see how poor we are to know that. What we need is to develop the organizational techniques so that these things can move into the market in some kind of serious way, so that we can keep some of the value of the products we produce. We also need things like good historians, who will tell history the way it happened, and not develop a history from some fantasy. We need serious and honest scientists. We want this alliance with other forest dwellers to go forward, and to develop ways of doing this kind of work. We want you to do what you do best, and use this knowledge in solidarity with us.

Interviewed and translated by Susanna B. Hecht

PART EIGHT
COMMENTS
AND
RECOMMENDATIONS

24

The Oaxaca Recommendations

The Oaxaca 67

Apart from their individual contributions, the participants in the Oaxaca 1988 workshop on the Conversion of Tropical Forests to Pastures in Latin America prepared the following recommendations for future research, policy goals, proposed institutional actions, and suggested alternative production systems.

Research

Research programs should facilitate cooperative, collaboration among scientists from diverse countries. Future programs should include graduate research training in Latin American countries and in the United States. They should also distribute bilingual reports. Bureaucratic hurdles and administrative difficulties in arranging cooperative research should be reduced.

There is an urgent need for papers to synthesize the information scattered in reports, government archives, conference proceedings, books, and journals and published in many languages and disciplines. As is evident in this volume, forest to pasture conversion takes place in a context of considerable ecological and social heterogeneity. Consequently, its study spans many disciplines. A program to prepare a series of synthesis papers should be initiated to critically evaluate and rescue data from these scattered sources and provide a stronger sense of the variables that influence the processes of conversion and the ecological outcomes of the conversion. The papers would include, but not be limited to, biological diversity, demography, land tenure, migration, ethnology of development strategies, characteristics of bureaucracies and institutions, determination of the causes of and human expectations from forest conversion, available markets for forest products, and procedures to integrate socio-economic and ecological criteria in the design of production systems.

Moreover, basic research is needed on:

- nutrient cycling, nutrient balances and nutrient dynamics;
- soil physical characteristics under various management practices;
- microclimatological characteristics under various management practices;
- humid tropical ecological systems, including wildlife;
- inventories of tropical flora and fauna, with attention to lower plants, canopy organisms and insects; and
- inventories and collection of germplasm, including trees, pasture species, and crops.

Applied research should focus on discovering:

- under what conditions can forests be reestablished from pastures;
- how can the sustainability of managed pastures be achieved;
- the conditions under which extensive livestock production in a tropical forest complements regional development and when it irrevocably hampers regional economic development;
- the proportion of carbon dioxide and ozone attributable to forest conversion versus industrial sources; and
- the social and economic dynamics that favor sustainable livestock and forest management systems.

Apart from basic and applied research, critical methodological problems include:

- determining ways to examine whole systems which cannot be subdivided for study without changing the nature and variances associated with the system; and
- determining the rate and specific locations of forest conversion and land degradation by using remote sensing, ecological models and geographical information systems.

Strategies

The Oaxaca group unanimously affirmed that cattle have an important role in tropical forests and that the area presently being used for pastures in Latin America was sufficient to meet domestic and export needs. There is no need to clear primary forest for new pastures. Cattle production should be limited to natural rangelands and intensively managed systems such as silvopastoral production, cut forage, or managed medium and small scale production.

The group also emphasized that it was fundamental to maintain tropical forest, promote human and biological diversity, and encourage the participation of local populations in determining the future of forest lands. To achieve these goals, policy initiatives should emphasize limiting physical access to the forest and increase the cost of converting forest to pasture.

Specific options include:

- reduce subsidies which the cattle sector has historically enjoyed.
- discourage new penetration roads and encourage alternative means of satisfying rural community needs by elaborating alternative forms of transport, and integrating existing highway systems more thoroughly into river transport. Many services demanded by rural populations do not require roads, and some of the most valuable commodities can be transported without recourse to roads.
- reduce colonization into tropical zones by eliminating formal colonization programs which attract huge numbers of spontaneous migrants. Address the social problems that drive migration to the tropics to already developed areas, by promoting agrarian reform.
- eliminate subsidies (i.e. credits, tax holidays, fiscal incentives) for forming new pasture at the expense of forest.
- use fiscal instruments to encourage intensification and forest conservation, such as land taxes, etc.
- encourage long term, usufruct land rights rather than outright ownership, to limit land speculation and the practice of clearing-for-claiming.

The Oaxaca participants were concerned about promoting biological and cultural diversity. Strategies for achieving this goal:

- create a large range of reserves, including those that incorporate sustainable human activities.
- encourage nations to develop an integrated mix of national parks, national forests, biosphere reserves, extractive reserves, community forestry, and peasant reserves in a variety of different ecosystems.
- identify areas which contain concentrations of endemic or threatened species, or areas of unusual concentration of economic species and establishing conservation priorities.
- strengthen the conservation and management related institutional capacity in universities, in government and other types of research institutions.

- empower local community institutions with conservation and management responsibility.
- develop financial mechanisms to support the recurrent costs of management, restoration and conservation.
- transfer financial resources from the developed world to humid tropical zones via mechanisms such as biosphere reserves, debt swap, international non-governmental organizations, and World Heritage sites.
- Increase returns on existing pastures and standing forest.

Biodiversity may also be promoted by intensifying cattle production in non-tropical forest regions and on existing pastures in tropical rainforest zones. This strategy would:

- promote consumption and production of alternative sources of protein, such as poultry and pork, goats and fish.
- research and development of marketing infrastructure (including cooperatives) for forest extractive products.
- develop alternative agricultural and livestock products from tropical areas, such as perfume essences, medicines, dyes, resins, oils, fruits, waxes, and husbandry of animals such as turtles, or iguanas.
- enhance secondary and tertiary processing within the forested area, so that jobs are created in tropical, especially humid tropical, regions.
- promote non-agrarian activities in tropical forest areas such as tourism, crafts, industries in minor forest products, and controlled sport hunting in specified hunting reserves such as that developed in the Cuyabeno reserve.
- allocate human and financial resources to better understand the ecosystem and sustainable uses.

Empowering Local Participation

Finally, the workshop participants recommended the promotion of biodiversity by empowering local participation in decisions over natural resources. The transformation of forest to pasture occurs within a dynamic, unstable institutional setting. Whether at the international or local level, few institutions are more than two decades old and inter-institutional relationships between regulatory agencies, businesses, and land owners are brittle. Old development formulas, including top down development planning and operations, is often problematic. Local level peoples are distrustful of forest development, which often serves as a pretext for clearing their land without reforestation. Non-governmental organizations have begun to play an increasingly important role in development by forging direct links to rural communities.

Few rural communities are directly benefiting from the transformation of forest to pasture. On the contrary, the existing forms of exploitation are seriously damaging the resource patrimony of what had been, heretofore, sustainable agricultural communities.

Local participation can be enhanced in several ways:

- recognize indigenous and local community rights to forest resources.
- promote mechanisms that directly finance community development.
- encourage the creation and training of local level organizations.
- facilitate the horizontal transfer and dissemination of information between local level organizations.
- encourage community participation in the definition and design of programs and projects which will affect their resources.
- adjust educational programs to local needs.
- facilitate the flow of price information to the people at the local level.
- recognize that forestry and livestock production are businesses to local level peoples and promote technological change and organizational structures which make this a sustainable business.

Alternative Production Systems

The Oaxaca workshop participants stress that the conversion of tropical forests to grazing lands destabilizes the ecological, social, and economic systems in the Latin American lowland tropics. It was apparent that the forest conversion process must stop and, in many instances, be reversed. Alternative production systems might involve integrated uses such as agroforestry and management of the present resources. New models for research and management of the tropical forests must focus on more integrated approaches with a stronger balance between conservation (wise use of resources) and management (sustainability of production systems). Alternative production systems must encourage diversity, optimize low input technology, and intensify management on existing pasture. Small ruminant systems and intensified management of rangelands should be encouraged to reduce pressure or need for more forest clearing. Multiple use, small scale management systems should be encouraged. Techniques should be developed to acquire economic returns from harvest of natural forest products and exploration of new products. Mechanisms for accomplishing the implementation of these alternatives should include ecological "zoning", strong involvement of local and community organizations, and direct forms of technical assistance suited to the local and community structure with financial support for these alternative approaches.

The Oaxaca Group of 67

Alejandro de Avila
Susan Abbasi
Eucario Angeles Martinez
Adan Aguirre
Paul Albrecht
Andres Aluja
David Barkin
Edward Bcalls
Theodore Bustamante
Judith Carney
Javier Castanea P.
Leon Jorge Castañeda
Heliodoro Cayetano
Alexander Cockburn
James Clawson
Theodore E. Downing
Gary R. Evans
Manuel Fernandez
Carmen Garcia-Downing
Vanessa Halhead
Susanna Hecht
Carlton Herbel
Otilio Hernandez
Helmat Janka
Donald A. Jameson
Jan G. Laarman
George Ledec
Jorge A. Lopez Garcia
Rodolfo Lopez
Gilberto Llescas
William Loker
Ariel Lugo
Theodore MacDonald
Carlos Marquez Aguilar

Ismael Martinez Santos
Fortino Matias
Mariano Morales G.
Katy Moran
Andres Mouat
Pablo Muench Navarro
Salomon Nahmad Sitton
James Nations
Ron Nigh
Benjamin Ortiz Espetel
Henry A. Pearson
Matthew Perl
Jesus Ramos
Angel Ramos Sanchez
Ivan Restrepo
Richard Rice
Arsenio Rodriguez
Nemesio Rodriguez
Jaime Ruiz Vega
Eneas Salati
Susana Sedgwick
Carlos Sere
E. A. Serráo
Marianne Schmink
Liane Simons
Reynaldo Soto J.
Nils Svanqvist
Jose Toledo
Victor Toledo
Fernando Tudela
Javier Trujillo-Arriaga
Fernando E. Vega
Charles R. Venator

Coda

What can I do?

Just days before I mailed this manuscript to my publisher, someone deeply concerned about tropical deforestation asked about the book. Pressed for time, I quickly reviewed its multiplicity of perspectives and problems. I was surprised to see her frustrated and perplexed. "I see", she said, limply dropping her arms to her side. "It all seems a big, hopeless problem. What can anyone do? What can I do?" Telling her that many scientists shared her frustration seemed only to deepen her anxiety. Assuming my professorial posture, I inquired about her skills and ambitions, hoping to encourage her to join the hopelessly small band working on the problems. I soon realized, however, that her concern was not over *how* she might help. Instead, she was concerned whether or not *whatever she might do would have any meaningful impact on the problem.* Fair enough. For her and those like her, I offer a coda.

An answer to her question might lie in an unlikely place, Chaos Theory (Gleick 1987). In 1979, a meteorologist turned mathematician, Edward Lorenz discovered that tiny differences in input could quickly generate overwhelmingly large differences in output (Lorenz 1979). Lorenz called his notion the "Butterfly Effect." Serendipitously, he choose a metaphor apropos to our theme, entitling his paper "Does the flap of a Butterfly's wings in Brazil set off a tornado in Texas?" His answer — it could. Mathematically, Lorenz demonstrated that the outcomes of complex systems are difficult, if not impossible to predict, since they are sensitive to minute changes in initial conditions. Whereas most flaps do little more than propel the creature, a few flaps might influence the time, place, or strength of Kansas tornado.

You cannot predict the consequences of your actions. Be the action infinitesimally small — such as whether or not to read an assignment — or large — such as dedicating a lifetime to a particular scientific problem or political cause, you cannot predict whether or not your actions will have a meaningful consequence in the long run or on the big picture. The consequences of inaction, however, are silence and death. Whether or not you precipitate a tornado or simply flutter to another limb, as most of us will, is immaterial. What matters is that you tried. Explaining this perspective, my answer to the young lady and you, is

"Flap your wings!"

- Theodore E. Downing

Gleick, James. 1987. Chaos: Making a new science. New York: Viking.
Lorenz, Edward. 1979. "Predictability: Does the Flap of a Butterfly's Wings in Brazil Set Off a Tornado in Texas?" Address presented at the American Association for the Advancement of Science, 29 December.

About the Contributors

MARY HELENA ALLEGRETTI is the President of the Institute of Amazon Studies, a non-governmental organization that has been instrumental in implementing extractive reserves in the Amazon Basin.

DAVID BARKIN is professor of economics at the Xochimilco campus of the Universidad Autonoma Metropolitana, Mexico, and director of the Morelia office of the Centro de Ecodesarrollo.

JAVIER CASTAÑEDA is a geographer specializing in forests with broad experience in several states of the Republic of Mexico. He was one of the initial promoters and advisors to the UCEFO S.C. described in Chapter 20.

THEODORE E. DOWNING is a Research Professor of Social Development at the University of Arizona. He specializes in the institutional dimensions of agricultural development and has worked on the development of Mexican coffee producers, irrigation's impact on society, and the human rights of cultural groups in Latin America.

GARY R. EVANS is Special Assistant for Global Change issues at USDA, Washington, DC. He is responsible for planning and coordination of all global change programs across the independent agencies of USDA, represents USDA in the planning and coordination of the global change research programs within the federal science agencies and serves as a member of the U.S. delegation to international organizations coordinating global change research programs and response strategies throughout the world.

CARMEN GARCIA-DOWNING works with Native American populations for the Rural Health Office at the University of Arizona Medical School and is an agricultural specialist in animal science and range management. A native Zapotec Indian, she also coordinates a non-profit organization, the Nine Points Alliance, which focuses on development of Native American populations and resources in southern Mexico.

JURGEN GLAESER owns and operates a private electric fencing and agriculture consulting business. He also operates a non-profit agriculture training school.

VANESSA HALHEAD specializes in social/community aspects of resource use and conservation. She currently runs a rural development project on this topic in northern Scotland. In the early 1980s she carried out a two year research project into the socio-political aspects of forest use in Mexico and has worked in an advisory capacity on forest management.

SUSANNA B. HECHT is an Associate Professor in the Graduate School of Planning at UCLA. She is a specialist in tropical forest development and has worked extensively on the environmental and social dynamics of livestock in Latin America.

CARLTON H. HERBEL is a Range Scientist (Emeritus) and former leader of the Jornada Experimental Range, Agricultural Research Service, USDA at Las Cruces, New Mexico. His research emphasizes soil-plant-animal-weather relations. He is one of the authors of *Range Management Principles and Practices*.

DONALD A. JAMESON worked for the USDA Forest Service, Flagstaff, Arizona from 1956-68, specializing in ecology of semiarid savannahs. From 1968 to 1989, he served as Professor of Range Management at Colorado State University, where he developed several large scale computer modeling and operations research projects. Beginning in 1989, he moved to the USDA Forest Service Computer Science staff in Washington, D.C., where he works on university liaison and technology forecasts.

LOVELL S. JARVIS is Associate Professor of Agricultural Economics at the University of California at Davis. Within his work on development economics, he has undertaken a range of studies and consultancies for international agencies on the economics of livestock development. He is noted for his major study for World Bank that resulted in the publication *Latin American Livestock Development*.

JAN G. LAARMAN is professor of forestry at North Carolina State University. His research explores the role of forests in regional economic development.

GEORGE LEDEC is an Environmental Officer in the Latin America Environment Division of the World Bank. His doctoral research with the University of California at Berkeley concerned the role of bank credit for cattle raising as a factor in deforestation in Panama.

THOMAS LOVEJOY is Assistant Secretary for External Affairs at the Smithsonian Institution.

ARIEL E. LUGO is director and project leader of the Institute of Tropical Forestry, USDA Forest Service in Puerto Rico. His research in tropical forest ecology spans three generations.

THEODORE MACDONALD is the project Director for Cultural Survival, Cambridge Mass., and a Research Associate in the Department of Anthropology at Harvard University. His current applied research and program activities focus on indigenous peoples' rights and uses of their common property, particularly land and natural resources.

FORTINO MATIAS is an Indian farmer in the village of Diaz Ordaz, Mexico. An impressive community leader, he has attempted to increase the awareness of his people to the need for sustainable agriculture and forest conservation.

EUCARIO ANGELES MARTINEZ grew up as one of the poorest among the poor in a small hamlet in the Quiatoni region. His brothers and he left the community, which provided only a first and second grade education, and worked as household servants and studied in Oaxaca City. Following training in community organization in the Catholic church, he returned to his homeland, organizing an unfinanced, non-denominational, non-governmental (i.e., bootstrap) cluster of development projects. Like many indigenous community developers, Eucario's enthusiasm and "can do" attitude is matched only by the poverty of his community and Solidarity group.

ISMAEL MARTINEZ SANTOS was born and farms in his small community of 5,000 Zapotec speaking Indian-peasants in the Central Valley of Oaxaca. He has served in a variety of community leadership positions, including that of village judge.

KATY MORAN is program analyst for the Assistant Secretary for External Affairs at the Smithsonian Institution. As an applied anthropologist, she spent several years working for different members of the U.S. Congress. She recently completed a book on *"Culture" the Missing Element in Conservation and Development*.

JAMES D. NATIONS is Vice-President for Latin American programs for Conservation International in Washington, D.C. He has studied the human use and conservation of tropical ecosystems in Latin America since 1974.

HENRY A. PEARSON, was Supervisory Range Scientist, Southern Forest Experiment Station, USDA Forest Service, Pineville, Louisiana. He conducts research dealing with forest-range management, agroforestry, and ecological, environmental, and socioeconomic relationships among trees, livestock, wildlife, and watersheds.

IVAN RESTREPO, founder and former Director of the Centro de Ecodesarrollo, is one of Latin America's most published advocates for environmentally sensitive development. Not only has he published scores of scholarly books and articles but he has successfully translated and interpreted his colleagues and his own research for the Latin American public in hundreds of newspaper editorials and magazines articles. For this reason, his colleagues named him Honorary President of the Oaxaca Workshop.

RICHARD W. RICE, Professor of Animal Science at the University of Arizona, is noted for his research on livestock grazing behavior, comparative behavior of domestic and wild herbivores, and livestock production from grazing animals. He chaired the Grazing land Directorate of the U.S. Man and the Biosphere from 1985-1986.

ENEAS SALATI currently heads the National institute for Amazonia Research (INPA) in Manus, Brasil and has been a consultant for the Inter-American Development.

CARLOS SERÉ is an independent agricultural economics consultant specializing in livestock development and agricultural research issues in Latin America. As a senior economist at the Center for International Tropical Agriculture, he worked extensively on pasture development strategies in savana and rainforest regions of South America.

E. ADILSON SERRAO is Senior Research Agronomist at the Agricultural Research Center for the Humid Tropics, EMBRAPA, in Belem, Brazil. He has been very active doing research on pasture development in the Brazilian Amazon over the past 15 years and also has research experience in other Latin American countries.

REYNALDO SOTO is an employee of the Mexican Federal Government Forestry Secretariat with vast experience in Mexican rural development. He also works part-time in the Chemistry Department in the University of Veracruz.

NILS H. SVANQVIST is Assistant Director for Reforestation and Forest Management of the International Tropical Timber Organization. He has worked for the last 25 years with technical assistance projects in South and Southeastern Asia. His main area of work has been sector analysis and sector planning in forestry.

JOSE M. TOLEDO is the Executive Director of FUNDEAGRO in Lima, Peru. He has carried out pasture and agrosilvopastoral research for oxisols and ultisols of the savannas and forests of tropical America, working at IVITA, Pucallpa, Peru (1966-79) and at CIAT, Cali, Columbia (1979-90).

VICTOR M. TOLEDO is a full-time researcher in the Centro de Ecologia at the National University of Mexico (UNAM). He has extensively published in such areas as ethnoecology, biological conservation, and political ecology of Mexico and Latin America. Presently, he is coordinating a research project on the economic potential of tropical rain forestd.

JAVIER TRUJILLO-ARRIAGA has taught agroecology in different universities and is presently teaching at the Colegio de Postgraduados, a Mexican agricultural graduate school. His research on traditional resource management focuses upon sustainable agriculture.

CHARLES R. VENATOR is a private consultant. He has worked for AID and the U.S. Forest Service on forestry and agroforestry projects in Latin America.

Subject Index

Name Index